THE ART OF FEATURE WRITING

THE ART
OF FEATURE WRITING

From Newspaper Features and Magazine Articles to Commentary

Earl R. Hutchison

Tennessee Technological University

New York   Oxford
OXFORD UNIVERSITY PRESS
2008

Oxford University Press, Inc., publishes works that further Oxford University's
objective of excellence in research, scholarship, and education.

Oxford   New York
Auckland   Cape Town   Dar es Salaam   Hong Kong   Karachi
Kuala Lumpur   Madrid   Melbourne   Mexico City   Nairobi
New Delhi   Shanghai   Taipei   Toronto

With offices in
Argentina   Austria   Brazil   Chile   Czech Republic   France   Greece
Guatemala   Hungary   Italy   Japan   Poland   Portugal   Singapore
South Korea   Switzerland   Thailand   Turkey   Ukraine   Vietnam

Copyright © 2008 by Oxford University Press, Inc.

Published by Oxford University Press, Inc.
198 Madison Avenue, New York, New York 10016
http://www.oup.com

Oxford is a registered trademark of Oxford University Press

Library of Congress Cataloging-in-Publication Data

Hutchison, Earl R., 1926–
   The art of feature writing: from newspaper features and magazine articles to
commentary / Earl R. Hutchison.
      p. cm.
   Includes bibliographical references and index.
   ISBN-13: 978–0–19–517938–5
   1. Freelance journalism.   2. Journalism—Authorship.   I. Title.

PN4784.F76H87 2007
808'.02—dc22   2006052011

Printing number: 9 8 7 6 5 4 3 2 1

Printed in the United States of America
on acid-free paper.

CONTENTS

CHAPTER 8   THE ART OF INTERVIEWING: THE ONLY WHEEL IN TOWN   225

CHAPTER 9   THE SEARCH FOR INFORMATION   254

CHAPTER 10 FOCUSING, OUTLINING: PULLING IT ALL TOGETHER 270

CHAPTER 11 TO MARKET, TO MARKET: THE BUSINESS SIDE OF FREELANCING, PART I 281

PREFACE

Thank you for reading these sentences. Few persons read prefaces, and that realization, as you know, has a chilling effect on the creativity of any writer—or professor. It's much like the feeling you have when students in a classroom chat merrily with their neighbors as you attempt to engage them in subject matter of some note. Nevertheless, I take some comfort from E. M. Forster, when he notes at times like this, that although things are pretty much in a muddle, there you are and here I am. Knowing you are there, I am determined to make this preface worth your reading.

You'll want to know what I've planned for this text, and how this "planning" will keep students so rapt in these pages that if thay pass notes to their neighbors, the notes will have been generated by what they are reading or have read. (No small task, you'll admit.) Here's what I've done in this regard:

From a list of roughly 380 features, articles, commentary and notes, I've selected those that reflect issues of deepest concern to our country: freedom of expression, gender equity (a majority of journalism students are now women), other workplace concerns, wayward governments, environment, economy, love, and mental and physical health. The items selected are most likely to entertain and interest your students while instructing them—a subversive thing to do, I admit, but these are treacherous, partial-attention times. An illustration:

While channel surfing last weekend, I settled on an interview of Anderson Cooper by Larry King—ostensibly about *Dispatches from the Edge*. (King is not my idea of an interviewer, and I was ready to surf on, but the scrolling type at the bottom of the screen mentioned something about Gloria Vanderbilt's husband's suicide.) I was surprised to learn that Cooper was the son of Gloria Vanderbilt (and also surprised at my ignorance of this fact). King was soliciting intimate information not only about Cooper's father's suicide but also about his brother's suicide and about his mother's feelings about those suicides. Cooper bore up fairly well until King asked him if he had been close to his brother. An answer was not readily forthcoming.

If you didn't see the interview, just imagine Anderson Cooper, a recently annointed CNN anchorman, asked to talk about his mother's description of his father crawling over the balcony railing, hanging on with one hand, while Gloria begged him to "come back." While all these vivid details were being elicited by King, the scrolling type at the bottom of the screen ran this sports item: "BARRY BONDS HITS NUMBER 17 IN PURSUIT OF HANK AARON'S HOME RUN RECORD."

Such "partial-attention" artifices/distractions, which this generation has been reared on (and which partially accounts for their "partial attention"), will be countered by this textbook. While I'll admit the key points under that attractive Chapter 1 title, "On the Path to Becoming a Freelance Writer," are not all that stimulating, from Chapter 2 on you'll have a difficult time finding another text with such interest-provoking key points as "Dog Bites Man—Dog Dies"—an Oliver Goldsmith item cited to help explain the difference between a straight news story and a newspaper feature.

A wide range of interesting features, articles and commentary exemplifies the instruction being presented. The variety of subject matter of those features and articles is designed not only to engage the imagination of the students but to represent the even more diverse areas that can be plumbed by the freelance writer or carved out and claimed as her/his domain or territory for publication possibilities.

This textbook will take the student by the hand and act as a guide through the various steps/phases of freelance writing: the idea, the research involved, the interviewing process, the organization of the materials and the writing of the freelance piece. The text continues with the revision process, the market selection process, and the marketing of the work. To assuage egos bruised by the rejections students will most assuredly receive, the text acquaints them with well-known authors such as James Lee Burke, Mary Higgins Clark and William Faulkner, and the numerous rejections they've had dumped on them. And that's not all. Students are shown how those rejections will earn them money-making deductions at income tax time.

All of this, I reiterate, is accompanied not only by articles and commentary designed to enhance instruction, but by pertinent commentary by freelancers and comic strips that will serve as scrolling type—all related to the subject matter being read! The Associated Press style is also followed throughout. Although the student has no doubt become acquainted with copyright, ethics and libel in previous courses, problems arising from violating them are briefly revisited so that when the student leaves the classroom for the wide world, the move will be relatively painless.

Complementing the key points at the opening of each chapter are summaries at the end emphasizing those points. (Old army training: Tell 'em what you're going to tell 'em. Tell 'em. Tell 'em what you told 'em.) And that, once again, is not all. A plethora of exercises follows that underscores the instruction presented, which proceeds from the simple to the complex, starting with the newspaper feature, moving on to the magazine article, and then to the commentary and "The Art of Writing" chapter.

A word of explanation about the inclusion and organization of some chapters:

Why include a whole chapter devoted to identifying a newspaper feature? In preparation for the writing of this text, I reviewed major texts in the field and discovered that the definition of a feature was obscure, buried, or missing. My upper-level freelance course students, I also discovered, had trouble identifying features in a newspaper. Regular news stories with featurized leads and book reviews that started out as a feature story were more often than not categorized as feature stories. After three identification exercises, almost half of them still made those mistakes. They also had difficulty identifying the three elements in the lead of a feature: the narrative hook, the idea, and the transition to the body of the feature. (These were intelligent students who had already taken newswriting and reporting and copyediting courses.) And so, the inclusion of a chapter defining a feature.

Why are there *two* chapters on writing a feature story? First of all, if the chapters were combined, you would have a bulky 80-page chapter viewed with horror by the students.

The chapters thoroughly explore basic and complex feature writing instruction, which transfers beautifully to instruction on writing the magazine article—the lead for both, for example, is essentially the same. As a matter of fact, currently the newspaper feature and magazine article have become so similar that they are prime examples of convergent journalism. The second feature chapter has an example that could also be published in a magazine. (Bill Rivers quotes Grant Dillman, former bureau chief at United Press International headquarters in Washington, D.C., as saying, "At least 25 percent of our effort now goes into in-depth, magazine-type stories." Carrying this point a bit further—although this is a stretch for some people—radio and television features are also examples of convergent journalism because the basic structure of the newspaper feature and magazine article may be noted in radio and television. The differences, of course, are the broad auditory and visual accommodations that must be made.)

The "Focusing, Outlining: Pulling It All Together" chapter, recapitulates the structures for the various forms of writing covered earlier for a number of reasons. First, the student retention span is treacherous—it cannot be trusted. In the classroom, their attention, unless harnessed, skitters around like a water spider on a lake during a hailstorm. (I've also discovered that the weeks between semesters make terrible inroads upon this retention.) Perhaps it's a result of information overload. Or perhaps it's iPods flushing out of the brain much of the instruction positioned there. To stress the importance of outlining, then, and at the risk of being overly redundant, the various outlines presented earlier are revisited to make two major points: (1) the importance of the outline in writing and (2) the use of the outline as an organizational tool in research. When you read that chapter, you'll more readily see what I mean.

Finally, the last chapter is on income tax, "Home Again, Home Again … The Business Side of Freelancing—Part II." One reviewer questioned whether it was necessary, since all freelancers keep receipts and file for income tax deductions. (My experience with freelancers, however, has been different. Invariably freelancers who have not published do not file for deductions. Many of those who have published sparingly do not take all the deductions allowable.) While this may be the case for seasoned freelancers, students entering the freelance field are not aware of allowable deductions (newspapers, magazines, television and radio sets, for example) and even if they are aware, but have not published, they are fearful of filing for these deductions.

In any event, I, too, wondered about having a separate chapter on income tax—but my concern was whether it might be boring for students. So in my most recent freelance course, I announced that I was giving them a printout of an income tax chapter and a subsequent quiz on it in the next class period. The pre-quiz announcement was greeted with foreboding. I had clearly given the class a mind-set designed to color what they were being forced to read. Imagine my surprise when, unsolicited, numerous students said the chapter was one of the most interesting and enjoyable chapters. (I discounted the idea of the *preceding* chapters being *uninteresting* and *unenjoyable,* and so influenced their judgment on the tax chapter.)

One reviewer noted this text encourages a high level of consideration of the crucial elements of freelance writing. I am particularly pleased that the text embraces a literary and sophisticated approach that is characterized by the counsel to the student, in "The Art of Writing" (Chapter 7), "to write as poetically as the subject matter and the audience can *endure*" (although I dislike the inference that hovers over this word).

Used judiciously, this text, I am confident, will do everything I say it will. If you adopt the text and find differently, however, let me know where I went wrong. I will not only appreciate it, I will make amends.

To get your course off on the right footing, you might ask your students to read "A Note to the Student," which follows on page xv.

ACKNOWLEDGMENTS

To fail to recognize the many persons who helped make this book possible would be unforgivable. My colleagues and friends who reviewed the manuscript and offered valuable suggestions were Dr. David G. Clark, retired Vice Chancellor for Academic Affairs, Colorado State University System, and Dr. Dwight Leland Teeter, Jr., University of Tennessee. The late Clay Schoenfeld, a University of Wisconsin professor whose textbook *Effective Feature Writing* launched me into the freelance field, should be noted.

Thanks go also to those professors who read this manuscript for Oxford University Press.

The excellent staff of Oxford University Press, Higher Education Group, who gave me aid and comfort include: Peter M. Labella, Senior Editor, who had the wisdom to select my proposal and follow it through to publication; Emily Pillars, Development Editor; Chelsea Gilmore, Assistant Editor who took care of permissions; Shiwani Srivastava, a former Editorial Assistant; Christine D'Antonio, Senior Project Editor; and Amy Krivohlavek, Copywriter.

Helping me tread the dangerous ground of permissions were: Amy Blackburn, Permissions Coordinator of Reprint Management Services, who handled the Associated Press permissions; Jan Bunch, Tribune Media Services; Raegan Carmona, Universal Press Syndicate; and Heather Penn, United Media.

At Tennessee Technological University keen eyes helped me clean up manuscript errors: Judy Hees, secretary III and proof reader par excellence; Erin Phillips, student; and Tracey Lefevre, Public Affairs Writer.

Among the administrators always encouraging me in my writing was Dr. Leo McGee, Associate Vice President for Academic Affairs. Those computer specialists who invariably answered my may-day calls of distress were Billy Sells and Elaine Wells.

The luxury of selecting features for this text from a bank of more than 375 came about because these workstudy students set most of them: Amanda Michele Amonett, Brandi C. Barnes, Keyna Davis, Shauna Dennison, Kelli Henry, Josh Hayes, Nicole Hinson, Matt Hutcheson, Ashley LaFever, Peggy Perdue and Meredith Purcell.

Others should be mentioned here but please forgive me because I've run out of this valuable space.

A NOTE TO THE STUDENT

Even if you don't read this, I want to let you know that this ain't no stodgy text—I mean, it won't bore you. Well, maybe a section or two in a chapter. But if that's the case, it'll probably be because you aren't into being a freelance writer. You're only taking the course because it's required. (In your heart of hearts, you're really a closet-accountant, waiting to do post-grad work in the college of business.)

Why won't this text bore you? I've selected the most entertaining, interesting, and instructive newspaper features, magazine articles and commentary from a file of more than 380. (That's three-hundred-and-eighty documents! Can you grasp that?) And what's more important, I've tested this stuff on my freelance students over the past five years.

So, if you really want to be a freelance writer, this textbook is guaranteed to prepare you, overtly and covertly. For example, you will be taken step by step through the writing of the simple newspaper feature to the more complex newspaper feature. Nothing serves more effectively as the basic foundation for writing the magazine article. Once you've mastered those writing forms, you're moved on to commentary: the writing of editorials, columns, essays, and book reviews. I mean, your plate will be heaping, but not intimidating. That's because the text has been organized and written so well. You'll feel confident tackling each new assignment as it materializes. You'll absorb the instruction, practice it, and excel. At the end of the course, you'll be so proud of yourself you will bore your friends and parents with your swagger. (Sorry about that. It's one of the drawbacks of using this text.) The material is all in Associated Press style, so you'll be eased painlessly into the writing world of newspapers and magazines (as well as public relations).

I make all these claims because I've written a text that reflects the trust in and affection I have for students. (You are my colleagues. Only a few years and a degree or two separates us.) Throughout the years, students have endured and enlightened me. During dreary days, they have been a source of delight. They have been a source of faith and protected me from cynicism. For all these reasons, I have dedicated this textbook to the students.

But (we're not through yet) when you get out into the wide world, let me know where I've succeeded in writing this text (that will put me in the proper frame of mind to receive adverse criticism), and what I need to do to improve it.

CHAPTER 1

ON THE PATH TO BECOMING A FREELANCE WRITER

WHY SEEK THE PATH OF A FREELANCE WRITER?

Why set out on the path of a freelancer? What is there about the title "freelance writer" that is attractive? The title *does* have an attraction for *you*, right? It does for me. Why is that so? Perhaps the title gives us a glimpse of a life free from the humdrum, stifling bounds of society? Is it also because "lance" suggests a knight questing for the holy grail or jousting for social justice? A Joan of Arc? A Sir Lancelot? That *must* be part of the attraction: being such a knight. "Lance" is even in the name Lancelot! Imagine! A career that frees you to write as you please, when you please, in the cause of justice!

However, if you choose a freelance writing career, some drawbacks are attached. Unless you're already wealthy, there's the problem of living a life in something other than squalor. Full-time freelancers will tell you that unless you've published books that are bringing in substantial royalties ($40,000 to $50,000 a year), you'll need another job to give you a livelihood you'll enjoy. And if you're married and want to send your kids to college, you'll need still more. Or you'll need to be associated with or have a contract with a magazine that will bring in that kind of money. (Seymour Hersh, whose articles I see regularly in *The New Yorker*, comes to mind.) Unless you're writing under these conditions, it's a hard rain falling. (You'll get some idea of what I mean when you read the brief portraits of freelancers later in this chapter.) In the beginning, there'll be a lot of scurrying around until you've settled into an area of expertise that brings your name to editors' minds when that "area" calls for an article.

Initially, then, the ideal course of action for you might be to land a job on a newspaper or magazine as a reporter (or as a staff feature writer, if you can swing it), or in public relations, and to moonlight as a freelancer. Then you can thrill to having a feature or article published with your byline and fully revel in the glory of publication without worrying about when the next paycheck is coming in.

WHAT DISTINGUISHES A GOOD FREELANCE WRITER?

Freelance writers call upon imagination and reason based upon experience, as much as memory, when writing. They write not only for themselves but for a specific audience, and that depends upon the subject matter and the medium it's being printed in. Freelance writers who are self-indulgent will not be remembered. But freelancers who write as poetically as the subject matter and the audience can bear will command an audience no matter what the topic. Among the multitude of journalists who have left their signatures on history's register are William L. Shirer, Winston S. Churchill, William Manchester and David Halberstam. The journalists' impact upon our society is colossal. As Paul Starr notes in *The Creation of the Media,*

> Zenger and Franklin and Jefferson and Paine, all journalists at heart, built this country. Crusading journalists ended slavery, urban graft, official indifference to [the Great] Depression poverty, McCarthyism, the Viet Nam War, and the Nixon Administration.

> (Quoted by Nicholas Lemann in a book review, *The New Yorker* [April 12, 2004], 84.)

WHERE ARE YOU NOW?

By this time many of you are developing or have developed a sense of what is news and a desire to right the wrongs of society—a sense of social justice. You've also, no doubt, developed a relentless curiosity—all trademarks of a professional writer. You probably derive a satisfaction from writing that no other activity provides, and that has propelled you into journalism. You've discovered there's a meditation involved in writing that generates an amalgam of sensations, emotions and associations that evolve into thoughts and ideas. And those move you to fashion words and sentences to express those feelings. When that happens, when you write those feelings on paper as a feature, a letter, an article, a poem, an essay or a commentary, you experience a pleasure, a delight, a fulfillment that leaves you content until another day.

Having just decided your life must include writing of some kind, at what writing milepost are you now? Have you just finished basic newswriting and reporting courses at a university? Most of you probably fall into this category. Many of you may have also acquired added experience by writing stories for your high school, university or hometown newspaper.

Kim Swint and Sameh Fahmy

Are you nontraditional students, about to immerse yourself still more in freelance writing in an effort to brighten your workday world—the way Kim Swint, an accountant, did? Until recently, she wrote two weekly columns for *The Tennessean*—one on running, another on fitness.

> At an awards ceremony for the Frostbite Half-Marathon Race I got an unexpected surprise of placing fourth in my age division (25–29). After complaining to the *The Tennessean* sports editor, Jimmy Davy, about the poor coverage of the race, he invited me in for an interview and gave me a job as a columnist. Luckily, I had a little help from other sports writers and editors.

Or perhaps you have had a Sameh Fahmy experience? Fahmy earned a degree in biology, intending to do research in aquatic ecology, but discovered he wanted to spend

more time in the community rather than in a lab. Texas A&M was among a handful of universities with a program in science and technology journalism. (Basically, the program trains people with science backgrounds to write in a journalistic style.) He then covered health for two years for a small paper in northeastern Louisiana, and served for a couple of years as a consumer health reporter for *The Tennessean* in Nashville. In March 2006, he moved to the University of Georgia to fulfill his first career choice, science writer. He now writes articles for newspaper and university publications about the research going on there. Fahmy's experience personifies the career versatility of a freelancer.

TWO VETERAN FREELANCE WRITER PORTRAITS

Susan Freinkel

My degrees are a B.A., Wesleyan University, 1980, in history, and an MS, Columbia University School of Journalism, 1984. I am married and have three children, ages 15, 13 and 9.

Although I can't give you a list of *all* the articles I've written, some of the publications I've written for include *Smithsonian, Discover, Health, Real Simple, Readers Digest, Organic Style, OnEarth, New York Times, Parents, Family Fun.* I'm just completing a book tentatively titled *The Perfect Tree: The Life, Death and Rebirth of the American Chestnut*, University of California Press, 2007.

I am a freelancer and have been full-time for the past six years. Prior to that I was a staff writer for *Health* magazine for three years, freelanced for a few years before that, and prior to that worked in daily journalism. However, the financial effects of spending two years working on a book are forcing me to contemplate a return to the world of what one friend calls "wage slavery."

How did I come to be a freelancer? Time Warner Inc., the owner of *Health* magazine, decided to move the editorial offices from San Francisco to Birmingham, Ala. I, along with the entire editorial staff, elected not to follow. Not that many magazines still publish in San Francisco, so finding another staff job seemed unlikely. I decided to try freelancing and found that the life suits me well.

I've never been tied into any news organization, though I would love to find some regular gig. My area of expertise is science, medicine and consumer health. Lately, thanks to my book, I've been writing a lot about trees.

Do news organizations come to you or do you go to them?

When I was regularly freelancing, that is, before this book project, it was about a 50/50 split as to whether news organizations came to me or I queried them. A number of editors I regularly worked with either contacted me or I would pitch stories to them.

The freelance life is not for everyone. There are great advantages; the one I cherish most is having a schedule that I control. As a parent of three kids, having a flexible schedule makes my life far less stressful. On the other hand, there's no discrete end to my workday. If I knock off at 3 p.m. to take one of my kids to the dentist, I may have to put in hours at night to meet a deadline. There's no neat dividing line between weekdays and weekends. If you're someone who wants a certain and regular routine, freelancing may not be for you.

To be able to survive and stay happy as a freelancer, you have to be very organized and self-disciplined—the sort of person who can get up in the morning and get herself to work even though there's no one checking to make sure you get to work on time.

Freelancing can be very isolating, and it can get downright depressing if you work out of your home. If you can afford to, get an office of your own or share a workspace with other people. I also belong to a writing group that meets twice a month, and it's an invaluable source for feedback, networking and general support.

Financially, freelancing can be tough. If you want to make it work, you have to be able to juggle multiple projects at once, so that as you finish one story you've got several others in various stages. Some writers do a lot of recycling of material: plumbing the same subject for multiple stories. I've never been good at that, but it is an efficient way of making money.

In getting established, it's helpful to have a particular expertise: Editors are always keeping an eye out for writers who cover their areas. This advice may be a no-brainer, but you should make sure to familiarize yourself with a publication that you want to pitch stories to. Nothing turns off editors faster than getting a query from someone who has clearly never read their magazine. Check to make sure your idea hasn't already been covered, and make your pitch as compelling and precise as you possibly can.

Freelancers are in a vulnerable position: We are always worried about doing anything negative that might cost us work or bump us out of an editor's Rolodex. But, on the other hand, I think it is important for freelancers to have a sense of our own value and to try to stick up for our own rights. It's a balancing act you have to work out over and over again. To that end, one issue I have had to deal with increasingly is the work-for-hire contract, which essentially forces the writer to abdicate his or her intellectual property rights in the story. As a matter of principle, I try not to sign such contracts whenever possible. Many publications have more than one type of contract in their files; if you don't want to sign a work-for-hire contract, some will send you one without that clause.

Vince Passaro

I received my bachelor's degree in English from Columbia College in 1981, and my MFA in Creative Writing (Fiction) from Columbia University's School of the Arts in 1988.

In my own mind, I am first and forever a writer, which is inherently freelance, but I've also taught and, for 12 years, worked full-time as a university administrator, specifically, as a communications director/public affairs officer, first for Adelphi University, then for Baruch College/CUNY. I stopped doing that a year ago but am looking for full-time work again. Writing just can't pay the bills.

How did I come to be a freelancer? The director of the writing program I attended back in the '80s recommended me to various folks who started using me to do book pieces and literary journalism shortly after I got my degree. I've been fortunate to have had relatively steady work since then.

I'm not under contract or anything with any specific organization, though I am still listed as a "contributing editor" to *Harper's Magazine*, where I used to publish regularly.

Being by vocation a novelist and reader, I have many interests and ideas but little expertise. It's a condition of that job to be both engaged and at the same time inexpert. I lucked into some very fine training in critical thinking by being able to study extensively as an undergraduate with Edward Said at Columbia, who remains for me, by a long way, the finest literary mind I was ever in the presence of. I think a lot about literature, about how it works and how it is made, and make fairly good use of that knowledge as a critic. I also write about politics and culture, from an informed layman's point of view.

Sometimes editors come to me, sometimes I reach out to them. In the latter case, basically, I meet people and they encourage me to be in touch, or I approach people who I think will know who I am. It's much easier to get work from people who in some sense know you. Getting to be known is the very hard part. It involves luck, savvy, and most importantly, when you finally get your chance, doing good work that people admire.

SO, YOU WANT TO BECOME A COLUMNIST?

Becoming a regular writer for a newspaper may not be all that difficult. *The Nashville Banner* asked me to contribute a monthly commentary after the editors read my letter to the editor titled "Lyle Starr Is Dead." (You can read it later in Chapter 6.) Once a month, I sent in a column of 700 words.

Editors, on occasion, will solicit writers. Newspaper editor Wes Swietek published this in a 2006 column:

Help Wanted: A Few Good Writers

One of the things that makes a community newspaper unique is the way it represents the voices in its community. The usual vehicle for those voices is letters to the editor and in columns.

Wes Swietek has been a professional journalist for 18 years. He currently serves as managing editor of the *Herald-Citizen* in Cookeville, Tenn. He previously served as the editor of newspapers in his native Illinois and in Georgia.

That's where you come in: While we always encourage folks to express their opinions via letters to the editor, we're also looking to add some community columnists to our pages.

The only qualifications are dependability, basic writing skills and having something to say. You don't have to be a professional wordsmith to write a column; in fact, some of the best community columnists I've ever read have been retirees, preachers, teachers and community activists. We're simply looking for folks who would be interested in writing a few hundred words a few times a month on general interest topics—preferably with a local tie-in. . . .

So, how do you become a community columnist? It's simple: send a note telling us about yourself and why you'd like to write a column, along with at least one sample column of 400–500 words, to my attention, *Herald-Citizen*, 1300 Neal Street, Cookeville, TN 38501.

Or e-mail the same to editor@herald-citizen.com.

But you don't have to wait for an invitation. Once you've developed the skill to write in various areas, solicit the editor yourself. (Once again, you can read more about this in Chapter 11 "To Market, to Market.")

No matter where you find yourself now, this freelance writing text is designed to introduce you to different writing forms and to take you to a different and, perhaps, a higher plane of writing. And it will.

BASIC CHARACTERISTICS OF MASS COMMUNICATION WRITING

What precisely does writing for mass communication entail? Because the next six chapters are devoted in various ways to this topic, the following characteristics are treated cursorily. (Most of you are probably already familiar with some of the characteristics, so this brief recounting may simply serve as a refresher.) Accuracy and objectivity are prized in mass communication, with clarity and succinctness treasured. Discipline is demanded. As if all this weren't enough, many times, even though you are a freelance writer, you'll find yourself called upon to write under pressure.

Accuracy: An Essential

How important is accuracy? The following error affected not only the national, but the international, scene. Although the desecration of the Koran had been noted numerous times before, when *Newsweek* published an erroneous account of American interrogators flushing a Koran down a toilet to torment captured Muslims in Guatanamo Bay, Cuba, the report triggered rioting in Pakistan and Afghanistan that killed 17 people. Numerous news stories and commentary followed.

Newsweek's momentous error, unfortunately, followed "a seemingly endless series of scandals involving plagiarism, nonexistent or unreliable sources, phony memos, sensationalized stories, inflated circulation figures and other misdeeds that have besmirched some of the most prestigious names in journalism—*The New York Times,* CBS News and *USA Today,* among them." Ron Hutcheson of Knight Ridder News Service also noted a steep decline in media credibility, based upon an annual State of the News Media report by the Project for Excellence in Journalism. And numerous polls, revealed the following:

> People have long considered the press sensational, rude, pushy and callous, but in the last 17 years, they have also come to see the press as less professional, less moral, more inaccurate and less caring about the interests of the country.

(*The Tennessean*, May 18, 2005)

How do we remedy all this? Perhaps by tilling our own garden? We can start at the very beginning (at the local level) and then branch out into the world, spreading the word on the importance of accuracy.

Basic, concrete, verified details are the credibility foundation of every news and feature story, magazine article, and commentary. Attention to details—or lack of it—will affect a writer's reputation and, ultimately, career. How, for example, did you feel when you last saw your name misspelled in a letter, in a student directory, in a newspaper, or on a certificate or an award presented to you? Errors turn off readers, viewers, listeners and editors. Attention to detail (citing of sources, for example) is important. When we later write about an event or incident, we tend to neglect details.

Accuracy is aided at the basic level by careful direct observation. If you are interviewing a person, ask yourself, how genuine is the greeting? Is the handshake firm? The smile forced? Are eyes evasive? Listen carefully to the words and how they are spoken. Lou Dobbs of CNN, questioning one of the guests on his program about immigration policy, remarked, "Yes, I hear what you're saying, but I also noticed you scratched your neck a couple of times while you were saying it." If a person rubs her or his nose a couple of times before (or while) answering a question, it's an indication of (1) lying, (2) being uncertain of what is being said, (3) being uncertain about how the information is being received or (4) an itchy nose. You may then want to question that person again to see if the answer is modified or changed.

Objectivity: A Sisyphean Goal

Objectivity, another essential, may be more easily approximated if you understand, first of all, that absolute objectivity is unattainable. Nonetheless, like the mythological Sisyphus, you continually strive to roll that objectivity boulder to the top of the mountain. It's not easy. Writers (and, no doubt, you as well) are usually more sensitive than the average person. You have emotions and feelings that may be stirred more deeply. When you are seeking the truth and objectivity, these feelings should be detached as much as possible from the gathering and writing of information.

In some areas, however, subjectivity is permissible. You can hardly be other than subjective when writing about experiences in an article titled "Twenty-four Hours in an Emergency Room" or in an article about a childhood bee-fighting rite-of-passage ritual. Charged with displaying your views on a particular subject to your readers in the form of essays, columns and reviews, subjectivity not only is permissible, but necessary. When you are not engaged in such writing, however, to achieve the utmost objectivity you must be aware of how personal feelings muddy the waters.

Generally speaking, the more sources you consult and the more sides you hear, the better your chance of presenting a thorough and objective view of an event or issue. Records, documents and other published facts all aid in attaining objectivity.

To convey a sense of accuracy and objectivity, note the source of all information that is not common knowledge. The fact that the country is emerging from an economic recession may be common knowledge *if*, for the past six months, economic indicators such as unemployment figures, housing starts and consumer buying underline the fact and *if*, for the past six months, various economic experts and market analysts have been making statements to that effect. However, if the indications are less clear, a statement about the degree of economic recovery would require verification from an economic authority. Similarly, the fact that a frightful toll of lives is taken on our highways annually is common knowledge. But if you write that the average weekend death toll on the highways is 500, you would be obligated to attribute the figure to an authoritative source, such as a highway safety authority. Ideas that are not your own should be attributed to their originators. Proper attribution conveys the sense that not only are you striving for accuracy and objectivity, but that you are fair and honest.

When you interview persons or witnesses—other people's observations to provide you with an accurate estimate or description of a situation or event—note their credentials. A political candidate will rarely level with you about the state of a political race if it is not favorable. Rarely will a person fired from a position for harassment be able to present you with an unbiased account of the reasons for the dismissal. Knowing the background and credentials of the witness enables you to assess more accurately the truthfulness of the facts and picture being conveyed to you. You also have to make allowances for the fact that different people see the same things in different ways.

To illustrate, let's say you're writing a feature or a commentary about lawmakers' problems with obeying speeding laws. You want to begin with an incident involving former Senate Majority Leader Howard Baker and his encounter with the law:

Baker Fined for Speeding

JACKSBORO, Tenn. (AP) — Senate Majority Leader Howard Baker ran afoul of the law this week by speeding 16 mph over the limit, but says he declined a traffic officer's offer to let him go without a ticket.

Instead, the Tennessee Republican said he wanted to be "treated like any body else" and was issued a $55 citation. . . .

It seems obvious what happened, doesn't it? But the Jacksboro chief of police offers another version of the incident varies: "Officer Jim Lindsey said that it never entered his mind to turn Baker loose. 'That was a lie,' Lindsey said. 'I did tell him that he knew I wouldn't be doing my job if I didn't give him a ticket.' Lindsey said the senator told him to give him his ticket and let him go."

Who are you to believe? Different perspectives may provide conflicting versions of incidents. Baker, expecting to be given a ticket option, may have interpreted Lindsey's remarks in that light.

HUMAN NATURE AND REALITY

It's human nature to rearrange and adjust the world of our reality, to see things in balanced ways and in completion. We constantly do this. We tend to fill in gaps and persuade ourselves that things are *not* what we perceive them to be but are, in effect, our desired reality. Learning to counter this wish-fulfillment part of our intellectual and emotional makeup is a major undertaking and an essential part of becoming a mature writer. Most media researchers agree that half of all major news stories contain some type of error. A research report for the American Newspaper Publishers Association indicated that a large number of psychological factors contribute to these distortions of reality. Among them are the following:

1. Fantasies that reporters allow to form in their minds about an event to dispel the internal stress of cognitive dissonance (mind-disturbing elements)
2. Authoritarianism, dogmatism, or open- or closed-mindedness of the reporter covering the event
3. The orientation or predisposition a reporter has about the source and/or the news message

All this means that the more you know yourself, the more you will be able to appraise an event or issue and write about it realistically. (Further discussion of accuracy and objectivity will come in Chapter 8, "The Art of Interviewing" chapter.)

JOURNALIST AND SCIENTIST METHODOLOGY

In the search for truth, meaning, and significance, in the attempt to determine and describe reality, the media writer engages in some of the same processes as behavioral and social scientists. Through investigation and observation, both journalists and scientists attempt to gather reliable data objectively. Both attempt to report their findings objectively. The major difference between the journalist and the scientist lies not in the attempt to report the truth, but in the strength and scope of the investigation. Although the journalist, because of limited time and resources, may at times generalize from a particular set of facts, she or he is many times compensated by arriving at a truth not available to the scientist. The journalist may allow emotion and intuition to enter into various stages of investigation and reporting. Both are valuable in arriving at that approximation of the truth. The scientist, meanwhile, is hampered by the scientific data obtained by observations, investigations, and experimentation.

In determining truth or reality, then, the journalist enjoys some of the advantages of the poet. The journalist may bring intuition as well as common sense and intelligence to the facts discovered by observation and investigation. The whole of the journalist's intellectual, intuitive, and imaginative faculties are employed in this search.

BEING ATTENTIVE TO YOUR AUDIENCE

When you write for mass communication, knowledge of the different media and their unique different communication characteristics is important. Brief descriptions of three—the print media and two electronic media (radio and television) follow. Through typography, headlines and clear writing, the print media seek to capture readers' attention and stimulate their desire for details. Freelance writers also know there is a "sound" or "echo" to the words they write, and this sound, along with flow and rhythm, is wedded to the "sense" of what is being communicated. If you were writing a feature story about a seemingly unending string of bank robberies, for example, you might include in the lead of that story this report of a holdup that was over almost as quickly as it began:

> Three bank robbers slipped into the First American Bank this morning, jumped over the counter, herded five employees and customers into a vault, and made off with $20,000.
>
> "It took less than three minutes," Dr. Jack Ross, a customer, said. "When I saw those criminally close eyes backing up those guns, I ran for the vault."

The major action of the robbery was telescoped into one sentence. If that robbery had been more casual, and slightly different, it might have been written like this:

> Three bank robbers walked into the First American Bank this morning and robbed it of $20,000. One of the robbers herded five bank employees and customers into a vault while the other two gathered small bills in two pillowcases.
>
> "Oh, they took their time about it all right," Dr. Jack Ross, a customer, said. "But when I looked into those criminally close eyes, I knew they meant business."

However, long, flowing, descriptive sentences, ideal for describing pastoral scenes and leisurely events, rarely rest easily in a feature about a robbery or a riot in a ghetto.

Successful freelance writers specializing in the print media are familiar with the different communication styles of other media. Radio appeals to the "ear," while television appeals primarily to the "eye." The skills that support those two media writing styles tend to be the same as those of the freelance writer for the print media. For example, you've just read a paragraph about wedding the sense of what you're saying to the sound. The rapidity of the robbery, in essence, appeals to the "ear" of the reader. When you write, you want to create images in the reader's mind, appeal to the mind's "eye." You have an example of that image making in the robbery description when you read about the robbers "jumping over the counter" and about a customer's comment: "When I saw those criminally close eyes backing up those guns, I ran for the vault."

TRACKING A FEATURE: USING IMAGINATION AND REASON

The freelance writer calls upon imagination and reason based upon experience, as much as memory, when writing. As you track the feature, article or commentary, your imagination continually suggests alternatives, branches and development possibilities. When you sit down to write, the imagination supplies you with words, phrases and images. To illustrate the imagination and reasoning at work in developing material for a feature story or a magazine article:

University City is located in a dry county. Citizens used to drink alcohol purchased in cities as far away as 70 miles. One year ago, however, voters in adjoining Christian County had a change of heart and voted "wet." Subsequently, three liquor stores opened up a mere 12 miles away in Virden, a small town with a population of 3,000. City and civic leaders in University City deplored the opening of these stores. They predicted dire consequences: teenage drinking, drunken driving and an increase in drinking overall, not to mention the other generally accepted evils accompanying drinking.

You call up the local newspaper editor and suggest writing a feature about the effect on University City of those three liquor stores that were opened one year ago. "Go for it," editor Tony McCracken says, "but on speculation." (This response means the article may or may not be published. It depends on how well you develop and write it.) McCracken suggests quoting civic leaders from a year ago and interviewing them about the facts you've discovered one year later.

What additional steps should you take?

You check articles on file in the newspaper's library and newspapers at the public library to determine what the citizens feared one year ago. A number of articles verify that civic leaders predicted evil from liquor sales. You take notes on your laptop and photocopy three articles.

You check the liquor stores in Columbia 70 miles away, where most University City citizens bought liquor prior to Christian County voting wet. Sales are down 20 percent. You drive to Virden and ask the liquor store owners what percentage of their liquor sales are attributed to University City residents. They estimate that more than 40 percent of their liquor is sold to people from University City.

You drive back to the University City and interview Police Chief Robert Himell. Has there been an increase in public drunkenness from last year? No. Has there been an increase in domestic disturbances resulting directly from drinking? No. Has there been an increase in drunk driving arrests? Not significantly. Has there been an increase in drunk driving by underage drivers? No. The state highway patrol corroborates the police reports: no increase.

You check with Dr. Joseph Greek, dean of men, and Dr. Carol Harwood, dean of women, at the university. Any discernible increase in drinking noted by their offices? No.

You check with Dr. Cynthia Webster, director of the counseling center. Any increase in the counseling of students with drinking problems? No.

The University Safety and Security Department reports no increase in rowdiness or disorderliness as a result of drinking.

High school principals report an increase in the use of marijuana, "ice" and methamphetamine, but not liquor.

Five of the city's ministers did not note any increase in the use of liquor by members of their congregations.

You check with garbage collectors. Any noticeable increase in discarded liquor bottles? No.

What you can infer from this series of observations is that University City citizens are buying liquor from Virden liquor stores—saving gas and driving time by buying there rather than in Columbia. The change in purchasing site also gives you another item to test: Have liquor sales fallen in Columbia? University City citizens and students, despite this shorter driving distance, apparently have not increased their liquor consumption. The city leaders' earlier fears stemming from the prospect of more accessible liquor appear unfounded. You schedule interviews with Mayor Charles Womack and civic leaders of University City. When you write your feature, you cite your investigation, liberally quoting the people you interviewed.

You have a feature story for your local newspaper that may be picked up for state distribution by The Associated Press, and a possible magazine article for a state magazine.

As you have seen, an ongoing process of evaluating and judging takes place in writers' minds when they are deciding what is or is not important information. Freelance writers and journalists who are news reporters and editors, as well as public relations writers who work for companies, engage in this process of evaluating, then processing and finally communicating what is of interest to their audiences. The process involves sifting the routine and the repetitious (those events that represent the cycle of life: births, deaths, anniversaries, etc.) and the nonroutine and nonrepetitious (arson, business mergers, odd crimes, freak storms, scientific breakthroughs).

NEWS INTERPRETATIONS MAY DIFFER

All those factors to be considered when deciding what to write about will be discussed in more detail in the chapters ahead, but it would be wrong to leave you with the impression that every writer sees the same thing in the same event. As indicated earlier, different persons perceive different things in different ways. It all has to do with varying experiences and lifestyles. As a result of those experiences, our brains have different screens through which these perceived events pass. We tend to see what we've been exposed to. If you have a friend who is a heart surgeon, your friend may perceive the man across the street who stoops down to tie a shoelace as having a heart attack—a natural reaction. Stop at a gas station and ask directions to some location. Chances are the attendant will say, "Drive down the road a couple of miles till you come to a Mobil station, then hang a right." Your particular mind-set or screen may let you see a Christmas tree as a beautiful decoration, while your environmentalist friend will see it as wanton destruction of nature's resources. So will it be with interpretations of events.

That's why, as a freelance writer, it pays to know your biases and prejudices. Bent on seeing a tennis ball hitting inside a line, you may see the ball as in when in fact it is outside that line. If you attend a meeting anticipating a confrontation between two factions, you may perceive, in any dialogue between those factions, animosities and hostilities where perhaps only minor differences exist. Or look at what happened to two foreign correspondents covering a meeting in Vienna of the Organization of Petroleum Exporting Countries. They wrote straight, no-nonsense news story leads unembellished with any frills:

Robert Burns of The Associated Press:

OPEC prices for their oil likely are stuck right where they are for a while, a leading oil minister said yesterday.

Thomas J. Lueck of *The New York Times*:

The stability of the international oil market is being threatened by mounting dissension among members of the Organization of Petroleum Exporting Countries.

Western experts believe that disputes among the 13 nations could lead to lower prices for consumers, but would pose severe economic problems for several oil producers.

Both stories were published in the same edition of a newspaper!

The moral: Sometimes you can place trust in your sources. At other times you might better place your trust in still other sources. Both of the reporters at the OPEC meeting would have served their readers better if Burns had mentioned what "Western experts" think might happen at the meeting and if Lueck had included what "a leading oil minister" had to say about the meeting. That might have been more balanced, more responsible reporting.

Lueck, incidentally, was right.

AUDIENCES DICTATE DIFFERENT VOCABULARIES

The important facts gathered by freelancers, such as those about the question of change in alcohol consumption by University City residents, would be lost if the feature stories were not presented in an interesting way. Having collected the information and drawn their conclusions, writers must now write. One of the objectives of this chapter is to familiarize you with the attitude and preparation a professional freelance writer brings to each assignment. We can view the writer as a gatekeeper of information, an individual who possesses the power to influence the way readers, listeners and viewers interpret the world around them.

To establish credibility with readers, recognize and use the basic common language and symbols available. The medium you're communicating in determines to a large extent the kind of language structure you use: Simpler and shorter sentences are usually employed in newspaper features. Magazine readers are more tolerant of longer and more complex sentences and paragraphs. Readers also have a bearing on the language and symbols you use. Different words and phrases are used to address readers of *The Atlantic Monthly* and *The New York Times* and readers of a small weekly newspaper.

The subject matter itself also affects the choice of language. Explaining the aftermath of a raging chemical-factory fire may call for highly technical terms compared to the words describing a day at the St. Lawrence County Fair.

Your aim, or purpose, in writing will also influence your choice of words and language. Do you want to alert people to the environmental hazards of waste disposal? You will choose words that are more serious than if your article describes the operations of a local dating service. Whatever the subject matter, whatever purpose you have in writing, whatever medium you select, whatever audience you address, select the language appropriate for the story. Regardless of the subject matter and the publication, try to be frank and sincere—to write only what you believe to be true.

A WORD ON ETHICS AND LIBEL

Since most of you have already taken a newswriting or reporting course, you know that to maintain credibility with your readers your writing and behavior must be ethical.

All transactions and behavior that you would not be comfortable with bringing to the attention of your readers must be avoided. Copyright materials should be properly accredited. In all this, you're striving to keep your integrity from being impugned.

To keep yourself and the publications who have chosen to publish you free from lawsuits you must be wary of committing libel. Your writing must be fair and truthful, and, while factual, it should not cast an undue shadow on a person or organization that would tend to hold that person or organization up for ridicule or defamation of character or reputation.

The two preceding paragraphs are, as the section title suggests, only a "word" about ethics and libel. For more complete statements on ethics you may read in Appendix E the "Code of Ethics" adopted by the Society of Professional Journalists and in Appendix G the "Code of Ethics" adopted by the Public Relations Society of America. Appendix F contains The Associated Press (AP) statement on libel. Appendix D comprises the AP's statement on copyright. The "Top Ten Myths About Rewriting Someone Else's News Reporting" appears in Appendix C.

WHY IS ALL THIS IMPORTANT TO YOU?

If you observe and assimilate the instruction given you in this book, you will not only maintain professional integrity and credibility with editors, you will have an edge upon the majority of freelance writers already in the profession. In addition, you will be rewarded with publication. With your writing, and subsequent publication, you will move people. In one word, that is power.

SUMMARY

Freelancers do not write in a vacuum. Their work requires them to become involved with others, with people making news of local interest as well as with those making history. To perform effectively, they must be good listeners and reflective thinkers.

Freelance writers write not only for themselves, but for a specific audience. To fill that audience's information needs, it's important to develop keen powers of observation, curiosity, and skepticism. Those provide you with a broader understanding of human nature and the sensitivity to pick up on more subtle expressions of emotions. These traits help you cultivate sources, expand research skills, and compose features, articles, and commentary with objectivity and credibility.

This text teaches you how to embrace the craft and artistry of prose, fiction and poetry in freelance writing. Since poetry is the highest form of writing, you should aspire to be as poetic in your writing as the subject matter and audience can bear. Approaching writing in these ways will help initiate and reinforce the instruction presented in these pages.

EXERCISES

1. A writer's self-analysis exercise. (Note to instructor and student: This exercise is also listed as an option—exercise 1—in Chapter 7.)
   In the next few days, think about and analyze your life as a writer up to this point:
   a. early beginnings (inspirations, aspiration)
   b. persons encouraging or discouraging you
   c. failures
   d. successes
   e. weaknesses
   f. strengths
   - In writing this assignment, brainstorm, noting in a pad those things entering your mind at various times during this period.
   - Read about outlining on pages 271ff and chapter 10 "Focusing, Outlining: Putting It All Together." (You will create an outline similar to the one on pages 275–276, including the introductory paragraph and conclusion and hand it in with this assignment. Use Roman numerals, etc.)
   - Create an imaginative title that will provide you with added motivation to write this paper.
   - Compose your detailed outline before writing your analysis. You will hand this outline in with your analysis paper.
   - Your introductory paragraph to this analysis must begin with the following:
   "When I write, I . . . ." Then describe the feelings and emotions that run through you when you write (e.g., power? elation? etc.).
   (Note that this introductory paragraph and all the items mentioned in this assignment [items a–f] will be reflected in your detailed outline as major headings.)
   - Your concluding paragraph must note what you'd like this course to do for your freelance writing career.
   Following the outline carefully (but not slavishly), write your self-analysis paper. You may revise the paper immediately after you have written it. If you do, wait at least one more day and then revise it again. (Rarely should you hand in an assignment not revised at least twice. You may want to read "The Importance of Revision" on page 215ff and exercise 2 at the end of Chapter 7 for guidelines on revision.)
   After revising your paper, add a parenthetical appendage at the end, noting the steps or instructions *you failed to follow* in writing this assignment. Briefly disclose why you decided to ignore them. *However*, this appendage does not excuse you from the error of these omissions.

2. Recall some episode early in your childhood that has made a deep impression on you. Select a corner where you will not be disturbed by other people, music, or television. Concentrate deeply on each aspect of the episode for perhaps an hour, until the episode crystallizes in your mind and you see that crack in the sidewalk, the lampshade askew in the den, or some other image from the past. When you have relived the episode, write about it rapidly, skipping words that do not come readily to you. When you are through, read what you have written.
   Are there words and phrases that you don't recall having written? Were you able to recall little details, such as a chip off a stone step? If so, you are succeeding in recalling details which ordinarily would be lost without your concentration—without your plumbing of the deep well. (See Chapter 7, page 217ff, for a description of plumbing the deep well.)

3. Write a paragraph about a place—a park, a house, a restaurant—for these audiences:
   a. An entry in your journal
   b. A brief oral presentation to your classmates

   c. A brochure to attract tourists

   d. A newspaper feature story

4. From memory, write a description of the front of the building that your writing class is located in.

5. Take a pencil and pad and stand in front of the same building. Write a description of the building while you are observing it directly. Compare the two descriptions. In what ways are they different? Why? In what ways are they the same? Why?

6. Interview your friends and classmates about what they see when they look at the front of the building. Write a description based only on their observations. Compare this description, based on "indirect observation," with your "direct observation" description. In what ways are they the same? Why? In what ways are they different? Why? Would you have a better description if you incorporated your friends' descriptions with yours? Why? What does this tell you about the care you should take in gathering information for features and articles?

7. Write a one-sentence impressionistic description of the building—something like Carl Sandburg's "Fog" ("The fog comes on little cat feet") or Ruth Whitman's "Castoff Skin" ("She lay in her girlish sleep at ninety-six,/small as a twig."). Compare your description with those of your classmates. Which are most imaginative? Which are the best? Why? Are some better and even more truthful than the direct-observation descriptions? Why?

8. Be especially aware of your surroundings on your way to or from class. List details that had previously escaped your notice.

9. Study the drawing and the wording below for 45 seconds.

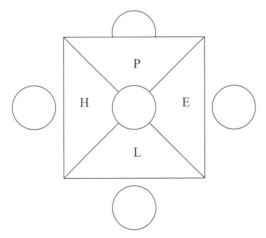

The Cow Jumped Over the Noon!

   (The instructor may time the whole class, if this is done in the classroom.)

   Close the text and reproduce the drawing and the wording on a blank piece of paper. How does your drawing and wording differ from the original? Do your classmates have similar reproduction errors? How do you account for the differences?

   Berko et al. believe the differences come from these concepts: We tend to see what we've been exposed to in the past: For example, "The Cow Jumped Over the Noon." We tend to see things in balanced ways: For example, your reproduction may be all half-circles or all full circles. We tend to see things in completion: For example, the circle in the center of the drawing is often bisected by slanting lines or it completely disappears. We tend to eliminate details in the restating: For example, fewer words, details in drawing. Our perceptions are influenced by our desire to see and hear what we want to see and hear.*

10. After reading the portraits of Susan Freinkel and Vince Passaro, you can see what an excellent source of information freelancers can be. Locate a freelancer in your community, published or otherwise (I know a person who has written eight novels and still has to find a publisher), and interview her or him. Perhaps the instructor might invite the freelancer to answer questions for 20 to 30 minutes of the classroom period.

---

*Roy M. Berko, et al. Handbook of Communicating: A Social and Career Focus, Houghton Mifflin Company, 1977, pp. 78–79.

CHAPTER 2

ON DEFINING A NEWSPAPER FEATURE

Dog Bites Man—Dog Dies

> When a dog bites a man, that is not news. . .
> But if a man bites a dog, that's news.
> —John B. Bogart, city editor,
> *The Sun* [1873–1890]

If a dog bites a man, that's not news . . . But if a man bites a dog, that is news. John Bogart's definition will be with us through the ages. However, today, when "a man bites a dog," that's a dog of a different color—not a newspaper story, but a feature.

Your previous writing experiences no doubt introduced you to a definition of a straight news story. Bogart's definition, even though it's erroneous, may be similar to the one you're acquainted with. His definition has dogged us through the years because it's so clear and graphic—on the surface. If we were to use Oliver Goldsmith's account of a dog biting a man in "An Elegy on the Death of a Mad Dog"—the man recovers but the dog dies—that, too, would not be substance for a straight news story. Once again it would be a feature, a form of news. Bogart is saying that if anything of significance varies from the routine, it's news. Of course, some routine, repetitious events are news (such as births, deaths and anniversaries). But Bogart was referring primarily to such events as crime, fire, emerging social issues, wars and the like.

Today, when we think of a feature, we automatically think of some thing or event that is humorous, unusual, unnatural, odd, awe inspiring or a Ripley's Believe It or Not! item. The way it is written, however, may place it in the category of a straight news story rather than a feature. A feature may also be a sidebar—an item accompanying a main news story—or a follow-up feature of a regular news story.

WHAT EXACTLY IS A NEWS STORY? WHAT IS A FEATURE?

A feature story is something other than a straight news story, both in structure and, most times, in subject matter.

A short feature story, for example, may be represented by a pyramid (not the inverted pyramid of a short news story, as discussed later in this chapter) creating a structure that piques the interest of the reader with the lead and increases that interest until the tension is released at the very ending. A short (or long) news story, meanwhile, is just that—a news story. After the lead (which may be "featurized," that is, written in the style of a feature story lead) the writer is relegated primarily to bare facts leading up to a no-nonsense conclusion. A feature, meanwhile, lures the reader in with a lead. Then, the writer, free to roam a literary field, builds on that interest to a climactic ending or to a climax and an ending that leaves a lingering impression.

While a news story is primarily concerned with the facts of what is happening and answering the five *w*s (who, what, when, where, why), and *h* (how) and significant questions, the feature story may be an adjunct of a major news story or may explore subject matter entirely independent of a breaking news story. For example, a major news story about forest fires raging out of control in California and adjoining states might evoke a feature story about the difficulty of detecting the arsonist who set the fires.

A stand-alone feature could be a how-to-do-it article on a home greenhouse, or an article on student graduation fears or surviving a divorce.

Whereas many news stories today have featurized leads, that, of course, does not qualify them as feature stories. Once through the news story feature lead, the reader faces bare facts with just a nod to setting or character description. But with a feature story, the lead entices the reader into a story that may be spiced with character and setting description as well as a wealth of writing that may be colorful and poetic, combined with a unity of impression that usually is entirely alien to the straight news story.

So when a man actually bites a dog, that event is not a news story but a feature—if it's written as a feature. Too many times the story is not written as a feature. The following variation of a dog-biting/man-biting event has feature story material. But as it's written, it crosses the great divide into a news story category:

"Man Grips Dog, Bites Man"

NORWALK, Calif. — A young man wanted for assaulting his mother-in-law was arrested early yesterday on charges he bit two sheriff's deputies as they tried to pry a police dog from his grip.

Charles Lamping, 22, was booked on two counts of assaulting a peace officer and a count of assault on his mother-in-law.

Deputy Robert Stoneman said officers responding to the assault report tracked Lamping down to a vacant home. Lamping, who was hiding, grabbed the dog, Captain, after the canine was sent in to find him. Captain's handler, Deputy John Falkner, and a second deputy, Thomas Rosas, were bitten by Lamping during a scuffle. The dog was freed just as Lamping blacked out, and was unhurt.

Falkner and Rosas were both treated at Whittier Presbyterian Hospital for bites on their right index fingers and were released. Lamping was hospitalized in the jail ward of County-USC Medical Center for treatment of multiple lacerations to his scalp. The circumstances of Lamping's fight with his mother-in-law were under investigation.

The reporter wrote this event as a straight news story. However, when the copy editor wrote the headline— "MAN GRIPS DOG, BITES MAN"—the play was upon the latent feature material in the event. The headline writer no doubt had Bogart's definition in mind. A good feature writer could have treaded that fine line between reporting and good taste in news events such as this and mined it for the feature material in it.

As noted previously, news events are frequently written in a straight news story format even when a feature story approach would attract more readers. The headline written for this next news story suggests a different lead is needed for it:

"Lions Chase Off Captors, Guard Ethiopian Girl"

By Anthony Mitchell
The Associated Press, July 22, 2005

ADDIS ABABA, Ethiopia—A 12-year-old girl who was abducted and beaten by men trying to force her into a marriage was found being guarded by three lions that apparently had chased off her captors, a policeman said yesterday.

The girl, missing for a week, had been taken by seven men who wanted to force her to marry one of them, said Sgt. Wondimu Wedajo, speaking by telephone from the provincial capital of Bita Genet, about 350 miles southwest of Addis Ababa.

She was beaten repeatedly before she was found June 9 by police and relatives on the outskirts of Bita Genet, Wondimu said. She had been guarded by the lions for about half a day, he said.

"They stood guard until we found her, and then they just left her like a gift and went back into the forest," Wondimu said.

"If the lions had not come to her rescue, then it could have been much worse. Often these young girls are raped and severely beaten to force them to accept the marriage."

Tilahun Kassa, a local government official who corroborated Wondimu's version of the events, said one of the men had wanted to marry the girl against her wishes.

"Everyone thinks this is some kind of miracle because normally the lions would attack people," Wondimu said.

Stuart Williams, a wildlife expert with the rural development ministry, said the girl may have survived because she was crying from the trauma of her attack.

"A young girl whimpering could be mistaken for the mewing sound from a lion cub, which in turn could explain why they didn't eat her," Williams said.

Ethiopia's lions, famous for their large black manes, are the country's national symbol and adorn statues and the local currency.

Despite a recent crackdown, hunters also kill the animals for their skins, which can fetch $1,000.

The girl, the youngest of four siblings, was "shocked and terrified" after her abduction and had to be treated for the cuts from her beatings, Wondimu said.

He said police had caught four of the abductors and three were still at large.

Another man-bites-man news event that a reporter failed to capitalize on follows:

"Although Victim Was Willing, Cannibal Sentenced for Slaying"

By Matthew Schofield
Knight Ridder News Service, Jan 31, 2004

BERLIN—A German cannibal will go to prison for eating a willing victim, but only for a maximum of 8½ years.

Armin Meiwes, 42, was sentenced for manslaughter in a case that has shocked, delighted and baffled Germany since his arrest in December 2002. News coverage had been intense because of the sensational nature of the crime, the eagerness of the victim and the fact that when Meiwes advertised online for a victim, he got more than 200 responses.

The trial in the 200,000-resident city of Kassel in central Germany also attracted attention in legal circles, as there's no law against cannibalism in Germany.

Prosecutors had hoped for dual convictions on sexual murder and disturbing the peace of the dead, which could have resulted in a life sentence.

Meiwes' attorney responded by saying his client had merely assisted in a suicide, a crime with a maximum five-year sentence. The panel of judges decided on a manslaughter conviction and a sentence of eight years, six months.

The sentence works out to a little more than a year for every 30 pounds of Bernd-Jurgen Brandes that Meiwes cooked and ate. He could be paroled in 2008.

According to a BBC translation, one of the judges told a packed courtroom Meiwes hadn't committed murder but "a behavior which is condemned in our society, namely the killing and butchering of a human being. Seen legally, this is manslaughter, killing a person without being a murderer."

Meiwes was relaxed during the reading of the verdict just as he had been throughout the proceedings, during which he calmly questioned witnesses against him.

For most, the case turned on the videotape that Meiwes and Brandes agreed to make of the killing and butchering. In the video, Brandes, 43, a software engineer repeated that being eaten would be the fulfillment of a dream for him. In responding to Meiwes' request for a human meal, Brandes emailed, "I am your meat."

The killing took place in March 2001. For Meiwes, eating another human was a merging of soul, and the one way to finally feel close to another person.

Both men were described during the two-month trial as having psychological problems. Meiwes said he believed he had become close to his victim after eating bits and pieces of him for more than a year and even that he had gained Brandes' English-language skills through the act.

This macabre story has to be handled carefully so readers won't be alienated by the gory material. Is that why the reporter failed to tread that fine line and write a good feature lead?

Missed opportunities like these occur day after day in the news media. Maybe it's because there's no designated feature writer on the newspaper or wire service. Here's another news event a reporter failed to capitalize on:

"Woman Accused of Trying to Kill Husband with Spiders"*

In Rutherford County, the woman accused of trying to kill her husband with poisonous spiders was in court Wednesday with her husband by her side.

Teresa Rivera's court appearance was delayed after she asked for time to get an attorney.

The Rutherford County Sheriff's department charged Rivera with attempted murder.

Detectives said she tried to hire a hit man [for $500] to kill her husband and then she tried to kill him with black widow spiders [while he slept].

Her husband said the allegations were not true and he wants the charges dropped.

"We've been let down by the system and now we're in the system as a criminal. She's not a criminal. She's not," said Emierto Rivera, the woman's husband.

The husband made the initial complaint against his wife.

The prosecutor said victims of domestic abuse sometimes change their stories, but the state decides whether to prosecute. They plan to move forward with the case.

*NewsChannel5.com (Nashville), Sept. 13, 2002

[At a later appearance the woman pleaded guilty and received probation.]

Not only did the reporter fail to capitalize on the feature material, the story began by answering the "Where did it happen?" question, rather than the "What happened?" question. To do justice to the story and to illustrate how to convert a feature story written as a straight news story into a bona fide feature, the lead could read something like this:

What took place in court today reminds you of the lyrics Percy Sledge sings so well:

"When a man loves a woman, she can do no wrong."

That's the kind of love Emierto Rivera displayed today when his wife, Teresa, was charged with trying to kill him.

The rest of the events then fall naturally into place for a feature.

One more example. A straight news story reports that a sneeze can eject particles from the nose at 103.6 miles per hour. A feature story writer would take that nasal material and run with it:

"AAAAAAHHHH . . . CHOOOO!!!!!"

If you're around a person with a cold and that person sneezes, you better move out. Fast!! Particles coming out of that sneeze have been clocked at 103.6 miles per hour.

As has been pointed out repeatedly, you can see that a feature story is indeed something other than a straight news story both in structure, and, most times, in subject matter. Let's list some of the differences.

A straight news story begins by answering six or seven questions in a straightforward manner, usually beginning with "What happened?" and, if appropriate, perhaps following with "What's the significance or consequences of the event?" Then, "Who was involved?" "When did it happen?" "Where did it happen?" "Why did it happen?" "How did it happen?" The straight news story's graphic representation is an inverted pyramid reflecting the idea that the most important facts go first. The rectangle the inverted pyramid rests upon, incidentally, represents the last paragraph of the news story, which should be something more than a trailing off of facts.

A short feature story, however, stemming from events that have human interest and/or emotional appeal and comic relief, mines the material for the utmost impression. The lead piques the interest of the reader. It saves, for the very end, a punch line or a ribbon that ties up the feature in a bow. The short feature story may also be represented by a pyramid—but not an inverted pyramid.

Straight News Story:
Simple Lead

Feature Story:
Suspended
Interest

The feature lead (rectangle) rests on the top of a pyramid—creating a lure that piques the interest of the reader and increases that interest until the tension created is released in the last sentence, represented once again by a rectangle. This sports event, written as a feature story, illustrates what I'm saying:

"Lou Piniella Kicks Hat—Ump Kicks Lou"

The Associated Press, Aug, 14, 2003

Lou Piniella put on quite a show for his Tampa Bay players and the fans at the Tropicana Field yesterday.

The excitable manager was ejected during a hat-kicking tirade in the ninth inning.

"That was a really good one," Travis Lee (a Tampa Bay player) said of Piniella's four-minute argument. "He spread it out over time. Just when you think he's done, he started up again. It's pretty impressive."

Piniella was tossed as the Orioles tied it in the ninth. Brian Roberts led off the inning with a single and Luis Matos followed with a single. Matos took a wide turn after his hit and had to hustle back to first—and when the second-base umpire Jerry Layne called him safe, Piniella flew into rage.

Piniella charged out of the first-base dugout, threw his hat and started arguing.

"I told Jerry he was out of position, and he didn't appreciate it," Piniella said. "That was a couple of expletives."

Piniella began kicking his cap, sending it flying from the infield grass onto the dirt.

"That hat was just laying there," he said, "it was begging for it."

It was the fourth ejection in Piniella's first season with the Devil Rays. Lee hit an RBI double in the 10th to give the Devil Rays a 6-5 victory.

Actually, the feature would have had a more humorous and dramatic ending had it concluded with the quote, and it would have had more unity of impression. But since the outcome of the game isn't noted elsewhere, I'm willing to settle for an anticlimactic ending, especially since Piniella's team won in the 10th inning. And, yes, an excellent photo accompanies the feature showing Piniella kicking his hat.

This feature story could have been written as a simple news story and lost much of its reader interest. The lead, for example, could have been the following:

Tampa Bay manager Lou Piniella was ejected for the fourth time yesterday.

Piniella was tossed out as the Baltimore Orioles tied it in the ninth. Brian Roberts. . . .

Another short feature illustrates what's lost when the feature fails to close with a "ribbon" paragraph:

"What's 'In' for a Name This Year?"

By Kasie Hunt
The Associated Press, May 13, 2006

WASHINGTON—When kids born in 2005 head to kindergarten in a few years, a lot of them will be raising their hands when the teacher calls out "Emily" or "Jacob." In border states, it will be hard to miss Jose, Angel and Mia.

For the 10th year running, Emily is the most popular name for infant girls in the United States, according to figures this Mother's Day weekend from the Social Security Administration.

The top 10 for girls in 2005: Emily, Emma, Madison, Abigail, Olivia, Isabella, Hannah, Samantha, Ava and Ashley.

For boys: Jacob, Michael, Joshua, Matthew, Ethan, Andrew, Daniel, Anthony, Christopher and Joseph.

For the reader of this feature, the lead lures the reader into the main paragraphs. And they are interesting enough. But then the reader is left hanging. No "ribbon" ties up and completes this feature. What might that concluding paragraph be?

LONG NEWS STORIES—LONG FEATURE STORIES

While we've noted the differences between the short straight news story and the short feature, what are the differences between the longer versions of news stories and feature stories? As in their shorter versions, the basic subject matter of both can remain essentially the same. However, the longer feature tends to explore more serious topics. Also, the structure of both is more complicated than mere graphic representations of pyramids.

A long news story, such as a story about a city council or school board meeting, will have three or more major news elements involved. The lead will have to reflect that complexity. Those major story elements will have to be mentioned within the first 2 or 3 paragraphs so the reader will know what's coming in the following 10 or 15 paragraphs. Those elements in the lead, and their relative places in the paragraphs following are illustrated by these complex news story graphic representations:

Complex News Story:
Summary Lead

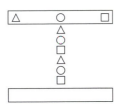

Complex News Story:
Salient Feature
Lead

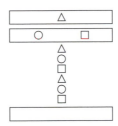

The circle in the top rectangle box of the summary lead may represent a proposed sales tax increase, the square may represent a recreational park being proposed, and a triangle may represent a hiring of a city manager. The way in which they will be taken up in the body of the story is represented by the order in which the symbols are listed. Or one element of the news story may be emphasized by noting it first in a lead paragraph as illustrated by the salient feature lead news story. The reader is then treated primarily to bare facts, with a nod to character and setting description, leading up to a no-nonsense conclusion, represented by a rectangle.

A long feature, meanwhile, lures the reader in with a feature lead. The writer is then relatively free to roam a literary field, building on that interest to climactic paragraphs and an ending that leaves a lingering impression. The long feature may be about the increase in motorists running red lights, stalking, or the Olympic Games of 3,000 years ago (taking advantage of the interest accompanying an impending Olympics). A graphic representation for a long feature may look something like this:

The left rectangle represents the feature lead. The undulating wavelike line represents valleys of exposition and peaks of reader interest generated by examples and illustrations of what was noted in the preceding valley of exposition. The line leads up to a rectangle representing the conclusion.

A FOLLOW-UP FEATURE

The news story below gives rise to a follow-up feature. The subject is Bobby Fischer, the chess champion:

"Fischer Expulsion in Check"

Tennessean News Services, September 9, 2004

TOKYO—Former chess champion Bobby Fischer won a reprieve from the threat of deportation yesterday when a court ruled he may stay in Japan until it considers a lawsuit he filed to block his ejection, his supporters said.

Fischer is wanted by the United States for violating international sanctions against Yugoslavia when he played a rematch there in 1992 against longtime rival Boris Spassky.

The Tokyo District Court granted Fischer an injunction barring his deportation from Japan until the court hears his lawsuit, Fischer's adviser, John Bosnitch, said. It could take about a year to hear the case.

Fischer was stopped at Tokyo's international airport July 13 trying to board a flight for the Philippines with an invalid passport. He has claimed the United States revoked his passport without following the due process.

A follow-up feature to this story begins like a true feature story. But then it fills in colorful background information before letting the reader see, in feature-writing prose, a ranting Fischer who is less than admirable.

"Fischer in Bizarre Endgame"

By Eric Talmadge
The Associated Press, July 17, 2004

TOKYO—In a bizarre end game, Bobby Fischer—the chess world's most eccentric star—was taken into custody after trying to fly out of Japan with an invalid passport.

Checkmate.

Wanted at home for attending a 1992 match in Yugoslavia despite international sanctions, the American former world champion had managed to stay one move ahead of the law by chess devotees.

It was not immediately clear if Fischer would be handed over to the United States under its extradition treaty with Japan. But his detention gives Japan a chance to show its cooperation with the United States just days before officials plan to bring an accused U.S. Army deserter, Charles Robert Jenkins, to Tokyo for urgent medical treatment—a case Japanese officials want Washington to overlook.

Jenkins, whose Japanese wife was kidnapped by North Korea in 1978 and returned home in 2002, is wanted by Washington on desertion charges for allegedly defecting to North Korea in 1965. He is suffering from complications after abdominal surgery in North Korea.

Fischer was detained at Narita Airport outside Tokyo after trying to board a Japan Airlines flight to the Philippines on Tuesday, according to friends and airport officials.

State Department spokesman Richard Boucher said yesterday that a U.S. consular official has visited Fischer in detention but that he could reveal nothing further.

Fischer "didn't know that his passport had been revoked," said Japan Chess Association member Miyoko Watai. "He had been traveling frequently over the past 10 years, and there was never a problem. I don't understand why his passport was revoked."

Watai told The Associated Press that she had talked to Fischer in custody. She said he was told that he would be deported and was planning to appeal.

Considered by many the best chess player ever, Fischer, now 61, became grandmaster at age 15. In 1972, he became the first American world champion and a Cold War hero for his defeat of Boris Spassky of the Soviet Union in a series of matches in Reykjavik, Iceland.

The event was given tremendous symbolic importance, pitting the intensely individualistic young American against a product of the grim and soulless Soviet Union.

It also was marked by Fischer's odd behavior—possibly calculated psychological warfare against Spassky—that ranged from arriving two days late to complaining about the lighting, TV cameras, the spectators, even the shine on the table.

Fischer was world champion until 1975, when he forfeited the title and withdrew from competition because conditions he demanded proved unacceptable to the International Chess Federation.

After that, he lived in secret outside the United States. He emerged in 1992 to confront Spassky again, in a highly publicized match in Yugoslavia. Fischer beat Spassky 10-5 to win $3.35 million.

The U.S. government said Fischer's playing the match violated U.N. sanctions against Yugoslavia, imposed for Serb leader Slobodan Milosevic's role in fomenting war in the Balkans.

Over the years, Fischer gave occasional interviews with a radio station in the Philippines, often digressing into anti-Semitic rants and accusing American officials of hounding him.

He praised the Sept. 11, 2001, terrorist attacks, saying America should be "wiped out," and described Jews as "thieving, lying bastards." His mother was Jewish.

He also announced that he had abandoned chess in 1996 and launched a new version in Argentina, "Fischerandom," a computerized shuffler that randomly distributes chess pieces on the back row of the board at the start of each game.

Fischer claimed that it would bring the fun back into the game and rid it of cheats.

A variety of long features will be presented in the next two chapters. For now, let's explore the ideas for features.

IDEAS FOR FEATURES: WHERE DO THEY ALL COME FROM?

A feature story may then be viewed as an umbrella term that embraces a multitude of experiences and interests. Feature ideas are like the cell phone—everywhere you look. The feature may be about nail biting, anorexia, memory problems, midlife problems, date rape, phobias, lying, cheating, blue jeans, a mayor, a janitor, a cat or a dog, a recipe for a chess pie. Also, snowstorms, power blackouts, bumper stickers. Or unusual occupations, hobbies or inventions. A calendar in a farmer's co-op provides a veritable future book for feature writers. National holidays, anniversaries and major events are noted on it.

Features can ride on the coattails of news events, as we've seen with the Bobby Fischer feature. A spate of forest fires may evoke related stories of secondary importance, as we will see in the next chapter. Facts revealed by the last census or a survey provide the feature writer with an opportunity, to render that information in a more palatable form. A homecoming football game may provide a color story on reminiscences by alumni cheerleaders invited to cheer one more time for the home team.

Personal experiences may generate feature story ideas, as they did for this former student, Nicole Upton Larsen:

"Living in Sin?"

Among the many reasons unmarried couples live together are economics, love, getting to know each other before marriage. Whatever the reason, more and more couples are turning to living together before marriage. Is this practice becoming more accepted or do people still look at this arrangement as living in sin?

"Breaking Up Is Easy to Do"

Most people have a hard time breaking up with their girlfriend or boyfriend, but some people seem to know how to let the ax fall gracefully. Here's a look at the flip side of breaking up. Instead of being miserable before, during and after a break up, see how the others did it and lived happily.

"Living with Chester, the Molester"

A big topic on talk shows these days is child molestation and the long-term physical and psychological effects it has on the adult survivor. Why do people repress these feelings? What are the effects on an individual?

"Before-the-Wedding Jitters"

Ever wonder what goes on in the mind of the bride to be? All thoughts are not of love and that special honeymoon night. No indeed. Some thoughts could even hover over hatred. Secrets of the bride-to-be.

"Please God, Don't Let There Be Something Under My Bed!"

Remember back when you were six years old and scared to death of what could be in your closet or under your bed? A comparison of what six-year-olds are afraid of these days with the older generation and their childhood fears.

-----
* Reprinted with the permission of Nicole Upton Larsen.

EPISODES IN YOUR LIFE

Growing up in Virden, Ill. I fought those big black-and-yellow bumblebees you find buzzing around flowers with wooden paddles slightly longer than Ping-Pong paddles. The article I wrote about it was published in a weekly newspaper, *The Potsdam Courier & Freeman*, and a daily, the *Watertown Daily Times* in New York, and then in *The New York Folklore Quarterly*. Years later, *Bee Culture* magazine paid $350 for a similar version. It then formed a chapter titled "On the Playing Fields of the Illinois Prairie: The Ritual of the Bee Hunt" for a book published by The Edwin Mellen Press titled *Growing Up on the Illinois Prairie During the Great Depression and the Coal Mine Wars: A Portrayal of the Way Life Was.*

Your life experiences may serve you equally well. I'm certain that as you read these last few pages, you recalled some of your life's events that could serve as feature story material. If an episode keeps coming to mind, chances are it's publishable. How you go about writing and marketing that experience will be treated at length in chapters like "The Art of Writing" (Chapter 7) and "To Market, to Market" (Chapter 11). Remember, whether you are on a visit to a friend's house or a grocery store, be alert for feature story material. Something probably will be there.

When things on the idea horizon look cloudy and gray, leaf through your local newspaper and look up "On This Date in History." You'll find a lode of historical feature ideas. (You can see an example in Chapter 5, "Magazine Writing and the Reader Interest Plane.")

SUMMARY

John Bogart's dog-bite news definition encompasses anything that varies from the routine (although some repetitive events—births, deaths and anniversaries—*are* news). Differences between straight news stories and feature stories lie in the subject matter, its treatment and the structure of each type of article. A straight news story begins by answering six or seven questions in a straightforward manner, usually beginning with "What happened?" The straight news story's graphic representation is an inverted pyramid, reflecting the idea that the most important facts go first.

A short feature story, however, stemming from events that have human interest and/or emotional appeal and comic relief, mines the material for the utmost impact. The lead piques the interest of the reader. Saved, for the very end, much like a joke, is a punch line or a ribbon that ties up the feature in a bow. The short feature story may also be represented by a pyramid—but not an inverted pyramid.

What are the differences between the longer versions of news stories and feature stories? The basic subject matter of both can be essentially the same. The structure of both, however, is more complicated than mere graphic representations of upside-down or right-side-up pyramids.

A long news story, such as a story about a city council or school board meeting, will have three or more major news elements involved. That means the lead will have to reflect the fact that the news event is a complex news story.

A long feature, on the other hand, lures the reader in with the lead. The writer is then relatively free to roam a literary field, building an interest to an ending that leaves a lingering impression. The graphic representation for a long feature may look something like a series of waves with rectangles at each end. One rectangle represents the feature lead. The undulating wavelike line represents valleys of exposition and peaks of reader interest generated by examples and illustrations of what was noted in the preceding valley of exposition. The waves lead up to a rectangle representing the conclusion.

Feature ideas may be as varied as life itself—and they're a part of our life. The feature may be about a mayor or a janitor, a cat or a dog, snowstorms, power blackouts, bumper stickers or unusual occupations, hobbies or inventions. A major source may be your own experiences or observations on life.

FEATURES FOR DISCUSSION

Which of these five features appeals least to you? Why? What would you change, if anything, to make one of them more appealing?

A. "Adultery Today and Yesterday"

By Courtenay Edelhart
Gannett News Service, March 23, 2005

There was a time when adultery was scandalous. Infidelity nearly ruined the career of Frank Sinatra after he left his wife for Ava Gardner. It didn't endear Eddie Fisher and Liz Taylor to the public, either.

Now adultery is hard to avoid in film, television or the real-life celebrity betrayal du jour in newspapers and magazines. The Internet is clogged with spouses cruising for discreet trysts. Many portals and dating services even specialize in facilitating such liaisons.

"I grew up in a neighborhood where there was a case of husband A running off with wife B, and it was a talked-about scandal for years afterward," says Tom W. Smith, director of the University of Chicago's National Opinion Research Center, which has researched adult sexual behavior. "It's just not shocking any more. Our TV images have gone from Ozzie and Harriett to Desperate Housewives."

Yet, 91% of those questioned in a Gallup Poll last year said affairs are morally wrong.

What gives?

Theories on who cheats and why abound among social scientists and jilted lovers, but those who have studied the issue are hard-pressed to come up with a one-size-fits-all answer.

Academics can't even agree on the extent to which adultery is happening. Various studies have found that anywhere from 15% to 70% of people have had sex with someone other than their spouse while married.

There is, however, consensus that men are more likely to be unfaithful than women, although the gap is closing. Couples in large, urban areas are more shaky than rural ones. And younger spouses are more likely to wander than those ages 50 and older.

In *Not Just Friends: Rebuilding Trust and Recovering Your Sanity After Infidelity*, author Shirley Glass identifies five motivators: emotional intimacy, love, sex, ego and revenge.

Generally, men and women cheat for different reasons, according to Ruth Houston, author of *Is He Cheating on You? 829 Telltale Signs* (Lifestyle Publications, $29.95).

"Women are usually looking for emotional fulfillment, and men are looking for sex," she says. "Women tend to do it as a last resort after they've tried everything else, but their words have fallen on deaf ears."

Houston became interested in the topic after a failed marriage to a man with a wandering eye. Her book is based on years of interviews with cheaters, divorce lawyers and private detectives.

Be cautious about gender stereotypes, warns San Diego psychologist David Wexler.

Sure, some guys are just selfish, lusty jerks, he says, but plenty of fundamentally decent men go astray, too, and blaming libido oversimplifies the issue.

In his book, *When Good Men Behave Badly* (New Harbinger Publications, $15.95), Wexler talks about "broken mirrors."

Men feel alive and worthy when they look into the eyes of a partner and see love, delight and respect mirrored back. A "broken mirror," then, is a partner's negative view.

"That makes him feel crummy, and many men don't react well to those broken-mirror experiences," Wexler says. "They can withdraw or get critical or sarcastic or even . . . abusive or violent.

"Or some men will choose to look for positive validation elsewhere. It's a dysfunctional and emotionally immature response, but it happens."

"Men will boast about their affairs, and women under-report," says Diane Shader Smith, author of *Undressing Infidelity: Why More Wives are Unfaithful* (Adams Media, $14.95). The book profiles 14 women who've had one or more affairs, as well as the author's own flirtation with temptation.

Many societies treat adulterous women more harshly than men. All the way back to biblical days, men could have multiple wives, but a woman who cheated was scorned or could even be killed.

It's no coincidence that infidelity rates among women have been creeping up since the 1960s, when women began entering the work force in large numbers for the first time, says Shader Smith. Now that many women are able to support themselves and in some cases avail themselves of no-fault divorce laws, they're more willing to take a chance.

"I like to say the reasons women cheat are as varied as the women themselves," Shader Smith says. "The common ones are boredom, loneliness and an unhappy marriage.

"Just about any parent would run into a burning building to protect their children from harm," she says. "Yet, they just don't see, or don't choose to acknowledge, that a broken family is every bit as damaging to those children emotionally."

B. "Everybody's Running Red Lights!"

Kevin O'Neal
Gannett News Service, March 7, 2004

David Potect tried not to get disgusted as he hauled possessions out of his wrecked Chevrolet recently. "There was nothing I could do," he said, "Nowhere I could go.

"She ran the red light."

It's a lament that police and sheriff's deputies know well.

In 2002, 42,815 people were killed in auto accidents and 3 million more were injured; 3,000 of those deaths and 476,000 of the injuries were related to drivers ignoring signals at an intersection, according to the National Highway Transportation Safety Administration.

The sort of "T-bone" collisions that result concentrate the impact at the doors, where cars have less strength to protect passengers, so such crashes can be particularly hazardous.

Nationwide, running a light is the most frequent cause of crashes reported to police, said Russ Rader, spokesman for the Insurance Institute for Highway Safety.

"Red-light running is a form of aggressive driving," Rader said. "They do it because there is a sense of a low likelihood of getting a ticket."

Fred Iknicki, who leads the Indianapolis Police Department's fatal crash investigators, says drivers might not realize the signal has changed because they are talking on a cell phone or otherwise distracted, or they might stomp on the gas when they see the light turn yellow in a rush to beat the red.

"It seems like it happens every day," said Indianapolis Police Department Patrolman William Slayton, as he filled out the accident form beside Poteet's mangled car.

The Insurance Institute for Highway Safety compiled the number of deaths per capita tied to red-light running in cities with populations of more than 200,000 from 1992 to 1998.

In the study, Phoenix, ranked first and Memphis second; Mesa, Ariz; Tuscon, Ariz; St. Petersburg, Fla; Birmingham, Ala; Dallas; Albuquerque, N.M; Louisville, KY; and Detroit rounded out the top 10.

Persuading drivers to obey signals is easier said than done, said Bryan Porter, an associate professor of psychology at Old Dominion University in Norfolk, Va., who has studied dangerous driving.

It still comes back to whether running a light lands someone in trouble.

"There's a disconnect between what people say is a problem and what they're actually doing," Porter said. "They figure there's not much chance of being caught."

Even the sight of patrol cars doesn't stop violators.

Precisely as Marion County (Ind.) Sheriff's Cpl. Clayton Willis pulled up recently to the intersection of Emerson Avenue and Southport Terrace, the light for Emerson turned red and a southbound Buick blew through the intersection.

"There are times when they argue so emphatically that you wonder if you saw what you saw," Willis said, after writing the driver the standard $150 ticket.

C. "What Is Stalking?"

The Tennessean, Nov. 23, 2004

Intrusive contact [or stalking] is when someone intentionally contacts or tries to contact you when you have asked that there be no contact.

The contact can be personal, such as phoning or visiting, or can involve leaving messages or sending emails. Sometimes, intrusive contact is just annoying (as when a person phones and then hangs up several times a day), but other times it can be frightening (as when a person appears at a bedroom window) or dangerous (as when a person physically hurts or threatens to hurt someone). Intrusive contact also includes:

- Insisting on talking with you when you do not want to talk
- Making a scene outside your home or dorm room
- Phoning or emailing repeatedly
- Phoning at inappropriate times
- Following you around
- Waiting to meet you outside school, work, or other activity

Stalking Myths

Myth: Only mean or sadistic people engage in intrusive contact with someone they used to date.

What we know: Some people who engage in intrusive contact are mean or sadistic; others are nice and are liked by others but cannot let go of the relationship.

What we do not know: We do not know who is likely to engage in intrusive contact and who is not. It seems as if almost anyone can engage in intrusive contact under certain circumstances.

Myth: The best way to end intrusive contact is to ignore it.

What we know: Intrusive contact will sometimes end if ignored for a few days or a week. Other times, however, the intrusive contact may increase to the point that it cannot be ignored.

What we do not know: We do not know which cases will end if ignored and which may continue or get worse.

D. "Does It Matter When You Were Born? First, Second . . .?"

Scripps Howard News Service
USA Today, Nov. 11, 2002

Growing up an only child, a first-born son or somebody's baby sister aren't just childhood labels. Birth order – the spot where a person is born in a family – can influence the adults we become and the choices we make.

First Born

First-born children are natural leaders. "For years they are told, 'Take care of your sister.' 'Take care of your brother.' They want to take care of people, be responsible for others," says Rev. George Doebler, director of pastoral care for the University of Tennessee Medical Center. Intense personalities, first-borns can be worriers seen as "bossy." "You don't want all first-borns working together. They have to have someone to direct."

The Only Child

Only children share many traits with eldest children. Confident and driven, these high-achievers mature quickly. Since they grow up without siblings, only children don't learn to fight or negotiate.

The Baby

A family's youngest child – the baby – is least stressed. Author psychologist Dr. Kevin Leman in his book *The New Birth Order* says last-born children are "typically the outgoing charmers, the personal manipulators."

Says Doebler: "When the oldest is done with a task, he goes on to the next. When the youngest is done, it's 'Good; let's celebrate.' That celebration may go on for days."

Somewhere in the Middle

Doebler says middle children – accustomed both to being bossed and having some-one to boss – are the most adaptable adults. Some middle children can have a "hard time finding their identity," Robertson says. "They may spend a lot of their time searching for their solid place."

Birth order characteristics aren't set in stone. Variables – including the number of years between children, a child's gender, a sibling's death or handicap – can alter the order. Two siblings born five or more years apart are more like two "only" children, Doebler says.

Love and Order

Birth order also influences marriages. When a first-born son raised with sisters mar-ries a woman who grew up with older brothers, they are "way ahead" in their rela-tionship, Robertson says. Each already understands how to relate.

Two only children may have a bigger adjustment. "If you know this, you can communicate about it," Robertson says.

ONLY CHILDREN

- Ambitious, enterprising
- Self-assured, leaders
- Organized, perfectionists
- Direct, logical, list-maker
- Haven't learned to negotiate
- "Little adults" who mature quickly, get along with older people

FIRST-BORN CHILDREN

- Reliable, aggressive, with leadership qualities
- Organized, goal oriented
- Younger siblings may call them "bossy"
- Intense, can be worriers
- Can be people-pleasers
- Perfectionists

MIDDLE CHILDREN

- Flexible, adaptable
- Good negotiators, mediators
- Loyal, friendly
- May be the first to leave home as an adult
- Mentally tough, independent thinker
- Unspoiled, realistic

LAST-BORN CHILDREN

- Charming, can be manipulative
- Outgoing "people person"
- Uncomplicated, affectionate
- Can be absent-minded
- Creative, entertaining
- Persistent, loves attention

E. "Women: Trying to Find Equality in the Business World"

By Becky Evans
The Tennessean, Nov. 21, 2003

WASHINGTON—Women earn about 20% less than men, even accounting for factors such as marital status and hours worked, according to a General Accounting Office report released yesterday.

The report found that the earnings gap had not shrunk in two decades despite efforts to improve gender equality in the workplace.

"The world today is vastly different than it was in 1983, but sadly, one thing that has remained the same is the pay gap between men and women," said Rep. Carolyn Maloney, D-N.Y., who commissioned the study along with Rep. John Dingell, D-Mich.

"After accounting for so many external factors, it seems that still, at the root of it all, men get an inherent annual bonus just for being men. If this continues, the only guarantees in life will be death, taxes and the glass ceiling," Maloney said.

The GAO said limitations in survey data and statistical analysis prevented a full explanation of the earnings difference but suggested that discrimination could be a factor.

"Discrimination resulting from societal views about acceptable roles for men and women or views about women in the workplace may affect women's earnings," it stated.

Decisions by women to trade higher earnings or career advancement for greater job flexibility could also explain the earnings gap, the GAO said.

The report found that women are less likely to work full-time then men and are more likely to leave the labor force for long periods of time.

Many working-class women are forced to take low-wage jobs in order to better manage their work and family responsibilities, said Beth Shulman, author of *The Betrayal of Work: How Low-Wage Jobs Fail 30 Million Americans.*

The trade-off gives women more time to care for their children, but their families still suffer because of low earnings, Shulman said.

EXERCISES

Note: The first five exercises call for a total of 15 feature ideas from three different areas. If this seems an inordinately high number of ideas, the purpose is for each person to lay in such a lode of feature ideas that they'll form an inspiration bank to draw upon when the urge to write later wanes.

1. List five ideas for feature stories from your personal experiences, in order of preference. Write them up in headline format, with a brief paragraph describing each paragraph as Nicole Upton did on page 30.

2. In class, swap with a classmate and discuss the ideas. Do you both agree on which feature ideas are best? (The instructor may ask that the best feature idea—selected by the classmate—be placed on the board for critique purposes.)

3. List five ideas for feature stories based upon your observations of various activities or events of the past month. List in order of preference and in the format prescribed in exercise 1.

4. Once again, swap with a classmate, different from the one with whom you previously exchanged ideas, and discuss them. Do you both agree on which feature ideas are best?

5. Select five ideas for features based upon historic events or anniversaries of the past. A narrow scope may be necessary. For example, the landing of the Mayflower would be too broad to treat in a feature. But a little-known incident affiliated with that landing might qualify, or perhaps an accounting of the death toll the crossing of the Atlantic took on the passengers.

6. Swap with a classmate the ideas from exercise 5 and discuss them. Do you both agree on which feature ideas are best?

7. Read the following news item:

> Nov. 2 marks the Mexican holiday called Dia de los Muertos, or Day of the Dead.
> Seemingly morbid, it's really a celebration of lives past, with special foods made and eaten at graveside parties.
> You can celebrate with pan de muertos, or bread of the dead, a round sweet loaf with bone shapes molded on top.
> It's available at La Hacienda Market, 2617 Nolensville Pike (256-5006), from now until supplies run out on Nov.1.
> (*The Tennessean,* Oct. 27, 2003)

Is the event a news story? Does it have unmined feature material? Give reasons for your answer.

8. a. Select three straight news stories from a local or national newspaper which could be modified or further investigated for rewriting as feature stories.
   b. Paste each on the left-hand side of a page. To the right of the news story, point out what could be modified or investigated for possible conversion into a feature story.
   c. In class, swap papers with a classmate. Do you both agree on the feature possibilities of the news stories?

9. After reading the following information about earthworm experiments carried out at the University of Wisconsin, write a satisfactory feature lead for the story from Berlin on cannibalism.

> Miewes' claim that he had gained the English-language skills of Brandes through his cannibalism is interesting. At the University of Wisconsin, more than 40 years ago, scientists experimented with earthworms and discovered that the worms could be conditioned to take a left fork of a channeled pathway if they underwent an electrical shock when they took the right fork. They then took an earthworm, so conditioned, cut it up and fed it to other earthworms new to the experiment. Those earthworms were then placed in the channel. When they came to the fork in the channel, they invariably took the left fork.

Exchange with your neighbor. Are the leads tasteful? Would they offend any person?

10. Write a concluding paragraph for the short feature on popular names for 2005 on page 26 of this chapter.

CHAPTER 3

WRITING THE NEWSPAPER FEATURE

What's in a feature lead? Three elements: a narrative hook, the idea of what the story is about, and a transition to move the reader into the main body of the story. Put the first letter of these words together and they spell HIT, an acronym to remind you of what should go into every lead.

What's in the feature itself? Connected nuggets of information that will inspire readers to read on for fulfillment. To satisfy them, avoid overly long expository paragraphs ("valleys of death") and make certain the high peaks of interest are composed of examples, illustrations and anecdotes. All of this should parallel a constantly mounting plane of interest.

Writing feature stories can be a most enjoyable experience. The writer becomes an interpreter or storyteller who, with imagination and resourcefulness, moves beyond the simple and the obvious to examine events from a different and sometimes deeper perspective. Features offer newspaper readers an opportunity to learn more about the human drama underlying an action or news event. Developing and composing features blends the best of journalistic prose with literary artistry. Falling stylistically somewhere between straight news stories and (prose) and fiction, features incorporate similar craft and writing techniques.

SOME FEATURE STORY CHARACTERISTICS: A RECAP

While many straight news stories today are leaning toward featurized leads, after the lead the reader faces bare facts with just a nod to setting or character description. As noted earlier, a feature story lead entices the reader into a story perhaps spiced with character and setting description, as well as writing that not only may be colorful and poetic but embraces a unity of impression alien to the straight news story.

While most feature stories stand alone in newspapers, some features may function as an adjunct of a major news story—exploring an allied subject matter aspect of the story. As noted in the preceding chapter, a major news story about an exploding chemical factory might evoke a feature story about a family forced to flee their home.

Examples and analyses later on of both short and long newspaper features will further illuminate the points presented so far. But now, let's examine more closely the feature lead.

FEATURE LEADS AND ANALYSES

If you want to involve readers in a short or long feature story, you need a lead to entice them—lure them into the story. The feature lead achieving that usually follows this pattern:

1. a narrative Hook for readers,
2. the Idea of what the feature is about and
3. a Transition into the body of the story.

To keep these lead elements readily in mind while writing a feature lead, think of the acronym HIT. The next four varied feature leads include these elements. As you read each lead, pick out the hook, the idea and the transition before reading the italicized commentary that follows.

"Against the Bubbling Tide"

EVANSTON, Ill. (AP) — Against the bubbling tide of liquor, wine and beer, the ladies of the WCTU bow their heads in prayer but never in despair.

They have been fighting the flood for a hundred years. They haven't stopped it. But it hasn't stopped them either.

The hook is the first sentence: "Against the bubbling tide of liquor, wine and beer...." The second paragraph makes more explicit the idea to be explored in the feature: a brief history of the Women's Christian Temperance Union (WCTU) and its fight against alcohol. The second paragraph also serves as a transition into the body of the feature by starting with the idea that the ladies of the WCTU "have been fighting the flood for a hundred years. They haven't stopped it. But it hasn't stopped them either."

Feature leads can be deceptively simple. Did the "bubbling tide" phrase come easily to the writer? The WCTU was founded in Cleveland, Ohio, in 1874. Every additional 25-year mark provides fodder for still another feature story. Get your laptop ready: In 2009, the WCTU marks its 125th anniversary. Anniversaries of significant events are sure things. Ten-year, 25-year, 50-year anniversaries provide a gateway to ideas for not only feature stories but magazine articles.

A first-person feature lead, an in-their-own-words lead, can be interesting, especially when it's as graphic as this lead:

"Under the Thumb: Battered Women"

"I don't remember what the argument was about, but, as usual, my husband was drunk. First he threw me on the hardwood floor and then against the wall. He ripped off my brand new sweater and the rest of my clothes.

"As he made threats against my life, I decided to run out the door. He grabbed me and dragged me to the shower, sticking my head under the cold water. I cried hysterically. Finally, I broke away and ran out of the room and the apartment, screaming, naked and dripping wet."

This is the story of Anne, as reported to psychologist Lenore Walker. It's a typical story of a battered woman....

The first two paragraphs are the attention-getters, the hook of the feature. The third paragraph serves as the idea element in the lead as well as the transition into the body of the feature story.

In what you've read so far, you've sensed from the lead whether the feature will be a light or serious feature story. The subject matter of the feature and how you intend to deal with it in the story is suggested in the lead. The next feature lead example implies that the feature will be humorous in tone.

"It's That Pesky Blue Clay"

It's that pesky blue clay over there in Ogdensburg that's causing all the trouble. As the *Courier* goes to press, that 300-foot tourist ship enters into its seventh day on a St. Lawrence River sandbar 150 yards off the Rutland Railway dock at Ogdensburg.

A herd of wild horses wouldn't budge her. You can believe that, for at last count, six tugboats with a combined horsepower in the neighborhood of 9,000 moved her only a degree or so.

The tone is set in the title and lead. The audience is prepared for a Mark Twain account of the efforts to dislodge the tourist ship.

"In Potter's Field"*

By Jim Squires

A man was buried in a muddy grave at Nashville's Potter's Field yesterday, without eulogy and without a name.

It was a $100 funeral. Nobody cries at a $100 funeral.

---

*Reprinted with the permission of *The Tennessean.*

There's nothing humorous about the subject matter. What transpires at a burial in Potter's Field is the idea. The last, one-sentence paragraph prepares us for what will follow. Knowing the etymology of Potter's Field leads to another feature idea: It refers to a field supposedly bought by Judas with his 30 pieces of gold for betraying Jesus, and was used as a burial ground in Jerusalem for paupers and strangers (Matthew 27:7–8).

SHORT FEATURE ANALYSES

The following analyses should clear whatever fog hovers over some of the previous explanations. For easy reference, paragraphs of the following short features will be paired with marginal analyses.

"A Skiing Accident Metamorphoses into a Business Break"

The lead does exactly what it's supposed to do. Readers wonder how can hitting (I like "crashing into" rather than "hitting") an evergreen be beneficial. They are lured into the story and the next paragraph is the transition into the body of the feature.

COLORADO SPRINGS, Colo. (AP) — Curtis Colligan got his big break in business after hitting an evergreen on a ski run.

Colligan retired to a ski-lodge bar after the accident.

"Two girls were sitting there, wearing casts," the 30-year-old Woodland Park resident said. "And every danged person who came in, whether they knew these girls or not, went over to talk to them."

And so was born Quik Curt's Casual Casts, a small mail-order business that sells fake arm slings and neck braces advertised as promising "dozens of dates!" and "sympathy galore!"

To keep things legal, he notes they're "good for everything except medical use."

The items are available at medical supply stores too, but Colligan's slings and casts—priced at $7 to $8.50—come complete with slogans such as "I Ski Moguls" and "Married Life Is Rough."

Colligan has run a variety of novelty businesses. He said this one, now five months old, is the break he has waited for.

"I've got orders piled up, waiting to be filled," he said.

The plot thickens. What's nice is that a direct quote does the work early in the feature. The readers say, "Okay, now what happens?" They quickly find out.

The concluding paragraph, and a direct quote at that, wraps up the feature neatly.

An analysis of another short feature reveals the same structure:

"Dark Mane Lions Preferred by Plains Janes"

By Paul Recer

The Associated Press, Aug. 23, 2002

WASHINGTON — On the Serengeti plain, the lady lion prefers a swain with a black mane.

That's the finding of a study analyzing how the dense collar of hair about the neck of male lions affects the love life of Africa's biggest cat.

Peyton M. West, a researcher at the University of Minnesota, said it's the mane color, not the length, that matters to the female lions.

"We were completely surprised by this," said West, first author of the study appearing in the journal, *Science*.

West said the female lions may instinctively be drawn to black manes because males with darker manes seem superior in a number of ways.

"A dark mane is apparently a marker the female uses to evaluate the fitness of the male," she said. This suggests that lions' manes evolved over time through sexual selection.

Dark-maned male lions generally have a higher level of testosterone "which means they are more aggressive fighters," said West, and this can be a key to raising cubs successfully.

An aggressive male is more able to chase away invading bachelors who try to take over the pride. This is important because if there is a change in male leadership of a pride, the new dominant male routinely kills all the young cubs sired by the deposed male. Thus, by choosing to mate dark-maned, aggressive males, a female lion gives her young a better chance of surviving, the researcher said.

Using a My Fair Lady allusion the writer not only casts a lure to the reader but reveals the idea of the feature.

The next paragraph provides the bridge into the main body of the feature.

The whole rationale is still something the reader wants revealed.

The reader says, "Yeah. Me too. But this suspense is killing me."

Reader: "This is more like it. Continue."

The conclusion wraps up the feature. Rationale explained. However, for more emphasis the last sentence could be rewritten. Take "the researcher said"—a phrase that deadens the ending of the paragraph—and move it to the beginning of that last sentence. In the process, delete "Thus," a stilted, pretentious word out of place here. (And most other places.) The concluding sentence is now more emphatic. (More about all this in Chapter 7, "The Art of Writing.") Although this suggestion runs counter to the previous attribution suggestion a couple of paragraphs earlier, do you see the logic of burying the attribution in the middle of the paragraph?

Let's look at another relatively short feature—about lying:

"Unmasking Liars"

By Christopher Newton
The Associated Press, June 22, 2002

The lead lures the reader into the story: Liars (all varieties) will find it more difficult to conceal their perfidy. In one sentence, Newton presents the hook, idea and transition leading into the body of the feature.

WASHINGTON—The world is becoming a trickier place for people who tell lies—even little white ones.

The technology utilized in this detection carries the reader still more into the feature, as does the next few paragraphs that list the people being affected.

From thermal-imaging cameras, designed to read guilty eyes, to brain-wave scanners, which essentially watch a lie in motion, the technology of truth-seeking is leaping forward.

At the same time, more people are finding their words put to the test, especially those who work for the government.

FBI agents, themselves subjected to more polygraph tests as a result of the Robert Hanssen spy case, have been administering lie detection tests at Fort Detrick, Md., and Dugway Providing Ground in Utah, bases with stores of anthrax. Nuclear plant workers also are getting the tests in greater numbers since Sept. 11.

The direct quote not only enlivens the feature but lends authenticity to the previous statements by citing an authority on the topic, Hetrick.

"There has been a reawakening of our interest in being able to determine the truth from each other," said sociologist Barbara Hetrick, who teaches a course on lying at Wooster College. "As technology advances, we may have to decide whether we want to let a machine decide guilt or innocence."

A historical perspective is provided and, in the next few paragraphs, the problems surfacing as a result of the astounding new technology.

The new frontiers of lie detection claim to offer greater reliability than the decades-old polygraph, which measures heart and respiratory rates as a person answers questions.

They also pose new privacy problems, moral dilemmas and the possibility that the average person will unwittingly face a test.

At the Mayo Clinic, researchers hope to perfect a heat-sensing camera that could scan people's faces and find subtle changes associated with lying. In a small study of 20 people, the high-resolution thermal imaging camera detected a faint blushing around the eyes of those who lied.

At this point a direct quote is badly needed and it comes in the next paragraph.

The technique, still preliminary, could provide a simple and rapid way of scanning people being questioned at airports or border crossings, researchers say. But would it be legal?

"As long as no one was being arrested or detained solely on the basis of the test, there is no law against scanning someone's face with a device," said Justin Hammerstein, a civil liberties attorney in New York.

More authorities are cited. And the direct quote is indeed welcome. However, the last attribution at the end of the paragraph kills an emphatic ending and is tautological. One attribution per paragraph is sufficient.

Barry Steinhardt of the American Civil Liberties Union said any technology that wasn't 100% effective could lead unfairly to innocent travelers being stranded at airports. "You would be introducing chaos into the situation and inevitably focusing on people who are innocent," Steinhardt said.

More astounding methods for detecting lying are revealed in this paragraph and the next. But rather than burying the quote in the preceding paragraph, the author should begin another paragraph with it to present a more typographically appealing story.

At the University of Pennsylvania, researcher Daniel Langleben is using a magnetic resonance imaging machine, the device used to detect tumors, to identify parts of the brain that people use when they lie. "In the brain, you never get something for nothing," Langleben said. "The process for telling a lie is more complicated than telling the truth, resulting in more neuron activity."

The concluding paragraph is unsatisfactory, focusing as it does on the brain waves technology alone. A more all-inclusive ending is needed. (In an exercise at the end of this chapter you'll be asked to write a better conclusion. After reading this chapter, you'll be able to do that.)

Even for the smoothest talker, lying is tough work for the brain. First, the liar must hear the question and process it. Almost by instinct, a liar will first think of the true answer before devising or speaking an already devised false answer.

All that thinking adds up to a lot of electrical signals shooting back and forth. Langleben says the extra thought makes some secretions of the brain light up like a bulb when viewed with an MRI.

If your region is prone to tornado touch downs, a brief feature on safety measures to be taken when a tornado is imminent and/or a sidebar on tornado violence such as this one might appear in your newspaper:

"When a Tornado Touches Down"

The Fujita Scale (Measure of a tornado's wind speed/power)
F0 (Up to 72 mph)
Broken tree limbs, signs
F1 (73–112 mph)
Trailer homes flipped, trees snapped
F2 (113–157 mph)
Roofs torn off, small buildings and trailers demolished
F3 (158–206 mph)
Roofs and walls ripped from houses, train cars knocked over
F4 (207–260 mph)
Frame homes leveled, cars thrown
F5 (More than 260 mph)
Homes and buildings completely blown away, cars disintegrated, ground scoured of trees, grass.

LONG FEATURES ANALYSES

You might consider the last major feature to be a segue to the following longer features. With its length, "Unmasking Liars" edges into this category. Strictly humorous feature stories can be based on a current fad, as in "Lawyer-Bashing." The following feature proved irresistible to editors across the nation:

"Lawyer-bashing"*

By Larry McShane

NEW YORK — Everywhere John Bracken turns, he hears another nasty one-liner: from his good buddy the doctor, from Jay Leno on The Tonight Show, even from his fellow attorneys.

There's just no justice when it comes to lawyer jokes.

"I can't go anyplace that somebody doesn't have a lawyer-bashing joke, or some comedian who unleashes a whole string of them," says Bracken, president-elect of the New York State Bar Association. "They cease to amuse me."

Bracken's not smiling, but a lot of other people are laughing out loud—especially those who've been sued, divorced, injured or indicted.

There's just something about barristers that brings out our basest instincts, says Jess M. Brallier, author of a new collection of lawyer lore through the centuries, *Lawyers and Other Reptiles*.

"Lawyers tend to inspire the creative juices of everybody," Brallier said. "The most inarticulate bum at the bar can throw a good zinger when it comes to an attorney."

The lead is the narrative hook. The following paragraph presents the idea and the transition into the body of the feature.

A peak in the feature. Excellent direct quotes opens the paragraph. And for maximum emphasis the attribution is buried in the middle.

Expository paragraphs that are needed to carry the feature along. The next few paragraphs, once again, provide a peak in the feature.

Q: What's the difference between a lawyer and a catfish?

A: One is a garbage-eating bottom-dweller; the other is a fish.

Brallier's inspiration came on the beach two summers ago, while listening to his brother, a physician, rail against lawyers. He began to think about a close friend who was going through an ugly divorce, and another friend, the target of a lawsuit.

A theme emerged.

"Within a matter of weeks, I was able to gather a great deal of material," Brallier said.

"I think we're the easy target," said Sandy D'Alemberte, [a former] president of the American Bar Association. "It's incredible. Lawyers are blamed for the failure of American business, the failure of the American health care system, the S&L failures. People attack lawyers for the most incredible things."

Q: What does a lawyer use for a contraceptive?

A: His personality.

Lawyer jokes cross all racial, ethnic and social strata. An attorney's suspenders are like crosshairs on his back. Lawyers are comedy's fish in a barrel. They are ridiculed as amoral, greedy, amoral, crooked, amoral, cold-hearted, and often, amoral....

But Bracken says lawyers are not the problem.

(And they're certainly not the solution, others might add.)

"'Anybody-bashing' falls into the category of scapegoating: 'Let's shift the focus from the real problems and do this.' It just happens," Bracken said.

It happens so much that Brallier is assembling a second volume.

"I've gotten letters from Canada, California, Savannah, Ga.," he said. "It really touches a nerve."

Q: How many lawyers does it take to screw in a light bulb?"

A: How many can you afford?

D'Alemberte says the lawyer jokes have replaced the ethnic cracks of the past.

"These are all retooled jokes. It's no longer politically correct to tell a Polish joke, so people say they're lawyer jokes," D'Alemberte said.

---

*Reprinted with the permission of The Associated Press.

After the preceding expository paragraphs, comes a peak in the form of an illustration through quotes.

This expository paragraph, with its vivid writing stands halfway between a peak and a dale.

A parenthetical gratuitous remark which obtrudes unnecessarily. It should be deleted.
This rationale for lawyer-bashing is expository. (And a little difficult to follow because of the phrasing.) The following paragraphs rise to a peak.

Somehow the concluding paragraph doesn't give me the satisfying feeling that a good conclusion should provide. How does it strike you? Perhaps an ending that incorporated these lines by Samuel Taylor Coleridge would give it more age-old spice:

He saw a Lawyer killing a viper ...
Hard by his own stable;
And the devil smiled for it put him in mind
of Cain and his brother, Abel.

A sidebar accompanies "Lawyer-bashing." It comes in the form of more lawyer jokes.

"Lawyer Jokes"

NEW YORK (AP) — There are almost as many lawyer jokes as there are lawsuits.
A random sampling:

Q: How can you tell when a lawyer is lying?
A: When his lips move.
Q: Why does New Jersey have the most toxic waste dumps and Washington
     the most lawyers?
A: New Jersey had first choice.
Q: If you were in a room with Hitler, Mussolini and a lawyer, and you had a
     gun with just two bullets, what would you do?
A: Shoot the lawyer twice.
Q: What's black and brown and looks good on a lawyer?
A: A doberman.
Q: What do you call 100 lawyers chained together at the bottom of the ocean?
A: A good start.

Love not only makes the world go round, but love and its consequences and offshoots
are fuel for a multitude of features in newspapers and magazines. When something new
about love surfaces, it's guaranteed publication. Such is the case with the next feature. But
the feature is, frankly, loveless. My introduction to the feature gives love top billing, but
that only adds to the ultimate disappointment. My introduction:

We now can disregard what Edmund Burke (the 18th-century British writer and statesman)
says about love in *On the Sublime and Beautiful:* "the passion of love is capable of producing very extraordinary effects, not that its extraordinary emotions have any connection
with positive pain." I suspect that Burke was never pierced by Cupid's arrows. Love, we all
know, can hurt. And now, we have the scientific proof of that fact provided by California
researchers (or do we?).

"Love Hurts—Really"

By Paul Recer
The Associated Press, Oct. 10, 2003

This lead is a perfect example of how the combination of the three elements (hook, idea, transition) in a one-sentence lead can lure the reader into a story. But, by now, you know that a much better lead is possible by simply having read what Burke said about love.

These two expository paragraphs provide the background for going to the more important idea presented in the lead—love hurts.

This paragraph is supposed to be a peak paragraph. And it is, but the reader wonders, "Where is this thing called love that I read about in the lead?"

More exposition! Now the reader is really down in the valley.

And more exposition, necessary but still frustrating. But for the reader there's light at the end of the expository tunnel.

For the reader, although this quote is supposed to function as a peak, it's pretty maddening. Where, oh where, is this thing called love?

This exposition is finally approaching the major idea? The reader hopes so. It's been a long wait.

Pretty dry, expository wordage compared to what we were lead to believe.

The reader says of this peak paragraph that ends the feature, mimicking Peggy Lee, "Is that all there is?" Certainly the reader deserves more. It now appears the author took the quotation provided in the last paragraph and ran with it, ignoring an exploration that would tie in more closely what has been discovered about love. An undeveloped feature.

WASHINGTON — A rejected lover's broken heart may cause as much distress in a pain center of the brain as an actual physical injury, according to new research.

California researchers have found a physiological basis for social pain by monitoring the brains of people who thought they had been maliciously excluded from a computer game by other players.

Naomi Eisenberger, a scientist at the University of California, Los Angeles, and the first author of the study to be published today in the journal *Science*, said the study suggests that the need for social inclusiveness is a deep-seated part of what it means to be human.

"These findings show how deeply rooted our need is for social connection," Eisenberger said. "There's something about exclusion from others that is perceived as being as harmful to our survival as something that can physically hurt us, and our body automatically knows this."

Eisenberger and her co-authors created a computer game in which tests subjects were led to believe they were playing ball with two other players. At some point, the players seemed to exclude the test subject from the game – making it appear the test subject had been suddenly rejected and blocked from playing with the group.

The shock and distress of this rejection registered in the same part of the brain, called the anterior cingulate cortex [ACC], that also responds to physical pain.

"The ACC is the same part of the brain that has been found to be associated with the unpleasantness of physical pain, the part of pain that really bothers us," Eisenberger said.

Eisenberger said the study suggests that social exclusion of any sort – divorce, not being invited to a party, being turned down for a date – would cause distress in the ACC.

"You can imagine that this part of the brain is active any time we are separated from our close companions," she said. "It would definitely be active when we experience a loss" such as a death or the end of a love affair.

In a commentary in *Science,* Jaak Panksepp of the department of psychology at Bowling Green State University in Ohio, said earlier studies have shown that the anterior cingulated cortex is linked to physical pain.

He said the study by Eisenberger and her co-authors demonstrates that the ACC is also activated by the distress of social exclusion.

"Throughout history poets have written about the pain of a broken heart," Panksepp said. "It seems that such poetic insights into the human condition are now supported by neurophysiological findings."

The next two features, however, are so powerful that years from now you'll remember them.

A Father's Tale*

PEORIA, Ill. (AP) — Donald Shreeves buried the last of his four daughters a week ago.[a]

"It's one of those things you figure, God, it can't be," Shreeves, a retired Army Corps of Engineers worker, said yesterday. "But it is."

All four of his daughters died violently at different times in different ways in less than a decade.

"Don't do nothing now, not a thing. Don't want to," he said. "I haven't been to bed all night. You just wake up in the middle of the night and walk the floor."[b]

His last surviving daughter, Candace Lang, 33, was buried last Thursday in a family plot in Iowa. Her husband has been charged with shooting her to death.[c]

Shreeves found out about her death Feb. 22 when he was listening to the car radio. He was driving from his new home in Princeton, Missouri, to Peoria to do some work on the old family house he had put on the market.

A few months ago, Shreeves and his wife, Bea, had given up their house there. It held too many bad memories, he said.[d]

The radio newscaster was saying something about a woman being shot to death in Schaeferville.[e]

"I knew that's where my last living daughter, Candy, lived," he said. "But I quickly dismissed it as impossible. It couldn't be Candy. A man simply does not lose all four of his daughters."

Shreeves lost his first daughter, Debbie, "the saint of the family," in a fiery car wreck in 1972. She was 19.

Beverly died in Chicago, where she had moved in the summer of 1977. A man in an apartment next to hers was killed in what people believe was an underground war. Beverly, then 27, opened the door of her apartment to see what the shooting was about. The killers saw Beverly, pushed her back into the room and forced her onto a bed. They put a pillow against her head and fired two shots into her skull.

Denise was two years younger than Beverly and followed her older sister everywhere. She moved to Chicago and tried to find out who killed Beverly.

Soon after she wrote her father that she believed she had found Beverly's killer, Denise was discovered dead in an elevator in Chicago. She had been injected with enough drugs to kill a horse, the medical examiner said.

But the father's tragedy did not end there. When Shreeves went to Chicago to try and find out what happened, he learned that his girls were not secretaries. They were prostitutes.

"I raised them since they were babies," he said, "I held down two jobs, washed their diapers and ironed their dresses. I thought I knew them."

So he and his wife moved to Missouri last October, to put it all behind them.

A week after burying his last daughter, Shreeves stares at an old portrait and says he can't believe all his girls are gone.

"It's like looking at a blank piece of paper," he said. "What the hell was wrong with us? That's what I'd like to know. Did we drink out of the wrong side of the cup or what?"

---

*Reprinted with permission of The Associated Press.

a. The hook of the lead is in these first three paragraphs. What a dreadful thing to experience. The idea of the feature is implicit in the first paragraph: "Donald Shreeves buried the last of his four daughters a week ago." The third paragraph is more explicit and serves also as a transition: "All four of his daughters died violently at different times in different ways in less than a decade."

Including the name of the father, Donald Shreeves, lends credibility and authenticity to the story. (Leading off with a name in a feature story does not necessarily violate good newswriting practices, as is usually the case in straight news stories.)

The impact of this feature is also increased by using the exact words of the father.

b. The direct quote and the effect of the deaths on the father stamp this as a peak paragraph.

c. It's difficult to designate paragraphs such as this or the following two paragraphs as expository because of the interest they generate.

d. The reader is momentarily confused by this paragraph standing alone. The unity of impression of this feature would be improved if the paragraph were grafted on to the paragraph preceding it. And put "Peoria" in brackets after "there" in the first sentence.

e. These two paragraphs are peak paragraphs, unfolding, as they do, the horror that is being awakened in Shreeves.

As we read the feature, ALL the paragraphs seem to be peak paragraphs, even as they move the feature along.

(See the preceding analyzing commentary.)

(Again, see the earlier commentary.)

The depth of the father's love for his daughters is fully revealed in this peak paragraph.

An expository paragraph bringing the feature up to the present.

All the anguish at the loss of four daughters is expressed eloquently in this paragraph. The concluding paragraph has a master's touch about it. Hemingway or Faulkner would have been hard-pressed to convey the father's feelings of loss and bitterness better than this. What these words from a simple man describe, what these figures of speech portray, are so moving that readers are led to the brink of tears.

The unity of this feature is assured by the author's focus on one man's grief over the death of his four daughters and the logical organization of the story. But to lead the reader from paragraph to paragraph and daughter to daughter, the 11th paragraph should start out with a clear transition: "Beverly, his second daughter, moved to Chicago…."

For clarity, the next paragraph, the 12th, should be revised to include stronger transitions, in this manner: "Denise, two years younger than Beverly, had always followed her older sister everywhere. After Beverly's death, she also moved to Chicago to try to find her sister's killers."

The major flaw in "A Father's Tale," however, is the omission of any mention of the mother. What was she doing all this time? The briefest inclusion would still allow the feature to focus on the father: While the father is relating the tale at the kitchen table, perhaps she's burnishing a copper tea kettle which doesn't need burnishing—a form of grief therapy, an objective correlative here, which also provides depth to the feature. (An "objective correlative" is an activity or thing that corresponds to what's taking place in the mind of a character. See Chapter 7, "The Art of Writing," for a more detailed explanation.)

Readers tend to forgive a writer's flaws if the story is dramatic, and this feature is, indeed, dramatic: Note that Shreeves is quoted profusely. The writer allows him to tell the story in his own words. The verbs are active. The writer is also conscious of word economy. The selection of words and details makes this a good feature. The final touch is the concluding paragraph.

The conclusion of your feature depends on the subject matter and the audience. Those elements generally dictate the ending.

The second unforgettable feature follows. (A movie was made about this town's villain in 1991: *In Broad Daylight: A Murder in Skidmore, Missouri,* by Harry N. MacLean. Brian Dennehy played the starring role.) So that you are able to feel the full impact of the feature, an abbreviated analysis comes after the feature rather than within.

However, notice how Jules Loh, starting with the lead, pulls you into the story and hurls you along—leaping over the valleys and skimming the peaks of the feature. By now, you can readily note them.

"The Saga of Ken McElroy"*

By Jules Loh
AP Special Correspondent

SKIDMORE, Mo. (AP) — No sooner had Ken McElroy walked out of the courtroom where they found him guilty of shotgunning the village grocer than, sure enough, there he was back at the D&G tavern.

He showed no remorse. He was sullen. When Ken McElroy was sullen, prudent people gave him room. Even when he was not sullen, tough guys in saloons all across Nodaway County called him mister. It was recognized as unhealthy to cross Ken McElroy.

"He never knelt down to nobody," his young, blonde wife of five years, Trina, reflected the other day. "He didn't care who they were or how many there were. He didn't need nobody beside him."

Just so. He was a big, thickset man of 47 ill-spent years, 5 foot 10 and 265 pounds, massive arms, low forehead, bushy eyebrows and sideburns.

He wasn't a street brawler. He was specific. He struck fear in your soul by staring you down, flashing a gun, occasionally using it. If you were his prey for today, he stalked you. He glared at you in silence, and when he spoke it was in a slow whisper. Chilling.

He was born on a farm just outside of town. When he was a boy, he fell off a hay wagon, requiring a steel plate to be implanted in his head. Some wondered if that was what made him so mean.

This is a small town: 440 people, filling station, bank, post office, tavern, black-top street, grain elevator. Beyond are rolling meadows, ripening corn, redwing black-birds, fat cattle, windmills and silos—a scene off a Sweet Lassy feed calendar. Ken McElroy jarred that pastoral serenity. So it is with outspoken relief that the citizens of Nodaway County now speak of him in the past tense. He is dead. The fear he brought them, though, still lingers in a new, unexpected form.

At the D&G tavern the day of his conviction, last June 26, he was very much alive, and he was decidedly sullen.

"I been fighting prosecutors since I was 13 years old and I'm damn near 50," he muttered in his beer. "This is the first time I've lost."

For the next two weeks the townspeople muttered, too. They wondered why Ken McElroy was in the D&G tavern in the first place, or anywhere else than where they had wanted him to be approximately since he was 13, which was a well-barred jail.

Here he was again, scot-free on a $40,000 appeal bond, terrorizing the country-side. Bond or no bond, he had swaggered into the D&G tavern toting an M-1 rifle with a bayonet on it.

"Same old story," Lois Bowenkamp said. "Police arrest him, courts let him go." Lois is the wife of Ernest Bowenkamp, known affectionately as Bo, the 72-year-old grocer who McElroy shot in the neck. Bo survived and is back at work.

On the day of a hearing to revoke McElroy's bond for carrying the rifle, July 10, about 60 men gathered downtown. They figured a big crowd at the hearing would impress the judge, and they figured to go to the courthouse together.

When the men got to town, though, they learned the hearing had been post-poned. Another maddening delay. In their frustration they gathered at the Legion hall, and invited the sheriff, to discuss how to protect themselves from the county menace. The meeting broke up when someone burst in with a message that more than once had cleared the streets of Skidmore.

"McElroy's in town."

This time they didn't clear the streets. This time they strode over to the D&G, and when McElroy finished his beer, they walked out with him. They stared word-lessly as he got into his pickup. Suddenly, someone put at least three bullets in McElroy's head.

Now a new terror grips the people of Skidmore. Having survived their fear of the lawless, they now fear the law. Not one person in that crowd has been willing to say who it was who shot and killed Ken Rex McElroy.

Trina McElroy, who was with him, told a coroner's jury she saw who it was and named his name. Nonetheless, the jury concluded McElroy was killed by a "person or persons unknown." Now a Nodaway County grand jury will investigate.

Trina was not McElroy's first wife. She was his fourth, the mother of three of the 15 children he fathered over the years.

They were married when their first child was a year old and Trina was 17— mar-ried under circumstances the prosecutor termed "suspicious." The townspeople had other words for it.

The prosecutor had charged McElroy with raping Trina. Trina says it was a lie, that they wanted to get married all along. Fair enough, except that Ken already had a wife and, besides, Trina would need her parents' consent, which they refused to give.

A few days before the rape trial, four things happened.

One, Ken got a divorce. Two, a house burned down. Three, Trina's parents gave their consent. Four, Ken and Trina found a magistrate in another county who married them. The house that burned down belonged to Trina's parents.

Thus ended the possibility of Trina's testifying against Ken. The rape charges were dropped.

Charges being dropped for lack of people willing to testify against Ken McElroy was the theme of his long criminal record. His lawyer said he had been run in and turned loose "for lack of a case" so many times he couldn't remember them all.

Rustling livestock, threatening people, molesting a minor, arson, you name it, McElroy had been charged with it, but witnesses had a way of backing off.

So it went, until he shot Bo Bowenkamp. Guilty. Finally.

"Oh, he was intimidating," Lois Bowenkamp said. "You can't know how awful it was. My neighbor and I took turns sleeping at night.

"Before the trial, he would drive up in his pickup at night and sit there. Occasionally he would fire a gun. We knew him, knew his reputation. It was frightening."

You could never know what small thing might set McElroy off. His falling out with Bo Bowenkamp resulted from Bo's clerk asking McElroy's daughter to put away a candy bar she hadn't paid for, or, from McElroy's view, "accusing her of raiding the store."

When McElroy roared into town in his pickup with the big mud flaps and the gun rack, his wife in a second pickup ("backup," she explained), everybody fled, not so much for their immediate safety but for fear they might see McElroy do something they would have to testify to later.

In fairness to the late Ken McElroy, it is also true that, like another who once prowled these parts and met his Maker just south of here, Jesse James, he was suspected of every crime in the county.

Especially rustling. Last year, Nodaway County led the state in stolen livestock—six times the thefts in any other county—and the ranchers who were aware of that were also aware that Ken McElroy always had a pocket full of money.

He lived on a small farm not likely to win any agricultural awards, so where did he get it all? He claimed also to trade in antiques, to which everybody said, but not to his face, whose antiques?

We're talking money. He paid for his pickups in cash. He paid his lawyer in cash. He tossed $8,000 on the bar at D&G and told the bartender, "If that ain't enough I've got a suitcase full at home." He peeled a hundred-dollar bill off his wad and told Lois Bowenkamp it was hers if she would try to whip Trina on the Skidmore street.

People here are looking to see what happens to the rustling problem now that Ken McElroy is laid in his grave.

It will be interesting to see what happens to Skidmore.

The McElroy shooting has thoroughly shaken this rural community. The townsfolk don't want to talk about who might have shot him, they don't want to talk about "the incident," as they refer to it, at all, not even among themselves.

"All we want to do," Lois Bowenkamp said, "is to go back to doing what we do best, which is minding our own business."

This feature blends the best of journalism prose and literary art.

The first paragraph provides a narrative hook hard to resist: Ken McElroy and the trouble he creates, and the transition to the body of the story: ... "there he was back at the D&G tavern."

The third paragraph starts with a direct quote from McElroy's wife that functions as an expository or valley paragraph. But the quote also characterizes the wife and her feelings about her husband. It is entirely appropriate to leave in her grammatical lapses. Loh renders the speech of the townspeople so faithfully that you can hear them talk. In the peak paragraphs that follow we discover why McElroy, "didn't need nobody beside him."

For impact, Loh uses fragmentary sentences. He ends paragraph 5 this way: "He glared at you in silence, and when he spoke it was in a slow whisper. Chilling."

The peak valleys end with paragraph 6. In paragraph 7, a valley paragraph, Loh paints a picture of the setting in which all this action takes place (a beautiful portrait in one small paragraph), and lets the reader know that McElroy is now dead, and then uses the transition into the next paragraphs: "He is dead. The fear he brought them, though, still lingers in a new, unexpected form." The reader is now ready for examples, in peak paragraphs, of how that fear lingers.

Loh flashes back to the day of McElroy's conviction and tells all that happened in the next few days in the present tense, for more impact. The feelings of the townspeople are explored. More quotes are used.

Paragraph 13 prepares us for the events that follow the hearing to revoke McElroy's bond for carrying the rifle. It functions primarily as a valley paragraph, moving the feature along to the climactic scene, when "Suddenly, someone put at least three bullets in McElroy's head." That sentence comes at the end of paragraph 17, the most emphatic position in a paragraph, and the reader is ill-prepared for the suddenness of McElroy's death. But that reflects the way it happened.

Paragraph 18, a valley paragraph, describes the new terror gripping the people of Skidmore—fear of the law. Loh notes this ironically: "Having survived their fear of the lawless, they now fear the law."

The following peak paragraphs explore that fear and, in the process, flash back to McElroy's wife's experiences with him and how charges of rape against him were dropped.

Paragraph 26, a valley paragraph, points out that charges against McElroy were always being "dropped," and the next peak paragraphs describe how McElroy operates to get them dropped. The occasion leading to McElroy's shotgunning of the grocer is included.

Valley paragraph 33 states that McElroy was, like Jesse James, suspected of every crime in the county. The next paragraphs touch on rustling, trading in antiques and the money he flashed around. They end with paragraph 37: "People here are looking to see what happens to the rustling problem now that Ken McElroy is laid in his grave."

The next two paragraphs function as valley paragraphs, touching on the fear that permeates Skidmore and the townsfolk's reluctance to talk about "the incident."

The concluding direct-quote paragraph illustrates the feeling of the townsfolk in this regard and ties up the feature in a neat bow: "'All we want to do,' Lois Bowenkamp said, 'is to go back to doing what we do best, which is minding our own business.'" To make the quote and the conclusion more emphatic, Loh buries the attribution, "Lois Bowenkamp said," in the least important place in the sentence and paragraph, the middle.

However, could the shooting of Ken McElroy be delayed and more effectively placed in the beginning of the climactic paragraphs? I think so.

Only highlights of the artistry evident in the writing of this feature have been noted.

TWO "COATTAIL" FEATURES

Earlier we noted that major news events could spawn features or articles of a secondary nature—sidebars or adjunct features. Just a small news story such as the following can justify a coattail feature:

"Wildfires Rage in Hot West"

Tennessean Services, June 27, 2006

Hot, windy weather hampered fire crews on Monday as they battled wildfires caused by lightning that had charred thousands of acres across northern Nevada.

Firefighters also were battling blazes that had led to evacuations in New Mexico, Arizona and Colorado.

Two Nevada brush fires that temporarily shut down parts of Interstate 80 on Sunday night near Elko, 290 miles east of Reno, continued to burn out of control Monday, said Bureau of Land Management spokesman Mike Brown.

The most disastrous wildfires in the history of California led to numerous adjunct features. The search for wildfire arsonists is just one such feature:

"The Search for Wildfire Arsonists"

By Joseph B. Verrengia
The Associated Press, Nov. 2, 2003

The lure, the suggestion of the idea of the feature, and the transition are all combined in this one sentence. The question, of course, segues the idea of the feature and the transition into the body of the story.

The writer wisely answers the question immediately in the paragraph following the opening one. (To keep readers waiting unduly for the answer to the question you pose is a perilous

Thousands of southern Californians helplessly watch their homes and hillsides devoured by flames, and ask, "Who could do this?"

The answer: Mostly careless hunters, campers, smokers, trash burners. But also angry, bored kids. Drunks. Ghostly psychopaths who vanish into the smoke. Too often—and most disturbingly—firefighters themselves.

If history is any guide, it may take years to arrest those believed largely responsible for a week of fire that has killed at least 20 people and destroyed 2,300 homes in what could be California's most expensive catastrophe. And they may never be caught. The typical rate of solving wildfire arsons is less than 10% a year.

Authorities in California are circulating a composite sketch of a young, long-haired, Jay Leno-jawed white man driving a light colored van. He is suspected of igniting at least one, if not more, of the 13 blazes that have burned in a hellish corridor extending from the mountains north of Los Angeles to San Diego and across the Mexican border.

Wildlife arson is a surprisingly common crime despite harsh penalties. In California it can carry a sentence of 10 years to life, plus murder charges when people die.

But it's one of the most difficult crimes to solve. That's because investigators are confronted with an incomplete puzzle of fragile clues such as ashes, matchheads and tire tracks, which can be obliterated in a single thunderstorm.

Witnesses are uncommon and their recollections hazy. In the West, where over-grown forests extend for hundreds of miles and mountains soar into the horizon, it's too easy to melt into the rugged background.

"The arsonist could drive to an adjacent ridge to watch his handiwork and you would never know," said Paul Steensland, a senior special agent with the U.S. Forest Service. "If they are serial arsonists, we will catch them. But it may take a number of years."

The nation has averaged 103,112 wildfires annually over the past 10 years, according to the National Interagency Fire Center in Boise, Idaho.

There are no firm numbers for wildfire arson incidents, arrests and convictions. Even a clear distinction between accidental fires and malicious ones is difficult to distinguish in the record-keeping. Experts say there just are too many jurisdictions and agencies to coordinate, from the Forest Service to county volunteer brigades, law enforcement and even the military.

But the problem is obvious. Investigators agree that human activities, not lightning, are responsible for nine out of 10 wildfires. That breakdown remains constant even in drought years such as 2000 and 2002.

The easy part, investigators say, is finding the fires' physical origins. Unlike structure fires, which tend to burn hottest where they start, wildfires usually begin cooler. They rapidly spread, propelled in a V-shape by the wind, terrain and fuel.

About three-quarters of the human-caused fires result from carelessness, fire investigators say. Hunters and hikers leave smoldering campfires, or grass brushes against the hot muffler of an off road vehicle. When the ignition point of dry forest litter is only 500 degrees Fahrenheit, it takes just a few seconds and a puff of wind for a spark to grow into a rising wall of flame.

Investigators look into every reported fire, but how to prosecute the accidents is left to local officials.

San Diego authorities say one of this week's fires that killed 12 and burned more than 1,000 homes was sparked by a lost deer hunter who set a signal blaze in the Cleveland National Forest. He was cited with a misdemeanor.

For investigators and homeowners alike, the most perverse category of wildfire arsonist are the firefighters themselves.

---

strategy. They may become impatient and move on to other news stories.)

The idea of the feature is brought to the fore: What are the problems encountered in discovering who sets wildfires?
The search for the arsonist forms a peak paragraph of interest.

The problems encountered in solving arson crimes are explained and form expository paragraphs carrying the feature along.

Direct quotes tend to elevate paragraphs into peak paragraphs of interest, as in this paragraph.

A historical overview of wildfires, expository paragraphs, provide background and importance to the feature.

The illustrations and examples in this paragraph, plus the buildup of the preceding paragraph, provide an unmistakable peak in reader interest material.

An expository paragraph that provides a flow or transition to the next paragraph.

With illustration or example, we have a peak paragraph.

The paragraph is expository, a valley or dale of interest.

Although this paragraph is a peak paragraph, it strays from the major idea of the feature—forest fires, who sets them, the difficulties apprehending them.

The feature comes back to forest fires with these two examples of firefighters setting forest fires. They are peak paragraphs. Although they are interesting, they do not function as a good conclusion for the feature. They are not tied into the major idea of the feature. A more proper conclusion might be the following:

"These firefighter/arsonists are the ones that were caught. Compared with those other arsonists who got away, they are pretty small fish."

(The analogy of "small fish" may not be the best, but you get the general idea.)

The most celebrated case was John Orr, an arson sleuth for the Glendale, Calif., Fire Department serving a life sentence for setting a 1984 hardware store blaze that killed four people.

He also was convicted of conducting a remarkable arson campaign that damaged 67 homes along with open land. He was arrested after penning a novel, *Points of Origin*, depicting a firefighter who torched a hardware store and other businesses for sexual pleasure.

In 2002 firefighters were responsible for two of the nation's largest wildfires. In Arizona, Leonard Gregg, a contract firefighter, was sent to a prison hospital for psychiatric evaluation after being charged with setting the Rodeo fire in the state's rugged eastern mountains. At its worst, the inferno spread 50 miles wide; one local fire chief described it as "walking down the aisles of hell."

In Colorado, former Forest Service seasonal worker Terry Barton pleaded guilty to starting the Hayman fire, which consumed 137,700 acres southwest of Denver and destroyed 133 homes.

And now one more excellent feature without interpolations:

"A Football Coach Does the 'Right Thing'"

By Steve Wilstein
The Associated Press, Nov. 24, 2002

Mike Slaughter wonders what it says about society when a football coach does the right thing and it gets treated like a big deal.

Congratulatory letters, faxes and cards are pouring into his office at Marquette Catholic in Alton, Ill.

Radio stations and newspapers are calling from New York to Los Angeles.

He's been coaching high school football in obscurity for 25 years, and suddenly he's a hero because he had the guts to suspend 16 starters arrested for underage drinking at a house party.

It would be nice, though perhaps naïve, to believe that every coach in the country would act the same way Slaughter did, especially in his circumstances—the team was 10–0 and poised to challenge for the school's first state championship.

This was his "once-in-a-lifetime" team, but the way Slaughter saw it, the way any coach should, is that he had no choice except to suspend the players, one of them his own son.

"It boils down to accountability," Slaughter said. "It doesn't matter if they drank a beer or a six-pack, they still broke the rules. I always told my boys that you get in trouble with alcohol, tobacco, drugs, I will suspend you from the team."

The lesson hit home for the players in this small Mississippi River town when they stood on the sideline the weekend before last, watching their teammates take a 63–0 pounding that ended their season.

"The players know they threw away a prime opportunity to make some history," Slaughter said. "They will be bothered by this for the rest of their lives. I feel sad for my son because I know that five, 10, 20 years from now he will always remember that he and his teammates ended the season under this cloud.

"For me, this was very sad. It tore me up. I'll always feel a sense of hurt and betrayal."

There have been other coaches, other communities, that have attached more importance to victory than following the rules. Offenses far worse than drinking a little beer have been swept aside, punishment postponed or ignored, in pursuit of championships. For Slaughter and the parents at Marquette, that wouldn't stand.

On the night of the party, Slaughter was called to the sheriff's office to pick up his son, a halfback celebrating his 18th birthday.

"He was very apologetic, very embarrassed," Slaughter said. "The biggest humiliation came in having to look his father, who is also his head football coach, in the eyes. On the way home, I said to him, 'Son, I'll always love you, but you need to learn from this.'"

Slaughter told the suspended players that they could skip the next playoff game because he didn't want to hold them up to further humiliation. But they all came, dressed, and rooted for their struggling teammates.

"It began the healing process," Slaughter said. "It gave these kids a chance to start making amends and start facing up to what happened and go out like men."

At the end, the players took off their helmets and held them to the sky as they had in victory, then went charging up the stairs to the locker room while the crowd of 1,300 gave them a standing ovation.

"The applause, the remarks from people, it was overwhelming," Slaughter said. "These kids had tears in their eyes, partly because of what had gone on but also because of the positive attitude that we got from the Marquette community. This could have been any high school in America. Drinking is a problem in a lot of schools. These were good kids. They made a mistake. They know that. They just need to be taught a lesson in responsibility."

Some have suggested that the suspensions, even the arrests at the house of a student whose parents were in Hawaii, were excessive, that the officers could have let them off with a reprimand.

"My attitude was no, they couldn't, and no, they shouldn't," Slaughter said. "If this party would have been allowed to continue, these kids would have been stumbling, fumbling, bumbling drunk. There were so many that surely a lot of them would have been driving home."

Slaughter has received several phone calls over the years informing him someone was killed while driving drunk.

"To a parent, that's the biggest fear in our lives," he said. "I told my son that at least I wasn't coming down to a morgue to identify his body. It could have been worse."

He can't understand why anybody, knowing how serious teenage drinking can be, would suggest that he could have done anything less.

"It's strange," he said, "that we get this much publicity for doing what we consider the right thing."

What is magnificent about this feature is the fact that those suspended football players suited up and rooted for their team, and when the game was over, held up their helmets as if that 63–0 humiliating defeat was a victory. But, of course, for those players, and the team, it *was* a victory. Perhaps that helmet display could have been more prominently displayed in the climactic paragraphs?

SUMMARY

A properly written feature lead contains three elements: a narrative hook, the idea of what the story is about and a transition to move the reader into the main body of the story. Put the first letter of these words together and they spell HIT, an acronym to remind you of what should go into every lead.

The feature itself will inspire readers to read on for fulfillment. Avoid overly long expository paragraphs ("valleys of death") and make certain the high peaks of interest are composed of examples, illustrations and anecdotes. All of this parallels a constantly mounting plane of interest.

Writers of features include details and vivid words, and especially active verbs. Direct quotations opening a substantial number of paragraphs break up long, gray columns of type. Each sentence and each paragraph should have a transition that keeps the feature flowing. The concluding paragraph delivers the feature to the reader in a neat bow.

FEATURES FOR DISCUSSION

Which of these five features appeals least to you? Why? What would you change, if anything, to make one of them more appealing? Which did you find most appealing? Why?

A. "What Happens Here, Stays Here?"

By Adam Goodman
The Associated Press, Feb. 9, 2004

LAS VEGAS — Lawrence Orae didn't come to the Las Vegas Strip looking to win big. He didn't come for the strippers or over-the-top shows.

He came to die.

Orae, 64, checked into the exclusive Four Seasons Hotel March 11 after driving his silver Jaguar from his condominium in Montecito, Calif. Five days later, a maid found the businessman in his room, slumped in a chair with a gunshot wound to the head and a suicide note in his leather briefcase.

"Las Vegas was one of his very favorite places," said his former wife, Long Charily, "They always treated him like a king. He loved Las Vegas."

Every year desperate men and women make the pilgrimage to the gambling capital to kill themselves. More than once a month, a visitor commits suicide here, according to Clark County coroner records dating to October 1998.

By comparison, Atlantic City had about one-third as many nonresidents take their lives during that period. In the same six years, no one committed suicide at Walt Disney World.

"They pick Las Vegas and kill themselves," former Clark County Coroner Run Feud said. "It's a fact."

But saying exactly why is not so straightforward.

Experts and family members have their thoughts—from the city's culture of anonymity to despair, in some cases over gambling losses.

But each case is different. As one suicide note said, "Here there are no answers."

———

Orae married Charily in Las Vegas three years ago and found the city luxurious.

"They always showered him with the attention he felt he deserved," she said.

The two had separated and planned to divorce, Charily said. Orae was also despondent over recent financial setbacks. But what he was thinking will always be unclear.

"Lawrence remained a mystery to those close to him," she said.

Four months after Orae's suicide, on July 19, 2003, Gloreah Hendricks, 30, jumped from the ninth floor of the Aladdin Hotel-Casino parking garage.

Her family thought Hendricks was on vacation in Las Vegas, which she considered beautiful, said her mother, Rosemary Pitts, of Montgomery, Ala.

In her car, police found a note that said, "One stop and away I go."

Matthew Naylor, 31, didn't leave a note before killing himself on June 21, 2002, at the Plaza hotel-casino.

The man died from a loss of hope, said his father, Lewis Naylor, an engineer in Baltimore. "He just had a lot of challenges in life and gave up. He couldn't see how it was all going to come together to make a life worth living."

David Strickland, 29, a Hollywood actor, whose wrists were scarred from previous suicide attempts, toured strip clubs and partied before he put a bed sheet around his neck at the Oasis Motel March 22, 1999.

Strickland was depressed because he "had fallen off the wagon," his friend and fellow actor Andy Dick told investigators. Strickland, who was in Alcoholics Anonymous, was worried his girlfriend would leave him after his relapse.

But why Las Vegas?

"I've asked myself that 100 times," said Judi Kagiwada of Middleboro, Mass., whose 39-year-old husband, Terrence, hanged himself at a downtown casino March 5, 2003.

Relatives suggest their dead loved ones might have been attracted to a place where you can get lost, and be found only when it's too late.

Experts say some might have been looking for one last sign not to pull the trigger or tie the noose. A jackpot, blackjack or smile. Anything.

"You're in a place that nobody cares. It's not famous for being warm and fuzzy. It's a place you can be anonymous and die," said David P. Phillips, a sociologist at the University of California at San Diego, who co-authored a 1997 study that found Las Vegas had the highest level of suicide in the nation for residents and visitors.

Still, he said, "I wouldn't bet big money on any particular explanation" behind the deaths.

Among the victims were a banker, musician, immigration officer, pharmacist, exotic dancer, taxi cab driver, disc jockey, car salesman, and professional gambler. Most came from California, same as the tourists. Others hailed from Texas, Wisconsin, New York, Utah, Kansas, Maine, 26 states and two foreign countries in all.

Almost all had medical, financial, or domestic problems. In some cases, victims appeared to suffer from gambling addictions or killed themselves only after Las Vegas took their money.

Elton Beamish, 24, drove to Las Vegas from Ann Arbor, Mich., where he was a student at the University of Michigan. He checked into a motel Jan. 12, 2000. Four days later he was dead. His checkbook told the story.

Beamish lost his financial-aid money and became depressed. He bought a 12-gauge shotgun from Kmart, put it in his mouth and pulled the trigger.

———

Suicide destinations exist around the world, the most famous being the Golden Gate Bridge, where more than 1,000 people have jumped to their deaths since the bridge was built in 1937. It averages about 20 suicides a year.

Other places resonate with the suicidal, such as Mount Mihara in Japan and the Empire State Building in New York.

Las Vegas is different. It has no association with death, even though in 2001 Nevada ranked third behind New Mexico and Montana in suicide rates, according to the American Association of Suicidology. For many years it was No. 1.

From 1991 to 2002, 4,994 people killed themselves in Nevada. Of those, about 11% of 547 were from out of state. Most suicides take place in southern Nevada's populous Clark County. Home to the Strip and its decadence and debauchery.

"Vegas is a canvas for American neurosis," UNLV history professor Hal Rothman said. "It's a place where we paint our hopes, dreams, fears and apprehensions. . . . It's the city of excess. What could be more of an excess than killing yourself?

"The average person who comes here still sees it as Sin City, where the rules of their lives have been suspended, where their actions have no consequences."

There are consequences to suicide, of course.

The body of William L. Mauldin III was discovered Aug. 2, 1999, in a swath of rocky dirt next to New York–New York Hotel-Casino's 10 story parking garage.

In the 32-year-old disc jockey's pocket was a note for his mother. "Tell her I'm sorry and I love her with all my heart. I have been depressed for almost a year now. Don't blame anyone but me."

Finding the body would have devastated family members, and that may partly explain why William chose Las Vegas, brother Rob Mauldin said. "He was probably trying to protect loved ones from the horror."

———

Alan Feldman, MGM Mirage senior vice president for public affairs, says that saving people who are suicidal once they arrive in Las Vegas probably is impossible.

"If a person's closest friends and family can't prevent it," Feldman said, "how is the bellman at the hotel all of a sudden going to have this miraculous cure? I don't know if there is very much we can do."

B. "On Lying and Dating"

By Alison Roberts
Sacramento Bee, Dec. 2, 2004

Much of the lying that goes on in dating is neither pathological nor cruel.

"Usually the lies that people tell to get a date are pretty harmless. People are just trying to please the other person," says Wade Rowatt, a professor of psychology at Baylor University in Waco, Texas. He studies deception, or lying, defined as "communication that's intended to mislead" (the delusional need not apply).

In his most recent study, college students were asked to describe themselves in writing to other students who were open to dating.

They lied. A lot. On average, they told two or three lies in their self-descriptions. "Almost every person used some deception," Rowatt says.

Some findings to consider from this and other studies:

- Men and women lied equally in their attempts to impress prospective dates.
- The more attractive the prospective date, the more lies they'll hear. This suggests that when it comes to being told the truth, you might be better off not looking too good.

Before you swear off dating, you should know that lying is not restricted to those looking for romance. We're all liars.

"The moral of the story is that people lie in everyday life," Rowatt says.

Studies have found that we lie in close to a third of our social communications in a given day, he says.

"Sometimes I feel like I'm studying the dark side of relationships, but lying and deception are common forms of communication," Rowatt says. (Lately, he's been taking a break by studying the psychology of humility: "I'm tired of vices; I want to study virtue.")

We're not as creepy as these findings may suggest. For one, when scholars such as Rowatt talk about lying, they include deception that most deem harmless. Makeup and girdles qualify as tools of deception, but most of us wouldn't say wearing them makes someone a liar.

There also are lies that actually are altruistic—to spare another's feelings.

"I actually see some benefits to the emotionally protecting lies that people tell," Rowatt says. "Think how awkward life would be if you told the truth all the time; the world would be almost uninhabitable."

You might as well decide to coexist with lies; you aren't even aware of most of them.

"There's good scientific evidence that it is very difficult for even trained professionals to detect deception," Rowatt says.

There are body-language indicators of stress that may indicate lying, such as fidgeting and blinking. But researchers say they are not reliable.

Studies have shown that people can discern lying only 54% of the time.

"There's no behavior that always means a person is lying," says Paula DePaulo, a social psychologist at the University of California–Santa Barbara and a leading researcher in the field of lying. "There's no Pinocchio's nose."

And, if you were in love with Pinocchio, you may well be the last to notice his nose is growing.

"People are more likely to be taken by their own romantic partner than by a stranger," DePaulo says. "You're just so invested in thinking your partner is honest; there's definitely this overconfidence effect."

As they say: Love is blind.

C. "Broken Hearts Are Real—And Can Be Treated"

By Linda A. Johnson
The Associated Press, Feb. 10, 2005

Confirming the wisdom of the poets and philosophers, doctors say the sudden death of a loved one can cause a broken heart.

In fact, they have dubbed the condition "broken heart syndrome."

In a study published just in time for Valentine's Day, doctors reported how a tragic or shocking event can stun the heart and produce classic heart attack-like symptoms, including chest pain, shortness of breath and fluid in the lungs.

Unlike a heart attack, the condition is reversible. Patients often are hospitalized but typically recover within days after little more than bed rest and fluids, and suffer no permanent damage to their hearts.

In their study, published in today's *New England Journal of Medicine*, doctors at Johns Hopkins University gave a name to the condition, demonstrated through sophisticated heart tests how it differs from a heart attack, and offered an explanation for what causes it.

For centuries, doctors have known that emotional shocks can trigger heart attacks and sudden deaths. Broken heart syndrome, technically known as stress cardiomyopathy, is a different phenomenon.

The Johns Hopkins doctors documented how a days-long surge of adrenaline and other stress hormones can cause a decline in the heart's pumping capacity. The researchers theorized that the hormones probably cause tiny heart blood vessels to contract, but other explanations are possible.

Until now, doctors "were trying to explain it away, but the pieces never fit," said Dr. Hunter Champion, an assistant professor. "By our ability to recognize it, we've saved people from getting unnecessary [heart] procedures."

Champion and colleagues treated 19 emergency room patients with the syndrome between 1999 and 2003. For reasons that are not entirely clear, nearly all of them were post-menopausal women.

Many were grieving over the death of a husband, parent or child. Others triggers included a surprise party, car accident, armed robbery, fierce argument, court appearance and fear of public speaking. MRIs and other tests showed they had not suffered heart attacks.

Other doctors have since told Champion that they have seen the same thing, and researchers in Japan and Minnesota have reported similar cases.

"This is probably something that happens all the time," but most people do not seek treatment, Champion said.

D. "The Lore of the New Year's Kiss"

By Amy Waddell
The Tennessean, Dec. 19, 2003

Smooch. Osculate. Smack. Peck. Lock Lips. Pucker up. Snog. Bouche. Kiss!

Whatever you choose to call it, the kiss is as much a part of New Year's Eve tradition as fireworks and noisemakers. Single people fret about finding someone to smooch and romantics go to great lengths to plan the perfect New Year's kiss. At the stroke of midnight, revelers around the world raise a ruckus, set off fireworks, pop open champagne, and kiss.

Most people know that they must secure a snog (as the Brits say) to ensure luck for the coming year. Throughout America, the Caribbean, Europe, Australia, Bali and New Zealand, people kiss at the breaking of the New Year. Even in Japan, everyone gives at least a polite peck. We don't question it, we just do it. It's tradition. Like knocking on wood or taking care not to step on a crack, the New Year's Kiss is deeply ingrained in our lexicon of popular customs. Though we're about to embark on 2004, we're carrying on New Year's Eve traditions that date back to antiquity.

The concept of making noise at the stroke of midnight on New Year's pre-dates the Middle Ages. People back then were always very concerned about the presence of evil and mischievous spirits. The noise was meant to drive away any lingering spirits of the old year, or to scare away any inquisitive ghosts or spirits that might have been drawn to the mortal's festivities.

Kissing itself is thought by scholars of antiquity to have originated in early Asia Minor as an expression of loyalty and sentiment. The lore surrounding the New Year's kiss may have come from some playful celebratory customs in Medieval Europe.

St. Sylvester was a Pope in the 1400's and New Year's Eve came to be known in Belgium, Germany, Austria and through the Alps as St. Sylvester's Night. It was popular custom at inns and taverns to have someone dress as St. Sylvester in a large cloak and a mask with a flaxen beard. One interesting thing is that this costumed St. Sylvester would also wear a wreath of mistletoe around his neck. Another wreath of pine would hang from the ceiling of the inn. The St. Sylvester figure would "hide" in a corner, and then jump out to impart a lucky kiss on any maiden or youth who walked under the pine wreath. At the stroke of midnight marking the New Year, the "Old Sylvester" would be chased out as a representation of the old year.

Historian Clement A. Miles tells us in "Christmas in Ritual and Tradition," first published in 1912, that as the tradition spread, a doll came to be used to represent St. Sylvester. The doll, also dressed in a cloak with a flaxen beard, would be hung in a wreath of mistletoe from the ceiling of an inn or home. Any maiden who stepped beneath the wreath was fair game for a kiss. At midnight, people would gather by the mistletoe to collect "lucky kisses" under the benevolent St. Sylvester. The doll was then tossed into the snow to confirm the passing of the old year. "Lucky" New Year's kisses under mistletoe! While most of us have never heard of St. Sylvester, we've certainly been caught for a kiss under the holiday mistletoe.

According to William S. Walsh in his 1897 book, *Curiosities of Popular Culture*, as time progressed, the lore of the lucky kiss spread throughout Europe. For example, as people milled about in 17th Century Edinburgh, Scotland, on New Year's Eve, any lady or maiden could be kissed by a youth for luck, even if the lady had an escort. Most tomes of folklore and superstition, including *Knock on Wood and Other Superstitions* by Carole Potter include specific instructions for a New Year's kiss. "At the stroke of midnight, make sure to kiss someone, or have someone kiss you," intone the encyclopedias of lore, "to ensure that you will be loved and kissed throughout the year." It is also popular belief that the one you kiss on New Year's Eve is the one you'll be kissing through the coming year.

We still ascribe a certain magic to the New Year's kiss, even if we pucker up to our husband or wife of 30 years. If you still have time, why not wrap a small doll in a dark green napkin or dish towel as a make-shift cloak and add some yellow yarn for a flaxen beard? Hang the homage to St. Sylvester amongst the mistletoe as a quaint conversation piece. Better yet, find a friend to dress up as the Saint and surprise your New Year's Eve party guests by carrying on the original tradition. Young maidens beware! Under the kind eye of the saint, your New Year's kisses may be especially lucky, and your party will certainly be remembered for years to come.

Sources:

The Dictionary of Omens and Superstitions, compiled by Philippa A. Waring, first published in 1978 by Souvenir Press, Ltd.

Miles, Clement A., *Christmas in Ritual and Tradition,* Reference book, originally published in 1912.

Potter, Carole, *Knock on Wood and Other Superstitions.* Sammy's Publishing, 1983.

Walsh, William S., *Curiosities of Popular Customs,* J Lippincott, 1897.

E. "Crunch, Crunch, Crunch, Nail Biters"

By Sandra Valdez Gerdes
Gannett News Service, Jan. 20, 2005

Crunch, crunch, crunch.

You can spot them anywhere; in a nearby car, on the bus, at the movies, in the library and even in the boardroom.

They're nail-biters. They sit and chomp away at their fingernails, often unaware.

The trigger can be stress, boredom or an action-packed flick. One thing is certain. Nail biting (or onychophagia) is an easy habit to start, but a hard one to break.

"Once I get started, I can't stop," says Margie Bissell, a 27-year-old mortgage funder and closer.

Bissell is attractive, outgoing, successful and drives a sporty BMW convertible. She has everything a young woman could want—except pretty nails.

She is a chronic nail-biter and she's not alone.

Nail biting, which includes biting the cuticle and soft tissue around the nail, is a common problem. As many as one in three Americans bites his or her nails, and the behavior crosses every social and economic barrier, according to www.stopbitingnails.com, one of the biggest online sources for nail-biters.

It is regarded in the medical field as the most common of the typical "nervous habits," which include thumb-sucking, nose-picking, hair-twisting or pulling, tooth-grinding and picking at skin.

Nail biting typically begins between the ages of 5 and 10. It often occurs as teens go through puberty.

Bissell, of Tucson, Ariz, started about age 8, probably because her older sister and mother did it, she says.

Bissell's boyfriend, Dustin Williams, 30, recalls starting back in high school, but he bites his nails to a lesser degree.

"I only bite to trim them. It's a ghetto-manicure," he says.

People attribute nail biting to many things, including old habit, stress, nervousness or behavior learned from family members.

However, there are no rules to suggest what causes people to bite their nails, says Dr. Norman Levine, professor of dermatology in the department of medicine at the University of Arizona College of Medicine.

"Sometimes it's anxiety. Only occasionally is it psychological. In most cases, it is not a serious problem," Levine says. "It's usually just habit. I think at one level we have habits because it feels good to do it. If it relieves stress I think that it's a coping mechanism. I think in most cases, people just do it because they do it, like cheek biters."

Most nail-biters do it mindlessly, while they are involved in other activities.

Nail salons report that between 25% and 70% of clients are nail-biters who are either trying to kick the habit or improve the appearance of their hands.

EXERCISES

1. Critique the published newspaper feature leads below. Are they effective? Confusing? Not interesting? Identify the narrative hooks, ideas and transitions in each of them. Sometimes they will be in separate sentences or paragraphs. At other times they will be combined in one or two sentences. Bracket them, labeling them "hook," "idea" and "transition." (For your aid in writing more attractive leads, sometimes additional paragraphs will be included.)

   a. *The European*

     STOCKHOLM — They are not very tall—less than a meter—and don't carry guns.

     But the governor of Berga prison in the south of Sweden is convinced that his new members of staff—10 domestic geese—are the perfect guards.

     Not only are the geese fierce, wakeful and alert, but they won't be demanding holidays or overtime pay. And they have cause to be grateful to their employers—their new jobs have saved the geese from the butcher's block.

     Warden Lars Sjoberg says: "We have such a small number of employees that we need this kind of help, especially at night."

   b. PARIS (AP) — Growls of protest resounded off the nicotine-stained walls when a tough anti-smoking law went into effect Nov. 1. But the government's enforcement efforts have been mostly smoke.

Cigarette-loving French have gone on puffing. No fines have been levied, and most cafes and restaurants have yet to provide no-smoking sections, although these are mandatory.

"A cafe is a place to relax," said Sophie Rochko, proprietor of a student hang-out called the Société Basile. "If one starts regulating relaxation, then it's not relaxation, is it?"

c. EYE, England — Deep in the heart of English chicken country, the abundant bird droppings have long been a smelly nuisance. Now they are an energy source.

More than 12,000 houses receive electricity from an innovative generating plant run on poultry litter—chicken dung plus soiled straw and wood shavings from the bottom of the chicken coops.

d. Your sleep problems are likely to become your spouse's problem, often making the partner irritable and affecting your sex life.

Researchers at the Sleep Disorders Center at St. Louis University School of Medicine found that half of the spouses of insomniacs and people with sleep apnea (sudden stops in breathing that result in snoring) said their partner's sleep problem affected their relationship.

e. "I don't know the name of the detergent," a shopper said to the clerk, "but I can hum the tune for you."

That highly resilient gag has been making its way up and down Madison Avenue for years, generating a few light moments in the intensely competitive business of providing music that sells soap—or anything.

f. By Jack Wilkinson
Cox News Service

SAND MOUNTAIN, Ala. — Who's killing the great cows of Sand Mountain?
Some suspect aliens in UFOs. Some say satanists. Or else it's government agents swooping down in helicopters for the kill. Or exposure to TVA high-power lines. Or it's cow murderers, impure and simple.

Whoever, it's udder chaos up here. As Ted Oliphant says, "There's strange things afoot." Ahoof, too.

Since October, 26 animals—nearly all cows—have been mutilated in several small, rural communities on this mountain in northeast Alabama. Nearly all have been killed in the same manner, with precise, bloodless, almost high-tech surgical incisions that removed various animal parts: tongues, teeth, eyes, ears, hearts and excretory and sexual organs.

And when the animals are found in pastures, there are no footprints. No tire tracks. No trails. No blood, either.

"It's pure Sherlock Holmes and one of the weirdest cases I've ever seen in my life," said Oliphant, a Fyffe policeman investigating the killings. "We've got no witnesses, no motive, no suspects. The only thing we've got is the animals left behind."

2. Give the third paragraph in exercise 1(a) more impact by burying the attribute.

3. Rewrite the lead in exercise 1(d) to make it reflect a feature focus.

4. What comment might be considered "offensive" or "insensitive" in the 1(f) feature?

5. Write a better conclusion for "Unmasking Liars" on page 44.

6. Write a better conclusion for the feature, "Lawyer-bashing" on pages 45–46.

7. Write a better conclusion for the feature on "Wild Fires" on pages 54–55.

8. a. Select three mediocre leads from three feature stories in your local newspaper. Paste each on the left hand side of a sheet of paper. Beside each, describe what is lacking in the lead. Underneath your statement, write a better lead.

b. The following grading form may be utilized. (Students exchange papers and use the form to grade each others' papers. The instructor can then grade the papers as well as the grading of the papers.)

Newspaper Feature Grading Form

Heading at top of page correct, single spaced, etc.?:
"Feature paste-up made easy"
A 150-word exercise
D.J. Anon   yes ____   no ____

Feature lead (1)

Pasted along left side of page?	yes ____	no ____
Hook, Idea and Transition clearly noted?	yes ____	no ____
Headline: What's wrong with this feature lead?	yes ____	no ____
Paragraphs pointing out deficiencies correct?	yes ____	no ____
Comments:		
Headline: A better feature lead?	yes ____	no ____
Paragraphs with feature lead an improvement?	yes ____	no ____
Comments:		

Feature lead (2)

Newspaper feature pasted along left side of page	yes ____	no ____
Hook, Idea and Transition clearly noted	yes ____	no ____
Headline: What's wrong with this feature lead?	yes ____	no ____
Paragraphs pointing out deficiencies correct?	yes ____	no ____
Comments:		
Headline: A better feature lead?	yes ____	no ____
Paragraphs with feature lead an improvement?	yes ____	no ____
Comments:		

Feature lead (3)

Newspaper feature pasted along left side of page	yes ____	no ____
Hook, Idea and Transition clearly noted	yes ____	no ____
Headline: What's wrong with this feature lead?	yes ____	no ____
Paragraphs pointing out deficiencies correct?	yes ____	no ____
Comments:		
Headline: A better feature lead?	yes ____	no ____
Paragraphs with feature lead an improvement?	yes ____	no ____
Comments:		

9. Write a feature story for this happening:

LAWRENCE, Mass. (UPI) — Steve Grabowski, a balding pro wrestler who fights under the name Steve Thunder, filed a $200,000 suit against the firm that attached his hairpiece.

Grabowski, 28, of Lawrence, paid $750 for a hair replacement that he says he was assured would be fixed tightly to his real hair. Four days later an opponent yanked off Grabowski's wig in the ring.

"Everybody was laughing at me," Grabowski said. "I was very embarrassed and quite humiliated, to say the least."

He said he can't get bookings because "I was a laughingstock."

10. Write a feature story for this news event:

> Edgar Jones, 28, of St. Louis, posing as a jogger, is accused of knocking down young women, removing their shoes and sucking their toes. Otherwise, they're unharmed. He's charged with assault, indecent exposure, and sexual abuse after eight victims ranging in age from 13 to 19 filed complaints.

11. Select a feature story from a newspaper and paste it on the left-hand side of a page. To the right, criticize it, paragraph by paragraph, listing the good and bad points of the feature.

CHAPTER 4

WRITING INVESTIGATIVE AND SURVEY FEATURES

FEATURES BASED ON SURVEYS

Features on survey results, medical findings and census results call for a skillful handling of the plethora of information. Unless you're careful, without good organization and adequate transitions the feature can degenerate into a series of choppy sentences—a mere recitation of facts. The following feature, on divorce, is a prime example. As unlikely as it seems, the divorce survey was funded by the Centers for Disease Control and Prevention. But let's look at how the feature plays out.

"Hoping to Avoid Divorce?"

By Laura Meckler
The Associated Press, July 25, 2002

The lead proves to be interesting. The hook is in the question as well as in the answers that follow. And those answers are transitions into the main body of the feature. The answers, however, tend to be listings and take careful reading by the reader—something that newspaper readers aren't particularly fond of doing. To clarify things, the last sentence could be broken into two.

The second through fourth paragraphs, while chockful of interesting information, discourage readers with what I call "choppy" sentences. Most are strung together without meaningful transitions.

This paragraph and the next one continue bewildering readers: The first paragraph has readers saying, "Yea! They got married." The next paragraph has readers saying, "Boo! They broke up." Such yea-boo sentences whipsaw readers. They loathe that treatment.

Once again, the readers are primarily led to believe they have the answers to a situation (Yea!), only to have the answers undermined by the last sentence (Boo!).

The feature now takes on a more orderly presentation by resorting to listings by groups that can be tolerated by readers.

WASHINGTON—Hoping to avoid divorce? It helps if you're wealthy, religious, college-educated and at least 20 years old when you tie the knot. Couples who don't live together before marriage have a better shot at staying together, as do those whose parents stayed married.

By age 30, three in four women have been married, but many of those unions dissolve. Overall, 43% of marriages break up within 15 years, according to a government survey of 11,000 women that offers the most detailed look at cohabitation, marriage and divorce ever produced.

Black women are least likely to marry and most likely to divorce, with more than half splitting within 15 years. Asian marriages are the most stable, with whites and Hispanics in between.

Women are waiting longer to get married than they used to, and after a divorce they are less likely to remarry than women once were. At the same time, couples are more likely to live together without getting married. Half of U.S. women had lived with a partner by the time they turned 30.

The survey, released yesterday by the Centers for Disease Control and Prevention, found that 70% of those who lived together for at least 5 years did eventually walk down the aisle.

These marriages are also more likely to break up. After 10 years, 40% of couples that had lived together before marriage had broken up. That compares with 31% of those who did not live together first.

That's partly because people who choose to live together tend to be younger, less religious or have other qualities that put them at risk for divorce, said Catherine Cohan, assistant professor of human development and family studies at Penn State University. That may not fully explain it, she said.

"Many people enter a cohabiting relationship when the deal is, 'If this doesn't work out, we can split up and it's no big loss because we don't have a legal commitment,'" she said. "The commitment is tenuous, and that tenuous commitment might carry over into marriage."

The report, based on 1995 data, found other groups facing a high risk of divorce, including:

Young People

Nearly half of those who marry under age 18 and 40% under age 20 get divorced. Over age 25, it's just 24%. The difference is maturity, says Chicago psychologist Kate Wachs.

"A lot of young people focus on right now, and if I'm not happy right now, I should get divorced," said Wachs, author of *Relationships for Dummies*. Older people have more life experience, he said, and realize "if I hang in there, it will probably get better."

After a plethora of expository paragraphs, the readers welcome these additional authoritative comments in the form of direct quotes. (And the attribution is rightfully buried in the least emphatic part of the paragraph—the middle.)

Non-religious People

Of those who don't affiliate with any religious group, 46% were divorced within 10 years.

Children of Divorce

Women whose parents were divorced are significantly more likely to divorce themselves, with 43% splitting after 10 years. Among those whose parents stayed together, the divorce rate was just 29%.

"You may have had a good model for conflict resolution," Cohan said. Or, she said, parents have taught their kids that "sticking to a marriage is important and divorce is bad."

Kids

Half of women who had kids before marriage were divorced in 10 years. Nearly as many couples who never had kids also wound up divorced.

Across the board, black women were less likely to marry and more likely to divorce. By age 30, 82% of white women have been married vs. 52% of black women.

The report suggests part of the problem is a lack of men in the "marriageable pool," with disproportionate numbers of black men unemployed or incarcerated. People with low incomes are also less likely to marry, and blacks tend to have lower incomes.

The conclusion deals with only part of the report: black women and their marriage pool. Are you able to see the problems that arise when too much information is thrown at the reader without adequate preparation and/or transitions? The writer appears to have suffered from an information overload.

The next survey report has similar problems of reporting, including a misinterpretation of the survey results.

"Do Virginity Pledges Taken by Teens Hold Up?"

By Todd Zeranski
Bloomberg News, June 20, 2006

Virginity pledges taken by teens don't reflect the sexual practices of young people, as many renege and others take the oath after having had intercourse, according to a study by the Harvard School of Public Health.

Harvard researcher Janet Rosenbaum found that virginity-pledge programs have a high drop out rate. She studied the responses of 13,568 participants age 12 to 18, from a 1995 national survey and compared them with the results of a follow up study a year later.

A virginity oath is defined as a "public or written pledge to remain a virgin until marriage." The results show the difficulty in accurately assessing the effects of the pledge on early sexual activity, Rosenbaum said.

"Research has to bear in mind that whenever we measure something that is sensitive behavior, there's a lot more uncertainty than we think there is," Rosenbaum

The lead should emphasize the drop-out rate for those taking the pledge—rather than focusing on one of the reasons for the drop-out rate. And the use of "as" rather than "because" gives the sense of things happening at the same time. Another lead possibility, probably the best one, can be composed from the next to last quote of this story: "Virginity pledges have limited effectiveness in delaying sexual intercourse among adolescents," said Monica Rodriguez...."

The lead might be: "Virginity-pledge programs have a high drop out rate, according to Harvard researcher Janet Rosenbaum.

"She studied the responses ... "

The writer displays aggressive reporting by interviewing Rosenbaum. In this paragraph, however, he fails to observe the "one attribution per paragraph rule" that I propound. And what does Rosenbaum mean when she says "focus on quality, not quantity"? Those teens taking the pledge?

The movement from survey to survey in the previous paragraphs leaves the reader's head awhirl. More lucid explanations are necessary.

Unruh appears to be addressing the "quality versus quantity" comment made earlier. (Note that the writer closed quotes at the end of a paragraph, although the quotation continued in the subsequent paragraph —an error growing more and more common.)*

I would be tempted to use the federal government spending $178 million paragraph as a conclusion. All that money! For what results?

29, said in a telephone interview. "Pledge programs need to focus on quality, not quantity," she said.

Her study found that 52 percent of all adolescents who made the pledge in the 1995 survey denied making such a vow one year later. Nearly three-quarters of those who broke their pledge denied they had taken such an oath in the second survey.

Adolescents most likely to retract virginity pledges were those who were newly sexually active or who had renounced a previous identity as a born-again Christian, the study found.

Almost one-third of non-virgins in the first survey who then took a virginity pledge disavowed their previous sexual experience in the second survey. Teens who admitted having sex in the first survey and later made the pledge were four times as likely to deny a previous sexual experience as those who hadn't made a pledge in the second survey.

"The study adds to the growing body of evidence that virginity pledges have limited effectiveness in delaying sexual intercourse among adolescents and that we need to continue to look for strategies that work," said Monica Rodriguez, a vice president of the Sexuality Information and Information Council of U.S., a non-profit sex-education group.

The federal government is spending $178 million in the 2006 fiscal year and the states are allocating an additional $37.5 million for abstinence education, the council said.

Leslee Unruh, founder of Abstinence Clearinghouse, a group that develops virginity pledge programs, said she "had not had any reports from anyone in the community that their kids had been in any study."

"The pledges that I know of aren't done in school, but where the parents are involved," she said.

The study is published in the June issue of the *American Journal of Public Health.*

---

* The quote rule, of course, is if the person speaking continues on to the next paragraph uninterrupted you do not close the quotes until the person is finished speaking in the next paragraph. And, you use quotes at the beginning of the next paragraph.

The next feature is handled much more adroitly than the previous survey features.

"Older Brothers Increase Gay Odds for Younger Brothers"

By Randolph E. Schmid
The Associated Press, June 7, 2006

Men who have several older brothers have an increased chance of being gay, researchers say.

The increase was seen in men with older brothers from the same mother— whether they were raised together or not—but not those who had adopted brothers or stepbrothers who were older.

"It's likely to be a prenatal effect," said Anthony F. Bogaert of Brock University in St. Catharines, Canada, who did the research. "This and other studies suggest that there is probably a biological basis" for homosexuality.

Bogaert studied four groups of Canadian men, a total of 944 people, analyzing the number of brothers and sisters each had, whether they lived with those siblings and whether the siblings were related by blood or adopted.

His findings appear in Tuesday's issue of *Proceedings of the National Academy of Sciences.*

S. Marc Breedlove, a professor in the neuroscience and psychology department of Michigan State University, said the finding "absolutely" confirms a physical basis.

"Anybody's first guess would have been that the older brothers were having an effect socially, but this data doesn't support that," Breedlove said in a telephone interview.

The only link between the brothers is the mother, so the effect has to be through the mother, especially since stepbrothers didn't have the effect, said Breedlove.

Tim Dailey, a senior fellow at the Center for Marriage and Family Studies, disagreed.

"We don't believe that there's any biological basis for homosexuality," Dailey said. "We feel the causes are complex but are deeply rooted in early childhood development." There have been a number of attempts to establish a physical basis, "and in every case the alleged findings have been severely challenged and questioned," he said.

"If it is indeed genetically based it is difficult to see how it could have survived in the gene pool over a period of time," Dailey added.

Bogaert said the increase could be detected with one older brother and became stronger with three or four or more. The effect of birth order on male homosexuality has been reported previously, but Bogaert's work is the first designed to rule out social or environmental effects.

Bogaert said he concluded that men raised with several older adopted brothers or stepbrothers do not have an increased chance of being gay.

"So what that means is that the environment a person is raised in really makes not much difference," he said.

What makes a difference, he said, is having older brothers who shared the same womb and gestational experience, suggesting the difference is because of "some sort of prenatal factor."

Side notes:

If the second and third paragraphs were transposed, the feature would establish the authority for the comments in the lead paragraph sooner. The reader is looking for this justification.

The reporter displays good news gathering techniques by bringing in other authorities to both buttress and question the findings of the study.

Breedlove and Dailey represent the sides that have been taken in this ongoing discussion of the causes for homosexuality.

In all fairness it's only right for the author of the research to have the last word, as he does here.

The next survey report, however, is more than acceptable and with a feature lead would be even more irresistible. A different conclusion would top off this superb feature material.

"How About a Woman for President?"

The Tennessean, Feb. 20, 2005

ALBANY, N.Y.—A majority of Americans say the country is ready to elect a woman as president in 2008—and even more said in a poll that they would vote for one.

The candidate's portrait as painted by 1,125 registered voters in a nationwide Hearst Newspapers/Siena College poll shows that she probably is a Democrat and is viewed as being at least as capable as a man on foreign policy. She's stronger on health care and education but somewhat weaker as commander in chief of the military.

The poll listed four prominent women—Secretary of State Condoleeza Rice and Sens. Hillary Clinton, D-N.Y., Barbara Boxer, D-Calif., and Elizabeth Dole, R-N.C.—and asked whether any of the four should run for president.

Clinton was the clear front-runner—almost four years from Election Day 2008—with 53% of those polled, including half of the men and 26% of the Republicans, saying she should run. Following Clinton was Rice, who first captured the national spotlight as President Bush's national security adviser. Forty-two percent of responders said she should run in 2008, including 30% of Democrats.

THE FEATURE ASSIGNMENT

Assignments for features may be suggested by news events. If you're a feature writer, and write on-call features for a newspaper, you may be given an assignment by an editor. Let's say, in this instance, an editor of an Albany, NY, newspaper calls you in Wednesday morning:

"Drive over to Hyslip, Conn., and find out what's going on there," Brenda Wilson says. "In the past three months Hyslip's been racked by a series of automobile accidents that have killed three high school students. And there's been heavy drinking and drug use, primarily meth. That's not quite the picture of suburban living that most people have in mind when they move to the suburbs. Most of the Hyslip citizens moved there to get away from the big city evils."

"Okay, I'll check with the police, school principal and newspaper editor," you reply. "Any other suggestions?"

"You might want to weave in some of the comments from the Sunday editorial of the Hyslip newspaper," Wilson said.

"When do you want the story?"

"We'd like it for the Sunday edition," Wilson replies.

Getting the Facts

After checking the newspaper library and noting the contents of four major stories on Hyslip's problem you know there's a notable feature on your agenda. You pack an overnight bag, pick up your laptop and drive to Hyslip.

You arrive there at twilight. The New England autumn eve is golden. You drive around the community of about 25,000, trying to get a feel for it. Some residents are burning leaves, no doubt ignoring a local ordinance banning the practice. Several wave to you with their rakes. A sports car full of young people zips past you.

At the Anchor Inn Motel, you wait to check in behind two high-schoolish looking couples. As you register, you ask the desk clerk: "Is most of your clientele as young as those kids who just signed in?"

The clerk smiles courteously and answers, "Yes."

The next morning you stop by the town's newspaper, *The Hyslip Courier*, the first stop of many in your efforts to research thoroughly the problems of Hyslip's youth. The path you follow is one taken by most writers of major features. The newspaper staff is receptive. The two reporters, Abbey Barnes and James Edmisson, brief you on some of the action taking place in Hyslip. You spend the rest of the day looking through the newspaper's computer files, including last year's editions. Late in the afternoon, the *Courier*'s editor, Allison Knell, gives you a copy of the Sunday editorial on the current trouble in Hyslip. You read it, then ask her questions that occurred to you as you were scanning the library's clippings.

How do the current problems differ from those in the past? What is causing the problems? What may be solutions to them? You list the people you're planning on talking to the next day and ask her if there are others you should see.

A feature story assignment such as this calls for extensive interviewing and investigation. After dinner you spend the night in the motel, going over your notes and writing down on 3-by-5 inch cards the questions you're going to ask the next day.

How does this high school population differ from those of the past?

How do these sons and daughters differ from those of a few years ago?

Are their relationships with the schools, churches and parents different?

What is the absentee rate? The dropout rate? The number of pregnancies?

How do the students regard the police, the laws of the community and the state?

You arrange the question cards in the order in which you plan to ask the questions of the police, principals, parents and church figures.

You go to bed knowing that the initial interviews will provide you with facts you can use in interviewing still other people and still more questions based on the answers you receive. You will have to listen carefully.

After breakfast the next morning, you drive to the police station and introduce yourself to the police chief, Justin Houston. You shake his hand.

"Allison Knell told me to come down here to check out some accident reports and talk about the kind of trouble the young people here in Hyslip get into."

"Police blotter's right there," Houston says. "You might want to talk to these two officers who are on duty at night."

He introduces you to Sergeants Paul Tsia and Juan Rodriguez. You talk to them about the auto accidents and about drinking and drugs among teenagers. You check the police blotter and the computer files. Later in the morning you ask Houston and other police officers more questions about the arrests and drug usage and the attitude of the parents and community toward those incidents.

You drive to the parish house of St. Thomas' Roman Catholic Church. Like the newspaper office building, the church architecture is elegant and stately. You talk with the priest, the Rev. Robert J. McCabe. You ask him about the role of the church in all this and the attitude of his parishioners. He is defensive and remarks that many of the answers are treated in the sermon he will be delivering this Sunday. You persuade him to give you a copy of the sermon.

You then stop by the high school and talk with the principal, Dr. Mildred S. Ross, about the discipline problems she's having and the parents' attitudes toward them. Although Ross is reluctant to talk at great length about the problems, you discover, among other things, that the parking lots have to be patrolled before classes, during lunch breaks and after classes because of the heavy necking and other things that go on during those times. In the hallways of the high school, between periods and at a lunch break, you talk to high school teachers and students about sex and drugs. You corroborate all that's been said to you about the lifestyle of high school students at Hyslip. You call the head of the Parent-Teacher Association, Emily McNeil. She puts you in touch with two concerned parents, Shannon Terry and Dorothy Boeker, and a minister of the Richard Street Methodist Church, Doña Watson.

On the way out of Hyslip, late in the afternoon, you cross the railroad tracks leading to New York City. The rusty-looking railway station can stand repairs: pigeon droppings, plaster, everything.

Outlining the Feature

As you drive to New York City, you mentally outline your feature. Some facts and statements fall naturally together into blocks of information: the car accidents, the arrests, the attitude of the community. Some remain stubbornly by themselves at this time: the roles of the newspaper, the church and the parents. You think about what will go into the feature lead to get the reader's attention. What will follow the lead? What goes after those paragraphs? You think about conclusion possibilities. Can the conclusion stem from the lead? You review the interviews to determine if you have left anything out of your notes. You retrace your drives through the suburban town. You are struck by the mixture of modern and old houses and by the incongruities of the various architectural settings and the community's jet-set lifestyle. Those architectural incongruities, you decide, will be the underlying and unifying motif of the feature story. They help tie in the roles of the newspaper and the church. By the time you arrive at your apartment at 10 o'clock you have the feature outline in mind. You can hardly wait to write the outline in detail. After a few revisions, the rough outline, although skimpy, looks good:

"Trouble in Suburbia" (outline)

I.   Introduction
    A. Autumn glory
    B. Eagle on Courier
    C. Leaf fires and turbulence
II. "Little Kinsey Report"
III. Auto accident deaths
IV. Citizens' reactions
    A. Father McCabe sermon
    B. Church architecture
    C. Hyslip setting, houses, etc.
V.   Courier editorial "On Name-Calling"
    A. Luxurious living
    B. Pampered children
    C. Good conscience not "bad press"

VI. Week's record of arrests
    A. Police blotter
    B. Police officers
        1. Paul Tsia
        2. Juan Rodriguez
VII. Conclusion
    A. Dull-red train station
    B. Tracks lead back to New York City (connects Hyslip)

First Draft

The next morning you sit down at the breakfast table with your laptop and a cup of coffee. Reviewing the outline, you make minor changes and add more details to each section of the outline. When you are through, you still don't like what you see. The more detailed outline is satisfactory, but you thought it would include more detail. You're uneasy be-cause you know the more detailed your outline is, the better your first draft will be. You know it's difficult enough just to put "proper words in proper places" without having to worry about where you are going and where you have been. You study the outline once more. Opening and closing with a setting description makes good sense. It helps unify the feature. Although your title, "Trouble in Suburbia," isn't likely to appear over your story when it is published (a copy editor will supply one), it keeps you focused on the subject of the feature.

You can't put it off any longer. You must write the first draft, a dreary task for you. But what provides you with impetus is that you know once the draft is written you'll be eager to add beauty to the writing through revision. As you wonder how to begin the feature, you recall the autumn scene in Hyslip. Your flair for the picturesque and your love of nature carry you away when you write the hook. It's what you call a "setting" lead.

"Trouble in Suburbia"

By Erin Phillips
The Massachusetts Intelligencer, Sept. 21, 2006

HYSLIP, Conn. — Streaks of rose lie across the western horizon at twilight in Hyslip in the evening, and the russet hills are pure New England glory. The weather-vane eagle, wings spread, on the roof of the *Courier,* seems made of freshly poured gold.

In autumn, this prosperous town is a beautiful haven from the noisy city. The tang of leaf fires rides the air. At night, long, low imported sports cars with loud engines, filled with young people, zip through tree-lined lanes.

The face of Hyslip appears serene. Underneath, however, lie agitation and turbulence.

The turbulence surfaced in May, when the Council of Hyslip School Parents published what one adult labeled "a little Kinsey report" on drinking, vandalism,

You know the hook is more "literary" than most newspaper features. But this is for your Sunday edition and, conse-quently, for readers who expect more from a feature and have more time to read it.

You then indirectly suggest the agitation underlying Hyslip, the main idea of the feature, by using leaf fires and sports cars zipping through the streets.

You like the idea of smoldering fires and loud engines in young people's cars to symbolize the underlying con-flict in Hyslip. It makes good, vivid reading.

Like a good feature writer, in the third paragraph you spell out the idea of the feature story and provide the transition for the reader to follow into the main body of the story.

The fourth paragraph really pleases you. Its expository prose is supposed to be a valley in the feature because it moves the story line along. But with the "little Kinsey report" and other examples in it, it represents a peak as much as a valley. The fifth paragraph, with its auto deaths, is definitely a peak. You also like the opening of the sixth paragraph: "Hyslip is self-conscious now.… " The feature is marching right along. The outline is doing its job.

These paragraphs about the sermon are peak paragraphs, representing reader peaks of interest. As you write McCabe's comments, you review the interview you had with him. You're never too concerned about the peak paragraphs; they tend to make interesting reading. And McCabe's "editorial guillotines" is wonderful color.

As you write this paragraph, a valley paragraph, you fear it will be the valley of reader-interest death. The exposition and the lengthy architecture description of Hyslip countryside may turn readers away and onto another story. You make a note in the margin to check it out closely when you revise. But if you've carried readers this far, you reason, you have their interest. That interest will probably sustain some of that long description. But you don't want the reader to suffer needlessly—to wallow through uninteresting detail.

A rush flows through you as you write the paragraphs. They're another peak.

So far, you've been doing what you should be doing as a feature writer. After the opening narrative hook, idea and transition—the lead elements—you've been alternating valleys and peaks, and you're now nearing the end of the feature. Brenda Wilson's editorial remarks make good copy—colorful and to the point. What's nice about them is that they also carry your story line along while entertaining the reader.

You move with confidence into the concluding paragraphs.

shoplifting, gang activity and sex play among teenagers. Some citizens called it unfair.

But three weeks ago, after two house parties, 16-year-old Shirley Atchison was killed at 3:55 a.m. in a station-wagon crash. As a result of this death, 13 adults, including business and professional men and their wives, were arrested and charged with serving liquor to minors. Four days later, Harvey Haddox, 17, died in another early morning car wreck in what authorities called similar circumstances.

Hyslip is self-conscious now, and a little angry. Some citizens feel it is being made to serve as a symbol of modern suburban moral decay.

"It could have happened in any one of hundreds of communities in America," The Rev. Robert J. McCabe said. He is pastor of St. Thomas Roman Catholic Church, a small stone building with a peaked roof and tower. At all masses last Sunday, he echoed an anguished truism:

"Editorial writers across the country have had a field day at our expense. They have made us the victims of their editorial guillotines."

But Father McCabe admitted that "in recent years there has been an ever-increasing disregard for law. In the eyes of some, all obligations are becoming a nuisance."

Suburban living and all its happy values seem to be summed up in the neatness and simplicity of the weekly *Courier*'s office. Published in a handsome, semi-colonial office, four wooden columns stand at the portico entrance. Those values also seem to be symbolized by the saltbox cottages with weathered shingles, lovely old wooden manors with tall pines towering over them, rambling suburban homes, and the long rock walls so familiar to New England.

But in a blistering editorial titled "On Name-Calling," the current issue of the *Courier* scolds some parents for pampering children.

"This sordid, tawdry spectacle, where children are allowed all sorts of excesses, includes too many material comforts and luxuries and too much license to do as they please."

Typical of the resident comforts is the listing of family after family on Buttonwood Lane with separate numbers marked "children's telephone."

"The standards and values this sad series of events exposed are false and superficial," the editorial adds. "We should be more concerned with real accomplishment than social status, with more worry about a good conscience than about a 'bad press.'"

Meanwhile, this week's record of arrests on the police blotter discloses that Juan Rodriguez, a policeman patrolling Weed Beach at night, came upon two 15-year-old girls with a bottle of rum and marijuana. Paul Tsia, another policeman, arrested a 21-year-old unmarried woman, of Middlesex Road, who was charged with secret delivery and concealment of birth.

Not too far from Weed Beach, at Hyslip's old, dull-red train station, not much more, really, than a bird roost needing several coats of paint, two tired, rummage-sale Victorian cast-iron benches face the New York–bound tracks—27 miles and 45 minutes from Grand Central Station.

Revision

You pour another cup of coffee, go back to the first paragraph and start revising. Back in college, one of your freshman English professors, Harry Shaw, said that all good writers go through a revision process: "There's no such thing as good writing. It's all good rewriting." You should have more time before looking over your first draft to revise effectively, but you like what you've written and you want to revise it now. Sometimes the flow and rhythm of the feature can be improved by revision immediately after the first draft. But you'll still let it sit overnight and revise it at least once more.

As you revise, you recall the scenes and the persons you interviewed as you come to them in the feature so that you can picture them more accurately if necessary and use still other quotes you may not have used in the draft. You keep in mind that, above all, you want economy, clarity and unity.

You check the lead—it has the three elements of HIT: hook, idea, transition. Your first paragraph serves as a good contrast to the concluding paragraph. You especially like the "freshly poured gold" phrase in the beginning. It symbolizes the Hyslip surface and contrasts beautifully with the "dull-red bird . . . roost" in the concluding paragraph, symbolizing the underlying corruption of values.

The lack of direct quotes in the first three paragraphs leaves something to be desired. You decide to pull "a little Kinsey report" from the middle to the beginning of the fourth paragraph. After that, the quotes appear liberally sprinkled throughout the rest of the feature. Quotes at the beginning of a paragraph provide the reader with a variety of typographical display. They make the long gray column of type less foreboding. And readers like to think they're reading the interviewees' exact words, not some paraphrase of them.

You check your verbs and substitute active verbs for passive verbs. Vivid words, along with specific details and figures of speech, make or break a good feature. You check for clichés. None. You read the feature aloud and listen to the flow and rhythm of it. You mark the sixth paragraph. The second sentence sounds stilted: "Some citizens feel it is being made to serve as a symbol of modern suburban moral decay." The phrase "it is being made to serve" must be changed. It's wordy. You draw a mental block on how to do it now, but you know that during tomorrow's revision session the words will come to you.

The valley paragraphs don't flatten out too much, and the following peak paragraphs nicely amplify, with examples, the exposition in the valley paragraphs. You're beginning to think you've written a good feature.

"Beware of overconfidence," you caution yourself. When you revise, you can't afford to don rose-colored glasses. Nevertheless, you're pleased.

You read the next-to-last paragraph. You compliment yourself on using details so well: If a woman has to be charged with concealment of birth, what better street for her to live on than Middlesex Road? If there are arrests made for rum and marijuana, what better place than Weed Beach? Since part of Hyslip's problem is one facing most American communities—the gap between youth and law enforcement officers who no longer know every person on their beat—what better names for policemen than Juan Rodriguez and Paul Tsia? After all, Hyslip is a WASP* community, and for those who read between the lines—the sophisticated reader—the names do not fit in. The paragraph's perfect.

"Watch that attitude!" you caution yourself again.

---

* White, Anglo-Saxon Protestant.

You look once more at the last paragraph. You started the feature with the eagle on the *Courier* building, the first stage of the architectural motif. The description of the Catholic church—the "small stone building with a peaked roof and tower" (paragraph 7)—suggests that the church is lagging behind the times: The church is not counseling its flock in the wise conduct of modern living. In the same fashion, paragraph 10, the *Courier* building's architecture—the "semi-colonial office, four wooden columns . . . at the portico"—suggests that the newspaper has failed to keep a surveillance on the community and let the citizens know what's going on. Instead, it has merely mirrored and reacted to events, not fore-warned the citizens of them. The mixture of saltbox cottages with rambling suburban homes suggests Hyslip's mingling of old values with new ones (paragraph 10). You have even mentioned the values in the paragraph.

You read the last paragraph and decide that the "Victorian cast-iron benches" evoke the Victorian era in England: On the surface, respectability was mightily striven for, while below the surface, morals were more than a little loose. The connection of the Victorian era with Hyslip may or may not be noted by the average reader, but it doesn't hurt the ending at all. The New York–bound railroad tracks, meanwhile, suggest to the reader that suburbia is still connected to the temptations of the big city. But the ending is still not as smooth as it could be. The next day's revisions will have to take care of that.

Overall, you are pleased with most of the paragraphs. But you know that as you revise, still more changes in imagery and details will occur to you. You take a last sip of coffee and place the feature aside until tomorrow.

ABOUT THOSE FEATURE CONCLUSIONS

In "Trouble in Suburbia," the last paragraph, as an ironic comment, calls to mind the pastoral setting in the first paragraph. How are you going to end your features? Let us count some of the ways.

Most feature endings fall into four major categories:

1. Sometimes the ending, as just mentioned, may be suggested by the lead of the feature. The unity of the feature may be assured by this circular organization. An example would be the ending of "A Father's Tale." The ending brings the reader back to the lead.
2. A note of finality may be added by describing what action is now being taken on the subject matter of the feature.
3. Conclusions can refer to what may be done in the future.
4. Another major conclusion category involves reader action. If you have been writing about the hazards of waste disposal you might end by asking the audience what they propose to do about it.

Most of the time your feature subject matter and your audience suggests the appropriate ending.

WRITING THE INVESTIGATIVE FEATURE

But let's look at a feature on "hate groups" in America by Judy L. Thomas, a writer who has earned a variety of awards, which should have included a Pulitzer Prize, for what she has written. Note the writing: how it flows from one topic to another, how direct quotes lead off paragraphs, and attributions are buried in the middle of the quotes. Those attributions sound natural: "he said" rather than the unnatural "said he." (Unless a long identification follows the quote.) Finally, note the number of major sources consulted and interviewed. Judy L. Thomas wrote this feature to coincide with the 10th anniversary of the Oklahoma City bombing. (How she went about writing and researching it is presented in a question-and-answer interview in Chapter 8.)

"Shadow of Hate Groups Lingers on the Landscape"

By Judy L. Thomas
The Kansas City Star, April 20, 2005

KANSAS CITY, Mo.—At the time, it was the deadliest terrorist attack on American soil.

April 19, 1995, a truck bomb destroyed the Alfred P. Murrah Federal Building in Oklahoma City, killing 168 persons and wounding hundreds of others. The catastrophe shocked the nation and turned the spotlight on a subculture that had been growing but operating off the grid: the anti-government movement.

Ten years later, that movement—which includes everything from the patriot and militia groups to the more violent white supremacists and neo-Nazis—is rudderless and in disarray, experts say. Many of its leaders are dead. Others are in prison, the result of a crackdown on anti-government activity after the bombing.

But those who monitor the movement say that is a cause for concern, not complacency. They say the lack of leadership has created a potentially explosive environment in which "lone wolves" are encouraged to carry out their agendas.

One such "lone wolf" was Eric Rudolph, who agreed Friday to plead guilty to a 1998 abortion-clinic bombing in Birmingham, Ala., the 1996 bombing at the Atlanta Summer Olympics and a blast at an Atlanta lesbian nightclub. Two persons died and one was maimed in those attacks. By pleading guilty, he avoided a possible death sentence but will spend life in prison with no chance of parole.

A disturbing new trend is that, a decade after that deadly day in Oklahoma, some groups are turning to the Internet to attract young recruits.

"Things are dramatically different," said Daniel Levitas, author of *The Terrorist Next Door: The Militia Movement and the Radical Right,* a book about militias and extremist groups. "The movement is but a pale shadow of its former self."

Among the reasons is that the emotional impact of the Sept. 11, 2001, terrorist attacks in New York, Washington and Pennsylvania, has made anti-government types think twice about a sales pitch that involves killing fellow Americans.

"On the other hand," Levitas said, "it's completely accurate to say that, although the movement is smaller and is faced with pretty significant institutional and ideological problems, what remains is in some respects deadlier, more dangerous."

Adding to that concern, experts say, is that after Sept. 11, 2001, federal authorities shifted their focus from domestic terrorism to foreign terrorist groups, allowing potential homegrown terrorists to slip through the cracks.

"The bulk of federal law enforcement attention certainly turned overseas," said Mark Potok of the Southern Poverty Law Center. "There certainly has been a tendency in the last few years to pay less attention than probably is needed."

Armed for Homegrown Terror

Consider the case of William Krar of Texas. In 2003, the white supremacist was caught with machine guns and other weapons, nearly 500,000 rounds of ammunition, more than 60 pipe bombs, remote control bombs disguised as briefcases and enough sodium cyanide to kill hundreds of people.

"You had a domestic terrorist actually having acquired weapons of mass destruction," Potok said. "A guy running around with an unassembled but still incredibly deadly sodium cyanide bomb. How did that happen?"

If Krar had been a foreign terrorist, Potok said, "it would've been shouted from the rooftops in Washington." Krar was sentenced last May to more than 11 years in prison, although he could have gotten a life sentence.

"As it was, it was a tiny little press release put out in Tyler, Texas, and nobody noticed it for a year," Potok said. "I would not attack the federal government for turning away from this completely, but I would say it's perfectly clear that the focus has shifted."

FBI officials said their focus did shift after the Sept. 11 attacks but dispute that they are ignoring domestic terrorism.

"We still have pending investigations of domestic terrorism cases, but obviously after 9/11 our primary focus became counterterrorism, counterintelligence and from a reactive to a proactive type of approach," said FBI spokesman Paul Bresson in the agency's Washington headquarters.

Bresson acknowledged, however, that fewer agents today are assigned to domestic terrorism cases.

"We've had to kind of shift resources in some ways because the threat from international terrorist extremist groups has become a much more grave concern," he said. "But at the same time, we're still focused on all the threats that exist out there. We know that the possibility for an attack from one of these domestic groups is always there."

Indeed, Bresson said, the Oklahoma City bombing changed the way law enforcement viewed terrorism.

"Oklahoma City showed it may only take one, two or a small group of individuals who could execute major attacks that profoundly impact the country," he said. "That was definitely when it became very prominent on our radar screen, the threat that domestic terrorism presented. And even more of a concern was the so-called lone-wolf theory."

No Time to Let Guard Down

Authorities say they will be especially alert in the days leading to the April 19 bombing anniversary.

"Anniversaries of significant terrorist events are always a concern," said FBI spokesman Jeff Lanza of the bureau's Kansas City office. "Our nation's perception of the threat in this country is defined by 9/11. And we should not forget there was another major terrorist attack in this country, on 4/19."

Despite disarray in the anti-government movement, no one should let their guard down, said Leonard Zeskind, director of the Kansas City-based Institute for Research & Education on Human Rights.

"At the end of the day, this movement never loses the impulse for violence," Zeskind said.

"They reconfigure it, and they think about whether they need small cells, big cells, underground armies, lone-wolf killers. But the fact of the matter is the pulse of violence just never goes out on this thing. And that's really the ugly truth."

Those left in the white-supremacist movement agree that the turmoil in their organizations could lead to increased violence.

"What's changed is that because of the way the country's going, it's basically sent the luke-warmers and the fence-sitters running for cover," said August B. Kreis III, national director of the Aryan Nations, a white-supremacist group. "And the only people that will really stay are the hard-core people."

But Kreis said he preferred it that way.

"I want the hardest of the hard," he said. "When enough white people say that we've had enough, we're not going to take it any more and we realize now that blood is going to have to be spilled, then it's going to get bad. I really believe that, and I'm really hoping I'm here to see that."

A former Kansas City Ku Klux Klan leader also says the movement today is not for "wimps."

"After the bomb went off in Oklahoma City, the White Knights completely collapsed," said Dennis Mahon, now living in Tulsa, Okla. "They shut down the post-office box, they shut down the hot line. They were scared to death. They just went down the hidey hole."

The militia movement went into hiding after the bombing, Mahon said. He said now a different strategy is needed.

"There'll be a time when we can go ahead and go with leadership movements," he said. "But right now, I think it's just we all want to overthrow the government and get a state of our own. There's many ways to do that. It's called small cells and lone wolfism."

Old Guard Is Decimated

The three main racially based hate groups left—the National Alliance, the Creativity Movement (formerly called the World Church of the Creator) and the Aryan Nations—have all suffered setbacks recently.

"I think what we've seen in the last few years is the decapitation of the major neo-Nazi groups," Potok said. "And that has really changed the shape of the movement in significant ways."

The National Alliance lost its founder, William Pierce, in July 2002. Pierce was the author of a book authorities say was a blueprint for the Oklahoma City bombing.

Potok said that before Pierce's death, the National Alliance had more than 1,400 members and 17 full-time national staff members. Now, he said, they have fewer than 700.

In recent months, the group has been making headlines by leafleting neighborhoods and putting signs on billboards in many states.

"Frankly, it's nothing new," said Devin Burghart, of the Center for New Community, a Chicago-based organization that monitors hate groups. "It's a publicity stunt."

The Creativity Movement was crippled when its leader, Matt Hale, was convicted in 2004 of trying to hire someone to kill federal Judge Joan Lefkow in Chicago. Lefkow's husband and mother were shot to death last month. Authorities investigated whether the murders were linked to white supremacists but later concluded they were committed by a disturbed man with no connection to the movement.

Potok said that when Hale went to prison, the Creativity Movement collapsed.

"It immediately dropped from 88 chapters to five," he said. But now it is up to 16—including a chapter in Springfield, Mo. "Most of the chapters are tiny, a handful of people, if that. Not only that; some of the chapters don't recognize the other chapters. The thing is falling apart."

Aryan Nations founder Richard Butler, whose followers have been convicted of murders, bombings and armed robberies, died last September. The loss of a $6.3 million lawsuit forced the group into bankruptcy and, after Butler's death, it splintered into two factions.

The Aryan Nations made headlines last month when The Kansas City Star reported that one faction was moving its headquarters to Kansas City, Kan. The group changed its plans after the publicity created intense community opposition.

Those deaths create a vacuum in the movement that authorities should carefully monitor, said Karen Aroesty, regional director of the Anti-Defamation League for Missouri and Southern Illinois.

"It's that kind of lack of strong leadership that has the potential to bring out the real radicals, because they're angry," Aroesty said. "They're frustrated. Matt Hale's in jail, Richard Butler died, William Pierce died. They're thinking, "Where's the vision? Where's the structure? Now's the time to do something.""

Militias, which enjoyed their heyday in the mid-1990s, have grown quieter in recent years.

"They're not even having the Preparedness Expos any more," Burghart said. "The gun shows still happen, but they're more for collectors and enthusiasts these days than they are the survivalist types. The survivalist types are probably still trying to get out of debt from Y2K, or they're still hunkered down."

New Blood Online

Since Oklahoma City, at least one troubling trend has emerged—an attempt to recruit young people through racist music and the Internet.

"That's creating a whole new generation" Burghart said. "They have been more successful than ever."

Groups such as the National Alliance with its company, Resistance Records, produce and distribute everything from comic books and video games to compact discs and T-shirts, Burghart said.

A Web site called Stormfront, which is based in Florida and run by a former Ku Klux Klan grand dragon, also is actively recruiting young people.

"It's become more and more like a group," Potok said. And although the Internet has not been as successful of a recruitment too as white supremacists had hoped, it has provided another opportunity to seek new converts.

"The Internet is very targeted at young, college-bound white kids who have always been hard to reach. So while mom and dad are making dinner, the kid's in his bedroom talking to Nazis."

What does it take to become a star writer on one of the most prestigious newspapers in the country? The following paragraphs about Judy Thomas gives you an idea:

"The Trek: From Kansas Farm Girl to Star Writer for *The Kansas City Star*"

Judy Thomas is not your traditional journalism school graduate. Raised on a farm in central Kansas, she graduated from Little River-Windom High School in 1977, then attended Hutchinson Community College, where she served as co-editor of the *Hutchinson Collegian*. After graduating, her career took a detour when she moved to Minnesota and became an over-the-road trucker, driving a semi cross-country for six years and hauling everything from race horse oats to steel coils. In 1986, Thomas moved back to Kansas and completed her education at Kansas State University. During her first year on campus, as a writer for the *Kansas State Collegian*, she exposed an air-line ticket scam that resulted in federal contempt charges against a California company. She also revealed that the county landfill was contaminating the water of residents living around it. Her stories led to an investigation by the attorney general.

Thomas served as editor of the *Collegian* in 1988 and graduated summa cum laude with a bachelor's degree in journalism the same year. Her first job was as a general assignment reporter for *The Wichita* (Kan.) *Eagle.* She later specialized in covering the abortion issue and right-wing extremist groups and was one of the first reporters in the country to track the rise of the citizen militias in the early 1990s.

In 1991, Thomas was *The Eagle*'s lead writer in its coverage of Operation Rescue's national abortion protests in Wichita. Thomas was again in the thick of the issue in 1993, when abortion doctor George Tiller was shot and wounded outside his Wichita clinic. Through close contacts with her sources, Thomas was able to get into the jail and conduct exclusive interviews with the woman who tried to kill Tiller. Her resulting stories—not only on the woman's confession to the shooting but also to a series of abortion-clinic bombings—prompted subpoenas from both the prosecuting and defense attorneys prior to the suspect's trial. Thomas was summoned to an inquisition and found in contempt of court when she refused to turn over her notes and tapes related to the case.

In 1995, Thomas covered the Oklahoma City bombing for *The Eagle* and continued to do so when she took a job with *The Kansas City Star* in June 1995. Her ongoing coverage of the right-wing movement has taken her to militia gatherings; gun shows; Elohim City, a white separatist compound in eastern Oklahoma; and Almost Heaven, a "covenant constitutional community" founded by patriot leader Bo Gritz in Idaho. In 1998, her coverage of a gathering in southwest Missouri resulted in a $4 billion class-action lawsuit filed by a group of "patriots" against *The Star* and other media outlets. A federal judge dismissed the lawsuit the following year.

Thomas is also the co-author of *Wrath of Angels:The American Abortion War*, a critically acclaimed book about the history of the anti-abortion movement. In researching the book, which was published by BasicBooks in 1998, Thomas became the only reporter in the country to personally interview the three anti-abortion activists convicted of shooting abortion doctors, including Paul Hill, who was on death row in Florida.

Though used to covering controversial issues, nothing could have prepared Thomas for the reaction she received when she wrote a series for *The Kansas City Star* about AIDS in the priesthood. The series—the most comprehensive study ever done on the Catholic priesthood and the AIDS epidemic—showed that hundreds of priests had died of AIDS and that little was being done to address the problem. Along the way, Thomas overcame numerous obstacles, including reluctant and hostile sources, and ferreted out information on the real cause of death for some priests whose death records and obituaries had been falsified. The project required extreme sensitivity and compassion—traits that proved essential after publication, when Thomas and *The Star* were deluged with months of backlash from some readers and church officials. The story was picked up in virtually every major market in the United States and in various outlets around the world. The series also sparked more than 3,000 phone calls and e-mails, about half negative and half positive. Despite the attacks—many of them personal and vicious—Thomas came back with a follow-up story in which she painstakingly examined death certificates and proved that priests were dying at a rate actually exceeding the projections and estimates reported in *The Star*'s original series.

More recent projects include a 2001 investigation of the trucking industry, in which Thomas temporarily returned to her previous career and hit the road in an 18-wheeler. She drove 6,000 miles through 15 states, delivering loads for a local charity in four cities, sleeping and showering at truck stops and talking to truckers along the way.

Thomas found that fatigue behind the wheels of 80,000-pound rigs was so pervasive on U.S. highways that drivers regularly nodded off and drifted into oncoming lanes or slammed into slower-moving vehicles. Sleepy truckers, driving far beyond their limits, caused hundreds of deaths a year, and perhaps thousands.

But at a time when truck traffic was on the increase, Thomas found that federal oversight was dwindling. Inspections of trucking companies were so few that three-fourths of all carriers had never been visited. And completed reviews were so weak that companies with documented problems continue to operate without sanctions. Moreover, the inspection stations on the nation's highways were frequently closed, allowing the average truck to travel more than 80,000 miles between inspections.

For that series, Thomas was named a finalist for a Scripps Howard Foundation National Journalism Award and a finalist for the national Gerald Loeb Award for Distinguished Business and Financial Journalism.

In 2003, Thomas wrote a series about Missouri's terrible roads and how they got that way. Her investigation found that Missouri's highways had tumbled from among the best in the nation to third-worst in less than a decade. The reason: an autonomous highway department that answered to no one, wasted money, lost records and offended voters—yet still boasted that it was doing a good job.

Reaction to the series was swift and strong. The state auditor immediately began an audit and called for the agency's director to step down and the six highway commissioners to resign. In early December, the director did step down, followed a week later by a key highway commissioner.

Thomas' most recent series, published in September 2004, was about the Missouri Department of Conservation, an agency that in the 1970s fought for a tax to restore the state's wildlife and natural areas. Her investigation found that the agency's goals had long been surpassed, yet the tax kept pumping millions into the department, allowing it to indulge in inventive spending. Thomas also discovered that the agency's internal auditor—hired to keep an eye on Conservation Department employees—instead had gone into business with many of them.

In February 2005, an investigation by Thomas found that more than 1,200 documents involving thousands of homes in the Kansas City area still contained racist language banning ownership by blacks, Jews and other ethnic groups. The racially restrictive covenants were routinely recorded in plats and deeds for the first half of the 20th century and placed in many home association documents not only in Kansas City, but nationwide.

Though ruled unenforceable by the U.S. Supreme Court in 1948 and later deemed illegal by the Fair Housing Act, many of the restrictions were never removed, mainly because they were crafted in such a way that they are difficult to get rid of.

After the story ran, the Missouri Legislature passed a bill to make homes associations remove the racist language.

SUMMARY

An extended investigative feature requires detailed preparation: research, a list of persons to be interviewed, areas to be probed, questions to be asked, details noticed—all of this with a mind toward what is pertinent to the feature.

After assembling all the information gathered, the actual writing begins with formulating a rough outline of the feature in your mind and then placing it on paper. Going over investigation notes allows you to fill in the outline spaces, producing a more detailed outline. "Putting proper words in proper places" is much easier when you don't have to think about where you've been and where you're going. While writing and revising, beware hubris—the tendency to look at your writing through rose-tinted glasses. Following these rules and procedures will help you to instill your writing with luster and impact.

FEATURES FOR DISCUSSION

Which of these five features appeals least to you? Why? What would you change, if anything, to make one of them more appealing?

A. "Women in Government"

By Dick Polman
The Associated Press, Nov. 3, 2002

With 10 women trying to break one of the toughest glass ceilings in politics, let us recall the rise and fall of their accidental trailblazer, Nellie Taylor Ross.

When her husband died after an appendectomy, she was asked to fill his job. Still clad in her mourning clothes, she took the oath as the governor of Wyoming in

1925—the first woman to run a state. But she lost the '26 election because the sympathy vote was too small, and she never ran for anything again.

Only 18 other women have governed since. But thanks to major shifts in the political culture—notably, the slow but steady ascension up the state executive ladder—the ranks of female governors are expected to swell rapidly. After Tuesday's elections, at least seven women could be running their states starting in January.

"This is shaping up as the Year of the Woman Governor," declared nonpartisan analyst John Kohut, who tracks gubernatorial races from Washington. "Every one of the 10 women candidates is either favored to win, or has a very good shot.

"This is a uniquely strong field. . . . They have had big state jobs—attorney general, insurance commissioner, treasurer—so that voters have gotten used to seeing women as executive decision makers."

Women have not governed in 33 states, and no more than five women have run states at the same time. Even the list of 19 governors is misleading because only 12 (including ex–New Jersey Gov. Christie Whitman) were elected in their own right—and that didn't start happening until 1974, when Ella Grasso won in Connecticut.

But 2002 could be a breakthrough. The current candidates, by dint of their resumes, seem poised to overcome the traditional view among many voters (particularly older males) that women can't do the big deals or kick butt in the backrooms of power.

Analyst Stuart Rothenberg said: "Attorney general, in particular is a great position. You're throwing the bad guys in jail. You get lots of name recognition, and you're not responsible for red ink in the budget."

Jennifer Granholm, the Michigan attorney general, is expected to be elected governor Tuesday. Arizona Attorney General Janet Napolitano and Kansas Insurance Commissioner Kathleen Seblius are similarly favored. All are Democrats who would replace Republicans. Granholm in particular is touted as a rising star, and Michigan is a key prize in presidential elections.

In Massachusetts, Democratic treasurer Shannon O'Brien could foil the candidacy of Olympics organizer Mitt Romney. In Arkansas, Democratic treasurer Lou Fisher is seriously threatening incumbent Mike Huckabee. In two strong Democratic states, Maryland and Rhode Island, Lt. Gov. Kathleen Kennedy Townsend and ex-state Sen. Myrth York, respectively, are banking on big turnouts.

In Alaska, Democratic Lt. Gov. Fran Ulmer is a tough-on-crime candidate who totes a gun while campaigning. And Hawaii is guaranteed its first female leader because ex-mayor Linda Lingle (the sole Republican in the women's field) is deadlocked with Democratic Lt. Gov. Mazie Hirono.

Here's the math: Five women now govern, but three are leaving office in January. That leaves Ruth Ann Minner of Delaware and Judy Martz of Montana. So if four other states plus Hawaii elect women—as analysts fully expect—that puts seven in power. That would please female activists, who point out that, since Jimmy Carter in 1976, governorships have become the prime route to the Oval Office.

The 2002 candidates are running strong because many have demonstrated on the job that they can handle state finances and law enforcement – two traditional hurdles for female aspirants. And generally, their male opponents have pounded them relentlessly, just as if they were men.

"That's really a great development," said Washington analyst Karen O'Connor, an expert on women in politics. "Because it wasn't so long ago that (the senior)

George Bush was trying to figure out how tough he should be on (rival 1984 vice presidential candidate) Geraldine Ferraro. This year the gubernatorial ads that guys are running against women are just as nasty as anything they would run against other guys."

But gender issues have not been totally absent. In Arizona, Republican Matt Salmon constantly touts his family in TV ads, as a way of pointing out that Napolitano is single and childless.

In Massachusetts, Shannon O'Brien—mindful that women make up 55% of the state electorate—has called attention to gender insults. She has been hammering Romney for alleged issue flip-flops. But after he protested in a debate last week that her tough questioning was "unbecoming," she said that he would never have used that word to rebuke a man.

If at least seven women are governing next year, Marie Wilson will be thrilled. As director of the White House Project, she wants to build a deep bench of hopefuls. And she said, "More women governors means more women in the pipeline. That's how we make history."

B. "What's So Tough About Being 25?"

By Alana Semuels
Pittsburgh Post-Gazette, Nov. 25, 2004

What's so tough about being 25?

Plenty, according to a Broadway play, an upcoming TV series and a best-selling book, all built around the premise that many people in their 20s waste the decade worrying about what to do with the rest of their lives.

"They tell you the world is your oyster," said Abby Wilner about the period after college when young people are supposed to be enjoying their freedom and settling into exciting lives. "Then you realize it's not quite true."

Wilner and Alexandra Robbins put a name to the mind-set when their book, *The Quarterlife Crisis*, was published in 2001. A workbook designed to help 20-somethings cope with the slippery slope they're on soon followed, as did the Tony Award–winning play *Avenue Q* and an ABC series that's in the works called *¼ life.*

And now there's a Web site:www.quarterlifecrisis.com, which provides an avenue for the 10,000 registered users to commiserate about their troubles and challenges.

Their angst screams out in the replies they post to each other.

One reads: "Let me tell you, I'm miserable. I'm 26 and have recently graduated with my master's in geology. I do have a job . . . great money and benefits . . . but I'm not happy. I usually feel bored."

Another quarterlifer replied: "I know exactly what you are going through. I have all the trappings of what a successful life is supposed to be and am miserable."

Experts are split on whether particular demographic trends have made the 20s a more challenging decade for young adults than it was for earlier generations or whether the "misery" some of them are feeling is of their own making, the product of having it a bit too good.

"The crisis part comes in the sense that freedom can be disconcerting," said Jeffrey Arnett, a psychology professor at the University of Maryland who has written a book on emerging adulthood and who looks at the idea of a quarterlife crisis with some skepticism and little sympathy.

"You have the responsibility to figure out yourself what to do, and that can be stressful and even depressing if you're not figuring it very well."

Some question whether the syndrome is new at all.

"My first reaction is that it's hardly novel," said Alan Waterman, a professor in clinical psychology at the College of New Jersey. In the 1950s and 1960s, sociologist Erik Erikson coined the term identity crisis to define people who are uncertain about who they are or what they want, Waterman said. From the 1967 movie *The Graduate* to the '80s hit *St. Elmo's Fire*, college graduates with angst have translated their woes into entertainment; its recent incarnations only gives it a name.

But recent findings released by the American Sociological Association suggest demographic currents may be redefining the lives and expectations of college graduates across the country in sometimes tumultuous ways.

A team of sociologists that examined the lives of young adults by comparing Census data since 1900 found that young people are making the transition to adulthood—which they define not by biological age but by societal milestones such as marrying, buying houses and having children—later and later. According to their benchmark, 65% of males and 77% of females had completed their transitions into adulthood in their 20s in 1960. In 2000, on the other hand, only 31% of males and 46% of females had reached these stages by age 30.

Young adults are marrying ever later, or not marrying at all, according to a report released by the U.S. Census Bureau. In 1970, the median age at which men were married was 23.2; now it's 26.8. Women got married at a median age of 20.8 in 1970; in 2000 the median was 25.1. What's more, the proportion of women ages 30 to 34 who had never been married tripled in those three decades, from 6% to 22%.

Many young people come out of college carrying debt loads never faced by earlier generations, in part because college costs have almost doubled over the past decade. A 2003 study by the Center for Economic and Policy Research in Washington found that debt for student loans is 85% higher among recent college graduates than it was for graduates a decade ago.

A report released by the American Sociological Association found that only 70% of men ages 24 to 28 earned enough to support themselves, while only half earned enough to support a family of three.

William Strauss, co-author of four books about generational trends, says previous youth waves—from Generation X to the Lost Generation of the, '20s—faced similar challenges, but that the current crop stands apart in some ways.

They have made it harder, he says, by putting more pressure on themselves and caring more about grades and name-brand colleges. A wave of second-generation immigrants has added to their numbers, and there are more college graduates today than ever before.

He sees today's typical 20-something wonder, "I had college and everything was planned, but now I am cast out into the work world. What am I supposed to do?"

C. "Divorce: What Do You Do? Who Gets the Friends?"

Joanne Mamenta
The Tennessean, March 8, 2004

Bellevue residents Candace and Carl Johnson recalled the day a friend stopped by their house to say his wife had left him.

"Everyone was stunned because the wife didn't contact us at all, and we didn't have any opportunity to see how she was doing. The husband was quite despondent and came by frequently, but it was uncomfortable because I felt like I was being disloyal to his wife, with whom I'd been friends," Candace said.

When friends are divorcing, what do you do?

Having been on both sides of that scenario, Pam Nixon, a former facilitator for the Divorce Care ministry, understands a friend's dilemma.

When she was going through her divorce, she had a group of girlfriends who recognized that what she really needed was compassion, support and someone to listen to her. And when one of her best friends went through a divorce, Nixon became that strong supporter.

"I had really close friends who I could call on at any time so not just one of them was hearing it all the time. And I tried to be sensitive to the fact that they had lives outside of my own," Nixon said.

Being available to listen is one of the best things friends can do, said Norm Anderson, director of Brentwood United Methodist Church's single adult ministry. But unless you're a counselor or attorney, "be careful of giving advice or getting involved too deep," he said.

Anderson recommends staying neutral. Sometimes that can be challenging if a divorcing friend starts to rely so heavily on friends that the friends become consumed with the divorce. That happened to the Johnsons.

"It was a lose-lose situation," Candace said. The friend wanted to talk about it all in detail, but they were hearing only one side.

Anderson recommends that friends state their positions on where they stand from the beginning. "You can tell both sides that you are friends with both and want to stay that way. Say that you will be there for each and will be compassionate and understanding with each but will not play one side against the other or betray either's confidence," Anderson said.

But despite your good intentions, friendships may end when the couple divorces.

"Lives are changed by divorce and so are social needs and agendas. Often it is the divorcing couple who drift away from their former couple's friends," Anderson said.

If friendships survive the divorce, new relationships can form. "You can keep individual friendships by inviting either one over for dinner with you and your spouse. In time, as they form new relationships, you can tell them to bring their new friends along," Anderson said.

D. "White Majority Steadily Shrinking"

By Genaro C. Armas
The Associated Press, March 13, 2004

WASHINGTON—For as long as there has been an America, whites have made up a clear majority. But that will change by 2050, when minority groups will be 49.9% of the population, the Census Bureau says.

Asians and Hispanics will see the most dramatic increases between now and mid-century, when the U.S. population will have grown by almost 50% to reach 420 million, according to bureau projections being released today.

America will get older, too. Nearly 21% of its residents will be 65 or older, compared with 12% now.

The data highlight trends long predicted. But racial and ethnic changes are taking shape faster than expected, due in large part to higher-than-forecast immigration rates for Asians and Hispanics, said Greg Spencer, a bureau demographer.

Whites now represent 69% of the population, but their growth is slowing because of low rates of birth and immigration. Their total will grow 7%, to 210 million, or 50.1% of the population, by 2050.

Those figures do not include Hispanics. The Census Bureau counts "Hispanic" or "Latino" as an ethnicity rather than a race, so they can be of any race, including white.

Between 2040 and 2050, the Census Bureau expects that the non-Hispanic white population actually will decline slightly because of a large number of expected deaths of baby boomers, who by 2040 will be at least 76.

Meantime, the Hispanic and Asian populations are expected to continue their explosive growth.

The Asian population is expected to more than triple to 33 million by 2050. Hispanics will increase their ranks by 188%, to 102.6 million, or roughly one quarter of the population.

"Historically, we've been a black-and-white country. That's not true any longer, and even less true in the future," said Roderick Harrison, a demographer with the Joint Center for Political and Economic Studies in Washington, which studies issues of concern to minorities.

"A good deal of social history in the next several decades will be reflected in how we sort that out, whether we achieve greater degrees of equality in these populations," he said.

The projections, the first released by the bureau since the 2000 head count, also show a burgeoning older population as healthier lifestyles and better medical treatment increase longevity. By 2050, 5% of the country will be 85 or older, compared with 1.5% now.

The bureau expects that the black population will rise 71%, to over 61 million, or about 15% of the population, compared with nearly 13% now.

Blacks would remain the second largest minority.

Asians would comprise 8% of the population, compared with 4% now.

"This means more of a mix of cultures and ethnic backgrounds," said Edward Kwanhun Rim, president of the Pacific Rim Cultural Foundation, Inc. in Barrington, Ill., and a member of a citizen advisory panel to the Census Bureau on the Asian population. "It will be a more colorful and bright future—we can hope."

E. "Give Me the Simple Life"

By Martha Irvine
The Associated Press, Jan. 26, 2004

CHICAGO—Sandi Garcia was living her dream—or so she thought. With a marketing degree from the University of Wyoming, she moved to Florida, started climbing the corporate ladder and was making good money.

There was only one problem: She was miserable. She was up at 6 a.m. and getting home from work just in time to watch the late-night news, and she often worked weekends, too.

"I've got burnt out pretty quickly," says the 26-year-old, who longed for a life that was "calmer and simpler." She found it back in her native Cheyenne, Wyo., where she has plenty of time to ski, volunteer at an animal shelter and see friends and family.

Experts say Garcia is one of a growing number of Americans—particularly people in their 20s and 30s—who are making a conscious decision to slow down and cut back on all that overwhelms them.

"It's true among people of all ages. But it's much stronger, much more notable among the younger generations," says Bruce Tulgan, a Connecticut-based consultant who tracks generational relationships and trends in the workplace.

They're simplifying at home. Pierce Mattie, 28, a New Yorker, recently sold his car, moved into a smaller apartment and gave away much of his wardrobe.

"It feels great!" he says, noting that having "so much junk I don't use" was stressing him out.

And they're dramatically changing their work lives.

Gregg Steiner, 29, in Sherman Oaks, Calif., escaped the busy high-tech world to work at home, and sold his beach home near Malibu. He says he grew tired of never having time to spend there. He also couldn't stand commuting two hours a day.

"I hate traffic. I hate dressing in a suit. I hate sitting under fluorescent lighting," says Steiner, who now does customer service via the Web for Pinxav, his family's diaper rash ointment business.

Tulgan says all those gripes are common for young professionals.

"The idea of working in a particular building with certain hours seems ridiculous to them," he says.

But he and other generational experts say that doesn't mean young people are lazy. They just want flexibility.

"It's much more likely they're going to tell you that they'd like more control over their schedule—and more time for the life part of life," Tulgan says.

Michael Muetzel, an author who has studied twenty-somethings, calls it a movement toward family and social activities.

"Why not put your trust and resources in things that you absolutely can trust?" he says. Young Americans are into local volunteering but have little faith in such institutions as Social Security or government. Many, given recent scandals, don't trust the political process or corporate America.

"A lot of us saw our parents or knew other people's parents who were laid off. There was loyalty to the company, and people were getting huge salaries, and all of a sudden it disappeared," says Garcia, who now works for the Wyoming Business Council.

While their parents' generation may have focused on trying to "have it all," many in Gen X and Y are taking a step back to prioritize.

"I see my parents. They just worked so much, and I don't think they had much of a chance to enjoy stuff the way they would have liked to," Garcia says.

Some researchers find benefits in a simpler life.

"The upshot is that people who value money and image and status are actually less happy," says Tim Kasser, a psychologist at Knox College in Galesburg, Ill., who has researched the phenomenon.

He says they often report being less satisfied with life and are more likely to experience depression, anxiety and such physical symptoms as backaches and headaches.

Those who weren't focused on possessions, fame and fortune were, overall, more content with life and felt better.

EXERCISES

1. Write a better lead for the feature on divorce.

2. Write a better conclusion for the feature on divorce.

3. Rewrite the following news story in a feature format:

"Bread of the Dead"

The Tennessean, Oct. 27, 2003

November 2 marks the Mexican holiday called Dia de los Muertos, or Day of the Dead.

Seemingly morbid, it's really a celebration of lives past, with special foods made and eaten at graveside parties.

You can celebrate with pan de muertos, or bread of the dead, a round sweet loaf with bone shapes molded on top. It's available at La Hacienda Market, 2617 Nolensville Pike (256-5006), from now until supplies run out on November 1.

4. Rewrite the following news story in a feature format.

"A Fishy Story"

The Tennessean, Feb. 11, 2004

EAGAN, MINN.—A smoke alarm summoned firefighters to a school in the middle of the night, but when they arrived, the flames had been put out.

Dory took care of it. Dory is a fish, a betta kept in a vase on a desk in a third-grade classroom at Trinity Lone Oak Lutheran School.

A forgotten candle started a small fire on the desk on Jan. 24, setting off the smoke alarm and shattering the fish bowl, spilling enough water to put out the flames.

Firefighters found a few embers still glowing on the desk—and Dory still alive in a puddle.

5. Rewrite the "Man Grips Dog, Bites Man" story from Chapter 2 as a feature story.

6. Rewrite the following news story in feature form:

"Man Accused of Stealing Shoes"

The Tennessean, Oct. 27, 2003

TOKYO — Police arrested a man for stealing shoes at a southern Japanese hospital then found a collection in his home of 440 women's shoes—all for the left foot.

The private hospital in Usu city, 500 miles south of Tokyo, began receiving complaints two years ago from patients and employees that shoes removed at the entrance hall were disappearing. Ichiro Irie, 45, was arrested Saturday on suspicion of having stolen two leather shoes the previous day during one of his twice-weekly hospital visits, a police spokesman said yesterday.

In Irie's home, police found a box in a closet overflowing with the left mate to 440 pairs of women's shoes, including high heels, patent leather pumps, sandals and nurses shoes. He told police he had "a penchant for women's feet," the Yomiuri newspaper said. It was unclear why he may have preferred the left foot.

7. Rewrite the following news story in feature form. Note the ambiguous observation about flower gardens and the effects of being pollinated. Is this fact necessary for this feature?

"A Social Insect"

By Harry E. Williams
University of Tennessee

Honeybees are social insects, with 50,000 to 100,000 living in a typical colony.

The worker bees may make 80,000 trips from the hive to flowering plants to produce one pound of honey. They fly a distance equal to three times around the world to produce one pound.

The bees use one ounce of honey to fly a distance equal to one trip around the world. This means about seven million miles of flight per gallon of honey.

The honey bees begin flying from the hive early in the morning before dawn. The last bees return to the hive just after dark. A few bees may remain out all night. On each of these trips the bees may visit several hundred flowers. However, on each trip the bee confines her visits to one plant species, collecting one kind of nectar and distributing one kind of pollen.

The honey bee's visit to the blossoms results in complete fertilization of the blossom.

The fruit set is increased, the quality improved and the yield increased when the plant is adequately pollinated.

A flower garden appearance is a sign of inadequate pollination. Flowers adequately pollinated will wilt a short time after pollination.

8. Recall your first kiss and write it up as a feature. *Or* go to exercise 9.

Here's a feature on a Bruce Springsteen first kiss:

"Bruce's First Kiss Was Really Dreamy"

The Tennessean, Nov. 13, 1996

Bruce Springsteen did his hometown gig in Freehold, N.J., and sang out this line about his first kiss: "Maria Espinosa, where are you tonight?"

Leave it to us media vultures to find her. *The Asbury Park Press* says she's now a 48-year-old grandmother who was 15 when she got the famed smooch.

"I can't believe he remembers my name," Maria Espinosa Ayala told the paper. She said she never talked about the kiss because her parents were strict, and she wasn't allowed to have a boyfriend at the time. When Bruce hit big, she was sure no one would believe her.

"It must have lasted about a minute," she said. "It was good. I dreamed about it afterward."

---

9. Describe how your love, or a love disintegrated.

10. Rewrite the following facts into a feature story that captures the spirit of the hoax and its consequences:

Craig Delk calls you at the city desk of *University Press.* He is public relations director of Memorial University, Potsdam, N.Y. It's the day after April 1 and *The Oracle,* the weekly student newspaper at the State University of New York, Potsdam, has printed a "hoax" front page.

The front page is full of hoax stories and features. Among them:

The Potsdam University dorms are reverting to male and female dorms.

Potsdam University is reverting to the quarter system.

Catering service for the cafeterias is going to be taken over by Bud's, a favorite local hangout for the students. "It'll be a real challenge," Bud said.

The major hoax story has caused a considerable uproar:

The Potsdam State University is going to take over Memorial University. (That's the other university, a private university in Potsdam.)

This major hoax story quotes President Kathryn Rust:

"I'm pleased the State Legislature has approved the funding to merge with Memorial University. The merger will be mutually beneficial."

The story also quotes Memorial University President Choi Yap:

"It was inevitable. When you have two universities in a small town such as Potsdam, and only two blocks apart, it's the economical path to follow. We look forward to the expansion promised with such a merger."

One of the wags (Denny Fry) at the local morning-cup-of-coffee-hangout, Ralph's, is quoted as saying of the whole affair and its aftermath:

"That's just the sort of thing you'd expect to happen here. Spell 'Potsdam' backwards and what've you got?"

Meanwhile, parents of the Memorial University students as far away as Long Island have been calling Memorial University to find out what the deal is. They've been wondering how it will affect their sons and daughters.

Faculty advisor of *The Oracle*, Kwun-Lon Ting, says, "Yeah, I knew of the hoax, even encouraged it when the students suggested the idea."

The president of the Faculty Senate of Memorial University, Joshua Gammon, calls the whole incident, "Unfortunate, from our point of view."

Student newspaper editor Bobbie Faye Hammock admitted it was her idea:

"We just got through studying famous hoaxes in the history of journalism course, and I thought it would liven things up a bit. The rest of the editorial staff thought it would too."

Jennifer Osburn, news editor, agreed:

"We tossed the idea around when we started making the paper up on Thursday night. Stayed up a couple of hours later to write the stories. We didn't think it'd be such a big deal."

It livened things up so much that President Rossie is no longer answering his phone. That's why Craig Delk is talking to you. He wants a story written to the effect that there's no way this merger story can ever come true. (In an aside, he says the story may affect their current fund drive.)

Both presidents refuse to comment on the story.

11. This feature-grading exercise enables students to earn a grade by grading a classmate's feature of 9a (or some other feature). Students grade in red pencil, and the instructor then grades the feature in green. Students are "self-instructed" by grading. Instructors learn if students are capable of writing better. (If students earn an "A" in grading, they should be capable of producing at least "B" papers.) **(The grading form can also be used by students in revising their own writing later on.)**

Your name: _____   Gradee's name: _____

Newspaper Feature Grading Form

Heading at top of page single spaced as per following example :
    "Featuring the Greatest of Grading"
    A 500-word feature

D.J. Anon	yes ____	no ____
Hook, Idea and Transition clear to you?	yes ____	no ____
Comments?		

An improved feature lead might be:

Is the feature coherent? (Logical sequence?)	yes ____	no ____

Comments?
A more logical progression of paragraphs, sentences:

The conclusion wraps up the feature in a neat bow?	yes ____	no ____

An improved conclusion might be:
Does the feature "flow" from sentence to sentence

and paragraph to paragraph?	yes ____	no ____
Are there similar paragraph beginnings?	yes ____	no ____

Overly short paragraphs?		yes ____	no ____
Is there a change in points of view?	pv	yes ____	no ____
Is there a change in the "tone" of the feature?	to	yes ____	no ____
Are attributions buried?		yes ____	no ____
Are "witches" negligible?		yes ____	no ____
(It is, was, we were, there are, they were, which was, were, he was, one is, etc., e.g., pronouns + verbs of being		yes ____	no ____
Passive verbs used instead of action verbs?		yes ____	no ____
Overused verbs like "get" or "set"?		yes ____	no ____
Are there trite phrases?		yes ____	no ____
Are there "be specific" possibilities?	bs	yes ____	no ____
Is there "telling" instead of "showing"	tell	yes ____	no ____
Possibility for better characterization	cd	yes ____	no ____
or setting description?	sd	yes ____	no ____
Concluding comments:			

12. Read exercise 5 on women in government in Chapter 9. You may want to pursue this feature idea at this time rather than after reading Chapter 9.

CHAPTER 5

MAGAZINE WRITING AND THE READER INTEREST PLANE

WHAT IS A MAGAZINE ARTICLE?

Writers will master the various leads and types of articles analyzed in this chapter as a matter of course. This mastery should come easily because of the similarity of the magazine article to the feature. Creative use of these lead styles can inspire the literary hook that carries readers into the body of the article. Using the reader interest plane, the writer then organizes her or his information notes, keying them to a mounting article interest ending with a lingering impression.

This close relationship between the feature and magazine article was indicated earlier, in Chapter 2. For example, a feature on "*Little Red Riding Hood*" was published in two newspapers and also featured in *Elementary English Magazine.* A ritual on kids fighting bees was published not only in a New York weekly newspaper, *The (Potsdam) Courier & Freeman,* and a daily newspaper, the *Watertown Daily Times,* but also in *The New York Folklore Quarterly* and *Bee Culture Magazine.* The subject matter, then, may be the same for articles as for features. Even the leads are essentially the same. Like newspaper features, magazine articles can also ride on the coattails of a news event, an individual personality in the news (Bobby Fischer) or a community interest that has surfaced—perhaps an environmental problem. Just what is different?

Usually it's the depth, complexity and length of the article. To emphasize that difference, here are two different graphic representations. The long feature, as you'll recall, has a square representing the lead and then a series of waves leading to the conclusion, another square.

Lead   Conclusion

The article graphic representation is the reader interest plane (RIP).

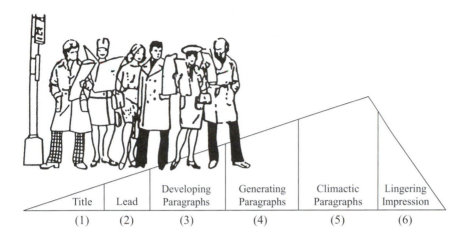

Title	Lead	Developing Paragraphs	Generating Paragraphs	Climactic Paragraphs	Lingering Impression
(1)	(2)	(3)	(4)	(5)	(6)

It's a solid ramp leading up to the climactic paragraphs. Then comes a slight drop-off indicating the "lingering impression" left with the reader.

One other important distinction: While both features and articles strive to attain a unity of impression, the reader interest plane offers a more rigorous plan to achieve it. You're focused on the idea in the lead. The RIP then forces you to add material that will begin to develop that idea. Once that's accomplished, you add generating paragraphs that develop or carry out the idea of the article still more. The interest now generated leads to the climactic point of the idea being pursued. Finally, a concluding paragraph adds the touch that will leave the reader with a lingering impression of what's been read. You get the idea we're talking serious development stuff involved in the article idea here? We are.

Whether the newspaper editor will tolerate the more in-depth study or complexity of the magazine article (if you also pitch the article to her or him) depends upon the editor. An editor of the weekly newspaper in Virden, Ill., found the narrative essays I wrote about life there during the Great Depression and the coal mine wars so interesting, he printed four or five of the longest—after they'd been printed in various magazines. An editor in Oregon or Wisconsin would not be so inclined.

The relevance for you of all this convergence between features and articles? Along with the writing latitude it gives you, it suggests multiple markets for what you write. But that's a topic for Chapter 11, titled "To Market, to Market." For now, let's scan the magazine scene.

THE MAGAZINE SCENE

Writing articles for magazines enables you to explore, in depth, subjects often given only fleeting coverage by other media with their hourly or daily deadlines. Many of the thought-provoking, informative articles and commentary that help shape people's opinions are published by magazines from *American Heritage* to *The New Yorker*.

Magazine publishing has exploded in the last couple of decades, with new titles being created to serve the needs of people who prefer to subscribe to several magazines with different specialties rather than to one or two very general magazines. This trend toward specialization can be seen in other magazine markets and on the Internet. In regional markets, city magazines have achieved a prominence vis-à-vis the national magazines in much the same way suburban newspapers have vis-à-vis big city newspapers. Indeed, local magazines are among the fastest-growing media in the United States. Their content varies from lifestyle and entertainment subjects to investigative features on local problems.

The trend toward specialization in media, led by magazines, indicates that magazines continue to be a popular medium for American consumers. If you can carve out a specialty for yourself that fits the profiles of magazines, you can anticipate considerable success in selling articles to them.

VINCE PASSARO WRITES ABOUT THE MAGAZINE SCENE

It's an interesting time, and not really a great one. When I started writing for magazines, almost twenty years ago, there were more general interest, high-quality magazines than there are now, by a good margin; each had more space for essays and serious reviews; the pay ranged from $2 a word at the best magazines, $1 being the minimum for any national glossy, down to say $300 dollars for a newspaper review.

The newspapers now commonly pay less than $200 (*Newsday*, as an example, paid me $350 for daily reviews and more for Sunday pieces in the early '90s, and now pays, I think, $175), and magazine pay has remained, after two decades, basically the same. So the money and the venues have essentially shrivelled to a mere fraction of what they were, and they weren't, in the late '80s, considered all that good compared to a decade before.

I would say that it is a moment now when the entire publishing industry should be reinventing itself; not only have people's reading habits drastically changed, but, for younger people, the whole culture of knowledge has been altered. It seems to me—watching my kids IM and text, and seeing how they read (they read online, in one sitting; and they read books; I can't tell you the last time I saw anyone under 25 sitting somewhere reading a magazine that wasn't essentially gossip or fashion that is flipped through and consumed, rather than read), and seeing how they talk and what they talk about and how they approach information, that consciousness itself is changing.

The essential solitude of the reading experience feels unnatural to them; they spend as much time reading the blogs (MySpace, etc.) of people they know as they do reading words written by strangers; for many young people, Everything is Social. So I would venture that now, the savvy young student journalists and writers will seek out venues and modes of writing that do at least a passable job of keeping up with these changes. Most of the publishing industry, like vague, out-of-it parents, remains clueless in the face of these changes.

SUSAN FREINKEL WRITES ABOUT MAGAZINE EDITORS

Magazines are editor-driven—much more so than daily publications. In my experience editors have a huge influence in shaping a story and determining how it ultimately turns out—for better and worse. It can be very frustrating to work with someone who doesn't really know what story he or she wants or who is a clunky or ham-handed line editor. So when I find an editor I really like, I will stick to that person like white on rice, and follow her or him from publication to publication, even if that means I end up writing for magazines I wouldn't have expected to.

MAGAZINE ARTICLE IDEAS

Where do ideas for articles come from? Like newspaper features, a better question might be, Where do they *not* come from? We live in a sea of ideas. Personal experience or narrative ideas may be the easiest to discover, develop, and write. Take an inventory of your life and the interesting experiences or thoughts you have had.

Here's an example of two articles that were written when I did just that:

"The Day the 'Reds' Came to Virden"

As a kid, I witnessed what happened when some "reds" from Chicago came to Virden, Ill., a day or so before the Fourth of July. Two men and a woman, about 30 years old, talked about the hard times we were going through during the Great Depression and what could be done about it, drawing comparisons between the Vanderbilts and ordinary people standing in welfare surplus lines. The citizens, however, didn't like that kind of talk. They also didn't like the "reds'" reply to their challenges, such as "It's a free country, and I can say what I want." As kids we were always saying the same things. I couldn't see what was the problem. The citizens, led by a guy who hauled coal in his truck, beat up the "reds," turned over their coupe, and ran them out of town.

About 15 years ago, I recalled that incident and wrote about it. I sent the article off to three editors. The Illinois Historical Society *Dispatch* editor published it in the Fourth of July issue (starting on the cover of it). No printed record of the incident existed. Gary DeNeal of *Springhouse Magazine* called one night and wanted to run the article after the Illinois historical magazine ran it. Two years ago, I got a check for $50 from Jim Villani, editor of the *American Dream* anthology. He included it in the volume. "The Day the Reds Came to Virden" was published as the lead narrative essay in *Growing Up on the Illinois Prairie During the Great Depression and the Coal Mine Wars: A Portrayal of Life as It Was*—my book, recently published by The Edwin Mellen Press. I read that essay at the Edinburgh International Festival of the Arts in Scotland in 2006 in a session titled "Keeping Memory Alive: The Mine Wars in the U.S. and U.K."

"Harold Proctor's Bull Comes A'Courtin'"

For 10 years I owned and ran a 130-acre cattle farm. One morning Harold Proctor's bull showed up in my pasture, enamored of one of my cows, "Barbara." How Harold separated the bull from my herd with his five beagle hounds and hurried it on home with bird shot furnished me with the material for an article that garnered $300 from *Inland Steel Magazine.* Then *Springhouse Magazine* published it. Now it is essentially a chapter in a novel under submission, titled *The Echoes from Ole Forge Hill.*

Check Out the Mall, and So On

Look around on your way to the mall. Note things that occur to you and tuck them away in your mind or in a notebook for further exploration. Look at the latest fashions. Listen to the latest sayings. When you get through with this observation and inventory tour, you may want to write an article about a day in the life of a cosmetic clerk where free perfume samples are available, or a day in the life of an undercover security agent.

While helping your mother plant her garden or your father paint the house you might think of a how-to-do-it article about how to get through the ordeal with a sense of enjoyment. Sort through the day's mail. If you've had the foresight to place yourself on the government's mailing list of periodicals, which include everything from building a solar energy unit to eliminating broom sage from pastures, you'll be able to mine ideas from those periodicals.

Science and health article ideas may stem from recently published books, phenomena reported by the press, or experiments being conducted in the science departments of major universities located near you. Travel article ideas crop up along the highways in the form of historical road signs, tourist information booths and chambers of commerce.

Checking through a big city newspaper will give you an Associated Press column on important dates—"On This Date in History." Note an anniversary date, a year or two later, or earlier (check past issues), that justifies a timely article recalling that event. Check the following list.

"On This Date in History"

The Associated Press

Nov. 24, there are 37 days left in the year.

1859—British naturalist Charles Darwin published *On the Origin of Species,* which explained his theory of evolution.

1863—The Civil War battle for Lookout Mountain began in Tennessee. Union forces took the mountain two days later.

1864—French artist Henri de Toulouse-Lautrec was born in Albi.

1871—The National Rifle Association was incorporated.

1947—A group of writers, producers and directors that became known as the "Hollywood Ten" was cited for contempt of Congress for refusing to answer questions about alleged Communist influence in the movie industry.

1963—Jack Ruby shot and fatally wounded Lee Harvey Oswald, the assassin of President Kennedy, in a scene captured on television.

1969—Apollo 12 splashed down safely in the Pacific.

1971—Hijacker D. B. Cooper parachuted from a Northwest Airlines 727 over Washington State with $200,000 in ransom. His fate remains unknown.

1985—The hijacking of an Egyptair jetliner parked on the ground in Malta ended violently as Egyptian commandos stormed the plane. Fifty-eight people died in the raid, in addition to two killed by the hijackers.

1987—The United States and the Soviet Union agreed to scrap short-and-medium-range missiles.

1993—Congress gave final approval to the Brady handgun control bill.

1998—America Online confirmed it was buying Netscape Communications in a deal ultimately worth $10 billion.

Note the 1971 date. D. B. Cooper is something of a folk hero. In 2006, the 35th anniversary of his jump, a recap of his exploits was printed in newspapers across the country.

Just scanning the *Writer's Market* and the descriptions of the sort of articles wanted by various magazine editors will generate article ideas for you.

But a giant word of caution: Once you have an idea, don't wait too long to write about it: While studying for final exams at the University of Wisconsin, I read about a slave, Nat Turner, who stirred a rebellion in Southhampton, Va., in 1831. I noted it in an "ideas for further exploration" manila folder. After I graduated and before I could turn to that manila folder, William Styron had published a best seller titled *The Confessions of Nat Turner.*

MAGAZINE ARTICLE LEADS

Like the leads written for newspaper feature stories, magazine article leads include a narrative hook, an idea of what the article is about and a transition into the body of the article. Newspaper features and magazine articles may both be connected with and exploit a news event or issue, an individual personality or community interest.

A wide range of approaches is available when writing magazine article leads. The following sample of leads illustrate this.

The Dramatic Lead

"Suicide in the Children's Ranks"

The Associated Press, Jan. 22, 1983

OSLO, Norway—His classmates called him "the leper," because measles had left his 12-year-old body scarred.

His mother said children tended to blame him when things went wrong.

One day, distraught, the boy in Tromsoe, Norway, took a rope and hanged himself.

In Manchester, Mo., a "nice boy" who had won a good citizenship award was taunted about his family by his junior high classmates before he pulled out a pistol and killed one student, wounded another, and took his own life, officials said.

The boy left a suicide note in his gym bag, police said.

These are just two of a growing number of cases of suicides by children, a phenomenon in our society.

The dramatic lead sets the stage for readers and draws them into the article immediately. The two examples of child suicide used in this lead might be called "minidramas." Where are the hook, idea and transition in this lead? The first five paragraphs form the hook. The sixth paragraph contains the idea and the transition. To flesh this lead out, a third example should be added to form a triad—something discussed later in "The Art of Writing" (Chapter 7).

The dramatic lead is an excellent way to draw readers into an article. This lead by John Gerstner from an internal publication of John Deere & Co. describes how employees brave unpredictable weather to service equipment in remote Alaskan villages.

"Beating the Bush in Alaska"

It was nearly closing time when Hans Hensen reached his office at the large Craig Taylor dealership on the north side of Anchorage. Jensen, manager of a new power system division, was greeted by Bob Combs, service manager, who handed him a telex. It began: "Hot, hot, hot," and went on to say that the single Deere engine providing all the electricity for the village of Kotlik (across the bay from Nome) was down. Hans would have to fly through a blizzard to fix the engine, canceling the travel plans he and I had made.

"Welcome to Alaska," he said with a grin, "where your plans change from minute to minute."

The Question Lead

Although question leads appear easy enough to write, the question should entice readers into the article.

"A Hard Rain A'Fallin'"

Acid rain—how much is falling and where? Where does it come from? Is the problem getting worse? Are its effects cumulative?

These are some of the questions two researchers at West Virginia University are attempting to answer in separate research projects on this problem that is causing worldwide concern.

Does this lead by William A. Aston in *The West Virginia University Alumni Magazine* interest you? When question leads are appropriate, they can be excellent. However, Dwight Leland Teeter, journalism professor at the University of Tennessee, noted he had a grumpy city editor who once said: "Readers want answers, not questions." A caveat to keep in mind.

The Setting Lead

The setting lead, similar to the one in "Trouble in Suburbia" (in Chapter 4), is difficult to write because it calls upon craft of fiction techniques. This article for *Family Circle* by Tracie Rozhon resulted from extensive interviews with one of the survivors of a plane crash. The article employs fictional techniques throughout its chronological story line.

"Icy Terror in the Potomac"*

By Tracie Rozhon

Thick, wet snow was falling on the nation's capital, and the freezing temperatures of one of the coldest afternoons of the century forced even well-wrapped pedestrians off the wind-swept streets. Commuters dashed through underground garages to their cars for an early escape across the 14th Street Bridge and the ice-clogged Potomac River to warm suburban houses in Virginia.

Priscilla Tirado, with her husband and two-month-old son, was riding to the airport in her grandmother's comfortably heated car. She was dressed in the in-between, layered style of Northerners flying south in wintertime: a long-sleeved red cotton top, black corduroy designer jeans and a patchwork leather jacket. As the Ford LTD cautiously maneuvered through the D.C. traffic on its way to National Airport, windshield wipers brushing away the swirling snow, she thought about what lay ahead in Florida: a new home; a new job for Jose, her husband. . . .

They pulled up outside the Air Florida terminal about 1 p.m., in plenty of time for the 2:15 flight to Tampa.

_____
* *Family Circle* (May 18, 1982) 56.

[That flight would end up in the icy Potomac River.]

The lead sets the stage for the reader. In this respect, it is similar to the dramatic lead. Rozhon is able to unfold her drama slowly, building suspense all the while.

The Combination Lead

Just as in writing newspaper feature leads, a number of openings can also be used in writing the magazine article lead. It depends on your material, the market you write for and your imagination. Scott Witte decided to start off this article in *Popular Science* with a combination lead—utilizing a direct quote lead and a question.

"The Ultimate Winter Adventure"

"You're going camping in the mountains, in the middle of winter? Wouldn't it be simpler just to hire someone to club you over the head?"

My friend's reaction was a typical one when I told him I would be spending my winter vacation ski mountaineering somewhere in the Rocky Mountains. It's a sport best described as the marriage between backpacking and cross-country skiing. Many enthusiasts consider it the ultimate expression of both.

After reading these leads, you may be thinking, as we indicated earlier, that there's not much difference between a newspaper feature lead and a magazine article lead. A great many newspaper editors feel the same way. The major difference, when it occurs, is length of the magazine article lead as illustrated in the setting lead and the article itself.

WHAT'S IN A TITLE?

Efforts on creating good titles for your magazine article are well spent. A good title not only attracts the attention of the magazine editor, it can provide you with the impetus to sit down and write the article. And titles not only open the wellsprings of creativity, they promote good writing. Unlike newspaper feature headlines—written by copy editors—your magazine article title, if it's appropriate and interesting, has an excellent chance of being used by the editor. Magazine article titles can be fun to create.

The primary function of the title is to attract the attention of the reader, describe or hint at what the subject matter of the article is about, and set the tone for the article. Look at the titles you have read so far in this text. Do they do that?

How were they created? The lead should provide you with an idea for the title. If there is trouble in "Hyslip," Conn., a natural title is "Trouble in Suburbia" (see Chapter 4). If an article is about going back to an old haunt, say, a lake, what is more natural than "Once More to the Lake," as in the essay reprinted in this chapter? Sometimes a celebrity's name is enough to provoke interest and indicate what the article is about: "Woman in the News: Julia Roberts." Most of the time, however, creativity is needed to come up with the best titles: "The House of the Dead," "The Dream of the Red Chamber," "Streams That Nobody Fords." Easily composed titles are rarely the best titles.

THE READER INTEREST PLANE

So, we're in agreement: Magazine article titles and leads require imagination and artistry. Let's say, you've done it: A great title for the article! A beautiful lead! But, alas. You have little time to bask in their glory. On the horizon, the rest of the article looms. Ominous. How should you go about writing the article itself? It's not quite like a newspaper news story where the lead provides a basic outline of what should follow. What to do? One method is to follow the peaks-and-valleys approach stressed in the chapter on newspaper features. However, that approach suggests a thin line model of the magazine article. Organizing your article along the reader interest plane, on the other hand, reminds you that the magazine article entails a more substantial organization and structure.

Check the figure on page 105 over again. How about a recapitulation? After the lead and idea there's a section titled "developing paragraphs." Simple enough: How do you develop the idea of the article? What will carry the reader deeper into the article? (It's just like telling your parents how you finally discovered the way to ace that history final.) Once you've roughed those paragraphs out in your mind, you're ready to create paragraphs creating even more interest, "the generating paragraphs" leading up to the climactic paragraphs—the ones that might be labeled the punch lines of the article. Once you've decided what those paragraphs will consist of, all that remains is the last touch, the concluding paragraph, which will leave a lingering impression upon the reader.

Another benefit from organizing your magazine article along the reader interest plane is that you'll discover if you have enough information to develop your idea fully. If you use up all your material in the generating paragraphs, you know you have to do more research.

But let's look at how the reader interest plane plays out in the following articles.

The Personal Experience Article

An examination of the next few articles reveals the reader interest plane prevailing as an organizational pattern—in some better than others.

You, of course, have personal experiences that, if written well, are publishable. The following article in *Bride* magazine stemmed from one of my students' frustration at losing close friends when she married.

"Gaining a Husband? Don't Lose Your Friends"*

By Cyndi Pritchett

I tried to include my best friend, Tammy, in all the plans when I arranged my June 24, 1989, wedding. Sometimes she gave me the impression she didn't want to help. I felt angry and betrayed. She accused me of confiding in everyone else before her. To be honest, I guess I did confide in others before her, but only because I felt she didn't care anymore.

The friendship changed due to our shifting personalities and a communication problem, according to Phyllis Davidson, Ph.D., assistant professor of child and family science at Tennessee Technological University in Cookeville.

"The relationship was based on conditional love," Dr. Davidson notes. If Cyndi didn't do as Tammy wanted, Tammy held a grudge. She was saying, "I'll love you if...."

In hindsight this makes sense. Tammy had always led: I followed. We were extremely close, but once I began planning my wedding, we lost the special communication we had before.

Some friendships endure after marriage. Carol, 22, a preschool teacher, says it took time to accept the fact that her best friend, Jessie, 23, a restaurant manager, was really married.

"We planned on going to college together, but we went our separate ways, and Jessie got married," Carol explains. "Since we communicate really well, nothing hinders our friendship."

Dr. Davidson believes that sustaining relationships "depends on a person's ability to form friendships, what she or he expects from them, and whether she or he can give and receive love." After marriage, women tend to become best friends with their spouses, Dr. Davidson says.

"Wives don't have as much free time as before; they can't be as spontaneous. It makes friendships different, and they don't always last."

After this lead, the following developing paragraphs discuss how friends may fall by the wayside when you marry.

The following generating paragraphs leading up to the climax of the article reveal more circumstances and how some friends remain and some go.

How to cope? "Keep the lines of communication open," advises Dr. Davidson. "Include your single friends in some plans with your husband early on, so they can develop a friendship with him, too."

The climactic paragraphs focus on marriages that lose friends.

Before Gina, 27, a journalism student, got married, her friends would call and ask her to go shopping. After she got married, the calls stopped. "They acted as if I couldn't leave home," Gina remembers. "My friends treated me as if [my husband] David and I were joined at the hip."

Gina isn't alone. Many single friends assume married women can't go out because they have chores and a husband to care for. Single women may not realize how neglected their married friends feel when they are left out. Even if they are busy, brides prefer the option of being able to say "yes" or "no" to invitations. "A single woman may fear her newly-wed friend isn't the same," Dr. Davidson says. "Maybe she is envious because she isn't changing."

"I see all my friends getting married," Debra, 22, a word processor in East Detroit, admits, "and I wonder if I ever will. I can't take vacations with my friends anymore because they're either getting married or having babies."

The lingering impression focuses on jealousy from the married person's viewpoint and how it is countered.

The jealousy can go both ways. Although I'm happily married, I sometimes envy my single friends' freedom and their lack of large debts. But I've learned to focus on common interests to keep my friendships strong.

———

* Reprinted with permission of The Conde Nast Publications, Inc.

The How-to-Do-It Article

If you can build a better mousetrap than anyone else, there'll be a magazine wanting an article about it. How-to-do-it articles (sometimes referred to as service articles) are one of the most popular types of articles. If, after reading how you can lose friends by marrying, you are still intent on marriage, Ellen Tien's article on how to get a commitment is an example of a how-to-do-it article from *Mademoiselle*. Let's see how this longer article rests on the reader interest plane:

"Hooking Him: A Last-Ditch Guide"*

By Ellen Tien

An excellent lead even though that "7,000 flushes" could be omitted because of the images it provokes. The idea and the developing paragraphs of the article follow.

A year or four ago, you and your boyfriend met and experienced that first exhilarating flush of new love. Now it's 7,000 flushes later, and the two of you know every humdrum, intimate detail of each other's lives (he showed you that funny, funny place where he has a birthmark shaped like Italy; you confessed to him that the hair on your upper lip isn't naturally blond). Lately, you've felt the powerful urge to take things a step further—maybe move in together or get engaged. He doesn't seem inclined to discuss it. You point out that Woody Allen (of all people) once said a relationship is like a shark: If it doesn't move forward, it will die. Your boyfriend continues to tread water. You try to be patient, but even chopped liver keeps for only so long.

Steady, girl. Before you whip yourself into a pâté, keep in mind that this is a man we're talking about, remember?

A normal, red-blooded, emotionally squashed, channel-flipping, ridiculously lovable human male. Of course he's a little commitment-shy! It's a natural part of the delightful, all-inclusive Y-chromosome package. More often than not, if you want a man to take the plunge, you'll have to give him a gentle push. And while you can't make a horse drink, you certainly can help him work up a thirst and then lead him to water.

But before you make a beeline for the stable (life), you have to do a little house-keeping of your own. Just because you've got commitment lust doesn't necessarily mean you've got to go for the gold. According to Judith Sills, Ph.D., a Philadelphia-based psychologist, there are three key questions every woman should ask herself, precommitment.

"First off," advises Dr. Sills, "figure out what compromise you'll make by being with this man. What fantasy of perfection are you willing to let go of?" Is he as smart, funny, ambitious or sensitive as you envisioned your future husband will be? Is he too neat, too messy, too hairy? "We all make some compromises, big or small, when we choose a partner," says Dr. Sills. "Your job is to identify what your biggest compromise is, and then not ask, 'Can I change that?' but rather, 'Can I live with that?' If you don't think you can, then he's not the one for you." Don't reject him because of a few niggling doubts, though. "You'll never be absolutely sure," says Dr. Sills. "Part of truly loving someone is being able to go on faith."

Question two: What compromise is he making by being with you?

"Compromise in relationships works both ways," notes Dr. Sills. "He's bound to be settling on some issue when he settles down with you." Can you name his sacrifice? If so, congrats—you have a level of insight and perception into your companion's psyche that bodes well for a healthy union. What's more, your awareness of that sacrifice provides strong, constant confirmation of his love. Look at it this way: If he's a health-food fanatic and he still picks up Cheez Whiz and Pop-Tarts for you, he's got to think you're the bee's knees, right?

Question three (perhaps the most important one): Can you make an honest assessment of your own expectations and/or fears when it comes to hitting the G-spot? "Keep in mind that you aren't committing just to a person, but to a completely different way of life," says Dr. Sills. "Ask yourself: How will the rules of the relationship change if we do this? How will I change? Will we become complacent? Will our sex life suffer?" Conduct a soul search to unearth your motives? Do you want to be married to him, specifically, or just be married in general? Do you equate commitment with security (as many women do)? If so, then it's time to check your math: Security comes from within. No other person can be responsible for your happiness and well-being. A mate shouldn't be there to hold you up, but to help you realize that you're strong enough to stand on your own. It's not that you can't survive without him; rather, you've chosen to survive with him. End of sermon.

So, if after all this self-analysis, you leave the couch still feeling that (a) he's Mr. Right, and (b) you want him to be Mr. Right Now, then it's time to start talking tactics.

"You can't force someone to commit," warns Dr. Sills. "It's an internal process every person has to go through individually."

Still, even the good doctor admits that there are ways to nudge the process along. Yes, in an ideal world, a perfect, solid union would evolve naturally, easily and with

---

An excellent lead that lures the reader in and puts the idea of the article and the transition to the body of it in the most entertaining and appealing language. Does the "emotionally squashed, channel-flipping, ridiculously lovable human male" description turn you off? Or tune you in to the flip tone of the article? As noted when discussing newspaper feature leads, article leads can be five or six paragraphs long. And now, the developing paragraphs.

The following enumerated tactics are the generating paragraphs leading to the climactic paragraphs.

considerably more speed than continental drift. Here on far-from-ideal Earth, all his dithering has pushed you into eleventh-hour mode. Desperate times call for clever measures.

Which is exactly what you'll find below. Since every woman has her own strategic style—from slow and subtle to bold and reckless—make sure you opt for the method that works best for you.

(Getting pregnant to force him to commit is nowhere on the list. Not only is it a bad idea, it's sociopathic.)

And whatever course you choose, don't forget that your real objective here is to help him see the true love-light, not hog-tie him like a calf at a rodeo. That said, it's time to get this show on the road. Happy trails.

No doubt about it: we're leaving the developing paragraphs and going into the generating paragraphs of the article. "Happy trails" is the tip-off. Does this transition appeal to you?

Make an Ultimatum

This is probably the most widely used and abused strategy among commitment-hungry women everywhere. As its name implies, you're establishing an ultimate condition: He must comply with (your requirement here) or . . . or . . . something really bad will happen and he'll be sorry, that much you know. Basically, you're finding a way to express those two little words of (exasperated) love: or else.

There are several variations on the ultimatum theme. Sarah, a 26-year-old medical student, gave her boyfriend of seven years a term limit.

"I'd had enough of his shilly-shallying," she says. "I told him if he didn't propose to me by my birthday, I would start dating other people."

All well and good, except that her birthday was a full nine months away. That meant an eternity of waiting and hoping and agonizing (her boyfriend waited eight and a half months to dangle that carat—round, solitaire, platinum setting—and pop the question). If you're going to set a deadline for him, make sure the time-span is a sanity-friendly one. Declaring, "Marry me by the turn of the century or I'm outta here" will hardly inspire him to hop-to.

"Marry me by the turn of the century or I'm outta here" and "Don't rush to fail" maintains the humorous and yet serious tone of the article. But then Ellen Tien is simply marvelous at producing phrases and imagery that entertain as well as instruct, such as in a later paragraph, after Erin's boyfriend proposed: "He was so proud of himself; he acted like it was all his idea."

On the other hand, unseemly haste isn't necessarily the answer, either. As some famous baseball coach once said: Don't rush to fail. Connie, 28, informed her boyfriend that she wanted a ring on her finger by the end of the year—meanwhile there were only eight more shopping days 'til Christmas. "Seeing so many of my friends get married put me in a huge hurry to join the nuptial ranks," she remembers. "I became a woman possessed—by the ghost of commitment future, I guess. He didn't respond well to the pressure I had placed on him, and finally bailed out on the whole relationship. I pushed him too hard, too fast."

When it comes to goal-posting, your best bet is to think not chronologically, but psychologically. Erin, 27, subtly couched her ultimatum in terms of her life rather than his, thereby absolving him of any feelings of obligation or pressure.

"I told him I knew I wanted children soon," she says. "But I also thought it was important to have at least two child-free years of marriage first. So, I said, "This is what I need to do with my life—but I would never want to push you. I love you and I know you love me, but if you feel this is not the right timetable for you, I understand completely. If you aren't ready, then no hard feelings.""

Two days later, Erin's boyfriend proposed.

"He was so proud of himself; he acted like it was all his idea," she recalls.

All his idea—in this simple phrase lies the key to a successful ultimatum. You have to let your honey feel as though he's the genius who cooked up this commitment plan—that he's the one at bat (even though it's really your ball game).

The upside of this approach is that it can make you feel that you're taking control of your life. Although you're still subject to a certain degree of suspense, at least it's at a fixed rate. Nonetheless, be aware that ultimatum making is the highest-risk game on the strip. Before you start issuing demands, be sure you're prepared—win or lose—to face the consequences. Once you've cast your die, you're on nonnegotiable turf.

Play It Cool

This strategy recognizes the basic nature of the male beast: He wants what he can't have. Conversely, he doesn't want whatever it is you keep shoving in his face. . . . Don't drop the slightest clue that the concept of a future with him ever entered your mind. In short, treat him to a crash course in reverse psychology.

"For the entire time we were going out, I told my boyfriend that he should feel free to have sex with anyone he wanted," says Vanessa, 28. "I said I didn't want either of us to feel trapped or constrained, and made it clear that we were free agents. Of course, if he had exercised his option, I probably would have been devastated. Luckily, he never did—as soon as he heard there were no strings attached, he became the most high-fidelity guy around. We had been going out only nine months when he proposed."

You know the old saying: If you love something, set it free. If it, or rather he, comes back to you, it's because you had the good sense to create an atmosphere of tolerance and open-mindedness in which your relationship could flourish. With a little luck, your original deception will become a reality: You'll go from pretending it to actually feeling it. That's certainly worth a thought.

Still, this approach works best for women who are naturally low-pressure, low-maintenance companions. If you're the kind of person who requires a minute-to-minute log of your loved one's activities, you'd better be a master thespian to attempt this free-and-easy ruse. Also, be careful not to overplay it: If you exhort him to enjoy his freedom too enthusiastically, he might take you up on your offer. Or, he might interpret your cavalier attitude as a sign that you don't really care about him—and thus decide to quit before he gets fired. You're supposed to play it cool—not freeze him out.

Be Simply Indispensable

The premise here is elementary: You make yourself an essential part of his life. Be forewarned that the process is a gradual one: You can't become a life-requirement overnight, so immediate-gratification seekers should shop elsewhere. If, however, you've got at least a little time on your hands, this could be your true commitment calling.

"My boyfriend was a corporate lawyer," says Betsy, 28. "He worked eighteen-hour days. Because of this, I usually ended up being the one who did errands, made sure the refrigerator was stocked—basically, I ran the household. I did it because I loved him and wanted to make his life easier. I really didn't have any ulterior motives. Then one morning I was cleaning out the coffee machine, and he came up behind me and said, 'You take such good care of me all the time. I don't know what I would do without you—and I never want to find out.' Needless to say, I never quite got around to making the coffee that day."

Unenlightened as it may sound, there is a certain joy to be had in nurturing the boy you love best. So if you're mopping and slopping and shopping because

Ellen Tien is well aware of how men are being portrayed in this article and so she cautions women about making demands if they're not prepared to follow up on them in these words: If he refuses to meet your terms, you can't very well giggle weakly and say, "Just kidding." Nobody respects a jellyfish.

you want to make his life sunnier, you're on the right track. If, however, your plan is to go through the domestic motions in an attempt to make him love you, don't even try. All the vacuuming in the world can't suck out an emotion that isn't there.

One important rule: When you do achieve compulsory status, don't wave it in his face. A man wants to see himself as independent; being informed otherwise will make him feel weak, emasculated—and resentful. He'd much rather wash his own clothes than have you cawing in his ear that you didn't go to college to separate the whites from the brights. And resist the urge to stray toward the Machiavellian. Do not hide his keys and wallet at night so you can be the hero who finds them the next morning. Remember: You're trying to help the guy, not dismantle him piece by horrible piece.

Finally, remember that there's no guaranteed payoff: A year's worth of hot dinners and tub scrubbings doesn't necessarily translate into a giant wedding reception at the Four Seasons. If he should happen to slip a diamond on your dishpan hands . . . well, that's ———

You can fill in the blank at the end of the paragraph. We're at the point of leaving the generating paragraphs and entering the climactic point of the article.

Help Him to Be Him

Before rushing into the fire of commitment, a fellow sometimes just needs someone to confirm his fears. So go ahead—give him your stamp of approval. "When your lover expresses his anxieties of commitment to you," says Dr. Sills, "the last thing he wants you to do is dismiss them as silly or inconsequential. When he says, 'I'm afraid marriage will turn us into our parents,' it isn't helpful for you to answer, 'That's ridiculous—why would you ever have such a crazy thought?'" Instead, says Dr. Sills, you should sympathize with him. "If you say to him, 'Honey, I know; my heart goes out to you. This is so hard for you, and I want to help you through it,' he'll feel reassured. He'll feel like you understand him—and that goes a long way toward making him want to have a future with you."

What you basically want to do is give the guy the psychological equivalent of a big bear hug. Keep a positive attitude: Avoid words like no, never, can't, won't, lamebrain, stupid jerkface, etc. Don't deny his emotions: accept them. By doing this, you'll create a climate for your partner in which he feels comfortable enough to express, confront and maybe even eliminate his anxieties. By helping him love himself, he'll love you all the more. Corny, but true.

Maintain Quality Control

When you're in a relationship—or almost any other life situation, for that matter—it always helps to put your best foot (and face and hair and behavior) forward. To wit: Pay attention to your personal upkeep. This doesn't mean that you should rush out and get implants or transplants or even houseplants. You're not supposed to put on a false front; you merely want to enhance your natural powers of attraction. A little fine-tuning can accomplish a lot.

"I made a real serious effort to look my best when I started dating Ron," says Beth, 26. "For the first time in my life, I didn't just talk about exercising. I actually did it. I firmed up, lost weight and looked great. I felt great, too, which did wonders for my confidence. And that confidence helped our relationship. He loved me all the more because I cared enough about myself to look after myself."

Quality control should extend beyond the physical. Do you tend to whine? Try to put a cork in it. Do you wield a sharp tongue? Then file away. Don't change your personality, just smooth out a few rough edges. Not only will you be more desirable to him, you'll be an all-around better person. Quite a mind-bending prospect.

Of course, sustaining sky-high standards is an enervating—if not downright bootless—endeavor. No one expects you to drop 20 pounds overnight or to take a crash course with Miss Manners. Also, don't set unrealistic goals that are more for him than for you, because you won't be able to sustain them—and that will make you look and feel bad. The point is, you're allowed to be less than perfect—hey, even Julia Roberts wakes up with morning breath. Just don't let yourself stray into the outer reaches of sloth (you know, a bikini wax every once in a while never killed anyone).

This whole thing isn't about a total rehaul; rather, you're doing the best you can with what you have. Which is really what you meant to do all along, anyway, isn't it?

The last paragraph falls into the lingering impression of the reader interest plane, leaving the reader, as it does, something that remains in the mind, that sums up the whole experience of the article.

———
*Reprinted with permission of *Mademoiselle.*

Other how-to-do-it articles treat such topics as dieting, exercising and kite-building. Sometimes they are mundane topics, at other times entertaining and serious topics, such as Ellen Tien's article. Photographs or illustrations are usually a must for most how-to-do-it articles. As a kite flyer, and one who used to make kites when I was a kid, I found this article on how to make a kite an excellent example of the no-nonsense, terse, how-to-do-it article.

Margo Brown, a McClean, Va., junior high teacher and former president of the American Kitefliers Association tells us how to make a kite:

"Go Ahead, Make My Kite"*

By Margo Brown

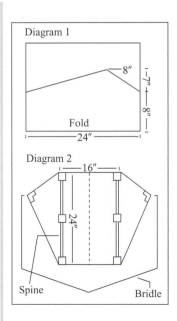

The sled design is easy to make and almost fail-safe to fly. Cut a pattern from posterboard using the dimensions shown in diagram 1 (it will look like half a kite).

Slit open the bottom of a plastic garbage bag. Put the pattern on the bag with the longest side on a fold. Cut along the two angled sides evenly. Uneven sides cause the kite to fall off right or left and split.

Open the sail face to show the full kite. Place your dowels (spine) as shown in diagram 2. Tape it in three areas: top, bottom and just above the center.

Make your string equal to three lengths of the dowel. There are only two points on your kite and they come out left and right. With masking tape, tape the bridle string to the two points (don't buy unbraided monofilament string, it will tear your fingers, 20-pound test is fine).

Find the center of the bridle string by holding the two wings together. Then tie a small loop.

You can add tail streamers on the bottom of the spine. Since this kite is light, crepe paper's fine.

Make them even three times the length of the spine, one on each side.

Tails add vanity. Kites are vain. If they're pretty, they love to fly.

———
*Reprinted by permission of *USA Weekend,* Feb. 27–March 1, 1987.

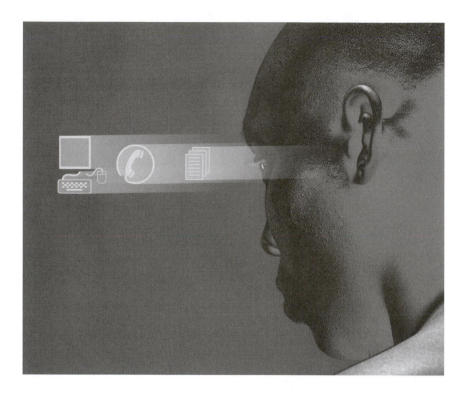

The Business Article

Most business magazines publish a variety of articles on topics as varied as Boston's St. Patrick's Day parade or the nation's problem with illegal aliens. *The Economist*, for example, explored the effects of divorce on children. **Job***postings*, however, keeps its editorial content on business.

For a student looking for a job, this lead paragraph, starting out with "When you are job searching," is no doubt interesting and informative. I'd like to make the introduction more readable by starting the second paragraph with "It's not only the way you appear for the job or information interview that counts in this job search arena, it's also your cover letter, your resume, your e-mail confirming a meeting and your thank you letter afterward which also weigh in heavily." Because these elements are in a different communication arena than the "first impression" interaction, they are important enough to call for a separate paragraph with more parallel constructions. Notice that the order of appearance of "cover letter" and "resume" has been transposed to correspond to the order in which they will be discussed in the next paragraph.

Important information is given to the jobseeker in this developing paragraph. I'd

"Successful Business Communications: A Career Zone Job Search Series from Job*postings*"

By Barbara Kofman and Kaitlin Eckler

When you are job searching, effective communication can be a deal maker or breaker. The axiom "You only get one opportunity to make a first impression" is ignored at your peril. When you interact with someone, how you communicate and the way you choose to present yourself makes a lasting impact. In the job search arena, it's how you write your resume, cover and thank you letters, that short e-mail you send confirming a meeting, and the way you appear for the job or information interview, that count.

A dynamic cover letter should always accompany your resume when responding to a job posting. Few employers will seriously consider you if you haven't taken the time to include one. It should be written in a professional manner, with a suitable heading, and be addressed to the appropriate person. (You may have to call the company and find out who that is.) It must encourage the reader to progress to your resume by describing your suitability for a specific role and detailing your qualifications as they match the targeted job and requirements of the company. A cover letter usually consists of four paragraphs. The first grabs the reader's attention and explains the purpose, the second details your competencies and experiences as they relate to the job, the third expands on your personal attributes without repeating your resume, and the last, thanks the employer, asks for an interview and makes clear your follow-up plan. A direct ending means you don't have to wait to hear from the employer and provides you with the opportunity to take the next step.

Always write a thank you note after you have met with someone, whether for an interview or to gain insight into your job target. While this may seem obvious, it's surprising how few people bother to do this. Begin by thanking the individual for taking the time to meet with you and point to something of importance that was learned during the exchange about the company and/or the job. If you are writing in response to a job interview, reinforce your suitability for and interest in the position and take this opportunity to correct any perceived interview mistakes or shortcomings. End by presuming further communication will take place. If you met with more than one person, send letters separately to each interviewer. These days thank you notes are often sent via e-mail, but depending on the culture of the organization and timing, mail may be more appropriate.

How you appear, when meeting with a potential employer also communicates messages. Research suggests that 55 percent of the impression you leave relates to how you present yourself. Typically, whether for an information or job interview, it's advisable to dress in business attire. Dressing appropriately visually transforms you from being a student to a professional. Always wear clean, well-pressed and stylish clothes. For men this means either a suit or dark pants and a sports-jacket with a plain shirt and traditional tie. For women, a conservative suit jacket with pants or a knee length skirt, stockings and shoes with a practical heel. Jewelry and hair are best kept conventional. Skip the cologne or perfume. Check yourself in a full-length mirror to ensure all is in order, and that you're sure to produce a great first impression.

Taking the time to write powerful letters and making certain that when you meet an employer you come across positively will go a long way towards convincing them that you just may be the person to meet their needs.

Kaitlin Eckler of KE&A Consulting and Barbara Kofman of CareerTrails are career management professionals with extensive experience in the youth and employment marketplace. Kaitlin can be reached at career@sympatico.ca and Barbara at www.careertrails.com.

Side notes:

whet the anticipation of the job-seeker by using a periodic sentence at the beginning: "When responding to a job posting, your cover letter escorts your resume to the employer." If you start out designating the "employer" as the recipient of all this attention, continue. In this paragraph the instruction switches to "reader" and then back to "employer." Consistency keeps the reader's mind from wandering back and forth.

This paragraph, if placed on the reader interest plane, would be a generating interest paragraph leading to a climactic paragraph.

This "appearance" paragraph somehow fails to fall into the category of a climactic paragraph for the reader interest plane organizational plan. Why is that? If you were to follow the organization of this article indicated by the order in which the topics were introduced in the beginning paragraphs, the paragraph on physical first impressions logically follows the introduction. Just copy and paste it there. Nothing else needs to be done. The next and concluding paragraph now provides the lingering impression of the reader interest plane.

You will notice that this concluding paragraph now follows the "thank you notes" paragraph beautifully.

Paragraphs will sometimes skip into an article out of order. That's frequently what happens when you write. One of the reviewers of this text pointed out that the beginning paragraphs of my summaries should actually be moved to the beginning of the chapters. "The reviewer is right!" I exclaimed—and then moved each one to the chapter beginnings. (I can take instruction.)

The List Article

Ellen Tien's article on "Hooking Him" was not only a how-to-do-it article, it was a "list article." Charles V. Main believes a list article is one of the easiest articles to research, write and sell. He not only explains why that is so, but presents valuable information about the wide possibilities of subject matter for articles for magazines of general interest, business, entertainment, and so on.

(We'll leave any further explications of how articles fit in the organizational pattern of the reader interest plane to the later articles "Billy Carter," and E. B. White's "Once More to the Lake.") For now, Charles Main presides:

"The Nearly Perfect Article"*

By Charles V. Main

If I were asked to list the components of the nearly perfect article from the writer's point of view, I would say:

- The article would be easy to research.
- The article would be easy to write.
- The article would be easy to sell.
- The article would appear in a list format.

The "list article" is one that unifies several units of information under a single theme. After selling about 50 such articles to national magazines ranging from religious publications to in-flight magazines, I have found the list article one of the most profitable. List articles take only a few hours to research and write.

List Item #1: The Idea

Good writing is important in a list article, of course, but at the core of the article is information. List articles are designed to solve problems, present information, and otherwise help the reader. This article I'm writing now is, of course, a list article. Keep the information angle in mind when looking for ideas for this type of article. Ask what problems must be solved, what procedures must be explained, what needs must be fulfilled.

First, ask those questions of other people. One conversation I had with a friend, a sales trainer for an insurance firm, resulted in a . . . sale. I asked him what problems he would like to see addressed in print. He said that one of the biggest problems new salespeople face in closing a sale occurs when customers say they wanted to think about the deal. Two months later *Specialty Salesman* magazine bought my article, "Handling the World's Toughest Objection," which listed several ways to encourage a buying decision when the customer is unsure.

Ask those questions of yourself, too. Your own problems, concerns and pet peeves can produce ideas for list articles. A couple of years ago I was bothered by the fact that many churches gave their youth little opportunity for creative expression. So I wrote an article that listed ten forms of creative worship activities to be used with church youth groups. The article sold to *The Youth Leader* on the first submission. Ask yourself, "What things bug me that I've been able to handle effectively?" The answer to that question may result in a sale.

By far the best source of list article ideas is the magazine you want to write for. Study a few back issues and note the titles of all list articles. Then change the titles by substituting a word here and there. For instance, a house-and-garden magazine may carry an article titled "Ten Ways to Improve your Lawn." You could change this to "Twelve Ways to Improve Your Vegetable Garden." Assuming the magazine doesn't have a similar article in stock, and assuming the information is sound, the editors will probably be interested in your variation on the theme of outdoor improvement.

In fact, I've found several list article title formats useful in gathering ideas. These are:

_____Ways to Improve _____ _____Ways to _____
Better _____Ways to Save Money on _____

List Item #2: Research

The nearly perfect article will be easy to research. Again, the focus of the list article is information. Where that information originates is relatively unimportant, as long as it is fresh, useful and accurate. Your most important sources are:

Yourself. I have drawn on my experiences as salesman, advertising consultant, Sunday school teacher, and drama coach to write articles for a variety of specialized publications. You don't need to be a "recognized expert" to write for specialized publications, as I proved with my "Toughest Objection" article for *Specialty Salesman*.

Experts. Don't think you must find someone with a long list of formal credentials. The purpose of a list article is to convey information. The purpose of your interview is to collect that information. You are less interested in finding quotable quotes than you are in finding valuable information. With this in mind, the definition of an expert changes from a person with certain credentials to a person who has the information you need to write your article.

Your expert could be a friend whose hobby or job relates to the subject you're writing about. Your expert might work for some governmental or quasi governmental agency like the police or fire department, the Consumer Protection Agency, or the post office. Or your expert might be a college professor who has studied the subject in question. Schools are repositories of experts on all sorts of subjects. If no one at the university or college can help you, someone can probably tell you where to go for the information you need. A few months ago, I was writing an article about shyness. As it happened, the nearby university employed a professor who made a special study of shyness and worked with people to help them overcome their own shyness. The information I gained from an interview with her resulted in two articles. One was a list article for *American Way. . . .* If you want to know if a university has a resident expert on a certain subject, call the appropriate department, the school's public information center or news bureau.

Published sources. An afternoon in the library can often provide you with enough information for certain kinds of articles. For instance, if you were writing an article on "Ten Organic Ways to Protect Your Vegetables From Insects," you could probably find all the information you'd need in textbooks on gardening. If you have trouble finding the information you need, [go on the Internet or] ask a librarian.

When doing library research, learn to look beyond the obvious for sources of information. Many libraries have cassette tape libraries that contain information on all kinds of subjects. Others have computer terminals connected with data bases that allow you quick and easy access to abstracts of difficult-to-find information. Microfilm files often contain otherwise unpublished information. Some major university libraries are depositories for U.S. government documents.

List Item #3: Writing the Article

List articles consist of four parts:

1. The introduction
2. The theme
3. The list
4. The conclusion

The introduction should entice the reader to read the article and tell the reader what the article will be about. Your introduction should be short and to the point. For instance, the lead to my article for *In Business*, "Eight Ways to Cut Advertising Costs," emphasized the main benefit of reading the article—saving money:

> They say it pays to advertise, but the truth is that you pay to advertise. As a salesman for several advertising media, I have discovered eight ways the average small business person can cut advertising costs substantially without reducing advertising effectiveness. By using these cost-cutting techniques, you can conserve your cash flow and increase your profit.

This introduction not only gives the reader a reason to keep reading, but it also sets forth the theme of the article. Most list articles state the theme within the first few paragraphs. The theme is the entire thrust of the article stated in one sentence. In the above example, the theme is: "I have discovered eight ways the average small-business person can cut advertising costs substantially without reducing advertising effectiveness." The rest of the article is designed to support that assertion. Stating a theme orients your reader toward what is to come and gives you a focus for your article.

List Item #4: The List

The list itself forms the bulk of the article and its structure varies with the type of article you are writing. Of the four common types of list articles, each has a slightly different structure.

1. The Helpful Hint List. This is perhaps the most ubiquitous of all list articles. I found five such articles in just one issue of *Good Housekeeping*. The helpful hint list consists of short tips on how to save money, do a better job, make improvements around the house, and generally live a happier, healthier, more prosperous life.

Each entry in your helpful hint list should start with a short imperative sentence that capsulizes the hint. Then briefly explain the hint. For instance, the following hint comes from a sidebar to an article on business fraud I wrote for *PSA Magazine*. The article was a modified list article describing various forms of business fraud. The sidebar discussed ways businesses could protect themselves against such fraud. Such as the following:

Deal with companies you know. Acquaint yourself with the major firms that sell the supplies you use. If a new firm places an order, investigate whether the firm is legitimate by checking with the Better Business Bureau in the hometown of the company.

In organizing the helpful hint article, I like to place my two strongest hints at the beginning and end of the list so the reader is enticed to keep reading at the start and feels satisfied at the end.

2. The Problem-Solving List. This is similar to the helpful hint list and some problem-solving lists can be considered forms of the helpful hint list. However, the problem-solving list generally takes a little different approach. In the lead, you set forth a common personal, family or even societal problem. This is followed by a description of the extent and nature of the problem. Next comes your list, which suggests how the problem can be solved. My article on shyness took this form. The first half of the article discussed the latest research on shyness, focusing on the nature and extent of the problem. The last half suggested ways the reader could handle shyness.

3. The Step-by-Step List. This list article style differs slightly from other list articles in that each component is necessary and the order of presentation is vital to the article. When organizing this type of article, break down the process you are

describing into individual steps. Each of these steps should describe a single procedure in such a way that the average reader of that publication can duplicate it. You
want to keep your steps as simple as possible, considering the probable skills possessed by your readers. For instance, you could write, "Make a dado joint," if you
were writing for a carpenter's trade journal. However, you would probably have to
break the process down into simpler steps if you were writing for a more general
magazine. Under each step, explain any procedure that might be necessary to complete that step. Anticipate any problems that may arise in completing each step, and
explain the solutions to these problems.

If the process you are describing produces a physical product, accompany your manuscript with artwork (either photos or drawings) illustrating each step in the process.

4. The General Information List. Some list articles round up general information about people, places, lifestyles, trends, new products and events. Travel magazines run articles on restaurants, campgrounds, tourist attractions and events. Home
and garden magazines list new products for the home. Consumer publications evaluate different brands of the same product. Many of these articles might be called "best
of" lists. They describe the best places to go, the best things to do, the best products
to buy. When writing a "best of" list, be specific. Why are the items you choose the
best? Why should they be included in the list and not others?

List Item #5: The Perfect Query

Even though list articles are generally short (800–1,500 words), I recommend that
you propose the article to an editor in a query rather than taking the time to write the
complete article.

I begin my queries with the lead I plan to use in the article. I follow this with a
transition line that explains the working title, the theme of the article, and a proposed
word length. Then I briefly describe the segments I plan to cover in the article. If I
haven't worked with the editor before, I conclude with a brief list of credits and any
special qualifications I have for writing this article.

Another Conclusion

Now you know just about everything I know about writing and selling list articles.
You know:

- How to generate ideas.
- How to research your subject.
- The types of list articles.
- How to organize and write the article.
- How to sell the article.

In keeping with my previous advice, go to it.

---

*Reprinted with permission of *Writer's Digest*

The Personality Profile

The challenge for the writer doing an article about someone who's been written about many
times is to find an original lead, something that points readers to something new. The next
article, a feature on Billy Carter, the brother of former President Jimmy Carter, written during President Carter's term in office, could also have been published in *Time* or *Playboy*.

In this magazine-style article of *The Washington Star*, excellent characterization, setting description and, above all, details are blended together to paint a colorful portrait of a colorful man. Pertinent paragraphs will be noted for commentary on the artistry of the author and how the article lies on the reader interest plane by marginalia.

"Billy Carter"*

By Michael Satchell

PLAINS—Last Sunday, says Billy Carter, was just too much.

"Used to be at 10 o'clock on a Sunday morning, you could walk out onto Main Street and [urinate] and nobody would see you," he grumbled.

"Last Sunday there must have been 2,000 damned tourists here. I couldn't stand it. I went off to the bootlegger, bought me a fifth, drove around the rest of the day and got good and drunk."

If Jimmy Carter represents the clean-cut, God-featuring, modest-mannered New South, Brother Billy epitomizes the old. He's an absolute original, a good ol' boy as Southern as sawmill gravy and fried white meat, with a passion—but not necessarily the capacity—for strong drink and good conversation. Lots of it.

> Miss Lillian, a loveable Mom, is not too happy with Billy's drinking. The author lets us know by including the repetition of her reservations (three times) in her direct quote. And by her sighs accentuated by the interpolation of the attribution in the middle of a quote.

"Billy," sighs Miss Lillian, "drinks too much. He's a wonderful boy and he's really my favorite son, but he drinks too much. Jimmy never tells him off for it and neither does his mother. But he does."

"Yes, Sir: I'm a real Southern boy," Billy chortles. "I got a red neck, white socks and Blue Ribbon Beer." And to the guffaws of his gas station cronies, Billy shows off his sun-drenched neck, his white socks, and snaps the tab off his can of the beer. It is 6:30 p.m., 90 minutes since work ceased and relaxation began for Billy and the boys.

> The narrative hook of this personality profile runs some seven paragraphs—not unusual for a magazine article lead. The eighth paragraph and transition into the idea and the developing paragraphs is, What influence does Billy "have over the next president? Will he try to exercise it?" Can you determine what makes Jimmy tick by examining Billy? The next paragraph continues the development of the idea: "There is only one way to examine Billy Carter close at hand and that is to drink with him after work, a risky venture at best." The writer evidently did what he had to do, drinking and all. We discover what that's like in the next developing paragraphs.

Ordinarily, Billy Carter would be just another slice of local color in a rather drab little town. But as the brother of the world's most powerful leader-elect, questions arise.

What influence does he have over the next president? Will he try to exercise it? What are his concerns about national or international problems? Will he try to profit from his brother's exalted position? And by examining Billy can one detect any clues as to what makes Jimmy tick?

There is only one way to examine Billy Carter close at hand and that is to drink with him after work, a risky venture at best.

He runs the family peanut farm and warehouse and regards his stewardship of the Carter family business interests as his contribution to his brother, because it has freed Jimmy to concentrate full-time on politics.

Billy works from 5 a.m. or so until 5 p.m., works hard, works seriously, and will entertain no nonessential visitors. From dawn to dusk six days a week, Billy is a tough, shrewd, no nonsense, very successful businessman.

> After luring you this far, the writer figures you're in for the duration. In the following generating paragraphs it's safe to discuss the background of the character, usually not very interesting stuff. Those two expository paragraphs are quickly disposed of. The succeeding paragraphs continue generating

But come 5 p.m., Billy locks up the peanut warehouse, hurries across the street to his gas station and relaxes. With a vengeance.

In the back part of the station, half a dozen, sometimes more, of Billy's pals gather each evening after work to drink beer and jaw about nothing in particular. They are all working men, wearing coveralls and red caps that say "Funk's Hybrid" or "Standard Oil." One wears an ABC television cap he conned from a cameraman.

No special deference is shown to Billy and he doesn't expect it. He plays the role, not of the President-elect's brother, but more the saloon keeper. Because there is no tavern for whites in Plains (there is a black club), Billy's gas station is essentially the town bar. Until 7 p.m., at least, when the gas station closes and everyone goes home to eat supper.

The station is impossibly cluttered with tools, tires, cans of Campbell Soup and 10W40 oil all mixed up. On the wall is a saucy pinup calendar from the Keena Auto Parts Co. Atop an 8-track tape deck, dusty and unused, are tapes by Lynn Anderson and Tammy Wynett.

At 5:02 p.m. precisely Billy bounces in, dives into a huge cooler, pulls out a handful of cans of beer, pops a couple, lights up a Pall Mall, sucks hard on it, gives a tubercular wheeze, and downs the can in a single guzzle.

"Boy, I needed that," he said. "Here, have another."

Billy, 39, is the youngest of Lillian Carter's four children. He was raised, like his brother, on the family farm at Archery, Ga., and was 14 when the family moved into Plains.

After high school he joined the Marine Corps and married his childhood sweetheart, Sybil Spires, 16, the day after graduating from boot camp. They have six children, ranging in age from 20 to one month, and Billy is said to be the consummate family man, caring deeply for little else but his wife and his children.

Physically, Billy resembles his brother closely, although he is shorter, wears glasses and is a lot thicker around the middle than Jimmy. Unlike the president-elect, Billy disdains the church. "Bunch of damned hypocrites down there at that Baptist church," is Billy's view. "The only time I ever go is when one of the kids is baptized."

Miss Lillian's recollection of Billy's childhood is naturally glossed with a mother's concern for projecting only the best of images. But Billy, being Billy, tells it like it was.

Jimmy, Ruth, and Gloria all graduated first or second in their high school class. I was 25th out of 26. It didn't bother me none though.

"I joined the Marines because I wanted to be a bad _____. First time on leave I tried to whip five or six sailors and found out I wasn't as tough as I thought."

Did he ever get into trouble?

"Well, I once did 30 days in jail in South Carolina for speeding. And I went to jail in Daytona Beach for drinking in public. Nothing serious though. You ready for another?"

Billy made several campaign appearances on behalf of his brother, clad often in his yellow leisure suit, yellow shoes, and pink shirt, but he says he "hated it."

"I don't like to go anywhere where I can't get back to Plains the same night," he said. "I was the token redneck on the campaign. But I think my main contribution to Jimmy was staying home." Er, yes.

"To keep the business running smoothly so Jimmy could be free." Oh, of course.

Billy said he has been to Washington only once.

"I was at National Airport for 10 minutes on my way to somewhere during the campaign," he recalled. "The other time was when I drove up to Montreal with my wife and three kids. I got lost in DeeCee and spent four hours driving around. I finally hired a taxidriver to guide me out to that ring road [the Capital Beltway].

---

interest in Billy and carry the reader to the climactic part of the feature.

A beautiful description of an old country gas station. Anyone who has been in one can vouch for the authenticity of this.

The author weds the sense of what's happening to the "sound"—that is, he telescopes what could be expressed in six or seven sentences into one sentence to indicate the rapidity and eagerness with which Billy wants that beer and cigarette. (The wedding of "sense to sound" will be discussed at greater length in Chapter 7, "The Art of Writing.")

The gratuitous remark by the author ("Er, yes") and the one in the following paragraph ("Oh, of course") on the way to the climactic paragraphs, are unnecessary and momentarily confuse the reader. They detract from the unity of the article.

"Well, I ended up going the wrong way on it. Finally found us a motel and when I hit the bar I had to have a triple to calm me down. Here, want some of this?"

After a tug on a Seagram's Crown Royal bottle, Billy continued: "My only regret about Jimmy being elected is that I wished he had lived in Atlanta. Plains has gone straight to hell. I went to a meeting the other night of landowners and property owners. I was the only one voting against commercialization. I'm the only person in this whole town who isn't selling peanuts to tourists. I really regret what's happening to Plains."

Just then another friend strode into the gas station. From the crook of his right arm hung a 270-Ruger with a scope site. He had returned from an unsuccessful day of deer hunting.

"You loaded?" asked Billy

The friend pointed the rifle into the ground and clicked the trigger.

"Nope."

"Well, I am," Billy giggled, opening another can.

Despite the ready laughter, the constant stream of four-letter words, the role-playing and the booze, Billy Carter is no buffoon.

For the last eight years, with his brother campaigning or serving in public office virtually full time, Billy has built the family's peanut business into a very profitable venture. He reads four or five books a week from the Americus Public Library and subscribes to eight newspapers and news magazines.

In a quiet moment, he will discuss serious matters—the economy, world affairs—with a sound depth of knowledge, but he's happiest when talking about crops and farm problems.

"I have absolutely no ambition beyond Plains," he said in answer to a question about his future role. "I'm just an unambitious person. Jimmy and I are very good friends and we talk for hours, just shooting the bull, but I don't try to influence him and I don't think I could. The only thing I'd like to see him do when he gets to the White House is appoint a working farmer as secretary of agriculture, that's all."

According to Miss Lillian, Billy and his brother are as close as two peanuts in the shell. "Billy is always the first person Jimmy wants to see when he returns to Plains," she said. "They spend hours together walking in the woods and fields. They need each other."

The last three or four paragraphs—the climactic paragraphs—answer the questions raised in the lead idea. The last sentence leaves the lingering impression in the mind of the reader.

If brother Billy has any role to play in the Carter administration it will be to keep on doing exactly what he has in the past. Jimmy Carter is a good example of the old axiom that you can take the boy out of the country but not vice versa. As long as Billy is around, the next president of the United States will be able to sit in the White House and still keep a few peanut husks under his boots and a little bit of red Georgia earth beneath his fingernails.

*Reprinted from *The Washington Star,* Nov. 14, 1976. Copyright © 1976 Reprinted by permission.

Until you've mastered the art of magazine article writing—and even after that time—the organizational path that promises the most success is the reader interest plane. If you organize your materials on this plane and acquire a good grasp of the writing principles stressed later on you should be on your way to a successful magazine-writing career.

CHARTING THE READER INTEREST PLANE

If you are now thinking there's a great deal being made of the reader interest plane, you're right. The reason: If you get in the habit of following it—incorporating it into your writing habits—you'll vastly improve your writing and your publication possibilities. The next few pages, however, are the last RIP lap. First, we want to illustrate how to simply outline an article along the reader interest plane, using E. B. White's great *New Yorker* article, "Once More to the Lake," as an illustration. (The article, by the way, explores how a parent—father or mother—attempts to live on, become briefly immortal, through the son or daughter. Some of you may be experiencing that now.)

"Once More to the Lake" (outline)

I. Narrative Hook
    Reminiscence about childhood and lake in Maine
II. Developing Paragraphs
    A. More reminiscence about lake
    B. Setting description of lake
    C. Illusion of dual existence—he being his son
        1. Same illusion—no passage of time motif
        2. Enchanted sea—no passage of time motif
    D. Dinner at the farmhouse
III. Generating Paragraphs
    A. Summertime! Life indelible!
    B. More remembrances
    C. Motorboat noise
        1. Sets years moving
        2. Dying flywheel revolution—reversing years
IV. Climactic Paragraphs
    A. Description of week at camp—illusion persists
    B. Thunderstorm on lake presages father's fate?
V. Lingering impression and Concluding Paragraph:
    As son pulls wet swimsuit on, the father feels in his groin the chill of death.

Prior to the writing of the first draft, as more recollections surface, this rough outline would no doubt be replaced with a more detailed outline, which would assist the author immeasurably in the writing of it.

Now read carefully "Once More to the Lake." Written by one of the most notable essayists of the last century, E. B. White describes how a man (symbolic of all people) tries to stop time—the aging process—to attain some sort of immortality through a son and fails. E. B. White also examines the cycle of life. Note how the article is unified through repetition of details and the insistence, repeatedly made, that there has been no passage of years since he has last been to the lake.

White's reminiscences about childhood in the beginning—replete with concrete details—form an excellent narrative hook. All readers will recall similar childhood experiences.

"Once More to the Lake"*

One summer, along about 1904, my father rented a camp on a lake in Maine and took us all there for the month of August. We all got ringworm from some kittens and had to rub Pond's Extract on our arms and legs night and morning, and my father rolled over in a canoe with all his clothes on; but outside of that the vacation was a success and from then on none of us ever thought there was any place in the world like that lake in Maine. We returned summer after summer—always on August 1st for one month. I have since become a saltwater man, but sometimes in summer there are days when the restlessness of the tides and the fearful cold of the sea water and the incessant wind which blows across the afternoon and into the evening make me wish for the placidity of a lake in the woods. A few weeks ago this feeling got so strong I bought myself a couple of bass hooks and a spinner and returned to the lake where we used to go, for a week's fishing and to revisit old haunts.

I took along my son, who had never had any fresh water up his nose and who had seen lily pads only from train windows. On the journey over to the lake I began to wonder what it would be like. I wondered how time would have marred this unique, this holy spot—the coves and streams, the hills that the sun set behind, the camps and the paths behind the camps. I was sure that the tarred road would have found it out and I wondered in what other ways it would be desolated. It is strange how much you can remember about places like that once you allow your mind to return into the grooves which lead back. You remember one thing, and that suddenly reminds you of another thing. I guess I remembered clearest of all the early mornings, when the lake was cool and motionless, remembered how the bedroom smelled of the lumber it was made of and of the wet woods whose scent entered through the screen. The partitions in the camp were thin and did not extend clear to the top of the rooms, and as I was always the first up I would dress softly so as not to wake the others, and sneak out into the sweet outdoors and start out in the canoe, keeping close along the shore in the long shadows of the pines. I remember being very careful never to rub my paddle against the gunwale for fear of disturbing the stillness of the cathedral.

The lake had never been what you would call a wild lake. There were cottages sprinkled around the shores, and it was in farming country although the shores of the lake were quite heavily wooded. Some of the cottages were owned by nearby farmers, and you would live at the shore and eat your meals at the farmhouse. That's what our family did. But although it wasn't wild, it was a fairly large and undisturbed lake and there were places in it which, to a child at least, seemed infinitely remote and primeval.

I was right about the tar: it led to within half a mile of the shore. But when I got back there, with my boy, and we settled into a camp near a farmhouse and into the kind of summertime I had known, I could tell that it was going to be pretty much the same as it had been before—I knew it, lying in bed the first morning, smelling the bedroom, and hearing the boy sneak quietly out and go off along the shore in a boat. I began to sustain the illusion that he was I, and therefore, by simple transportation, that I was my father. This sensation persisted, kept cropping up all the time we were there. It was not an entirely new feeling, but in this setting it grew much stronger. I seemed to be living a dual existence. I would be in the middle of some simple act, I would be picking up a bait box or laying down a table fork, or I would be saying something, and suddenly it would be not I but my father who was saying the words or making the gesture. It gave me a creepy sensation.

We went fishing the first morning. I felt the same damp moss covering the worms in the bait can, and saw the dragonfly alight on the tip of my rod as it hovered a few inches from the surface of the water. It was the arrival of this fly that convinced me beyond any doubt that everything was as it always had been, that the years were a mirage and there had been no years. The small waves were the same, chucking the rowboat under the chin as we fished at anchor, and the boat was the same boat, the same color green and the ribs broken in the same places, and under the floor-boards the same fresh-water leavings and débris—the dead helgramite, the wisps of moss, the rusty discarded fishhook, the dried blood from yesterday's catch. We stared silently at the tips of our rods, at the dragonflies that came and went. I lowered the tip of mine into the water, tentatively, pensively dislodging the fly, which darted two feet away, poised, darted two feet back, and came to rest again a little farther up the rod. There had been no years between the ducking of this dragonfly and the other one—the one that was part of memory. I looked at the boy, who was saliently casting his fly, and it was my hands that held his rod, my eyes watching. I felt dizzy and didn't know which rod I was at the end of.

We caught two bass, hauling them in briskly as though they were mackerel, pulling them over the side of the boat in a businesslike manner without any landing net, and stunning them with a blow on the back of the head. When we got back for a swim before lunch, the lake was exactly where we had left it, the same number of inches from the dock, and there was only the merest suggestion of a breeze. This seemed an utterly enchanted sea, this lake you could leave to its own devices for a few hours and come back to, and find that it had not stirred, this constant and trustworthy body of water. In the shallows, the dark, water-soaked sticks and twigs, smooth and old, were undulating in clusters on the bottom against the clean ribbed sand, and the track of the mussel was plain. A school of minnows swam by, each minnow with its small individual shadow, doubling the attendance, so clear and sharp in the sunlight. Some of the other campers were in swimming, along the shore, one of them with a cake of soap, and the water felt thin and clear and unsubstantial. Over the years there had been this person with the cake of soap, this cultist, and here he was. There had been no years.

Up to the farmhouse to dinner through the teeming, dusty field, the road under our sneakers was only a two-track road. The middle track was missing, the one with the marks of the hooves and the splotches of dried, flaky manure. There had always been three tracks to choose from in choosing which track to walk in; now the choice was narrowed down to two. For a moment I missed terribly the middle alternative. But the way led past the tennis court, and something about the way it lay there in the sun reassured me; the tape had loosened along the back line, the alleys were green with plantain and other weeds, and the net (installed in June and removed in September) sagged in the dry noon, and the whole place steamed with midday heat and hunger and emptiness. There was a choice of pie for dessert, and one was blueberry and one was apple, and the waitresses were the same country girls, there having been no passage of time, only the illusion of it as in a dropped curtain—the waitresses were still fifteen; their hair had been washed, that was the only difference—they had been to the movies and seen the pretty girls with the clean hair.

Summertime, oh summertime, pattern of life indelible, the fade-proof lake, the woods unshatterable, the pasture with the sweetfern and the juniper forever and ever, summer without end; this was the background, and the life along the shore was the design, the cottages with their innocent and tranquil design, their tiny docks with the flagpole and the American flag floating against the white clouds in the blue sky, the little paths over the roots of the trees leading from camp to camp

The generating paragraphs leading to the climactic paragraphs, which start with the next paragraph. When White speaks of "the fade-proof lake, the woods unshatterable," he is repeating, in different words, that there has been no passage of years.

and the paths leading back to the outhouses and the can of lime for sprinkling, and at the souvenir counters at the store the miniature birch-bark canoes and the post cards that showed things looking a little better than they looked. This was the American family at play, escaping the city heat, wondering whether the newcomers in the camp at the head of the cove were "common" or "nice," wondering whether it was true that the people who drove up for Sunday dinner at the farmhouse were turned away because there wasn't enough chicken.

It seemed to me, as I kept remembering all this, that those times and those summers had been infinitely precious and worth saving. There had been jollity and peace and goodness. The arriving (at the beginning of August) had been so big a business in itself, at the railway station the farm wagon drawn up, the first smell of the pine-laden air, the first glimpse of the smiling farmer, and the great importance of the trunks and your father's enormous authority in such matters, and the feel of the wagon under you for the long ten-mile haul, and at the top of the last long hill catching the first view of the lake after eleven months of not seeing this cherished body of water. The shouts and cries of the other campers when they saw you, and the trunks to be unpacked, to give up their rich burden. (Arriving was less exciting nowadays, when you sneaked up in your car and parked it under a tree near the camp and took out the bags and in five minutes it was all over, no fuss, no loud wonderful fuss about trunks.)

Peace and goodness and jollity. The only thing that was wrong now, really, was the sound of the place, an unfamiliar nervous sound of the outboard motors. This was the note that jarred, the one thing that would sometimes break the illusion and set the years moving. In those other summertimes all motors were inboard; and when they were at a little distance, the noise they made was a sedative, an ingredient of summer sleep. They were one-cylinder and two-cylinder engines, and some were make-and-break and some were jump-spark, but they all made a sleepy sound across the lake. The one-lungers throbbed and fluttered, and the twin-cylinder ones purred and purred, and that was a quiet sound too. But now the campers all had outboards. In the daytime, in the hot mornings, these motors made a petulant, irritable sound; at night, in the still evening when the afterglow lit the water, they whined about one's ears like mosquitoes. My boy loved our rented outboard, and his great desire was to achieve singlehanded mastery over it, and authority, and he soon learned the trick of choking it a little (but not too much), and the adjustment of the needle valve. Watching him I would remember the things you could do with the old one-cylinder engine with the heavy flywheel, how you could have it eating out of your hand if you got really close to it spiritually. Motor boats in those days didn't have clutches, and you would make a landing by shutting off the motor at the proper time and coasting in with a dead rudder. But there was a way of reversing them, if you learned the trick, by cutting the switch and putting it on again exactly on the final dying revolution of the flywheel, so that it would kick back against compression and begin reversing. Approaching a dock in a strong following breeze, it was difficult to slow up sufficiently by the ordinary coasting method, and if a boy felt he had complete mastery over his motor, he was tempted to keep it running beyond its time and then reverse it a few feet from the dock. It took a cool nerve, because if you threw the switch a twentieth of a second too soon you would catch the flywheel when it still had speed enough to go up past center, and the boat would leap ahead, charging bull-fashion at the dock.

We had a good week at the camp. The bass were biting well and the sun shone endlessly, day after day. We would be tired at night and lie down in the accumulated heat of the little bedrooms after the long hot day and the breeze would stir almost imperceptibly outside and the smell of the swamp drift in through the rusty screens.

White's sensibilities and better judgment start making inroads on his euphoria in the next paragraph. The illusion he is trying to sustain—the dual existence with his son—is shattered from time to time by the "nervous sound of the outboard motors" that "set the years moving." Describing the old one-cylinder motorboat of his day, White says that "you could have it eating out of your hand if you got really close to it spiritually." This paragraph comes close to being the climactic paragraph of the article.

All that White is attempting to do, living on through his son, is described symbolically in how he used to dock the old motorboat. White wants us to associate this reversal of the "dying revolution of the flywheel" with his own aging and his attempt to reverse the aging process in himself. The next paragraph reiterates, for the last time, the illusion he is trying to sustain: "Everywhere we went I had trouble making out which was I, the one walking at my side, the one walking in my pants."

Sleep would come easily and in the morning the red squirrel would be on the roof, tapping out his gay routine. I kept remembering everything, lying in bed in the mornings—the small steamboat that had a long rounded stern like the lip of a Ubangi, and how quietly she ran on the moonlight sails, when the older boys played their mandolins and the girls sang and we ate doughnuts dipped in sugar, and how sweet the music was on the water in the shining night, and what it had felt like to think about girls then. After breakfast we would go up to the store and the things were in the same place—the minnows in a bottle, the plugs and spinners disarranged and pawed over by the youngsters from the boys' camp, the Fig Newtons and the Beeman's gum. Outside, the road was tarred and cars stood in front of the store. Inside, all was just as it had always been, except there was more Coca-Cola and not so much Moxie and root beer and birch beer and sarsaparilla. We would walk out with a bottle of pop apiece and sometimes the pop would backfire up our noses and hurt. We explored the streams, quietly, where the turtles slid off the sunny logs and dug their way into the soft bottom; and we lay on the town wharf and fed worms to the tame bass. Everywhere we went I had trouble making out which was I, the one walking at my side, the one walking in my pants.

In these climactic paragraphs and the concluding paragraphs leading into the storm on the lake and its aftermath, White realizes that his fate is inescapable: He will die.

One afternoon while we were there at that lake a thunderstorm came up. It was like the revival of an old melodrama that I had seen long ago with childish awe. The second-act climax of the drama of the electrical disturbance over a lake in America had not changed in any important respect. This was the big scene, still the big scene. The whole thing was so familiar, the first feeling of oppression and heat and a general air around camp of not wanting to go very far away. In midafternoon (it was all the same) a curious darkening of the sky, and a lull in everything that had made life tick; and then the way the boats suddenly swung the other way at their moorings with the coming of a breeze out of the new quarter, and the premonitory rumble. Then the kettle drum, then the snare, then the bass drum and cymbals, then crackling light against the dark, and the gods grinning and licking their chops in the hills. Afterward the calm, the rain steadily rustling in the calm lake, the return of light and hope and spirits, and the campers running out in joy and relief to go swimming in the rain, their bright cries perpetuating the deathless joke about how they were getting simply drenched, and the children screaming with delight at the new sensation of bathing in the rain, and the joke about getting drenched linking the generations in a strong indestructible chain. And the comedian who waded in carrying an umbrella.

When the others went swimming my son said he was going in too. He pulled his dripping trunks from the line where they had hung all through the shower, and wrung them out. Languidly, and with no thought of going in, I watched him, his hard little body, skinny and bare, saw him wince slightly as he pulled up around his vitals the small, soggy, icy garment. As he buckled the swollen belt, suddenly my groin felt the chill of death.

---

*"Once More to the Lake" from *One Man's Meat,* text copyright © 1941 by E. B. White. Copyright renewed. Reprinted by permission of Library House, Publishers, Gardiner, Maine.

The rhythm, flow and unity of this article come not only from the majestic pacing and flow of the words but also from the repetition of details and the motif—no passage of time: "there had been no years." And the artistic weaving in of nature imagery creates and maintains the unity of impression so vital to an article such as this. The craft of fiction is so evident that "Once More to the Lake" could easily be classified as a short story. When you search for a nonfiction effort that blends the best of journalistic writing with literature, no better example exists than E. B. White's article.

SUMMARY

As you can see from the pages of this chapter, the magazine article is quite similar to a newspaper feature. Mastery of article leads and structure should come easily because of this similarity. Creative use of these lead styles can inspire the literary hook that carries readers into the body of the article. Using the reader interest plane, organize your notes, keying them to a mounting article interest ending with a lingering impression. In selecting markets, be aware of the trend toward specialization among magazines. Paying close attention to a magazine's requirements will help you produce articles that will sell. More instruction on these points comes in Chapter 11, titled "To Market, to Market."

ARTICLES FOR DISCUSSION

Which of these five articles appeals least to you? Why? What would you change, if anything, to make one of them more appealing?

Dumpees, dumpsters

■ Men ▢ Woman

I have been dumped by others more often than I have dumped someone

30%
21%

I have dumped others more than I have been dumped

35%
45%

I have have been dumped and done the dumping about the same

16%
12%

Don't know the answer

19%
22%

A. "Crimes of the Heart"

By Karen S. Peterson
USA Today, Feb. 4, 2002

Delia Coleman says when she was in her 20s, it was the men who were doing the dumping, ending a romance.

"The guys wanted to rack up the numbers" of women who had succumbed to their charms, says the 32-year-old Chicago single.

But now that she is in her early 30s, it is the women who dump the men, she says.

"Women are much quicker now to move on, to get impatient with the process. We have our friends, our lives to live, other things to do. If I am maybe two months into a relationship and I don't get that feeling that this might last, then that person gets moved out of the lover box into the friend box."

An interest in who dumps whom—and the etiquette, or lack thereof—is a pop culture phenomenon. Dumping is a prevalent topic on the Internet. Pop the words "dumped" and "dating" into the search engine Google, and you get 46,700 Web sites.

Some sites will do your dumping for you by e-mail, including www. wasniceknowingyou.com, complete with a voodoo doll to stick it to him or her.

Internet sites offer endless stories of being dumped, coupled with suitably lame excuses. Did you hear the one about the guy who broke up with his girlfriend because her second toe was longer than her big one?

Dumping actually has drawn the attention of a prestigious polling organization, which today is releasing results of what one might call an anti–Valentine's Day project.

Overall, the perception is that women and men dump each other with equal zeal, says the poll from Public Opinion Strategies:

- About 36% say women dump more often.
- About 34% believe the reverse is true: Men dump women more often.
- About 40% see themselves as dumpsters: They have dumped more often than they have been dumped.
- About 25% are usually the dumpees, getting the heave-ho more often than not.

Overall, about a quarter of those polled (22%) say they have broken up with from six to 10 romantic interests. And 46% say they have been the victim about two to three times in their lives.

The poll of 800 adults has a margin of error of 3.5 percentage points.

The legions of the canned get together on the Net. Thea Newcomb runs www.soyouvebeendumped.com from Glasgow, Scotland. She has formed "a global support group" for the unceremoniously dumped. The pained reaction to a crime of the heart "is something universal, whether you are in England or Alaska, regardless of age, profession or sexuality," she says.

And the boot does often come around Valentine's Day, as couples re-evaluate their relationships, Newcomb says. "One woman posted she got dumped four hours after her grandfather's funeral on Valentine's Day."

Some of the nastier breakup lines recorded on her Web site include:

- I'm sorry. You are just too boring to be my girlfriend.
- We are happy, but we are not very happy, so I think we should see other people.
- If I have to choose between you and this glass of wine, I will choose this glass of wine anytime.
- You are not attractive enough for me anymore. My standards have changed.

Normally, the pollsters at Public Opinion Strategies would embrace dumping with the same enthusiasm as they would a rabid porcupine.

"We do polls for political campaigns and on public policy issues," says Bill McInturff, one of the firm's partners.

However, a couple of months ago, McInturff got ticked off listening to a staffer laugh about breaking up with her boyfriend. His comments lead to a genuine fracas between the male and female researchers—and to this poll.

"We do all sorts of research, and nothing has generated so much buzz in this office."

McInturff, 48, still recalls when he was dumped at 15.

"My worst moment occurred when I was a sophomore in high school. I really liked this girl, but she dumped me saying 'Bill, girls marry guys like you, but they don't date them.' It was a teen tragedy for me."

Regardless of sex, the dumping is not always done gracefully. Steven Smith, 32, of San Diego, collects pathetic excuses to dump a partner at collegeclub.com. One of his favorites is the guy who was told by his girlfriend that she was breaking up with him because he just couldn't respect her being in the Amway army.

Smith reports that another guy compared his partner to a Trans Am that was being traded in on what the man had always really wanted: a Corvette.

"You really love your Trans Am because it is the best car you've ever had UP TO THIS POINT," the guy messaged to his girl. But he was ready to move on to another chassis, and she basically had become a used car.

Collegeclub.com is a division of Student Advantage, Inc., which markets to college students. Jim Styn, 28, is something of a legend in the San Diego offices of Collegeclub, thanks to his tale of severing ties with his girl.

"I took my girlfriend to go fly a kite," intending to let her know that indeed she was supposed to take the activity literally and go fly a kite. "It didn't go as quite as smoothly as I had hoped."

The story is told that he eventually cut the kite string in front of her, explaining that he was letting her go, but he claims that never happened.

So much for his veiled attempts to be clever. Now if he wants to end a relationship, Styn admits, "I just dodge her phone calls. I'm not proud of that. My maturity level is not that high."

Breaking up with someone has gotten easier in the era of Caller ID, Styn says. You know who is calling without picking up the phone.

Another little helper is e-mail and instant messaging, he says.

"That is heartless. But it works if you have trouble facing someone or are nervous about what he or she might do. It can be a safe way to do it."

Then there are the Internet sites that will provide today's 50 ways to leave your lover. One can click on "dump" at www.wasniceknowingyou.com and take advantage of their claim: "We're happy to do the dirty work for you."

Rejectionline.com lists a Manhattan phone number that provides "premium rejection services" with "rejection specialists." (Caution: It is very hard to get through until the wee hours of the morning, and it is not toll-free.) The service is used to dump, although co-founder and stand-up comic Chelsea Peretti says the number is mostly intended as a joke, to "give to someone you have just met who is coming on too strong."

Some of those who were polled by Public Opinion Strategies are rather philosophical about ending romances.

Ray Shaun says women have an easier time dumping men than the other way around.

"Women can say things easier than men can in a relationship," says Shaun, 21, of Greensboro, N.C. "A guy will go ask someone how to do it, but a woman will just know how to come right out and say it."

Shawn Hill has done some dumping—but he prefers the term "breaking up"—in his time, but it's only after "turning every stone" to see if a relationship would work. He wants a "soul mate," says Hill, 38, of Englewood, Calif. But if the outlook appears bleak, he will lose interest and may start complaining about little things.

"I'll become less tolerant. It's my indirect way of saying I don't want to be together anymore."

David Zierman and Kimberly Allario of Sacramento are getting married Feb. 16. But not all his relationships have been fodder for Valentine's Day romance.

He intended to break up with a different lady a few years ago at Thanksgiving.

"But when she told me that the most unhappy time in her life was when this guy broke up with her at Christmas, I just couldn't do it," says Zeiberman, 38. "I rode it out until the end of January. But I got out before Valentine's Day. It was a touchy few months. I was stuck, wedged between holidays."

Allario, his fiancée, has perhaps the ultimate breakup story. A few years ago she was involved with a guy who said he was a federal agent and couldn't talk much about his life hush-hush job. "It was so highly secretive and yada, yada, yada," says Allario, 33. One day, after about a year of serious dating, she picked up a phone message canceling their date for that night.

She never heard from him again.

As it turned out, he "was on the lam. Everything he told me was a lie." Eventually he was arrested for fraud involving a "Beanie Baby Internet scam."

It sounds hilarious now, she says. "But at the time, it was just surreal." At least, she says, she knows what legions of the dumped need to know: Splitting up "really wasn't about me."

B. "Got a Baby Face? Forget About Politics"

By Donna Cassata
The Associated Press, June 10, 2005

WASHINGTON—The term *baby face* is ideal for cooing infants, or as a nickname for singer-songwriter-producer Kenny Edmonds. In politicians, though, it's often a losing look.

Scientists have found that voters often pick the candidates with more mature looks, exuding competence, over those who have certain features —round face, big eyes, small nose, small chin—in other words, a baby face.

Every election, campaigns spend millions on advertising that features photos of smiling candidates. A study in today's issue of the journal *Science* suggests that if the politician has cheeks worth pinching, the effort may be a lost cause.

"We show that inferences of competence, based solely on the facial appearance of political candidates and with no prior knowledge about the person, predict the outcomes of elections for the U.S. Congress," the scientists wrote.

They found that a quick look at the candidate's photograph—a one second exposure—created an initial impression that often lasted through the deliberative process that helps a voter decide.

Competence was an overriding trait, and the politician perceived that way, even based only on looks, left a lasting impression.

Psychologist Alexander Todorov of Princeton University had volunteers look at black-and-white photos of House of Senate winners and losers from elections in 2000 and 2002, and the competing candidates prior to the 2004 contests. The faces had to be unknown to participants; images of Sens. Hillary Rodham Clinton, D-N.Y., John McCain, R-Ariz., and John Kerry, D-Mass., for example, were immediately eliminated.

"It was just on facial appearance, it could not be influences by any other information," Tordorov said.

The study found that the candidates perceived as more competent was the winner in 72% of the Senate races and 67% of the House races.

In an analysis of the study, Leslie Zebrowitz of Brandeis University and Emerson College's Joann Montepare said the perception extended to all demographic groups and even affected well-known politicians.

When images of former Presidents Reagan and Kennedy were altered to give them more baby-like features, "their perceived dominance, strength, and cunning decreased significantly."

So what's a politician with a baby face to do?

The optimum strategy is to argue that the campaign is less about experience and more about character, said David Eichenbaum, a political media consultant.

"Play to strengths, assume you have a baby face with character."

C. "The Rise and Fall of the Chestnut Tree"

By *Smithsonian Magazine*
for AP Weekly Features, Sept. 14, 2004

James Hill Craddock calls himself a chestnut breeder, but a truer description would be a chestnut evangelist. For the better part of his 44 years he has been preaching the virtue of the genus Castanea.

"I think the world would be a better place with more chestnuts," Craddock told *Smithsonian Magazine* for the September issue.

His particular concern is the American chestnut. Once known as the redwood of the East, the tree ruled forests from Georgia to Maine until it was devastated by chestnut blight in the first half of the 20th century. By 1950, the fungus had killed some four billion American chestnut trees, "the greatest ecological disaster in North America since the ice age," Craddock says.

Today, the towering American chestnut of old is very rare, and hardly an acre of its natural habitat is blight free. Yet Craddock, a biologist at the University of Tennessee at Chattanooga, persists in his optimistic mission of restoring the vanquished tree. At several experimental orchards outside Chattanooga, he is breeding scores of chestnuts in an effort to develop blight-resistant hybrids that could be planted in forests, helping reestablish what was once, he says, "the dominant tree in the canopy."

The tree once played a critical role in American life in the eastern United States. The nuts that rained down each fall fed nearly all the inhabitants of the forest. The trees grew fast and tall and straight, reaching more than 100 feet high and as much as 9 feet in diameter in 75 to 100 years. The wood resisted rot and warping, making it a favorite for fencing, utility poles and furniture. People built homes from chestnut logs, buried their dead in chestnut coffins and fattened their hogs with the tree's nuts. In Appalachia, the blight dealt a blow as crippling as the Great Depression.

The disease was first observed in 1904 at the Bronx Zoo, and scientists soon determined that it was caused by a fungus that had arrived in America on chestnut trees from Asia. In its native habitat, the fungus, Cryphonectria parasitica, is relatively benign. Asian chestnuts can shrug off an infection, but the American chestnuts quickly succumbed. The fungus, whose spores infiltrate tiny cracks in a tree's bark, can kill a healthy tree in a year.

The blight moved with heartbreaking speed, carried by the wind, animals, insects and humans. Despite efforts to stop the pandemic, "it spread about 30 miles a year in concentric circles from New York City," says Craddock.

However, there is hope.

Craddock follows breeding procedures championed by corn geneticist Charles Burnham, who helped found the American Chestnut Foundation in the early 1980s. Since that time, the foundation has led the effort to breed blight-resistant hybrids at its experimental farm in Virginia.

In the technique, known as backcrossing, the idea is first to transfer blight-resistance characteristics to the American species, then phase out all other Asian traits by subsequent crosses with American chestnuts.

Scientists predict it will take at least five generations of crosses to produce a highly resistant tree. Even so, the odds are daunting: for every hundred trees produced, only a handful acquire resistance.

The program expects to have its first blight-resistant nuts ready to test in forests by 2007 or 2008.

D. "How Does a Mockingbird Know What Song to Sing Next?"*

By Roy Reiman, Publisher

Some time ago, I was playing a round of golf when I became aware of a northern mockingbird in a tree just above the green on the seventh hole, singing its heart out. You couldn't help but notice him as he switched from one tune to another.

A member of my foursome, knowing I'm the "bird nut" in the group, asked me what kind of bird it was. I told him and explained the bird got its name because it doesn't really have its own song, but "mocks" the songs of other birds it hears.

As that bird kept cheerfully chirping away, singing what I recognized as the songs of a half-dozen well-known birds, I recalled reading about a naturalist who reported a mockingbird imitating songs of 32 different birds in 10 minutes.

Thinking on that, this question suddenly occurred to me: How does a mockingbird know what to sing next?

Think about it. Most birds just have one song, and every time they open their bill the same song comes out. But a mockingbird has a whole songbook to choose from. He has to make some decisions; which of those numerous tunes is he going to sing next?

A Few Fascinating Facts

This interested me enough to do a little checking, and here are a few amazing things I learned:

Researchers have found there appears to be no limit to the number of songs a mockingbird can pick up. Most are able to master at least 180 songs in a few months!

And during an entire mating season, it may master more than 400 songs! A virtuoso mocker can run through its entire repertoire for almost an hour with little repetition.

The male mockingbird does most of the singing during the mating season when he uses his whole songbook of medleys to lure a mate. To a female, a vast repertoire suggests he is wise to the world, has survived for a while and has established a territory with plenty of food.

A mockingbird can imitate more than just other birdcalls. It can also mimic squirrels, frogs, crickets, sirens, bells, home alarms, a rusty gate and even the whirring and squeaks of a washing machine.

According to National Wildlife, one mockingbird near Miami mimicked an alarm clock so perfectly that it awakened residents early every morning.

No other animal on earth comes close to the ability of the mockingbird when it comes to copying the sound of its environment. Parrots can be taught to mimic, but only in captivity. Thrashers and catbirds—which are mockingbird relatives—will do some good imitations.

But when it comes to mimicking other sounds on its own, nothing else matches the incredible natural mimicking ability of the mockingbird.

Evidence of this unique talent was shared in a recent letter from subscriber Suzette Ivill of Clermont, Florida:

"We love all birds, but particularly enjoy mockingbirds for the way they imitate other birds. Here are two experiences I've had.

"Three years ago, we put up a purple martin house. Martins don't have a very elegant song, but we were thoroughly amused to hear them chatter back and forth to one another.

"I knew it wouldn't be long until the mockingbirds would duplicate that chatter exactly. And I was right! In no time at all, you couldn't tell martins from mockingbirds.

"And here's my other mockingbird tale: My aunt, who knows I love birds, gave me a refrigerator magnet that makes bird songs when it's pushed. So when I heard mockingbirds in this area, I sat on my screen porch and kept pushing the magnet. In only a couple of days, the mockingbirds could duplicate those songs exactly. They're amazing!"

They truly are. Hopefully, these facts will add to your enjoyment the next time you "listen to the mockingbird." But, even though we now know all this, how it decides which tune to sing next still remains a personal secret.

---

*Reprinted with permission: *Birds @ Blooms* (Collectors Edition, August/September, 2002, p. 19).

E. "The Art of Setting Traps "

By Keith McCafferty
Field and Stream (October 2003) 27–28.

I once attended a seminar hosted by Dr. Florence Dunkel, the entomologist whom the producers of *Survivor* turn to for advice about bug-eating challenges. Halfway through the wax-worm fritter I remember thinking there had to be a more palatable way to obtain protein from the woods in an emergency.

There is: trapping. Not only do you end up with a hearty meal, but compared to the hours of energy expended while foraging or hunting, traps take little time to set, and unlike firearms or fishing rods, they work for you while you sleep. But to trap animals with enough regularity to feed yourself you need to heed these three principles as you set up:

1. Location. Rabbits, muskrats, groundhogs, and other animals make distinct trails that they use over and over. These trails are the best places to set traps, but they can be difficult to see in bright sunlight. Search for them early or late in the day, when the shadows that define them are longer.

2. Direction. Where possible, narrow an existing trail by brushing vegetation or driving a couple of small sticks into the ground to direct the animal into the trap, or place a horizontal stick at the top of the snare so that the animal must duck slightly, ensuring that its head will go right into the noose.

3. Size. Scale your trap correctly. As a rule, the noose should be one and a half times the diameter of the head of the animal you wish to capture and made of material that will break should you inadvertently snare, say, a cougar's foot.

The most important tool you can carry for catching dinner is a spool of snare wire (26 gauge is about right for all-purpose small-game snares; use 28 gauge for squirrels, 24 or heavier for beaver size animals). Soft single strand wire is superior to nylon monofilament because it holds its shape and game can't chew through it. Snares can also be made from braided fishing superlines or 550 parachute cord, depending on the trap you're making.

The five traps illustrated on these pages will work in a variety of habitats and conditions. Check your state trapping regulations before trying them out.

Squirrel Snare

(1) Make a small loop by wrapping the snare wire around the pencil-diameter stick twice, then turning the stick to twist the wire strands together. (2) Pass the long wire

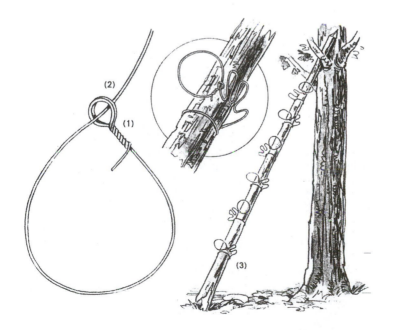

end through the loop to form the snare. (3) To build a squirrel snare, attach a series of small wire snares around a long stick propped against a tree. You can catch several at a time with this setup.

Twitch-up Snare

(1) Tie a small overhead loop knot in your parachute cord, then fold the loop back on itself to form Mickey Mouse ears and weave the tag end through the ears as illustrated. (2) To build the twitch-up snare, use more cord to tie a spring pole or the

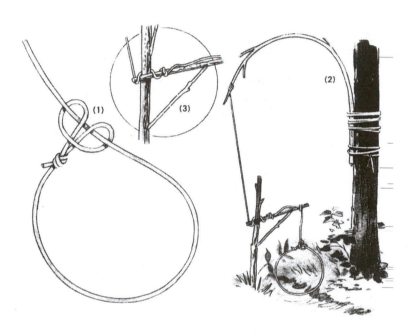

branch of a small tree in tension. (3) Set up a trigger mechanism like the one shown. When the animal's head goes through the loop, the trigger is released, and it snatches the animal into the air, out of reach of other predators.

Ojibway Bird Trap

This works best when set in a clearing where the trigger stick offers a handy perch. The slightest weight on the trigger should cause it fall and the noose catch the bird by its feet. (1) Cut a small 1/4-inch-diameter hole through one end of a stout 3-foot-long pole with a knife. If necessary, shave the sides of the pole to make it thin enough to make the hole. Sharpen the bottom end of the pole and drive it into the ground. (2) Whittle the end of the trigger stick so that it resembles a pencil with the point cut

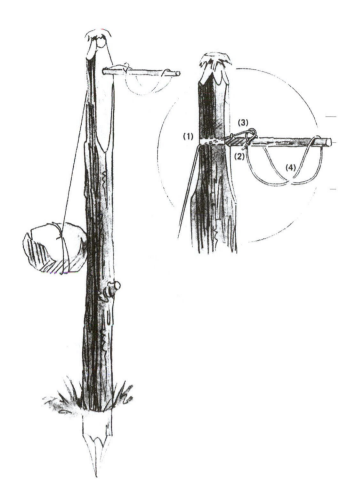

off. This end should fit loosely inside the hole in the pole. (3) Insert thin cord or fishing line through the hole and tie an overhand knot. Beyond the knot, form a noose. Tie the other end of the cord to a rock. (4) Drape the noose over both sides of the trigger and insert it into the pole (if it's breezy, wet the cord with saliva to help it stay put). Draw the cord until the knot catches at the point where the trigger fits into the hole, to keep it from falling back through—until a bird alights on the small stick.

Two-Stick Deadfall Trap

Your intention here is to create a precarious balance, so the slightest jostling of the trigger will cause the trap to collapse. (1) Cut a shallow groove in one end of both upright sticks. (2) Insert the trigger stick between the grooves. The upright sticks should not meet at the center of the trigger. (3) Balance the sticks as shown under the weight of the deadfall.

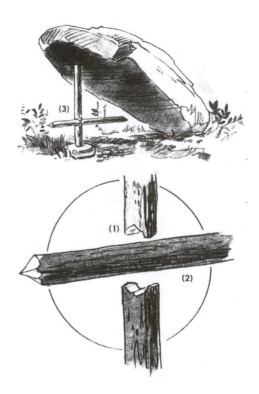

Fish Trap

After dark, fish often cruise the shorelines of a lake or the shallow inside bend of a stream—ideal places for a trap. (1) Build it as shown with the materials at hand: logs, rocks, or stakes driven into the bottom. (2) The diversion arm of the trap directs the fish into the V entrance. Most won't be able to find their way out. Close the entrance and net the fish with a seine made by tying a shirt between two poles. This is much more effective than trying to spear fish or catch them with your hands.

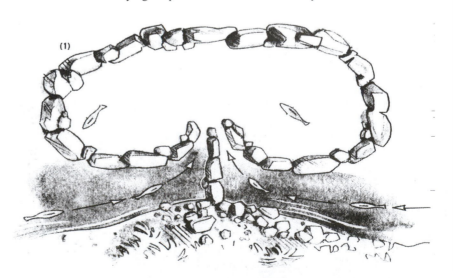

EXERCISES

1. List five magazine article idea possibilities derived from your personal experiences. Under each, list up to five of the articles in the *Readers' Guide to Periodical Literature* or on the Internet which have explored a similar or related idea in the last two years. Include full bibliographic data for the articles.

   a.

   b.

   c.

   d.

   e.

2. List five ideas that stem from your observations of life around you that are suitable magazine article material. Check the *Readers' Guide* for the last two years to determine if other articles have been written about the subject matter of the first two. Include the bibliographic data of the articles.

   a.

   b.

   c.

   d.

   e.

3. List five ideas that stem from a calendar that notes holidays, anniversaries, and the like. Include the angle from which you will write the article.

   a.

   b.

   c.

   d.

   e.

4. Using *Writer's Market*, select three magazines for each of three article ideas you listed in exercise 1. Repeat the article ideas here, listing three prime markets for each. Note the pay you'd expect to receive from each.

   a.

   b.

   c.

5. Compose a detailed outline of an article, from exercise 1 or 2, indicating at one side where parts of the outline fall on the reader interest plane. Include a tentative lead and conclusion.

6. Write the article you've outlined.

7. Reread the gas station description in paragraph 15 (p. 123) of the article on Billy Carter. Write a similar description of some place of business in your hometown in 50 words or less. Compare descriptions with your classmates.

8. Reread the small town description of Skidmore, Mo., in Jules Loh's "The Saga of Ken McElroy" in Chapter 3 (the first seven lines of paragraph 7, p. 150). Write a similar description of a small town you know, keeping within the word count of Loh's description.

9. Note on page 287 in Chapter 11, "To Market, to Market," how the feature outline "Butterflies and Dragons—Graduation Daze" is to be developed. Interview sources noted for the article. Gather information from other sources. Develop a detailed outline along the RIP. Write your article.

10. Student grading: The following magazine article grading form may be used by the instructor by having students exchange papers and grade them. The instructor then grades not only the student's papers but the grading students.

Would it be wise to precede the grading by calling attention to this quote from Franklin P. Jones? "Honest criticism is hard to take, particularly from a relative, a friend, an acquaintance or a stranger." And an addendum: The criticism received in the course will probably be the most honest criticism they'll receive.

(Students may also find the grading form helpful in revising their own articles.)

Magazine Article Grading Form

Heading at top of page single spaced as per following example:
"Featuring the Greatest of Grading"
A 2000-word article
D. J. Anon

		yes	no
Hook, Idea and Transition clear to you?		yes ___	no ___
Comments?		yes ___	no ___
An improved magazine lead might include:			
Is the article coherent? (Logical sequence?)		yes ___	no ___
Comments?			
Are there developing, generating, climactic grafs?		yes ___	no___
No? Which are needed?			
The conclusion leaves a lingering impression?		yes ___	no ___
An improved conclusion might include:			
Does the article "flow" from sentence to sentence and paragraph to paragraph?		yes ___	no ___
Are there similar paragraph beginnings?		yes ___	no ___
Overly short paragraphs?		yes ___	no ___
Is there a change in points of view?	pv	yes ___	no ___
Is there a change in the "tone" of the article?	to	yes ___	no ___
Are attributions buried?		yes ___	no ___
Are "witches" negligible?		yes ___	no ___
(It is, was, we were, there are, they were, which was, were, he was, one is, etc., e.g., pronouns + verbs of being)			
Passive verbs instead of action verbs?		yes ___	no ___
Overused verbs like "get" or "set"?		yes ___	no ___
Are there trite phrases?		yes ___	no ___
Are there "be specific" possibilities?	bs	yes ___	no ___
Is there "telling" instead of "showing"?	tell	yes ___	no ___
Possibility for better characterization or setting description?	cd sd	yes ___	no ___
Diction problems?		yes ___	no ___
Illogical statements?	ill	yes ___	no ___

Concluding comments:

CHAPTER 6

COMMENTARY

Editorials, Columns, Essays, Reviews

PREPARATION FOR THE COMMENTARY

Definitive guidelines for writing commentary are nice to have around when you first start out. The best advice for writing commentary is this: Collect facts, ideas and thoughts you want to include in your work. Devote time to reviewing them and establishing their importance. Compose an outline.

The training and experience you receive in writing feature stories and magazine articles provide you with a basic foundation: A more fully developed curiosity and sensitivity to life's experiences is necessary. Your feel for words and how they flow to express your views to various audiences needs to be considered. All easily said, right? But not easily done. The next few pages, however, should help place you on track.

IDEAS: AGAIN, WHERE DO THEY ALL COME FROM?

"You cannot be in my business long without being asked the question: Where do you get your ideas?" columnist Ellen Goodman recently wrote. "The answer, alas, is a secret known only to me and an oracle that lurks in Boston Harbor."

The answer also lies in keeping a keen eye on the day's events and the ensuing sparks those events may evoke. Your imagination and resourcefulness may then be called upon to explore those sparks. For example, this news feature about researchers who may have found a genetic basis for monogamous bonds could evoke a creative spark in you. Let's see if it does:

"Researchers Find Possible Genetic Basis for Monogamous Bonds"

By John Jurgensen
The Hartford Courant, June 17, 2004

HARTFORD, Conn.—Commitment is a curious thing. What transforms a stranger into a lifelong friend, confidante or lover? And just [as] intriguing, what prevents some people from building such bonds?

The answers could hinge on a genetic trait in the pleasure center of the brain, say scientists who study the social and sexual habits of a mousy creature called a vole.

These animals, like humans, are among the fewer than 5% of mammals that form monogamous bonds. But what makes voles interesting to researchers is [that] not all of them prefer to settle down.

The meadow vole is a rodent that gets around. After sex, the male quickly loses interest in its partner and starts the hunt for another.

Not so for its close cousin. The prairie vole is almost identical to the meadow vole except that it's the family type. The male sticks with its mate, stays close to the nest and helps raise the babies.

But by "infecting" the promiscuous vole with the single gene that makes the monogamous variety want to pair up, researchers at Emory University in Atlanta were able to make the meadow vole more committed to its mate.

When Larry Young, a researcher at Emory University in Atlanta, who conducted the experiments, discusses his work with the public, he often gets approached by people hoping for a pill they might slip to a wayward lover.

But that's not what these findings, published this week in the journal *Nature*, are necessarily about, Young said.

"It looks like we're studying the basis of love, but we're really studying the basis of social behavior," he said. "I do feel strongly that there is a genetic basis that causes us to tend to form bonds with a partner. The variation that we see (in levels of commitment) is probably a combination of the environment interacting with those genes to shape our behavior."

From previous experiments, Young knew that the prairie vole, the monogamous species, had receptors for a hormone called vasopressin in one of the primary reward centers in its brain. Mating releases vasopressin, which makes the male associate the female's identity—namely her smell—with the good feeling of sex.

"It's sort of like a drug," Young said, "a kind of addiction and a habit. They associate that particular female with the pleasure that comes from mating. It usually lasts for the rest of their lives."

The meadow vole, often called a field mouse, has no such receptors in that part of its brain. Sex is a fleeting pleasure not connected with any particular female.

But after Young and his partners injected a virus carrying the vasopressin receptor gene into the pleasure center of the male meadow vole's brain, it was more likely to bond with its current partner than to run off to a new female.

Despite the deeper intricacies of human relationships and the cultural forces that influence them, Melvin Konner, a professor of psychology and neurology at Emory who wrote an article commenting on Young's research, said that genes certainly could help power the inscrutable magnets that draw people together for good.

"There's something mysterious about a couple that stays together for 50 years through thick and thin," Konner said. "And then when we see how many couples don't, it's hard to imagine that it's just a question of different beliefs. I expect that we'll find out that there's some core biological component."

What idea occurred to you to write about when you read this? Have you had or know of any experiences bordering on this subject matter? Do you want to answer this question before going on to the next paragraph?

Perhaps this article provided an impetus to write a column or essay about men and commitment because of what you've experienced or known about relationships?

But let's look at three broad categories of commentary on the next few pages and the subject matter some authors chose to write about.

THREE BROAD EDITORIAL AND COLUMN CATEGORIES

The line of demarcation between editorials and columns is wavy at best, another sign of convergence journalism. (Even newspaper articles are beginning to take on the characteristics of editorials, as we shall see later on.) The major distinction between editorials and columns is that columnists speak for themselves. As a result, their comments tend to be more personal. The editorial writer, meanwhile, most often writes anonymously for a newspaper, radio or television station. Editorials and columns generally fall into three broad categories: persuasive, informative and interpretive. "Humorous" could be added as a category, but what the humorous editorial or column is attempting to do falls into one of the three other categories. Some editorials and columns hopscotch around, informing and interpreting at the same time—and employing humor while doing so. Others may simultaneously inform and persuade. The discussion and examples in this chapter attempt to illustrate these models.

If a complicated health care bill has been passed by Congress, an informative editorial may direct and explain the implications of the bill to the public in a more detailed manner than a news story. If the president presents a budget to Congress, various terms of that budget may call for interpretation and discussion. What, for example, does "supply-side economics" really mean? An interpretive column may explain that the concept is based on what is called the "trickle-down" theory, and detail what that means to the rich and the poor in this country. A persuasive commentary may try to convince an audience through various arguments and emotional or intellectual appeals that supply-side economics is doomed to failure. A humorous commentary by the editorial cartoonist and columnist Herblock may bring a smile to your lips while explaining and simultaneously persuading by proposing a "trickle-up" theory—giving tax breaks to the poor which gives them money to spend which will benefit the rich.

Writing to Persuade

No one formula exists for writing most commentary. However, it's important to remember that commentary, like all writing, should embrace the general rule of unity of impression. The subject matter and the audience usually dictate the form, and the reader interest plane provides valuable guidance without dictating specific structure. When writing persuasively, however, you will have difficulty improving upon the following instructive matrix:

1. The opening paragraph(s) states the problem or situation and outlines the position you are taking.
2. The next few paragraphs present arguments, illustration, examples, evidence and other support for your position.
3. The succeeding paragraphs present the major arguments or evidence counter to your stand, along with the refutations to them. Try not to dwell too long on opposing arguments. (Why give aid and comfort to the opposition?)
4. The concluding paragraph reemphasizes, *in different words*, the stance you took in the beginning.

The reason for presenting the major arguments or evidence opposing your stand in paragraph three is that the Yale one-side, two-side series of studies on persuasion revealed that a sophisticated audience—which includes most readers—may recall the unmentioned opposing arguments and become suspicious of your presentation, undermining its effectiveness.

Lee Garland's letter to the editor is a good example of the persuasive form. With little modification it could be an editorial for a newspaper:

"Don't Fly Me to the Moon"

Lee Garland
The Tennessean, Jan. 8, 2004

To the Editor:

I have long been a devotee of both science and science fiction, especially in the areas of space and physics. I thoroughly enjoy an episode of *Star Trek* or a spectacular photography taken by the Hubble Telescope. Nevertheless, I have begun to question some of the world's space ambitions.

When mankind faces so many threats on Earth, would not much of the world's space budget be better spent here? I refer in particular to the recent hoopla over the two Mars missions; Beagle failed, and Spirit is a success so far. It is certainly fascinating to speculate about current or past Martian life, but what possible use would knowing either way be? If life were discovered, we would know we are not, or haven't always been, alone in the universe. Probability theory already allows us to make that assumption to a high degree of certainty.

The United States has spent billions of dollars and more than a few lives on failed extraplanetary missions. Yes, many wonderful industries and inventions have arisen from the space program; however, physics tells us that by far the greatest chance for "contact" is the SETI project, at a much lesser price. Even if we should detect a planet with extraterrestrial intelligence, we could not go there. The technology does not exist. Assuming theoretical possibility, to develop and build it would bankrupt entire nations.

Garland's major premise is in the last sentence of this paragraph.

Garland supports his position by facts and argument.

The second sentence admits there are some arguments or evidence in opposition to the stand he has taken, and then immediately refutes them. Note that after "space program" a period would be more effective. That allows the refutation, the next sentence, to stand alone as an independent sentence and, as a result, it makes a more powerful statement.

The last two paragraphs sum up, in different words, the stance taken in the initial paragraph.

The pursuit of knowledge is one of humanity's highest callings. Is it not possible, however, that all that money could be better spent on things like medical research, the environment, poverty, hunger and energy development?

Perhaps we should dream less about other worlds and more about this one. None of us will be permanently departing anytime soon.

If you happen to agree with Lee Garland's commentary, you no doubt see this as a magnificent letter that could easily be amended to an editorial.

Anna Quindlen generally follows the persuasive form in her *Newsweek* editorial. (You'll no doubt note that *Newsweek*'s editorial space titled "The Last Word" allows Quindlen a more personal approach that tends to erase the "wavy line" between editorial and column mentioned at the beginning of the section about the three categories.)

a. The play on the "F word" lures the reader into the primary theme of the editorial.

b. The editorial topic—the plight of women today—is made explicit.

Quindlen marshals support for her opening statement in this and the following paragraphs.

"Still Needing the F Word"

Anna Quindlen
Newsweek, CXLII (Oct. 20, 2003) 74

Let's use the F Word here. People say it's inappropriate, offensive, that it puts people off. But it seems to me it's the best way to begin, when it's simultaneously devalued and invaluable.[a]

Feminist, feminist, feminist, feminist. Conventional wisdom has it that we've moved on to a postfeminist era, which is meant to suggest that the issues have been settled, the inequities addressed, and all is right with the world. And then suddenly from out of the South like Hurricane Everywoman, a level '03 storm, comes something like new study on the status of women at Duke University, and the notion that we're post-anything seems absurd. Time to use the F word again, no matter how uncomfortable people may find it.[b]

Fem-i-nism *n.1*. Belief in the social, political and economic equality of the sexes.

That wasn't so hard, was it? Certainly not as hard as being a female undergraduate at Duke, where apparently the operative ruling principle is something described as "effortless perfection," in which young women report expending an enormous amount of effort on clothes, shoes, workout programs and diet. And here's a blast from the past: they're expected "to hide their intelligence in order to succeed with their male peers."

"Being 'cute' trumps being smart for women in the social environment," the report concludes.

That's not postfeminist. That's prefeminist. Betty Friedan wrote *The Feminine Mystique* exactly 40 years ago, and yet segments of the Duke report could have come right out of her book. One 17-year old girl told Friedan, "I used to write poetry. The guidance office says I have this creative ability and I should be at the top of the class and have a great future. But things like that aren't what you need to be popular. The important thing for a girl is to be popular."

Of course, things have changed. Now young women find themselves facing not one, but two societal, and self-imposed, straightjackets. Once they were obsessed about being the perfect homemaker and meeting the standards of their male counterparts. Now they also obsess about being the perfect professional and meeting the standards of their male counterparts. In the decade since Friedan's book became a best seller, women have won the right to do as much as men do. They just haven't won the right to do as little as men do. Hence, effortless perfection.

While young women are given the impression that all doors are open, all boundaries down, empirical evidence is to the contrary. A study from Princeton issued at the same time as the Duke study showed that faculty women in the sciences reported less satisfaction in their jobs and less of a sense of belonging than their male counterparts. Maybe that's because they made up only 14 percent of the faculty in those disciplines, or because one out of four reported their male colleagues occasionally or frequently engaged in unprofessional conduct focusing on gender issues.

Californians were willing to ignore Arnold Schwarzenegger's alleged career as a serial sexual bigot, despite a total of 16 women coming forward to say he thought nothing of reaching up your skirt or into your blouse. Sure, they're only allegations. But it was Arnold himself who said that where there's smoke, there's fire. In this case, there was a conflagration. The fact that one of the actor's defenses was that he didn't realize this was objectionable—and that voters were OK with that—speaks volumes about enduring assumptions about women. What if he'd habitually publicly humiliated black men, or Latinos, or Jews? Yet the revelation that the guy often demeaned women with his hands was written off as partisan politics and even personal behavior. Personal behavior is when you have a girlfriend. When you touch someone intimately without her consent, it's sexual battery.

The point is not that the world has not changed for women since Friedan's book lobbed a hand grenade into the homes of pseudohappy housewives who couldn't understand the malaise that accompanied sparkling Formica and good-looking kids. Hundreds of arenas, from government office to construction trades, have opened to working women. Of course, when it leaks out that the Vatican is proposing to scale back on the use of altar girls, it shows that the forces of reaction are always waiting, whether beneath hard hats or miters.

The anti-arguments are presented in the second sentence and immediately refuted.

But the world hasn't changed as much as we like to tell ourselves. Otherwise, *The Feminine Mystique* wouldn't feel so contemporary. Otherwise, Duke University wouldn't find itself concentrating on eating disorders and the recruitment of female faculty. Otherwise the governor-elect of California wouldn't be a guy who thinks it's "playful" to grab and grope, and the voters wouldn't ratify that attitude. Part fair game, part perfection: that's a tough standard for 51 percent of everyone. The first women's rights activist a century ago set out to prove, in Friedan's words, "that woman was not a passive empty mirror." How dispiriting it would be to those long-ago heroines to read of the women at Duke focused on their "cute" reflections in the eyes of others. The F word is not an expletive, but an ideal—one that still has a way to go.

A companion piece to Anna Quindlen's persuasive commentary is this column by Leonard Pitts of the *Miami Herald*.

"Is This Social Justice?"

By Leonard Pitts
The Miami Herald, May 21, 2004

A few words on behalf of Dixie Shanahan.

Granted, some might consider her a less-than-sympathetic figure. After all, two years ago, Shanahan, 36, from Defiance, Iowa, killed her husband with a shotgun blast to the head. She left his body decomposing on the bed for a year.

But there is, as you might expect, more to the story.

Shanahan, backed up by friends, police reports and photographs of her own blackened eyes, testified that her husband Scott beat her repeatedly for years. She said he threw her down stairs, slammed her into walls, chained her in the basement for days at a time, shoved her head in the toilet and once hit her over the head with a plate because his mashed potatoes were runny.

The day she killed him was especially awful. He had been beating her for three days, she said, angry that she was pregnant with their third child. She says her husband had demanded that she get an abortion. When she refused, he vowed to beat the baby out of her, hammering her repeatedly in the stomach.

Shanahan fled the house. Her husband knocked her down and dragged her back inside by her hair. Shanahan says he pointed a shotgun and said, "This day is not over. I am going to kill you." Then he unplugged the telephones and took them into the bedroom.

What happened next is in dispute. Shanahan says she went into the room to call police. She says Scott made a threatening move and she grabbed the shotgun. Prosecutors say Scott was actually asleep when his wife shot him in the back of the head.

They offered a plea bargain that would have freed her in as little as four years. Shanahan turned it down, gambling that she could avoid a conviction. She could not. She was sentenced Monday to 50 years in prison. The sentence was non-negotiable under Iowa's mandatory sentencing laws. It'll be 35 years before she's eligible for parole.

Many observers are horrified. As one put it, the sentence "may be legal, but it is wrong." This was Charles Smith, the judge in the case. The sentence, said Shanahan's attorney, was like one last beating.

Could she have found a legal way to escape her husband? Yes. But the judgment of battered people is often unsound.

Should she have taken the plea bargain? Definitely. But you know what they say about the accuracy of hindsight.

The point is, even if you accept the prosecution's theory of the crime, this sentence is not justice. Not even close.

But then, justice has become a rarer commodity since the "get-tough-on-crime" movement swept the nation during the Reagan years. Declaring the courts too soft on crime, state legislators around the country divided—judgment was too important to be left to judges. They enacted mandatory sentencing guidelines that were supposed to produce tougher and more uniform sentences.

Instead, those guidelines produce travesties. Consider the Connecticut college student who was peripherally involved in her boyfriend's drug ring—never sold drugs, never used them, had never been in trouble before.

The next few paragraphs present the opposing arguments to Pitts' contention, and then immediately sweep them aside.

Twenty-five years.

Then there's the Iowa man who kicked a door in.

Another 25 years.

And let's not forget the California man who stole a slice of pepperoni pizza.

Twenty-five to life.

Like the zero-tolerance school policies they resemble, mandatory-sentencing guidelines leave no room for compassion or common sense. And you have to wonder how many more of these tragic absurdities it will take before legislators concede the obvious: These are awful laws.

While we await that attack of courage, Dixie Shanahan is filing her appeal and beginning her sentence. Anyone who thinks that's justice doesn't know the meaning of the word.

> The final paragraph ties the commentary together by referring to the beginning paragraph as well as impressing upon us the main theme of Pitts' commentary.

Is there ever a time when you're in the persuasive mode when you don't include the opposition's arguments? Yes. Here is an occasion:

"Thanksgiving? No Thanks!"

By Albert Bender
The Tennessean, Nashville Eye, Nov. 24, 2004

The much heralded mainstream holiday, Thanksgiving, indeed never happened as celebrated and in fact marked the beginning of genocide against the American Indian with the first recorded near extermination of an American Indian nation, the Pequot in 1637. The Pequot were goaded into war, ruthlessly and barbarously attacked and massacred until only a remnant survived.

> The beginning sentence, emphatic as it is, would be more emphatic if a period were placed after "celebrated." Then begin the next sentence: "In fact, it marked. . . "

The largest massacre of Pequots was at Mystic Ford near Groton, Conn. Hundreds of men, women and children were burned alive in a Pilgrim attack. To commemorate this "victory over the enemy," the governor of the Massachusetts Bay Colony in 1637 proclaimed the first official, "Thanksgiving Day," which was celebrated for the next 100 years.

Proof of Thanksgiving's origins was found in the 1970s by a Penobscot Indian professor, William Newell, in documents in Holland libraries as well as in letters, reports and journals written in the mid-1600s.

The Pequots' near annihilation, which spawned Thanksgiving, set the tone for a policy of genocide waged by Euro-Americans that roared like a veritable "white tornado" across the length and breadth of the land. By 1900, U.S. Census records could find only 237,000 Native Americans left alive from a pre-Columbian population that by current estimates numbered anywhere from 40 million to 60 million.

This holocaust was finally over as far as outright mass killing, and it settled down to the slow genocide of starvation, inadequate medical care, cultural eradication and other overall U.S. government imposed conditions of life designed ultimately to destroy the Indian survivors.

Small wonder the term "the vanishing American" came into popular vogue.

The Euro-American policy of indiscriminately killing Native women and children was a war crime atrocity meant to terrorize, but even more so it was intentionally genocidal, for a people cannot survive if its women and children are killed.

This paragraph interrupts the flow of the main theme by the way it is introduced.

This brings to mind an episode in Tennessee history in which Cherokee war chiefs left a letter for militia commander John Sevier apologizing for the killing of women and children in the storming of a settler fort as it was an "accident" and that Cherokees "unlike the white people do not kill women and children in war."

George Washington and Thomas Jefferson were vocal advocates of Indian genocide. Washington advocated a "war of extermination," and Jefferson said, "In war they will kill some of us; we shall destroy all of them." Moreover, we can never forget Andrew Jackson, who cranked up the early 19th century genocide machine to its highest volume with the Trail of Tears.

Moving westward, in California, the landscape was transformed into "vast killing fields" of Native people, where the hunting of Indians was a sport on the level of shooting wild game. In 1849, there were over 100,000 Indians alive in the state; 10 years later there were less than 30,000 survivors. Then-Governor Peter Burnett announced in his 1851 legislative message that a war must "continue to be waged between the races until the Indian becomes extinct."

There has to be an accounting, there has to be a starting point for justice, and what could be more appropriate than the canceling of the Thanksgiving holiday, which marked the beginning of genocide, in favor of one that honors Native Americans and recognizes, not the myth of Indians feasting with the Pilgrims, but the fact that Indians survived the Pilgrims.

Al Bender is a Cherokee Indian and lawyer whose legal career has focused on Native American law. He has been head of various American Indian legal aid and service organizations. He is also a political columnist and book reviewer for various national American Indian newspapers.

This persuasive commentary omits the third step we suggested for articles trying to persuade an audience: Present opposing points of view and refute them. Sometimes, it's inappropriate or illogical. In this instance, like the Holocaust, the theme of a later column in this chapter, what could an opposing point of view possibly be?

Writing to Inform

The informative column or editorial generally eschews choosing sides on a issue and sticks to the main task of informing the readers of what's taking place in the nation or world.

Syndicated columnist Mona Charen primarily does that in the following column. The opening paragraph states what's going to be explored. Succeeding paragraphs develop that theme and increase reader interest up to the climactic paragraph. If the reader interest plane were followed, the last paragraph would leave a lingering impression on the reader. My preference is to use the reader interest plane as a guide when writing most articles, especially informative ones. Let's see how that plays in this column. My commentary annotates pertinent paragraphs.

"Cohabitation—With Children"

By Mona Charen
March 17, 2003

The census brings news that cohabiting couples are now almost as likely as married ones to be raising children. While the majority of children continue to be raised by married couples, the past decade has witnessed a 72% increase in the number of unmarried couples who are deciding to have children.[a]

Nationally, 46% of married couples are raising children vs. 43% of cohabiting couples—and while in absolute numbers, the children of married parents still far predominate, the trend toward unmarried child-rearing is on the increase.[b]

From one point of view, the prevalence of unmarried parenting could be interpreted as good news, since a preciously unmeasured number of biological dads seem to be taking part in the upbringing of their illegitimate children.

But the comfort is cold, as cohabiting couples have such a high rate of separation—much higher than the already lofty levels of divorce among married couples. As Kay Hymowitz reports in *Commentary*, only one-sixth of cohabiting couples remain together for three years and only a tenth for 10 years.

So while biological dads may be present at the creation, it's extremely unlikely that they will remain in their children's home for the full 18 years of childhood. Because serial cohabitation is so common, 70% of the children being raised by cohabiting couples are the biological offspring of only one partner.

Nor is it the case that a home with unmarried parents is as wholesome for kids as those with married parents. Whether cohabiting couples decline to marry because they value their sexual freedom, are less inclined toward long-range planning, have negative feelings about family life based on their own childhood experiences or for some other reason, they tend to be less supportive of children (note the word "tend"—individual cases will vary).

The Institute for American Values has surveyed the literature on marriage and finds that couples who live together without benefit of clergy report more conflict, more violence and lower levels of satisfaction in their relationships than married couples. See "Why Marriage Matters," www.americanvalus.org. The children of these couples also show many of the same troubles that children of divorced or single-parent families display—a higher infant mortality rate, lower grades in school, a higher tendency to repeat a grade and a greater drop-out rate.

a. The subject matter in the ensuing paragraphs, it is made clear, is about unmarried couples who have children.

b. The statistics are enough to lure readers into the body of the column. Now they're wondering, where is this going?

These developing paragraphs continue the exploration. The following question is now raised: What's going to happen to the children?

These generating paragraphs explore the complexities of cohabitation, increasing still more interest in the column.

Cartoon of bride and groom with backs to you.
Behind them a child with arms stretched out
as if to gather them together.

Children of divorced or cohabiting couples are also more likely to experience depression, drug abuse and other mental illnesses. When they become teen-agers, boys who do not grow up with their married parents are more likely to get into trouble with the law, while girls are more likely to become pregnant. Children who live with cohabiting adults are also at a much higher risk than the general population to be sexually abused—the so-called "boyfriend problem."

One study found that a preschooler living with a stepfather was 40 times more likely to be sexually assaulted than one living with both biological parents. Another study suggests that boyfriends are responsible for half of all reported cases of child abuse by non-parents.

Children of non-married parents are worse off even in terms of physical health and life expectancy. In Sweden, where heath care is socialized and payments to single mothers are generous, adults raised by unmarried parents are more inclined to suffer poor health and to die early.

The adults in these temporary unions are hardly better off. Married mothers have far lower rates of depression than divorced or cohabiting mothers. Married women also experience less domestic violence. The National Survey of Families and Households found that cohabiters were more than three times as likely to report physical violence as married couples.

Married couples build more wealth than cohabiters. They are more likely to own their home and to receive financial support from both sets of grandparents. As Charles Murray once put it: A man will bring his son-in-law into the family business but not his daughter's live-in boyfriend. Married men are healthier and less likely to abuse alcohol or drugs, be unemployed or get into trouble with the law.

Don't marry any old jerk just to be married, but be aware that cohabitation is often a dead end.

> The previous three or four paragraphs form the climactic part of this column. But with the depressing description of cohabitation preceding them, they tend to be anticlimactic.

> The concluding paragraphs leave an impression that will linger with the reader. The last paragraph, however, jars the reader by changing the tone of the article with this sentence: "Don't marry any old jerk just to be married." The advocacy in the paragraph and the use of the color words "old jerk" undermines the whole of the informative column and, indeed, the credibility of the columnist.

Norman Lockman's column falls into the slot between being informative and persuasive.

"What Is a Liberal?"

By Norman Lockman
News Journal, Oct. 28, 2004

What's a liberal to do? George W. Bush and his bully boys (and girls) think liberals are bad people, given to fast living, loose morals and un-American behavior like wind-surfing (snicker, snicker) and (horrors) speaking French. Worse, liberal bashers believe liberals are socialists, which as far as they are concerned, is just about the same thing as being a communist.

Don't accuse liberal-bashers of being too nasty. Some of the nicest people I know bash liberals. You just have to realize they weren't paying much attention in seventh-grade civics class. That's about the first time teachers start talking seriously about American democracy. (They still do that, don't you think?)

Had they been paying attention, they would know that the United States of America was founded as a liberal democracy where individual freedoms are guaranteed by a revolutionary set of rules called the Bill of Rights. It was appended to a document called the Constitution, which is the most liberal governing matrix since the Magna Carta.

This would come as a great shock to the civics-challenged except for the fact that American democracy is so steeped in liberalism that we don't even have to take daily note that our house has a roof.

All those clauses ratified by the Continental Congress Sept. 17, 1787, make us the bastion of liberty. All are based on liberal principles. The first 10 amendments (the Bill of Rights) were added Dec. 15, 1791, guaranteeing our freedom of speech, the right to bear arms, the right to privacy, the right to avoid self-incrimination in court, the right to a jury trial, and all other undelegated powers "to the people." All these very liberal principles are still the wonder of much of the rest of the world.

This liberal vision of the Founding Fathers produced a remarkable nation. We sing songs about it and get teary over *God Bless America*, (which incidentally is a 20th century Broadway show tune). We would not have it any other way.

Now here comes the funny part. While George W. Bush is whipping up wrath against liberals at home, hoping it might keep our minds off the mess in Iraq and save his job, while he is poking fun at liberals in general and at one tall liberal from Massachusetts in particular, he is trying to establish liberal democracies in Afghanistan and Iraq, because he thinks the freedoms they mandate can jump-start peace in the Middle East.

Every time he goes off about the power of free elections, guaranteeing women access to political process in those desperate lands, children the right to education, families the right to health, prosperity and happiness through democracy, then starts beating up on liberalism, I start laughing.

Where was Bush during all those expensive classes at prep school and Yale that he fails to recognize he is currently the leading proponent of enforced liberalism in the world today? Don't you think Condi Rice (who didn't miss any of her civics lessons) should take him aside and tell him?

The president falls into the standard liberal-bashing trap. He equates liberalism with weakness while forgetting how much courage it took to produce and maintain a liberal democracy in America while most of the world thought it was a notion that wouldn't last.

Take a good look at the American flag. It is the banner of liberalism. President Bush should notice.

Lockman pulls no punches in his writing. However, using terms like "bully boys" and cute parenthetical asides like "(snicker, snicker)" and "(horrors)" before settling down to a more solemn discourse creates something akin to disquiet in the reader. Once he settles down, he delivers a different kind of punch from Mona Charen's "old jerk."

The following newspaper article by Jeffrey Fleishman falls into that narrowing chasm between news articles and informative editorials. Certainly with a headline stressing that after more than 60 years the Red Cross has finally unsealed records of the Nazi Holocaust, the article hints at a miscarriage of justice. Why did the Red Cross wait so long? Ironically, it appears that Germany—the nation fostering the Holocaust—was one of 11 nations behind the delay. German confidentiality laws were called upon to conceal these records. The Red Cross and the rest of the nations fell into line with this reasoning for concealment. This informative newspaper article tells of the horrors:

"Red Cross Finally Opens Files on Holocaust Horror Kept Sealed Since 1943"

By Jeffrey Fleishman
Los Angeles Times, June 18, 2006

He was a Jew with missing teeth and flat feet, married with three children. He fixed heaters, wore reading glasses and wheezed with bronchitis. On March 28, 1943, he surrendered his trousers, winter coat, socks, slippers and shaving kit and stepped into Auschwitz.

The man known as Max C. is a ghost of pencil and ink, shreds of his memory preserved by the notations of those who made up the Nazi bureaucracy of death. These officers, guards and clerks logged the mundane and the mesmerizing across millions of pages, their meticulous keystrokes and ornate penmanship belying the brutality of their trade. Max C's Auschwitz medical card listed a cursory history: hand injury, missed five days of concentration camp work, Dec. 31, 1943; open head wound, March 31, 1944; Gangrene May 16, 1944; Virus July 9, 1944.

He was transferred to Buchenwald. The last medical report is for a back injury on March 30, 1945—two weeks before the camp was liberated. There is no mention of Max C. after that.

Such stories are stacked in files here at the Red Cross International Tracing Service, which houses one of the largest collections of documents on World War II concentration and slave labor camps. The service was founded in 1943 to search for missing persons. It has unearthed facts and fates of millions on Nazi victims, and this year it is expected to open its archives to historians and scholars for the first time.

A *Los Angeles Times* reporter recently was shown samples of the papers.

Jewish organizations and Holocaust survivors long have sought to study the 50 million documents and 17.5 million names of those the Third Reich considered undesirable. But the service, overseen by a commission representing 11 countries including Germany, which has strict confidentiality laws, has restricted access for decades.

In April, Germany agreed to open the files, though the commission is still debating questions about privacy. "Given the number of documents I personally believe we'll have a new understanding of the Holocaust," said Dedre Berger, director of the American Jewish Committee in Berlin. "We'll see what the victims had to endure, and the details will sharpen the horror of what happened. Historical documents always cast new light."

Along rows of dull metal filing cabinets, past maps and artifacts, past sepia papers and brittle photographs, is a room where scanners click and spin, turning fading documents into computer bytes. The room is crowded with boxes, binders and shelves, and the paper work seems as constant as ocean tides. The people working here don't look up much.

Their sounds linger down the hall and into another room, where Gabriele Wilke spends her days cataloging the section on concentration camps and deportations. She is a detective, twisting strands of symbols and words into short narratives.

She knows that a black upside down triangle sewn on a camp cloth signified a gypsy; a pink triangle a homosexual; a red one a political prisoner; a star a Jew. Her finger runs over lines of ink that dried more than half a century ago: A Slovakian Jew born in 1923, died at 8:40 a.m. on Aug. 6, 1942.

"It's a special thing to touch such an original document," she said. "After a while you develop a routine and it's work, but every now and then something jumps out and touches you. I do this person the best favor I can if I can say I found something, if I have some piece of evidence. Nothing is more sad than closing a file that says, 'Nothing Found.' I have been not only amazed by the amount of paper work the Nazis kept but the meticulousness of it."

Every year the service accumulates thousands of new files, many of them combed from archives and folders in the former East Bloc. The Red Cross has responded to more than 11 million requests from 62 countries since documents seized by the Allies at the end of World War II were first stored in a former Nazi SS barracks in this

Baroque spa town. The center had 151,000 queries last year, many from former slave laborers with compensation claims or children and grandchildren of Nazi victims.

"The Nazis documented any tiny thing," said Maria Raabe, who has worked at the service for 36 years. "For some concentration camps we have all the names but not all the documents. In parts of Eastern Europe we have very little. We almost have no documentation from the Nazi run camp Gross-Rosen. But what we do have from there are documents specifying how many lice were found on inmate's heads and this may be the only paperwork to show that this person was here when."

A page in the Gross-Rosen entry reads: Lice List, Block 8, 886 prisoners, 12/20/1944." Fifteen lice were found on the heads of 11 inmates; each inmate's name is listed along with the number of insects plucked from him. There is nothing else on the page, which lies in a cabinet next to a small box holding a silver pocket watch, a few rings, a cigarette case with faded engraving, trinkets pulled from dirt and ash.

Shaded by oaks and set behind a bike path, the service's main office, which has housed the archives since 1952, has many windows and looks like a hotel. Walking through rooms of binders and encroaching paperwork, one is struck by all that is still unknown about the lives that disappeared and the enormity of what took them. Similar details taken from those killed around the world in terrorist attacks since 2001 would fill a small fraction of this space.

Opening the files may divulge secrets and lies; the Nazis often embedded slander within their paperwork. There also may be references to inmates who acted as informers and conspirators to survive amid mud, frost and smoke of the camps. Such potential information, emerging decades later in a different world may not later provide an accurate picture of the pressures and fears many faced. It is one reason countries such as Germany and Italy have stressed confidentiality when rousing the past.

"Painful choices had to be made in those days of life and death," said Berger. "These files will help us humanize them."

But now, onto a lighter topic and still another example of journalistic convergence. When was the last time you put a rod into the water hoping to land a fish? After reading the next news feature/editorial and looking at the fish called "Albert" that guides soccer balls into a goalie's net, you'll think twice before doing it again. This feature/editorial brings to light things we never dwelt on before. It falls into the informative/persuasive category of commentary.

"Is It a Crime to Kill a Fish?"

By Paula Moore
Senior Writer, People for the Ethical Treatment of Animals (PETA)

Should a person be sentenced to prison for killing a fish? Anglers, enjoying the start of a spring fishing season, would say, "Of course not." But what if the fish is a little boy's friend?

In a recent landmark decision, a New York appeals court upheld the cruelty conviction and sentencing of a fish killer to two years in prison. Pointing out, as it

Albert Einstein, a fantail goldfish, pushes a soccer ball toward a goal. It will get a piece of food as a reward from its owner, Dean Pomerleau. (SHNS photo by Lake Fong / Pittsburgh *Post-Gazette*)

does, a growing awareness of the intelligence of these animals and the importance they have in some people's lives, the court decision is worth noting.

The incident occurred in 2003 in the New York City apartment that Emelie Martinez shared with her boyfriend Michael Garcia and her three children, Juan, who was then 9-years-old, Crystal, 8, and Emaleeann, 5. She also had two dogs, a cat and three goldfish, Junior, Crystal and Emma, who were named after the children.

One morning Martinez awoke to find the 6-foot-5 Garcia standing over her, holding the fish tank. He hurled the tank into the television, shattering both and warning Martinez, "That could have been you." Juan rushed into the room to see what was happening. Garcia asked the boy, "You want to see something awesome?" before stomping on one of the fish, killing her instantly.

"My sisters were very upset. They were crying," Juan recently told reporters.

Garcia was convicted of assault for punching and choking Martinez, and of felony animal cruelty for killing the fish. His lawyer argued that the cruelty charge should be reduced to a misdemeanor, if not tossed out all together, because the victim was, after all, just a fish.

The court disagreed. It recognized what children all over the country, and some adults, already know: Sometimes fish are friends, not food.

Ask Dr. Dean Pomerleau and his 9-year-old son, Kyle, who taught their pet fish to swim through hoops and push fish-sized soccer balls into nets. Dr. Pomerleau and his son got the idea after Kyle won two goldfish at a school fair. "After watching them for a couple weeks, we came to suspect that there was more going on in their little brains than most people give them credit for," the Pomerleaus write on their Web site, www.fish-school.com, http://www.fish-school.com/about.htm.

Although stomping on a fish in the abstract does not seem all that cruel (fishermen knock fish in the head all the time once they land them on board), readers will probably react in horror to what took place in the Martinez apartment. It tends to detract from the main thrust of the commentary. Perhaps it could be played down, telescoped?

Recent studies show that fish have long-term memories, "talk" to one another underwater, form complex social relationships, use tools, learn by watching what other fish do and experience fear when being chased and pain when impaled on hooks. Dr. Phil Gee, a psychologist at the University of Plymouth in the U.K., says that fish can even tell what time of day it is, and he trained fish to collect food by pressing a lever at specific times.

Other countries are using this information to encourage citizens to extend the same considerations to fish that they do to dogs and cats—and to treat them like living beings, not toys or household decorations. If you live in Rome, you may face a hefty fine for keeping goldfish in tiny bowls, where they are doomed to swim in endless circles. It is illegal to hand out goldfish like trinkets at fairs and carnivals. The city of Monza, Italy, has also banned keeping goldfish in bowls. As one sponsor of the law points out, these cramped containers do not meet fish's needs, and they give fish "a distorted view of reality."

Perhaps we humans are the ones with a distorted view. We argue, as Garcia's lawyer did, that fish are not companions like dogs or cats, then decide, as the appeals court did, that they are, then change our minds again and conclude that, well, maybe some are, but others—the fish on our plates, for example—are not. But fish are fish—whether we think of them as friends or as food. If you wouldn't cook your child's goldfish for dinner—or hook your dog in the mouth for "fun," for that matter—then why would you do these things to other thinking, feeling beings?

The local aquarium man here, Michael Consallas, told me that when he turns the television on at home, the fish in his aquarium line up in the tank—all of them looking at the television screen. Then, when he walks over to the cabinet and reaches up for the fish food, a feeding frenzy occurs in the tank.

Writing to Interpret

The next column, by Kathleen Parker, describes hysteria over a revelation by *The New York Times* and the *Los Angeles Times* of government encroachment upon the privacy of individuals. Kathleen Parker told me the column didn't make her many friends. Strong stands such as Parker's can bring about those things. It's an informative/interpretive column salted with a cry for a return to a more sane way of viewing things.

"Safety Versus Security in a World Gone Mad"

By Kathleen Parker
Herald-Citizen (Cookeville, TN), June 28, 2006

Hey, buddy, can you spare a towel? Not since Cujo showed up for a blind date with Lassie has so much froth and spittle saturated the airwaves. This time, it's Big Government and Big Media circling the hydrant.

Hysteria is the only word to describe reaction from all sides to the recent *New York Times* revelation that the U.S. government has been monitoring international financial transactions in attempting to track terrorists.

Without defending the *Times'* decision to publish classified information, a reasonable person could begin to wonder whether everyone has gone barking mad. From the right, we hear charges of "treason" against the *Times* and other papers that ran the story, including the *Los Angeles Times* and *The Wall Street Journal*.

From the left, we hear reiterations of "Bush is evil," from which, presumably, we are to infer that mining bank data is also evil. In truth, of course, if Bush were not tracking terrorist financing, they'd be even more hysterical.

The dots, man, why aren't you connecting the dadgum dots?

All of which underscores how ridiculous American political debate has become.

To be clear, I think the *Times* was wrong to reveal the program as long as it was still useful, as it reportedly was.

It was also apparently legal and effective—a few terrorists have been captured as a result of the program, preventing who knows what havoc and how many deaths. Several members of Congress had been briefed about the program, and safeguards were in place to protect Americans' privacy.

Only if you believe President George W. Bush is determined to rule the world's oil supply is it possible to believe that he's interested in your recent wire transfer to your Swiss mistress.

Even so, all Americans should be concerned when executive powers are expanded, especially when predicated on something as amorphous as the "war on terror," a disconcertingly fluid enterprise lacking clear boundaries or a foreseeable end.

To judge the debate thus far, there are apparently only two possible schools of thought: Bush, Cheney and Rumsfeld are the axis of evil and therefore everything the administration does is bad and must be exposed as such.

Or, we're at war and anything the government does to protect us is justified and the media are a bunch of traitors. Despite his obvious displeasure, Bush has been more restrained than others fogging the mirrors of America's green rooms.

While Bush said the *Times* actions were disgraceful and reckless, Rep. Peter King, R-N.Y., wants to see *Times* Executive Editor Bill Keller strung up for treason.

Claiming that the *Times* violated anti-espionage laws, King has called for an investigation and possible criminal prosecution of Keller, as well as *Times* publisher Arthur Sulzberger and the reporters and editors who worked on the story.

King's outrage is doubtless shared by many Americans who simply hate the Times for its perceived elitist, left leaning coverage of the war and other issues. But treason?

Are we really quite ready for our government to put reporters and editors to death for revealing government activities that pre-9/11 would have been beyond unacceptable?

Perhaps we could behead them for state-sponsored television audiences.

Breathing deeply, we might ask ourselves: Is it possible that no one is evil or treacherous, but that both the White House and Times are right and by degrees wrong—in their own way? That both, in doing their jobs, are trespassing on sacred turf?

We're all on unfamiliar territory these days—at war with a phantom enemy that stalks our national psyche like some lunatic poltergeist. Bush, whose misfortune it was to become president at the moment when those nebulous forces organized them-selves into a lethal instrument, has used every tool at his disposal to thwart another attack.

It would seem he has done his job.

But the media also have a job to protect the public interest against unchecked government power. Balancing that interest against broader security concerns is not a scientific process, but a subjective decision guided by long-held principles that in today's paranoid environment seem to many outdated or irrelevant.

Critics of the *Times* say that Keller and Co. have put America at greater risk, while equally strident Bush critics insist the administration's expansion of executive powers endangers the freedoms we seek to protect.

Each side is both partly right and partly wrong. But the greatest risk to our country is us, as Pogo would put it. Our increasingly polarized and draconian nature weakens us as it strengthens our enemies, who have no quarrel with the gallows for a free press.

The following article on date rape, by Molly Secours, might very well segue into the review segment of this chapter. While bordering on a movie review, it falls into the interpretive mode, with a cry for action.

"A College Campus Epidemic: Date Rape"

By Molly Secours
The Tennessean, April 5, 2005

If you've been meaning to call Oprah and have been waiting for just the perfect excuse, look no further.

Tonight, a young Fisk University graduate named Rel Dowdell is screening his latest film called *Train Ride* on the Fisk campus during the two-day Cartlon Moss Film Festival. The film adeptly takes on a subject that everyone needs to know about but doesn't want to discuss: the epidemic spreading throughout college campuses involving the date-rape drug Rohypnol.

If we were to chart this commentary on the reader interest plane, the following developing paragraphs dispel doubts about the authenticity of the "epidemic" by citing research in the area and the deadliness of the date rape drugs.

If you think your son or daughter is immune to being drugged by a stranger or so-called "friend" while away at college, think again. According to research by the University of South Florida, FBI and U.S. Department of Justice, drug-induced rapes are on the rise. The studies revealed that 25% of college woman have been victims of rape, and of those, 84% knew their attacker and 44% have considered suicide as a result. And those are only the rapes reported. Often times shame and humiliation prevent young women from ever reporting the rape.

Rohypnol, GHB and Ketamine are known as "date rape drugs" or "predatory drugs" because they are used to incapacitate someone for the purposes of committing a crime, often sexual assault. These drugs are odorless and colorless and are particularly dangerous when combined with alcohol. They can cause dizziness, disorientation, loss of inhibition and a loss of consciousness. And there's more bad news: These drugs are easy to come by.

In *Train Ride*, Dowdell incorporates two things: the date rape drug Rohypnol—which is easy to slip into someone's drink without him or her knowing it—and the rampant use of videotapes for recording sexual activities performed once under the influence of the drug.

According to Dowdell, video has become a lethal weapon. "If they get you on tape performing a sexual act, it can hurt you down the road. If you want to get into broadcasting or politics—anything in the public eye—you might be inhibited from fulfilling that dream." Worse than that, warns Dowdell, is the destruction of one's reputation and self-respect and the permanent emotional scars left by such humiliation.

Consider the *Girls Gone Wild* videos—which are widely advertised on television. They depict college-age women performing wild sexual acts in various states of intoxication. What is equally disturbing is that the video is reported to have grossed over $90 million dollars in sales which means that young women caught drunk and reckless on video is big business.

Dowdell says "what most people refuse to believe is that whatever you do in college has permanent repercussions on the rest of your life."

After seeing what happens to Katrina, *Train Ride*'s leading actress (played by rapper M. C. Lyte), most would agree. Katrina is a college freshman—and by all definitions a "good girl"—who gets charmed and snared into the malicious plan of a "cool" senior named Wil (played by Wood Harris, star of HBO's *The Wire*). After being drugged, Katrina is raped by Wil and his two friends who have been convinced by Wil that Katrina requested to have sex with all of them (aka a "train ride") before falling asleep. After lying to his friends, Wil then videotapes the two young men having sex with Katrina.

What is so compelling about *Train Ride* is that Dowdell manages to do what many filmmakers strive to do but often don't. Without gratuitous or explicit scenes in the film, Dowdell gives us chills at the horror of what is done to Katrina—all the while demonstrating complete respect and sensitivity for the characters and their individual plights. As each character in this tragic debacle begins to emerge, we see just how easy it is to get involved in a situation that you never dreamed could happen and how quickly the life you imagined for yourself is destroyed.

It was the filmmaker's respect for this subject matter that prompted Emmy award-winning actress Esther Rolle to rearrange her dialysis treatments in order to appear in the film in spite of her failing health. As it turns out, *Train Ride* was Rolle's last performance before her death in November 1998, and the film is dedicated to her.

Asked why he chose date rape, Dowdell says: "The bottom line is this: If the media doesn't start showing the true consequences of young men and women being sexually reckless, date rapes will continue to increase, not just on college campuses but everywhere: bars, parties, anywhere that young people socialize. The exploitation that's going on is creating a destructive generation."

Unfortunately, it seems many parents are unaware of just how rampant date rape is or how easily their daughters or sons could become victims. Many college students are in denial that it could happen to them. Who knows how much grief might be avoided if every college freshmen were required to see this film on orientation day?

The next few generating paragraphs leading to the climactic paragraphs spell out the even more serious consequences of date rape.

Now the climactic paragraphs bring the commentary to a close.

The concluding and lingering impression paragraph, obviously, starts with the words: "Maybe Esther Rolle. . . ."

Maybe Esther Rolle will be looking down on the Fisk campus from heaven with pride tonight, urging someone in the audience who has Oprah's ear to make the call.

Molly Secours is a writer/speaker/filmmaker and frequent co-host of Behind the Headlines on Nashville WFSK radio. She is also an activist.

The next news feature is a sign that convergence journalism is thriving. It functions as an interpretive as well as a subtly persuasive editorial. In describing where women are in power throughout the world, it poses the mute question: How is it that our progressive country lags behind even third world countries when it comes to electing women to government offices? Read Robin Hinery's article and you'll find out. (Incidentally, and again, the article is an example of convergence journalism—news articles jump-roping over into editorial columns.) We'll leave commentary out of this one, except for the conclusion. But we'll revisit the article in the exercises at the end of the chapter.

"How About a Woman for President?"

By Robin Hinery
The Associated Press, June 22, 2006

For all the talk about Hillary Rodham Clinton and Condoleezza Rice battling for the presidency in 2008, the closest a woman has come to the Oval Office is actress Geena Davis, star of the recently canceled TV series "Commander in Chief."

Yet, in other nations, a female leader isn't just the stuff of television drama.

Countries as diverse as Britain, Chile, Liberia and Israel have elected women to their highest political office. When it comes to female representation in national parliaments, the U.S. ranks 68th in the world. A primary reason for the success of women in politics elsewhere, according to one observer, is the effort on the part of women themselves.

"Women in other countries have made more strong-willed efforts than we have," said Marie Wilson, head of the New York–based White House Project, a nonpartisan group that works to increase women's participation in politics. "They have gelled with each other to say: 'We know women matter in these positions. We must have more women.'"

No woman has ever led the presidential ticket of a major political party in the United States. Only one—Democrat Geraldine Ferraro in 1984—has been nominated for vice president by either the Republicans or the Democrats.

Clinton, a senator from New York and a former first lady, is considered by many a front-runner for the Democratic nomination in 2008. Rice, President Bush's secretary of state, is mentioned as a possible Republican candidate even though she adamantly denies any interest in national office.

In Washington today, 85 percent of Congress is male. As of mid-May, six months before the November elections, 175 women were considered candidates for the House and 18 for the Senate. In 1992, a record 222 women filed for House seats and 29 for the Senate.

While female representation in Congress hovered between 13 percent and 15 percent for the past five years, the presence of women has increased significantly in parliaments in many other countries.

Even the new democracies in Iraq and Afghanistan have a greater percentage of female representatives than does Congress, according to the Inter-Parliamentary Union, an international group based in Geneva, Switzerland. The organization ranked 188 countries according to their female representatives.

In 2005, the global average for female representation at the parliamentary level was 16.3 percent, an average that increased from the year before largely due to quotas put in place in several Latin American countries to promote the candidacies of women, according to the Inter-Parliamentary Union.

Such gains for women were not limited to the developing world. Quotas implemented in 2005 within Britain's Labour Party led to the highest number of women ever being elected in that country—128.

The U.S. has "gotten further and further behind as other countries have adopted quotas and other mechanisms to ensure they are using all their resources, meaning their women," Wilson said. "Those countries implemented quotas because they finally decided that political parity was important enough to be given some teeth."

The Inter-Parliamentary Union found that the average ratio of female parliamentarians in countries that used quotas in 2005 elections was nearly twice that of those without such special measures: 26.9 percent versus 13.6 percent.

In 2003, the number of women in Rwanda's National Assembly doubled, largely due to the creation of a constitutionally mandated quota. Since that year, Rwanda has been No. 1 in the global ranking of women in national parliaments, with 48.8 percent of its assembly made up of women.

Experts say the success of quotas does not tell the whole story.

Other factors helping female politicians outside the U.S. include financial support, women-focused reforms within individual political parties, and an organized effort by the media and the general public to champion political parity.

"The absolute most fundamental part of a successful policy for gender equality is to give opportunities for women to get economic independence," said Martin Nilsson, a Social Democrat in Sweden's parliament and his party's spokesman on gender equality.

"Major ingredients . . . are the creation of a well-funded service sector; individual, and not family based, taxation and social benefits; and finally, and most important, a family policy giving women a real opportunity to combine work and family."

Sweden ranks second in the Inter-Parliamentary Union's ranking.

Another common denominator among some of the governments with the highest rates of female participation was a shift in the political balance of power following a period of violent conflict, said Anders Johnsson, the secretary general of the Inter-Parliamentary Union.

"Some of the success stories we've seen are stories where women had to assume roles during conflict that were traditionally dominated by men," Johnsson said, singling out Rwanda, Mozambique and Burundi.

"When the conflict was over, the women were not willing to give up the power that they had attained, and they promoted systems that then allowed them to be elected into office," he said.

Experts point to a number of problems the U.S. needs to solve to bring more women into office: the cost of running a competitive campaign, re-districting that favors incumbents—most of them male—and stagnant numbers at the state legislature level.

Quotas appear an unlikely option for increasing female representation in American government.

"Some people have discussed it in the U.S.," said Debbie Walsh of the Center for American Women and Politics at Rutgers University, "but people in this country tend to run when you say 'quota.'"

> While the percentages thrown at us earlier in this commentary may be a source of some irritation, the reader welcomes the precise documentation of our tarrying in allowing women into the hallowed halls of governmental power. Imagine! Rwanda has 48.8 percent women in its National Assembly. And this was in 2003. In the concluding and lingering impression paragraph we are left with the thought that the situation appears nigh to hopeless.

The next news article can, without a doubt, function as an editorial or column. Comic strips didn't contain as much serious social commentary years ago as, for example, "Doonesbury" does today. This news story about comics reveals how a section of the population views the comics today, and how that vociferous few can cause great newspapers to discontinue some strips.

"Comics as Commentary"

By James Sullivan
San Francisco Chronicle, May 2, 2004

What's funny about losing a limb?

The funny pages took a dour turn in recent days as two daily strips, Garry Trudeau's *Doonesbury* and Darby Conley's *Get Fuzzy,* concurrently addressed the war in Iraq. Coincidentally, both strips featured characters who lost a leg serving in the military.

The strips join *The Boondocks,* Aaron McGruder's wickedly controversial daily feature, in raising grim wartime questions in that part of the newspaper traditionally reserved for lighthearted family squabbles and cutesy cat jokes.

> These two paragraphs introduce the theme of the commentary—the controversy stirred when comics comment upon serious social and political issues. Now follow the paragraphs developing that theme.

While Trudeau has long mined current events for outrage and inspiration, the award-winning *Get Fuzzy* is, as the name implies, typically unconcerned with politics or heavy contemplation. Its main character, Rob, spends most of his time coping with two lovably cantankerous pets.

But the wounding of his cousin Willie brings out the inner protester in Rob. Upon learning that Willie's Air Force jet arrives at 2 a.m., under cover of night, he demands an explanation.

"Shouldn't these guys be getting back when people could welcome them home?" Rob wants to know.

Iraq's arrival on the funny pages marks another milestone in the debate about serious subjects in daily comic strips.

"It's the same issue—what's appropriate in the comics and what isn't," said Rod Gilchrist, executive director of San Francisco's Cartoon Art Museum. Last year, Gilchrist curated "Hate Mail: Comic Strip Controversies," an exhibition that examined cartoon depictions of knotty issues such as racism, unmarried sex and extreme political views and the correspondence they generated.

"My personal viewpoint is that comics should reflect the world we live in," said Gilchrist.

Many readers and editors have historically disagreed. *The (New York) Daily News* dropped *The Boondocks* for a month when McGruder lampooned post–Sept. 11, 2001, patriotism in the strip. Trudeau is so accustomed to controversy that he has an online forum for reader response he calls "Blowback."

But Lisa Klem Wilson, general manager of United Features, the syndicate that distributes *Get Fuzzy*, said mail about Conley's commentary on the Iraq war have been surprisingly supportive.

"Most people think it's great he did this," she said. "Some people have said they think the funny pages should be reserved for humor, not political issues, but the response has been overwhelmingly positive."

The fates of combat veterans in *Doonesbury* and *Get Fuzzy* might be read as implicit criticisms of the administration's course in Iraq.

The notoriously press-shy Trudeau told ABC News on *This Week with George Stephanopoulos* that the image of the long-running, former football-playing character B.D. stripped for the first time of his trademark helmet was nearly as jarring for some *Doonesbury* fans as the fact that he'd suffered the trauma of amputation.

"The strips are about sacrifice, about the kind of shattering loss that completely changes lives," he said. "I have to approach this with humility and care. I'm sure I won't always get it right, and I'm also sure people will let me know when I don't. But it seems worth doing."

(*The Tennessean* elected to substitute another Doonesbury strip the day that B.D. discovered he had lost a leg in combat. The reason: not politics but language that editors didn't feel was appropriate for a page read frequently by children.)

Robert C. Harvey, author of *The Art of the Funnies: An Aesthetic History*, said comic-strip characters have gone to war nearly as long as there have been comic strips. Mutt and Jeff went to Europe during World War I; Barney Google and Joe Palooka served in World War II.

Having developed the theme, the next generating paragraphs carry the reader to the climactic point of the article.

The climax of the commentary comes with the following Trudeau statement, *The Tennessean*'s admission of declining to run the Doonesbury strip and Harvey's historical comment on strips in the past.

The last paragraph is a beautiful summation of the problem the strips bring to the surface—and a great lingering impression upon the reader.

But those strips weren't critical of a presidential administration or government policies. "By and large, their engagement has been patriotic in the sense that they're supportive of leadership," Harvey said. "Until quite recently."

Perhaps this is a good time to look at how the music scene, simply described by John Leicester, brings societal issues to the surface in France.

"Hip-Hop in Paris"

By John Leicester
The Associated Press, Nov. 22, 2005

The ghetto scene and the "wounded pride from the heart of France's ghettos" lure the reader into the commentary and keep the reader there with a direct quote.

PARIS—The beat is infectious, the music sensual. But the words are acid, a rapped cry of wounded pride from the heart of France's ghettos.

"Whatever I do, in France's mind I will always be just a kid from the projects," raps Disiz La Peste on his new album. "I know that I fascinate people because where I come from, succeeding is not easy, and I still bear the stigma of this environment, of my olive skin."

A description of the current unrest and the role music plays in the description generates still more interest.

Three weeks of riots, arson and attacks on police ripped the cover off of problems that French hip-hop artists like Disiz have been rapping and raging about for years. Racism, despair, anger, drugs, crime, hostility against police—issues thrust to the top of the national agenda by France's worst civil unrest in four decades—have been grist for these urban social commentators for years.

Disiz, whose real name is Serigne M'Baye, said it is too simplistic to say that French politicians now accused of having ignored the ghettos' problems for decades need only to have listened to rap to learn that the lid was ready to blow.

Instead, people need to examine themselves, their prejudices and their country, he says. That includes youths from poor suburbs who are too quick to write off their own futures, telling themselves "there is no point in fighting," and white French, he says, must ask themselves "Do we really accept immigrants who are French?"

Now that the reader is embedded in the commentary, brief expository historical paragraphs are acceptable.

"We speak in France of liberty, equality and fraternity. Liberty exists. No doubt there. Everyone can speak out. But equality and fraternity do not exist. We have to fight for them, but we have to fight together," he said.

Hip-hop crossed over to France from the United States in the 1980s. It quickly became a vehicle of expression for suburban youths, some of whom wove in musical and lyrical elements from their own North and West African backgrounds and helped make France a vibrant center of hip-hop culture.

Like other French artists, rappers benefited from legislation that obliges radio stations to broadcast a certain proportion of French songs to ward off English-language dominance.

As in the United States, French rappers appeal as much to rich white kids as they do to French-born children of immigrants.

Information about who listens to hip-hop and who the leading musicians are provides needed background for the commentary.

French pioneers included Supreme NTM. Their song *What are we waiting for* (*Qu'est-ce qu'on attend*), from the 1995 album *Paris bombed* (*Paris sous les bombes*), seems, in light of recent riots, like an early warning sign that was ignored.

"What are we waiting for to set everything aflame? What are we waiting for to no longer follow the rules of the game?" NTM rapped.

"We have nothing to lose because we had nothing to start with. I wouldn't sleep soundly if I were you. The bourgeoisie can quake, the scum are in town."

Scum. That word, used by French Interior Minister Nicolas Sarkozy two days before the rioting erupted Oct. 27, has been much in the news lately.

Sarkozy was referring to toughs and criminals who terrorize marginalized housing projects.

The final sentence alerts the reader to the continuing unrest that is coming.

But his comment was taken by many youths as a blanket slur.

THE ESSAY

What separates the essay from the editorial or the column is not the length, form, or even the subject matter—although more esoteric subjects may be treated in an essay than in an editorial or column. The major distinction may be much like that between poetry and prose. John Stuart Mill, in making that distinction, noted: More inner soliloquy is involved in writing poetry. Fresher channels of thought are explored. Poetry, Mill wrote, is more the fruit of solitude and meditation. The same may be said about essays. The essayist may sometimes simply be a better writer. At other times, better essay writing may stem from the fact that the essayist has the luxury of time and contemplation not available to the editorial writer or columnist who is chained to a daily grist mill.

An essay may be a personal reminiscence, a reflection on a worldly event, a political comment, a eulogy, an exhortation, a declamation, a pronunciamento.

What distinguishes it, generally, from editorials or columns might be the flow, dignity and artistry of the language when it treats a serious subject, and the sparkle, polish and wit displayed when the essayist engages in humor or satire. For a more complete grasp of what an essay is, and what it can be, you might pick up a modern anthology of essays or a collection of essays by George Orwell, E. M. Forster or E. B. White.

The essay generally follows the reader interest plane: The title is arresting, and the opening paragraph "hooks" the reader. The idea of the essay and the transition into the main body of the essay occur in the first paragraph. The second paragraph elaborates on the idea and launches the reader into the body.

The essay lends itself to a wide variety of topics, as indicated earlier—even the death of a friend. When Lyle Starr died, I wrote this for *The Nashville Banner*. (You could consider it a lead-in to the May Sarton essay that follows.)

"Lyle Starr Is Dead"

My friend, Lyle Starr, is dead. Although Lyle was only my income tax consultant, I thought of him as my good friend.

The opening paragraphs lure the reader into the body of the essay and set the stage for the following developing paragraphs.

Both my wife and I were shocked when we read about his recent death of complications from a neurological disease. We could not believe that his obituary would have such an effect upon us. We thought we had Lyle for life. And then he died.

If you totaled up the time I spent with Lyle, I only knew him for two days—the time it took to make out my income tax. Once a year for 25 years, I worried him with my deductions and figures—but for no more than two hours. Those two hours even included a phone call to set up an appointment. And to discover the latest tax code changes so I could keep the lecture on tax deductions to my freelance writing class up to date.

Lyle's wife, Marion, said Lyle never liked being complimented. He liked being in the background. But, perhaps, Lyle will forgive me for saying a few simple words like, "I miss him."

I've known friends much better and longer than I've known Lyle and do not consider them "good" friends. How could it be that, on this slimmest of acquaintanceship, I have trouble thinking of life without Lyle Starr?

Certainly, in this sense of loss, the reality that I left Lyle's office each year unburdened and accompanied by an air of relief is a factor. But it has to be much more than that:

Lyle Starr was a kindred spirit. He didn't mind driving beat-up old cars. (The latest was a 1979 Pontiac. His favorite, a 1969 Rambler he drove for 21 years.) He disliked the IRS almost as much as I did. I stumbled upon him in Nashville in a rambling old house converted into an office off Gallatin Road after having consulted a series of wimps masquerading as income tax consultants. But Lyle drew the line on deducting such things as the food and vet bills for the two dogs who rode with me to the cattle farm I ran for 10 years in Dickson County. Lyle had character.

The generating paragraphs beginning here lead up to the climactic paragraphs of the essay.

I stayed with Lyle year after year, to the new office he last leased on Trousdale Drive in Nashville. Even after I moved to Cookeville, 80 miles away. After every session, I would say:

"Well, we didn't get it ALL back, but next year we will!"

Lyle would reply, "There's only $200 that we didn't get." A trifle hurt that I was not completely satisfied.

"I know," I would say, "you done good, Lyle. But I want it ALL!"

That comment would mollify Lyle.

Lyle was one of those lights that E. M. Forster writes about in that essay "Three Cheers for Democracy." Those persons reflected a message, something to the effect that, "Yes, things are a muddle. But there you are and here I am and together we can bear up."

You could run a lottery with the cigarette tray on Lyle's desk: "Guess the number of cigarette butts in the tray and win a trip to Las Vegas." I often wondered how the huge schefflera plant in the corner survived in all the smoke.

"Those cigarettes are going to do you in, Lyle," I once said.

"Naw," he replied. "They're the fuel that keeps me going."

I'm pleased that I was wrong about the cigarettes.

Now come the climactic paragraphs.

Among the other regular desk items was a top. When you spun it, and it stopped, it told you to buy stocks or not to buy stocks. A kaleidoscope was another curio. Though we never confirmed it, Lyle and I saw the world pretty much the same way:

a configuration of bewildering shapes and colors that changed from moment to moment—a fascinating charade of characters and actions.

Under a shock of brown hair that fell across his broad forehead, that worldly kaleidoscopic vision caused a small wry smile to perpetually play on Lyle's face despite the Salem cigarette dangling from his lips.

The ancient Greeks believed that so long as a person is remembered—though he be dead—he will be immortal. Because of Lyle Starr, I am now more attentive to those momentary human contacts that I once so cavalierly took for granted. And in this small, desperate, way, I hope to keep Lyle alive—for just a little while longer.

> The final paragraph functions as the climax as well as the lingering impression.

When you read May Sarton's essay, you'll probably think of John Stuart Mill's comment about the essay being the fruit of solitude and meditation—one of the reasons I selected it. So that you may enjoy the unity of impression of this essay, commentary will come at the conclusion of the essay.

"The Rewards of Living a Solitary Life"

By May Sarton

YORK, Me.—The other day an acquaintance of mine, a gregarious and charming man, told me he had found himself unexpectedly alone in New York for an hour or two between appointments. He went to the Whitney [Museum] and spent the "empty" time looking at things in solitary bliss. For him it proved to be a shock nearly as great as falling in love to discover that he could enjoy himself so much alone.

What had he been afraid of, I asked myself? That, suddenly alone, he would discover that he bored himself, or that there was, quite simply, no self there to meet? But having taken the plunge, he is now on the brink of adventure; he is about to be launched into his own inner space, space as immense, unexplored and sometimes frightening as outer space to the astronaut.

His every perception will come to him with a new freshness and, for a time, seem startlingly original. For anyone who can see things for himself with a naked eye becomes, for a moment or two, something of a genius.

With another human being present vision becomes double vision, inevitably. We are busy wondering, what does my companion see or think of this, and what do I think of it? The original impact gets lost, or diffused.

"Music I heard with you was more than music." Exactly. And therefore music itself can only be heard alone. Solitude is the salt of personhood. It brings out the authentic flavor of every experience.

"Alone one is never lonely: the spirit adventures, walking / In a quiet garden, a cool house, abiding single there."

Loneliness is most acutely felt with other people, for with others, even with a lover sometimes, we suffer from our differences of taste, temperament, mood. Human intercourse often demands that we soften the edge of perception, or withdraw at the very instant of personal truth for fear of hurting, or of being inappropriately present, which is to say naked, in a social situation. Alone we can afford to be wholly whatever we are, and to feel whatever we feel absolutely. That is a great luxury!

For me this most interesting thing about a solitary life, and mine has been that for the last twenty years, is that it becomes increasingly rewarding. When I can wake up and watch the sun rise over the ocean, as I do most days, and know that I have an entire day ahead, uninterrupted, in which to write a few pages, take a walk with my dog, lie down in the afternoon for a long think (why does one think better in a horizontal position?), read and listen to music, I am flooded with happiness.

I am lonely only when I am overtired, when I have worked too long without a break, when for the time being I feel empty and need filling up. And I am lonely sometimes when I come back home after a lecture trip, when I have seen a lot of people and talked a lot, and am full to the brim with experience that needs to be sorted out.

Then for a little while the house feels huge and empty, and I wonder where my self is hiding. It has to be recaptured slowly by watering the plants, perhaps, and looking again at each one as though it were a person, by feeding the two cats, by cooking a meal.

It takes a while, as I watch the surf blowing up in fountains at the end of the field, but the moment comes when the world falls away, and the self emerges again from the deep unconscious, bringing back all I have recently experienced to be explored and slowly understood, when I can converse again with my hidden powers, and so grow, and so be renewed, till death do us part.

The adventure in solitary bliss awaiting the man at the museum is explored in terms of what will be revealed to him, as it has been revealed to May Sarton in those developing and generating paragraphs. The climactic paragraphs come with the last paragraphs dealing with loneliness, when the house feels huge and empty. The concluding paragraph is the climax: Sarton describes her rejuvenation, "when I can converse again with my hidden powers, and so grow, and so be renewed, till death do us part." With the last five words, "till death do us part," the reader is left to meditate and discern the full meaning of them. In doing so, the essay is assimilated. The reader is not likely to forget it.

REVIEWS

A Standard Review Format

Until you become more acquainted with reviewing, you'll probably feel more secure writing reviews if you have a format to follow. The review format in the following matrix provides you with a review "security blanket."

Similar to the reader interest plane, an appraisal of the work would form the introductory paragraphs. The intent of the artist and the synopsis of the work form the developing paragraphs. The generating paragraphs are composed of the evidence supporting the appraisal. The climax comes with the restatement of whether or not the artist accomplished

```
┌─────────────────────────┐
│      Appraisal          │
│      of the work        │
├─────────────────────────┤
│       Intent            │
│      of the artist      │
├─────────────────────────┤
│       Synopsis          │
│      of the work,       │
│      performance        │
│        exhibit          │
├─────────────────────────┤
│       Evidence          │
│      supporting         │
│      your appraisal     │
├─────────────────────────┤
│    Artist's intent      │
│    accomplished,        │
│   not accomplished.     │
│  Suggestions to the reader │
└─────────────────────────┘
```

the intent. That may be accompanied with a concluding paragraph suggesting whether readers will benefit or not from attending the event—a lingering impression.

Winthrop Sargeant, *The New Yorker*'s music critic for some 20 years, says this about reviewing:

> The critic's function is not to lay down incontrovertible laws or pronounce absolute truths. It is to reflect his [or her] personal taste. . . . and try to stimulate his [or her] readers into accepting or rejecting it according to their own lights. . . . Music, in particular, is an art that invites intuitive and passionate reactions rather than cold-blooded appraisals.

VINCE PASSARO COMMENTS ON BOOK REVIEWING

My editor at *Oprah Magazine**—or, as they like it to appear, "*O, The Oprah Magazine*"—is a woman deceptively soft at the edges and hard at the core, a brilliant editor with a very strong sense of the topography of prose, the hills and valleys of sentences and paragraphs. She edits literally word by word, which I find a profound and instructive pleasure. I first worked for her almost twenty years ago at a wonderful New York City weekly, edited by Adam Moss, called *7 Days*. She was the first editor to publish my work, largely book reviews with occasional essays and reported pieces, and she remains the very best editor I've ever known.

Since apparently she also likes my work still, after all these years, I do one or two books a month for *O,* where she is a senior editor with responsibility for books and many other things. I laid claim to the Colm Toibin novel as soon as I heard about it: it's a novel about Henry James, whom I love and about whom I'd written before, and Toibin himself is one of the most distinguished and interesting writers among a wonderfully large group of interesting writers who have spoken to us from Ireland over the last ten or fifteen years. I particularly admired *The Heather Blazing,* an early novel of Toibin's which I mention in the piece reprinted here.

The process of writing such a piece is at once simple and very obscure. Everything one does for a monthly magazine is rushed—more rushed than for a weekly or a daily, for peculiar reasons I can't really describe. Since I live in New York City, the books are messengered uptown to my apartment; I have about a week or ten days to read them and write a piece. That's not bad for one book, but if I'm doing two, which usually I am, it's the same time span. *The Master* was not a short book; I read it as quickly as I could. I don't very often take notes, though if I do, it will be a lead sentence that comes to mind while I'm reading; when I'm finished I'll have to see if that idea for a lead still holds up. The lead sentence is everything: it provides the angle and direction of the piece's movement and the momentum to take it to its conclusion. What most fascinates me about Henry James are his later years and his later work, which is notoriously difficult and wordy, isolating small moments of human interaction and dissecting them in their finest particulars. Fortunately, Toibin's fictional account of James' life also focused on the later years. That gave me a "subject," as it were. The piece, to do what I wanted it to do, needed a lead that would swiftly put across some notions introducing the reader to the issue of James' later years, notions that would open up into a brief discussion covering both James and Toibin's novel about him.

After that, it's just writing, and we all know how hard that is. Short pieces demand an inordinate amount of editing. Often we need to land on exact word count or very close to it (smart type/layout designers using good software can adjust for some overage by shrinking the spaces between words, fooling with small things like commas to pull up a word onto a previous line, gaining you slightly more space). But *Oprah Magazine* really cares about the quality of the prose and the depth of the ideas, so even as we cut things out (working together on the phone usually) we try to find some way to slip a key word or phrase back in elsewhere, where it won't need a whole sentence to support it. For instance, in this piece, you will a see a phrase about James, saying he "was incurably a celibate." This is a point of some controversy in James scholarship, whether he ever had a full-fledged romance with anyone. Toibin's novel (quite rightly, in my view) comes down on the side that he didn't; that he brushed along the sides of love but never met it face on. My original draft noted Toibin's distinct choice. We had to cut that sentence (perhaps it was even two sentences), but then we put in the word "incurably" in order to hint at the importance and conflict behind that issue. I enjoy re-reading the pieces I've written for *O,* because short pieces with real content are the tightest writing around.

---

*Vince Passaro's review of a Henry James biography for *Oprah Magazine* may be read later in this chapter.

Reviews do not readily lend themselves to formats or patterns. Critics may review works differently when they know their subject matter—when they have prepared themselves to be critics through education, reading, and viewing, and mastering books, music, cinema or theater.

Major newspapers, magazines and television stations have critics who review the arts for their readers and viewers. Many are freelance writers. Especially is this true on smaller newspapers, magazines or television stations. Having secured a position as a freelance critic, you might be called upon to "write a couple of paragraphs" about, say, the country music festival that night at the municipal auditorium.

"But I don't know anything about country music!" you protest.

"Just go there and act like a reporter," Cedric Parker, the editor, replies. "Tell what happened and how the crowd reacted to it."

With trepidation, you cover the performance. You write a reportorial review.

The Reportorial Review

Audience reaction usually forms the lead element in a reportorial review. A prototype of the reportorial review:

Open with a paragraph describing the crowd's reaction to the performance. Describe the program and the artists' performance and the crowd's reaction to various portions of it. End with a concluding paragraph highlighting the general feeling generated by the performance.

Pseudo Book Reviews

Akin to the reportorial review are the pseudo-reviews of new books being published widely today in newspapers. The review reads like a feature until the middle or the last few paragraphs. (I'm tempted to label them feature reviews.) The reader then discovers that the material comes from a book just published. An example is this pseudo-review based on Maggie Scarf's *Intimate Partners: Partners in Love and Marriage.*

"After the Marriage: The Masks Come Off"

By Vanessa W. Snyder
Gannett News Service, July 11, 1993

The peeling of the mask. That's what I call it.

It's the moment he lays back on the couch, slips his hand inside his pants and does his Al Bundy imitation.

Or perhaps it's the moment she feels comfortable enough to flatulate openly, without as much as a blush.

That's when you know you've started to peel back a piece of the mask.

What mask?

This big one. The pre-marital, I'm perfect, everything you want mask, of course.

Let's face it. Before marriage—and even as newlyweds—we wear masks to disguise those annoying habits.

Here's a few (from an informal random sampling):

— Falling asleep while I'm talking

— Making a slurping noise while eating soup or other liquid food

— Shaking ice in a cup incessantly

— Getting up in the middle of the night to go to the bathroom at least three times ("And I'm a light sleeper!")

— Dropping body powder all over the dressing table

Why do we hide these lovely personality traits?

Well, obviously you won't impress most people with the above habits, but beyond that, what's the big deal?

It's all about living up to the illusion, according to Maggie Scarf, author of *Intimate Partners: Patterns in Love and Marriage* (Ballantine Books, $4.95).

"We're really putting our best foot forward. If he says you're the most wonderful person in the world, you're trying to live up to that. There's a tremendous amount of idealization going on," she says.

But at some point the masks do come off and there's some disillusionment.

And while time has a way of making us less rigid, negotiation is the key in preventing these little things from turning into major problems.

You can understand how attractive this feature material is to a critic or a freelance writer. The reviews are so relatively easy to write (no research here) that you're persuaded to be put on a book publisher's reviewer list. Here is another pseudo-review:

"You Know He's a Keeper, You Know He's a Loser"

By John Boudreau
Knight Ridder News Service, March 4, 2004

It's easier to recognize a diamond once you've known a lump of coal. The handsome, sweet date did everything right—up until he admitted to his nightly abductions by space aliens.

Then there's the supportive boyfriend who loaned his girlfriend money so she could fly across the country to attend the funeral of her grandfather—then charged her interest.

And how about the guy who showed up for the first date with only a dollar in his pocket—and asked if his date had any money.

These tales from the dating front lines, as told by women, are detailed in *You Know He's a Keeper, You Know He's a Loser: Happy Endings and Horror Stories from Real-Life Relationships* (Pedigree, $12.95), by Linda Lee Small and Norine Dworkin.

The book underscores the axiom known to all who are engaged in the mating dance: You don't know how weird someone is until you date him (or her).

The book focuses on the stories of women because women talk about these things, Dworkin says. Male friends have asked her why she hasn't written about the sometimes clueless and strange behaviors of women.

Everyone we have talked to in the business says guys don't buy these books, the author explains.

The book isn't about bashing men, though Dworkin concedes it was easier to find "loser" tales than "keeper" anecdotes from women around the country, for helping sort out the good from the bad and the ugly.

"I'm sure guys are hungry for this information," she says. "Guys say they aren't sure what women want. Well, here you have close to 200 women basically laying out the qualities that make for a keeper guy and a loser guy.

"The writers interviewed strangers, friends and friends of friends of friends."

"I got a lot of my girlfriends to throw mini cocktail parties and brunches," Dworkin says. "We just got the girls talking. The women would just go on and on and on."

The writer was surprised that not one person said she looked for wealth in a man.

"Money was never mentioned by women regarding what makes a guy a keeper," she says, "No one said, 'My guy is a keeper because he's loaded.'"

In fact, women look for a different kind of generosity.

"One woman told us the story about her husband," Dworkin says. "He's a car aficionado. He dotes on every car. He names them, polishes them. They are like children to him. But she always gets into an accident with his car. And he never gets upset. He always says 'Are you OK? We can fix the car.'"

Conversely, the men who quickly end up in the loser column display a "stinginess of personality," she says. "It's this feeling that you don't matter."

One woman recalled a ski trip date. She had explained she wasn't a very good skier and didn't want to go down a challenging run. He promised he'd help her, and then abandoned her. Another woman dished about a similar situation. But her man carried her down the mountain—on his back.

The book, Dworkin says, is also a reminder to women like herself. She just got engaged.

"Having dated all these losers, once you find your gem, you really appreciate him. Expect happy endings with this Romeo."

What makes him a keeper:

He takes an interest in something solely because it interests his woman.

He's generous with his time and affection. Taking care of his sweetie when she's sick rates high.

Does the little things that make her feel special, such as buying her—unbidden—a telephone headset so she doesn't have to cradle the phone all the time and get a sore neck.

Even letting her pick the snacks at a movie shows a generosity of spirit and emotions.

He doesn't have to throw his money around but shows a willingness to pay for the meal.

An example of the more general and authoritative book review of a biography of novelist and critic Henry James is this one by Vince Passaro:

"Portrait of a Writer: An Indelibly Beautiful Novel Gets Inside the Mind of Henry James"*

By Vince Passaro

Although he was known to younger admirers as The Master, Henry James was little read in his later years, and he battled melancholy, solitude, and public neglect with a fervor that produced, in his last novels and stories, some of English literature's most remarkably nuanced masterpieces. *The Master* (Scribner), Irish writer Colm Toibin's fifth novel, gorgeously animates these years of James's life—holding our attention not through plot, for a writer's life rarely has much plot, but with the heartbreaking conflicts of James's psychological paradoxes. James was relentlessly social (you see him here at the dinners and balls, among the aristocracy, observant, witty, wise), but he was perennially lonely. He yearned for intimacy, and he was filled with desire: in fact he practically trembled with it, a condition he could capture in his fiction in a way more explicit writers never can, but he was incurably a celibate. He was warm and generous of spirit but ultimately unapproachable—all of which Toibin weaves into his story with seeming ease. There is a tragedy of human genius at the heart of James's life that has driven Toibin to write a beautiful and profoundly sympathetic novel. *The Master* is comparable to Michael Cunningham's *The Hours*, though not as narratively complex: It is about a writer and it is about literature itself, its grue-some cost and its near-divine grandeur. Toibin's own best prior novel, *The Heather Blazing*, is a most Jamesian book, subtle, silent, lovely, and immensely, almost blindingly painful; it concerns Ireland's long-delayed passage into modernity. Here Toibin recalls what it was like for a supreme writer of English prose to make that same passage, late in life, with mastery, and we are moved by it.

---

*O, The Oprah Magazine, V (June 2004), 144.

In the following review, Whitney Weeks, well versed on "chick lit" literature, com-ments first on the "chick lit" novel, outlining what's needed to meet the criteria of "chick lit," setting the scene for the ensuing evaluation.

"On Carrie Gerlach's 'Chick Lit' Novel"

By Whitney Weeks
The Tennessean, August 7, 2004

A chick lit novel must meet certain requirements including a heart-broken female protagonist actively seeking love in all the wrong places.

She must find a way to mention her weight, her favorite type of vodka and her signature Starbucks drink in at least one conversation each day. Her life should include a great career, two always-there gal pals and one fabulous gay guy who has nothing better to do than dote on his single, straight friend.

Though Carrie Gerlach's debut novel, *Emily's Reasons Why Not*, meets the technical requirements for the genre, it rarely moves beyond the most predictable situations and characters.

The flat storyline is especially disappointing given the novel's clever premise for telling this familiar tale of the pursuit of Prince Charming and Happily Ever After. Rather than follow her from man to man as so many of these sorts of books do, readers learn of Emily's misadventures in lovers as she recounts them during therapy, where she lists reasons why she shouldn't have dated each boyfriend.

Initially readers cheer for a main character brave enough to seek professional help as she struggles to understand why, as a beautiful, successful 30-something, she can't find a good man. But the cheering quickly ends.

Having Emily, in her early 30s, recall her dating misadventures from eight years prior makes it easy for a reader to see how little Gerlach develops her main character. Readers don't understand Emily's misguided quest for the perfect guy any better on Page 200 than they did on Page 2.

As she trades in her stilettos for pumps and her mini skirts for slacks, as her career takes off, as she fulfills her dream of owning a home, her willingness to date increasingly terrible men becomes frustrating rather than entertaining.

Emily's Reasons Why Not captures only moderately well the story of a "single successful woman" trying to figure out how to have it all. Undeveloped characters, a shallow protagonist for whom one has little sympathy, and an unsatisfying ending keeps this novel from standing out among dozens just like it.

Its one redeeming factor is the clever—and accurate—list of reasons why one shouldn't fall for a certain type of guy. For it, and for it alone, Gerlach deserves a toast with one of Emily's Absolut Citron martinis.

The length of a review can vary. The following review is short, sweet and relatively nonjudgmental.

"The Ups and Downs of Motherhood"

Anonymous
The Tennessean, Oct. 28, 2003

Do I want to spend 18 years or more taking care of someone else? Will I regret it if I don't have children? How can I tell if the sacrifices will be worth it to me?

These are the questions many women in their 20s, 30s and even 40s are agonizing over. *Do I Want to Be a Mom? (Contemporary Books/McGraw-Hill, October 2003, $14.95 hardcover)* offers information from the doctors, psychiatrists and other women who write about their experiences of motherhood or being childfree.

On Broadway (and elsewhere in the reviewing field), how much leeway does the experienced reviewer have? Jeff Baenen gives us an idea.

"Flying the Not-So-Friendly Skies"

By Jeff Baenen
The Associated Press, March 11, 2004

Do you have raspberry-kiwi iced tea?

Has anyone ever said you look like Monica Lewinsky?

Who's flying the plane?

Do you have a place where I can put my cheesecake?

Passengers have asked these and many other questions of Rene Foss as she scurried to fetch drinks, hand out their pretzels and pick up their garbage.

Foss, a second-generation flight attendant, has taken her 19 years of experience and turned it into a hilarious one-woman play and book, *Around the World in a Bad Mood* (subtitled *Confessions of a Flight Attendant*).

Foss still works at Northwest Airlines, where she started flying in 1985. She's quick to say that the airline of her play and book, WAFTI ("We Apologize For This Inconvenience Airlines") is not based on any specific carrier. She wears nondescript uniforms while performing and does not mention Northwest in the book or play.

"It's really a commentary on air travel in general," she says.

Flying these days isn't the same as it was when Foss' mother, Maxyne, worked as a stewardess for Northwest Orient Airlines in the 1950's. Flying then was considered a luxury; Rene Foss calls it the golden age of air travel.

"Instead of wearing white gloves, we're wearing rubber gloves. Instead of serving lobster thermidor, we're learning to put handcuffs on people. And instead of practicing the art of polite conversation, we're practicing the art of self-defense and disease control," Foss says.

On stage, Foss is a dynamic performer, throwing herself from a frenzied "safety demo" pantomime that opens the show to different skits that feature her as a flight attendant training supervisor with an accent straight out of *Fargo* or as a gun-toting pilot with a Southern drawl.

In one sketch, Foss uses puppets made of barf bags to reenact *Macbeth* as a comic duel between two passengers warring for the same first-class seat.

Foss, who stands 5 feet, 4 inches, hasn't had to cuff any unruly passengers in her career. But she understands how crowded airports, long lines and increased security can try passengers' patience.

"So you kind of get on the plane and you are hungry and you are tired," she says. "And now we don't even really serve food anymore.

"That's when passengers end up in a bad mood," she says. "And then the flight's full and there's no room to put your bag on because you're the last passenger, and then we're going to take away your bag and check it. And then the only seats left are center seats. And, well, 'Welcome aboard!'"

After Foss graduated from the University of Minnesota in 1984, her dad encouraged her to get a job with benefits. But Foss, who grew up in the Minneapolis suburb of Edina, had acting ambitions and set her sights on Broadway or Hollywood. The solution: a flight attendant's job that allowed her to live in New York.

She thought she could quit in six months. "Of course, 19 years later I'm still picking up garbage on the airplane," she says.

Foss says she was so down and out that she was ready to give up and move back home to Minnesota. But she decided to write a play and star in it, and chose flight attendants as her subject.

"I would be an expert, and I would know how to play that role because I've been doing it" she says. Foss got her actor friends to come over, and with piano player Michael McFrederick writing the music, came up with a five-actor revue. *Around the World in a Bad Mood!*—featuring songs about the safety demo and greeting passengers—debuted at a New York cabaret in 1998.

A *New York Times* article about the play caught the attention of Hyperion Books, which approached Foss about writing a book, which was published in 2002.

Meanwhile, Richard Frankel Productions, a producer of such Broadway hits as *Hairspray* and *The Producers,* suggested Foss trim her five-actor play to a one-woman show. She did, and now Foss plans to take her show to Los Angeles. She hopes it becomes a franchised theater piece and dreams of a TV sitcom. She also would like to do a sequel to the book.

"Instead of *My Big Fat Greek Wedding,* maybe it'll be *My Big Fat Airline Career,*" she says.

Entertainment Weekly magazine, after a lengthy review of a major music album, usually presents brief music reviews of a multitude of albums. Here's one:

"Telefon Tel Aviv: Map of What Is Effortless (Hefty)"*

Loneliness, loss, and the darker side of soul music are the subjects of Telefon Tel Aviv's second album, a stunning collision of techno blips, lush strings, and swooning R&B vocals. Though the mood is unsettling; it works as an apt metaphor for the decaying of male-female relationships. Not only for the broken-hearted, this is computer-driven soul for anyone who's spent too many nights in front of a flickering monitor: B+ —*ME*

———
*Entertainment Weekly, Feb. 13, 2004, 72.

The wide array of reviews presented gives you an idea of how to go about reviewing. One last word. How harshly the reviewer criticizes the work depends on whether the artists are amateurs or professionals. A circle theater group in University City would not be expected to attain a level of performance comparable to that of a professional troupe from New York or London.

SUMMARY

Definitive guidelines for writing commentary (editorials, columns, essays, reviews) are nice to have around when you first start out. Collect facts, ideas and thoughts you want to include in your work. Devote time to reviewing them and establishing their importance. Compose an outline.

If you're writing in the persuasive mode, and until you feel more comfortable writing in this mode, you may want to follow this four-part formula:

1. An introduction to the issue and your stance
2. Arguments in support of your position
3. Arguments in opposition to your position and a refutation of them
4. A reaffirmation of the stance taken in the opening paragraphs—but in different words.

With other categories of commentary, informative and interpretive, you may want to approach them with the reader interest plane in mind.

After outlining your commentary, write the first draft and revise according to the suggestions in this text. When writing a review, until you feel more comfortable without it, keep the review format in mind. A good way to learn how to write reviews is to study those reviewers who are generally considered to be the best in their fields.

COMMENTARIES FOR DISCUSSION

A. "Look Who's Taking on Bullies!"

By Craig Wilson
USA Today, Oct. 2, 2002

I haven't watched the Miss America pageant in years. I couldn't tell you last year's winner if you threatened me with a can of hairspray.

I'm not even sure if Miss America still has two first names. When I was growing up, she always did. You know, Vonda Kay, Laurie Lea. That kind of thing. She also usually came from places like Oklahoma and Mississippi. Big-hair country. And every last one of them wanted world peace.

So I was pleasantly surprised last week to see the newest Miss America making her rounds, talking about a different kind of peace. One more local than Baghdad or Tel Aviv.

She comes with the no-nonsense name of Erika Harold. She also comes from Illinois, a state not known for its hair. Not that she doesn't have nice hair. From her photo it looks like she does. It's just not Miss America hair.

But what intrigues me most about her is that her platform isn't literacy or saving the humpback whales. It's bullies.

She says she's going to spend her year as Miss America preaching against school violence, taking on good old-fashioned bullies. Her goal is to have every state pass anti-harassment laws for schools. At the moment, only 12 have them.

Harold says this is a natural for her. She was picked on in school because of her race. She's of mixed black, Native American and European heritage, and obviously she has not forgotten the harassment she received at school back in Urbana, Ill.

Millions of us have bullies in our past. I remember mine all too well. The ones who would bump into me in the hallway for no reason; the ones who would lurk, saying nothing because they didn't have to; the ones I didn't want to be left alone with for very long.

But one incident stands out. I was walking home from school into town, most likely to catch a ride home after missing the bus. I was with a friend when suddenly, from behind the stone war memorial monument in the town park, sprang two guys from school.

I don't know why they jumped me. I didn't really get the chance to ask. Maybe I was too bookish. Maybe because I was small and easy prey. Perhaps they knew before I did that I was "different," though anything out of the very narrow mainstream was considered different in those days. The wrong shoes made you different. Even the way you carried your books could brand you as bully material.

But I can remember it as if it were yesterday. One of them picked me up by the waist and twirled me around for what seemed an eternity. The other one knocked the books out of my hand. My friend probably was as embarrassed for me as she was scared.

I was lucky. They fled when a car slowed down and the driver yelled for them to stop. I picked up my books, collected what was left of my pride and shuffled on. I never mentioned it to my parents.

I'm old enough now to know that help often arrives in the most unlikely of packages. But little did I know then that one day, 40 years down the road, Miss America would be the one to come to the rescue.

Good for her.

B. "Splits-ville for Live-ins: Who Gets the Property?"

By Sharon Jayson
Gannet News Services, June 9, 2006

When couples who live together call it quits, it's not just the end of a relationship.

"Every part of your life is going to be affected by it: financially, socially, psychologically, emotionally," says Kate Wachs, a Chicago psychologist. "In the context of your world, it's a shakeup of your entire life."

The scenario depicted in the new movie "The Break Up" is increasingly common, say relationship experts who work with cohabiting couples such as Gary and Brooke, played by Vince Vaughn and Jennifer Aniston.

Almost 4.9 million unmarried opposite-sex couples lived under the same roof in 2005, according to U.S. Census data released last month.

Some see marriage ahead, relationship experts say. Others view cohabiting as temporary. Some live together to save on housing costs.

In the movie, Gary and Brooke have lived together for two years—one of the common relationship stress points, relationship experts say. They have bought a condo together, without a living together contract dividing assets. When their romance implodes, neither wants to move out.

Ann Rosen Spector, a clinical psychologist in Philadelphia, says cohabiting relationships often dissolve later than they should because the partners have a hard time letting go.

"They have a huge sense of loss, not only of the relationship but the dream of what might have been," she says.

The "anti-romantic comedy" illustrates a relationship unraveling as the couple becomes embroiled in arguments that sometimes lead to outlandish behavior.

Part of the couple's trouble stem from Brooke's desire to have Gary help out at home, a fairly typical situation, according to Charles Hill, a psychology professor at Whittier College in Whittier, Calif.

"If you're not living together, it's a lot easier to be equal," he says. "But if you're living together you're faced with certain tasks and decisions: the laundry, the dishes, scrubbing toilets, how to decide these things."

So at the point when breaking up is inevitable, that joint property ownership, as the movie shows, is the tie most difficult to undo, says Sharyn Sooho, an attorney in Newton, Mass., who has practiced family law for 30 years.

"Living together is not the big issue," she says. "It's acquiring property together and, maybe one party giving up a career to be a stay-at-home partner. If you're just moving into an apartment and signing a lease together—while there are some serious consequences—it's not as difficult to untangle.

"But if you're buying a condominium or a house or promising to support someone else," Sooho says, "you may want to think about calling a lawyer."

Plenty of web sites offer one size fits all contracts for cohabiting couples, which Sooho says work fine in some situations.

But Los Angeles attorney Mark Barondess, who handles plenty of cohabiting break ups, says such "boiler plate agreements" often don't work.

Live-in situations are so different from one another that a lawyer is often needed to get through the rough spots, he says.

Still Barondess says, unmarried couples who split have fewer problems than divorcing couples do.

"When you say 'I do,' all the rules change."

C. "Something About Christmas Ornaments"

By John Sergeant
The Tennessean, Dec. 23, 2003

Last week, for the 39th time, Carole and I decorated our Christmas tree. It's always special with the smell of the tree somehow canceling out the knowledge that by the time Christmas is over, we will be all too happy to lug it down to the recycling pickup area and get our house back to normal.

Christmas trees are one of a number of pagan practices that were absorbed into Christianity. In what is now Germany and in other parts of Europe, the practice of celebrating the winter solstice by brightening up the house with greenery was commonplace. When the area became Christianized, this tradition was adopted by the new religion. And although it's nice to have a religious connotation, the fact that the days are getting longer and spring isn't too far away is worth celebration in is own right.

So following first our pagan and then our Christian ancestors, Carole and I strung the lights on the tree, put a rather whimsical angel on top, then began putting on the ornaments.

One by one we pulled them out, dusted them off and paused to remember the story behind each. Most of our older ones were handmade, for reasons both personal and financial. We re-told the story of every one, thinking of friends, some from as far back as my internship year, whom we now remember only with the annual Christmas cards.

There were ornaments given to us by friends and relatives who have died, and each of those received a special place on the tree. There were ornaments representing weddings, the births of grandchildren and family vacations.

When we finished, our tree was a splish-splash of colors and decorations, but we decided it was perfect, although looking at all of those ornaments suddenly made us realize how much we've aged in nearly 40 years of marriage.

The process of aging is so gradual that we almost don't notice it. I know that the connective tissues around my joints get a little bit stiffer every day, that my maximum attainable heart rate declines in a straight line fashion year by year, that my ability to exercise and consume oxygen falls a tiny amount daily and I can't prevent it.

If you don't believe it, check the world records for the mile run or the marathon by age group.

So we merrily go along, skin sagging and hair graying each day by such a miniscule difference that we don't think about aging much at all. Then we do something like trimming a Christmas tree, and all those memories come flooding in.

For a while it seems almost more than we can stand—the dear friends, our wonderful grandchildren, the Christmases when we couldn't afford it but bought a tree just the same.

With all of those thoughts, the fact that we have aged is suddenly undeniable. Full of nostalgia, we think for a moment about how much we would like to have those years—and those friends and relatives—with us again.

It can't happen, of course, and we soon turn our thoughts to other matters. Before we know it we are getting out the toys for grandson Henry to play with when he comes the next day to be joined soon by his cousins Kathryn and Emmaline.

In this joyous anticipation—our aging doesn't seem so bad after all, less a curse than a blessing. We are at peace. Merry Christmas.

If you were to suggest revisions in the commentary, what would they be? In the next feature, commentary will, once again, be provided.

D. "Hoping to Avoid Divorce?"

By Laura Meckler
The Associated Press, July 25, 2002

WASHINGTON—Hoping to avoid divorce? It helps if you're wealthy, religious, college-educated and at least 20 years old when you tie the knot. Couples who don't

The opening paragraph, although not the author's intention, is crammed with data, heralding what the remainder of the article will be. The reader wonders, Where's all this stuff coming from? In the next paragraph, buried under still more "stuff," she or he will find out.

Rather than burying the source of the survey under data, the second paragraph should state forthrightly that this important governmental survey of 11,000 women was conducted by Centers for Disease Control and Prevention (CDC).

As it is, this CDC information is found in the fifth paragraph, far too removed from the opening paragraph. And the next few paragraphs, the developing paragraphs, simply ply the reader with more data rather than engage in a coherent development of the theme of the article.

The next paragraphs are generating paragraphs, generating increasing interest in the article up to the climactic paragraphs. Incidentally, the paragraph quoting Cohen has two attributions—one attribution per paragraph is the rule.

live together before marriage have a better shot at staying together, as do those whose parents stayed married.

By age 30, three in four women have been married, but many of those unions dissolve. Overall, 43% of marriages break up within 15 years, according to a government survey of 11,000 women that offers the most detailed look at cohabitation, marriage and divorce ever produced.

Black women are least likely to marry and most likely to divorce with more than half splitting within 15 years. Asian marriages are the most stable with whites and Hispanics in between.

Women are waiting longer to get married than they used to, and after a divorce they are less likely to remarry than women once were. At the same time, couples are more likely to live together without getting married. Half of U.S. women had lived with a partner by the time they turned 30.

The survey, released yesterday by the Centers for Disease Control and Prevention, found that 70% of those who lived together for at least 5 years did eventually walk down the aisle.

These marriages are also more likely to break up. After 10 years, 40% of couples that had lived together before marriage had broken up. That compares with 31% of those who did not live together first.

That's partly because people who choose to live together tend to be younger, less religious or have other qualities that put them at risk for divorce, said Catherine Cohen, assistant professor of human development and family studies at Penn State University. That may not fully explain it, she said.

"Many people enter a cohabiting relationship when the deal is, 'If this doesn't work out, we can split up and it's no big loss because we don't have a legal commitment,'" she said. "The commitment is tenuous, and that tenuous commitment might carry over into marriage."

The report, based on 1995 data, found other groups facing a high risk of divorce, including:

Young People

Nearly half of those who marry under age 18 and 40% under age 20 get divorced. Over age 25, it's just 24%. The difference is maturity, says Chicago psychologist Kate Wachs.

"A lot of young people focus on right now, and if I'm not happy right now, I should get divorced," said Wachs, author of *Relationships for Dummies*. Older people have more life experience, he said, and realize "if I hang in there, it will probably get better."

Non-religious People

Of those who don't affiliate with any religious group, 46% were divorced within 10 years.

Children of Divorce

Women whose parents were divorced are significantly more likely to divorce themselves, with 43% splitting after 10 years. Among those whose parents stayed together, the divorce rate was just 29%.

"You may have had a good model for conflict resolution," Cohen said. Or, she said, parents have taught their kids that "sticking to a marriage is important and divorce is bad."

Kids

Half of women who had kids before marriage were divorced in 10 years. Nearly as many couples who never had kids also wound up divorced.

Across the board, black women were less likely to marry and more likely to divorce. By age 30, 82% of white women have been married vs. 52% of black women.

The report suggests part of the problem is a lack of men in the "marriageable pool," with disproportionate numbers of black men unemployed or incarcerated. People with low incomes are also less likely to marry, and blacks tend to have lower incomes.

> As you can see, what could have been climactic paragraphs has degenerated into a listing of categories factoring into divorce. The concluding paragraph tapers off into still more data. Not much lingering impression there.

You have no doubt noted how Laura Meckler failed to handle this similar subject matter and material as adroitly as Mona Charen. What is it exactly that Meckler fails to do in this regard? Does the commentary in this feature ring true?

EXERCISES

1. Write a letter to the editor of your hometown newspaper on some topic of your own choosing. Use the persuasive format. (Or do exercise 2 instead.)

2. Write a letter to the editor of your hometown newspaper blaming women for the state of affairs in this country: They refuse to insist upon their rights for equal representation in our local, state and federal governments and elsewhere and for at least four justices on the Supreme Court instead of one. (Women make up 52% of the population.) Use the persuasive format. No difference in the structure or language should be evident. Incidentally, this topic guarantees publication.

3. Select one good and one poor example of an editorial, a column, an essay or a review. Paste them on a page and write a brief paragraph explaining why each is good or poor.

4. Write a commentary based on one of these brief news items (or a news item of your own choosing):
   a. Dear Abby:
      I need your help dealing with my ex-girlfriend, "Ashley." We were together off and on for 2½ years and lived together for a year. It was a new experience for both of us.

      About a year into our relationship, Ashley decided she wasn't sure that what we had was what she wanted anymore. I was OK with it. We split up for four or five months, and then we started talking and decided to try again. About three months later, she did the same thing.

      It has now been another three months, and supposedly she has a new boyfriend, but she's calling me. I love her and would do anything for her, but I just don't know what to do anymore. My romance with Ashley has caused a lot of arguments between me and my parents. Any advice would help.
      —Hurting in Pasadena
      Dear Hurting:
      Ashley appears to be too immature and indecisive for a serious commitment to anyone— her current boyfriend included. If it's love you're looking for, she isn't the girl who can provide it. The best advice I can offer is to admire her from a safe distance. She's a heartbreaker.
      Abigail Van Buren, *"Dear Abby," March 18, 2004*

b. Television viewers will be in for some unpleasant surprises in the coming year. TV producers are being pressured by advertisers to insert commercials in much the same way it is now being done in England. What this means is that in the middle of a discussion on what to do about Ruth Ann's impending crisis, the doctor may ask her if that aroma of Tastee Freeze Coffee isn't the best thing that's happened to her this morning and then invite her to have a cup. Filled to the brim.

5. Select a segment of Meckler's article on divorce (item D) and write a column about it.

6. Select an experience from your life that can be used in a reflective essay such as May Sarton's: perhaps it's a divorce you've endured or a friend's parents divorce, or the loss of a friend or of love, or even a search for identity or values.

7. Use May Sarton's article on solitude as a launching pad or explanation for the current widespread use of cell phones.

8. Write a review of a movie or a play. Compare it with a critic's review. How does it differ? Why? Are some comments in your review superior to the critic's?

CHAPTER 7

THE ART OF WRITING

The Echo of Words

> There is no conceivable
>   beauty of blossom
>   so beautiful as words—
>   none so graceful,
>   none so perfumed.
> —Thomas Wentworth Higginson

ASPIRING TO THE LEVEL OF POETRY

Writing is an art that requires not only a profound knowledge of the craft that goes into it, but discipline. With so much information moving over the wires and through communication satellites, editors are under tremendous pressure to select the most lively and significant fraction of available features, articles and commentary. As a consequence, freelance writers must develop ideas with succinct, varied and vivid phrasing.

We would like our words to move our loves and the masses, to approach a level of music from violins that will soar our readers to the heavens. But, alas, more often than not,

being poor mortals that we are, we produce jangles from banjos suitable only for clogging. What must we do to create a melodious composition, a symphony of sound? We will seek the answers to that question in this chapter.

DISCIPLINE

In an *Atlantic Monthly* article, Wallace Stegner, the great poet and novelist, wrote:

To a Young Writer

> For one thing, you never took writing to mean self-expression, which means self-indulgence. You understood from the beginning that writing is done with words and sentences, and you spent hundreds of hours educating your ear, writing and rewriting until you began to handle words in combination as naturally as one changes tones with the tongue and lips in whistling. I speak respectfully of this part of your education because every year I see students who will not submit to it—who have only themselves to say and who are bent upon saying it without concessions to the English language. In acknowledging that the English language is a difficult instrument, and that a person who sets out to use it expertly has no alternative but to learn it, you did something else: you forced yourself away from that obsession with self that is the strength of very few writers and the weakness of so many. You have labored to put yourself in charge of your material: you have not fallen for the romantic fallacy that it is virtue to be driven by it. By submitting to language you submitted to other disciplines, you learned distance and detachment; you learned how to avoid muddying a story with yourself.

> *The Atlantic Monthly* II (November 1959), 89.

The discipline that Stegner describes will do other things for you. Most writing experiences follow this pattern: Something happens that stirs your emotions or intellect. Perhaps you hear a sad call of a rain crow, view the soaring flight of a hawk, stumble upon a vine of wild roses or hear a familiar song on a radio. You want to describe that experience and your reactions to it. Whether your imagination is primarily auditory (stimulated by the ear) or visual (stimulated by the eye), these sparks ignite emotions, memories and thoughts that move you into a state of meditation that is preliminary to the writing stage.

In this meditation—a groping full of false starts and glimmerings of inspiration, a searching for relationships between thoughts—your ideas may be expanded by more illustrations, examples and incidents. Revelations follow that explore the significance of your initial experience more fully. While this is going on, you are also forming a rough image, a silhouette of how all this could be written.

The meditation may occur at any time or place—while you're bathing, applying mascara, shaving, driving an automobile or waiting in a ticket line. (James Thurber never quite knew when he wasn't "writing" in this fashion.) How do you harness this creativity? Through discipline.

The power of your words corresponds directly to your command of the English language. Knowledge of the craft of writing alerts you to, among other things, the value of active verbs and imagery and to "showing" rather than "telling." *The New Yorker*'s top writers and editors, discussing how their magazine's style of writing evolved,* observed that they drew heavily

---

*From "Made-up Stories," *The New Yorker* (June 27–July 4, 1994), 6.

from the techniques of fiction—"the setting of scenes, the delineation of character, the unfolding of narrative"—and that their reporting aspired to the level of literature.

Your writing, at the very least, should aspire to the level of literature. Not only are all of the techniques just mentioned within your grasp, in the following pages you will also become acquainted with even more sophisticated fiction and nonfiction skills and techniques, such as objective correlatives and wedding sense to sound.

What is this sense/sound thing? Briefly, here, more later:

"The sound must seem an echo to the sense," Alexander Pope, the English poet, noted. Novelist Henry James' words echo Pope's: The substance of what you're saying must be wedded to the form (the sentence or paragraph) in which you're saying it. How important is this "sound"? The words to "Somewhere Over the Rainbow" were written by E. Y. Harburg. Harold Arlen took those words and blended them to music that has transported us all "Over the Rainbow." The sound of Arlen's music conveyed the sense of what the lyricist Harburg wrote.

What does this "sound" require of you, the writer? When you're writing, you might think about how your words would sound with the lilt of piano keys or the strumming of a guitar. Perhaps, like music, the writing we are striving for must be composed by ear and feeling, and sometime with a flight of imagination akin to fantasy. Since poetry is the highest form of literature, perhaps we should endeavor to write as poetically as our subject matter and readers allow.

When you assimilate all these techniques, and your writing embraces the craft of fiction and poetry, you will not only enthrall your readers, you will have found your place among the elite of media communicators.

VARIATIONS IN SENTENCE PATTERNS

For now, however, let's start at a very humdrum beginning. The sentence, nevertheless, is a very good place to start.

No matter what the subject matter or what a freelancer's area of expertise, all writers rely on basic rules of sentence structure. Nothing labels writing "elementary" more clearly than a series of subject-verb sentences strung together. Within the subject-verb construction are these variations:

> *Subject + verb + object:*
> She served the dessert.
> *Subject + indirect object + object:*
> He served her breakfast.
> *Subject + predicate:*
> He was an angry fool.

Though they appear to be different in complexity, all three sentences start with subjects (nouns) and are followed by verbs. They can be called "loose" sentences. While there's nothing wrong with using this "safe" construction—perhaps 90 percent of all sentences written follow this pattern—when they are strung haphazardly together, with little thought to the effect they create or to the relationships of the ideas in them, they can be repetitious. And boring.

They lack rhythm or flow.
They are short, choppy things.
They hit like a hammer.
They dull the senses.
They try readers' patience.

Notice how wearying the last five sentences are. They include only four or five words—elementary lengths. Your readers deserve more intelligent passages. If you don't render them, your readers will leave you for another feature or article or another form of mass media.

How can you vary your sentence patterns to enliven your writing?

1. Reverse the order. You can vary the subject-verb pattern by reversing the order. Begin with a verb: "Strive for sentences that flow." The subject in that sentence (you) is understood. It need not be stated. Most questions reverse the subject-verb order: Are your sentences varied? Do you now utilize questions in your writing? Used judiciously, questions can be effective.

2. Place the object first. You may vary the pattern by placing the object first: "That article's been revised five times."

3. Use intervening phrases and clauses. Although you essentially repeat the subject-verb pattern when you place a phrase or clause between the subject and the verb, the variation is so radical that you effect a pattern change: "The sentences, lacking rhythm and flow, are short, choppy things."

4. Use phrases and clauses at the beginning. To change the pattern completely, however, you can place the intervening phrase or clause at the beginning, like this: "Lacking rhythm and flow, the sentences are short, choppy things."

5. Combine the offending series of sentences. One of the obvious ways of varying a series of choppy sentences is to combine them. Look, once again, at the five sentences we are discussing:

1. They lack rhythm or flow.
2. They are short, choppy things.

3. They hit like a hammer.
4. They dull the senses.
5. They try readers' patience.

Some of the statements made in these sentences are more important than others. Yet, in their subject-verb constructions, they all appear equally important. All are independent clauses—they can stand by themselves and make sense. But if some statements are more important than others, why not relegate them to a less important status? Why not reduce them to phrases or dependent clauses? When you do that, the more important statements will receive more emphasis.

Look at the first two sentences: "They lack rhythm or flow." "They are short, choppy things." The second sentence is more emphatic or important than the first. Revise to reflect that importance by uniting the sentences: "Lacking rhythm or flow, the sentences are short, choppy things." The first sentence has been reduced to a participial phrase and introduces the second sentence, which now contrasts a phrase that suggests rhythm and flow—"Lacking rhythm or flow" (note the even beat and pleasant sound)—with a phrase that doesn't have any flow or pleasantness to its sound: "short, choppy things." (You've wedded the sense of what you're saying to the sound of how you said it! Just like that!) The grammatically necessary comma after "short" emphasizes the choppiness. The reader must pause in this sentence yet one more time.

Now let's look at the third, fourth and fifth sentences:

3. They hit like a hammer.
4. They dull the senses.
5. They try readers' patience.

All three are related to effect. Why not combine them into one sentence? How would you do that? Play around with different combinations and wording until you find the one that is just right.

Positions of Emphasis in Sentences

The position of greatest emphasis in a sentence is the end.

Positions of Emphasis:

_____(2)_____(3)_____(1)_____

The least important position (3) is the middle of the sentence. (That's a major reason for burying an attribution.) The least important element should be placed there. Is the statement "They try readers' patience" the least important of the three? Place it in the middle of the sentence. Is the most important statement "They dull the senses"? Place it at the end. That leaves the "hammer" statement for the next most important position at the sentence's beginning: "They pound like a hammer, trying readers' patience and dulling their senses."

In this revision—sentence combining—the opening of the sentence states an action, and the sentence ending emphasizes the most important result of that action. For more descriptive impact, the word "hit" was changed to the more concrete and colorful "pound," a word that seems more appropriate to use with the word "hammer."

Here's what we have just done: We have converted five short, choppy, elementary sentences into two more mature 10- and 12-word sentences. In one case we varied the sentence structure from a subject-verb pattern to an introductory phrase subject-verb pattern. In the other we moved from a subject-verb construction to a subject-verb-modifying phrases construct. What's most important, we combined the sentences to reflect the importance of the statements being made.

Beginning writers tend to write sentences and then act as if they were cast in iron. More experienced writers have little difficulty varying sentence patterns when revising because they realize that nothing is sacrosanct about sentences written in the first draft—or any draft. Most sentences can literally be cut up into words and phrases, put in a cup, shaken up and dropped on a table. Any way they fall, some sense can be made of them.

Take this truncated sentence, the first part of the opening of Charles Dickens' *Tale of Two Cities*: "It was the best of times, it was the worst of times. . . . " You could rewrite it in a number of ways:

1. It was both the best and worst of times.
2. It was the worst and the best of times.
3. The times were both the best and the worst.
4. The best and the worst of times it was.
5. Both the best and the worst of times were embraced by the era.
6. Timewise, it was both the best and the worst.

We have to credit Dickens with having considered some of these alternatives and discarding them in favor of his memorable beginning. Work hard enough at revising your sentences and you will arrive, with a small shock of recognition, at that one best way of phrasing your words for the greatest impression.

The Periodic Sentence

When you shape a sentence, priming it for maximum emphasis by leading up to the most important idea—withholding that idea until the end of the sentence—you create a periodic sentence. (The preceding sentence is an illustration.) You have created suspense and drama for your readers.

Creating a periodic sentence is no little thing. *The Encyclopedia Britannica* will tell you that Isocrates, a famous Greek orator, owes his eminence "to a prose style of his creation, based upon the periodic sentence, and subject to the rules of rhythm comparable to those of verse." Isocrates influenced Cicero and *through him the literature of modern Europe.*

You may be able to write periodic sentences more easily if you think of them in terms of placing the action (or verb) toward the end of the sentence. A prime example of a periodic sentence is this line: "Over the river, and through the woods, to grandmother's house we go." In a periodic sentence, vital information providing most meaning to the sentence is withheld to the end—like the punch line of a joke. (You, no doubt, know some persons who just can't tell jokes. They give the punch line away before the end.) Look at the "Dilbert"

comic strip on page 195. If the last frame of the strip were to come first, the humor of the strip would fall flat. Read it with the last frame first and you'll see what I mean.

To reiterate: The periodic sentence withholds the suspense until the end. The "loose" sentence version of the Thanksgiving Day song would read: "We go to grandmother's house through the woods and over the river." A dull rendering. Do you agree?

In usage then, note that "loose sentences" date practically every paragraph in town. "Periodic sentences" are more discriminating.

On the Use of Attributions

Attributions form an important part of reporting or describing an incident or episode. Readers want to know who said what, and with what degree of conviction. Occasionally, beginning writers believe they must vary the verbs they use in attributions. Although it's important to demonstrate variety in your vocabulary, it's best to use straightforward words for attribution. The all around favorite is "said." If someone is asking a question, however, it's all right to use, "asked." If someone is answering that question, it's all right to say "she answered" or "she replied." But unless someone actually shouts, don't say "he shouted." Unless someone actually makes a declaration, avoid the attribution "she declared" or "stated." Unless someone gives an order, avoid "she commanded."

Here is a list of verbs used for attribution, in order of their intensity (not of popular use), starting from the top-left column and going down, then starting at the top of the next column and working downward again, and so forth.

said	commented	concluded	commanded
added	explained	asserted	shouted
continued	remarked	averred	screamed
replied	suggested	declared	cried
answered	reported	stated	
asked	repeated	exclaimed	

Once again, this list does *not* suggest that variety of attributions should be used. "Said" is the all-around favorite verb to use in attributions.

To recapitulate (and to try your patience while making a point about attributions): The emphatic part of a sentence or a paragraph is the end. Next most important is the beginning. Least important is the middle. What this means is that you guard, zealously and jealously, the beginnings and endings of sentences and paragraphs. Bury unimportant details, attributions and transitions in the middle of sentences and paragraphs.

For example, why say *She said, "Your sentences have no rhythm or flow,"* when you can say *"Your sentences," she said, "have no rhythm or flow."* Placing that attribution inside the direct quotation even adds "sound" to the sentence by interrupting the "flow" of it.

Bury unimportant phrases like "as anticipated" and "at 2 o'clock, Thursday" in the middle of your sentences, after natural pauses. To determine exactly where they should be placed, read the sentences aloud. Place the unimportant phrases after a pause, where it sounds natural to do so.

The attributions themselves should be used logically. *"Drive on," he explained* makes little sense. *"Make up your bed," Mom declared* makes *just* a little sense. The verb "said" would be the logical substitution in both instances.

Attributions should also be used as you would use them in conversation. *"Write,"* she *said.* Not *said she.* *"Write,"* Mom *said.* Not *said Mom.* (When you're telling someone what your mother said—"Never run with scissors in your hand"—you would never end it with the unnatural "said Mom.") The only logical time to use the verb before the noun in an attribution is when the identification of the speaker separates the two at some length. For example, "*. . . and that's all*" *Captain Robert Hayes, commander of Company G, 325th Infantry Regiment, 82nd Airborne Division, said.* For better communication, and to tax the reader less, write *". . . and that's all," said Captain Robert Hayes. . . .*

Attributions and their placement can assist in varying the structure of sentences and paragraphs. For newspaper features, magazine articles and commentary, attributions can generally be placed in the middle of a sentence or after the quote has been completed, rather than at the beginning. For example:

> "We don't know how many people are still on board," one source said, "but the Coast Guard is hard put to rescue those remaining because of the forty-foot waves."

The first clause sets up the suspense. The attribution, in the middle position (the least important part of the sentence), provides a pause, building up the suspense, after which a conclusive statement can be made.

In the following example, the attribution appears after the quote, allowing the full impact of the direct quote to be made first: *"They're all saved!" he said.* With this quote, there's really no way to bury the attribution. After all, you can't be so gauche as to dig graveyards in the middle of *all* sentences.

On the Use of Direct Quotes

Of what importance are direct quotes? When you hear a story about a person being rescued from an avalanche, would you like to hear about the rescue from a person standing at the bottom of the ski slope? Or would you rather hear the account from the lips of the skiier who "rode" the avalanche halfway down the slope before being buried? Paraphrasing doesn't have nearly the appeal to readers that direct quotes do. Readers, like you, want to hear the exact words from the person telling the story. Direct quotes add not only authenticity but life to what you're writing.

Direct quotes also break up those long gray columns of type. For the same reason we use paragraph indentations to make those columns more typographically appealing and organized, use direct quotes at the beginning of those paragraphs. Note the graphic representation of three columns of type in the figure on page 198. The first column has no break in it. The second has paragraph indentations. The third has indentations and direct quotes. Which column is most likely to entice a reader into it?

The Importance of Transitions

Ideas of feature stories, magazine articles and commentary all flow into the body of the writing by way of a transition. The body of the writing then flows sentence by sentence, paragraph by paragraph, to the conclusion. That flow is derived from a logical organization of information connected by transitions.

As you read or write, you may find that some sentences or paragraphs do not flow naturally from one to the other. They seem to be disjointed parts of the writing. The connective tissue is missing—the knee bones are not connected to the thigh bones.

Transitions transport the reader from different facts and actions to still other facts and action. Some transitions are subject transitions. A repetition of a widow's name or a pronoun are examples of subject-matter sentence or paragraph transitions. Subject-matter transitions stem naturally from the subject matter of the story itself.

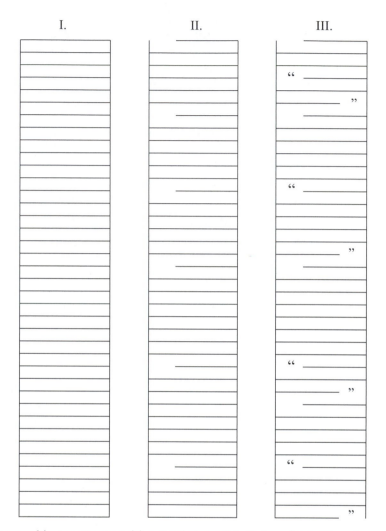

What are subject-matter transitions? Whatever it is that you're writing about. In the last two paragraphs, the subject we're discussing is subject-matter transitions. "Transitions" is an example of a subject-matter transition.

On the other hand, mechanical transitions may also be pressed into service for flow, continuity and clarity of expression. Although they may be more unnatural than subject-matter transitions, mechanical transitions still bring to the story a flow and continuity that all good writing has. What are examples of mechanical transitions? The first four words of this paragraph is an example of a mechanical transition: "On the other hand." While sometimes it is necessary to use mechanical transitions like "meanwhile" and "however," most of the time subject-matter transitions will serve just as well.

A TRIAD OF PARAGRAPH PATTERNS

The same principles and graphic representation of a sentence applies to paragraph patterns:

____(2)_____ \ ____(3)_____ \ ___(1)_____

Where you put your topic sentence in a paragraph creates different paragraph patterns. (A topic sentence presents the major subject matter of the paragraph.) Moving from a general statement (topic sentence) to the details or particular facts supporting that statement is the deductive reasoning pattern approach. If you reversed this pattern, starting out with details and leading up to the climactic topic sentence at the end of the paragraph, you would be using an inductive reasoning approach. Paragraphs are usually written using one or the other approaches. (Most writers use the deductive approach.) At times, however, the topic sentence may be placed in the middle of a paragraph. Sometimes the topic sentence may not even be stated: The idea is implicit or implied as the paragraph develops. You will want to vary paragraph patterns in much the same way you vary sentence patterns.

One obvious way to provide your readers with variety and relief from long paragraphs is to write short paragraphs. For emphasis, you might write a paragraph consisting of just three words or even one word:

I mean it.

Honestly.

As noted earlier, media requirements usually dictate sentence and paragraph lengths. The most finicky of audiences—those with the shortest attention span—are those of radio and television. That calls for shorter and simpler sentences and paragraphs. Newspaper and magazine readers tend to be more tolerant of longer and more complex sentences and paragraphs. The most tolerant of all are book readers.

TRIADS, TRIADS, TRIADS

> "What I tell you three times is true."
> — Lewis Carroll, *Hunting of the Snark*

In your writing you use examples or illustrations to emphasize the point you're making. When you do, try using multiples of three: the triadic structure. To the Greek mathematician Pythagoras, the magic number was three. In our rituals and our society, the number three figures prominently: We plan three meals a day. Our days consist of morning, afternoon and night. Our government is composed of three major branches—executive, legislative and judicial. One of our major religions speaks of a trinity—the Father, the Son and the Holy Spirit. Our dramatic productions usually have three acts. Series of books on one subject are often written in trilogies.

Most people feel an intuitive "rightness" about examples coming in threes. Just one example or argument is insufficient. Two examples help to prove a point. Three are convincing and, somehow, inexplicably—unless you're aware of the magic number three—satisfying. Four examples, many times, seem like overkill. (The recipient of all four examples may be inclined to throw up her or his hands and say, "All right! Enough already!")

Some examples of triads:

Writing about the global impact mass migrations are having, Ramon G. McLeod of the *San Francisco Chronicle* used a triad of fragmented sentences in the first paragraph of his lead:

> Chinese emigrants packed into the filthy hold of an old cargo ship. Hopeful campesinos crowded into shantytowns built on dumps outside Lima, Peru. A million Rwandans streaming into Zaire, turned into refugees by a savage war.

To population experts, these images are part of an unprecedented global phenomenon: a new age of migration, in which more than 100 million people have left their homes in search of economic opportunity or to escape war.

Driven by desperation and dreams, the immigrants are changing the face of nations—and causing an angry backlash in some. Experts in global demographics say they represent only the first swell in a wave of migration that may not crest for decades.

Many writers use the triadic principle—most, probably instinctively, and some not as effectively as others.

Marcia Muelengracht knew exactly what she was doing when she wrote on the inside of Hallmark's top valentine card of 2005, number V330-05:

Each time I see you, hold you, think of you, here's what I do—fall deeply, madly, happily in love with you.

The following writer, however, employs a triad anticlimactically:

By Tania Fuentez
The Associated Press, Dec. 6, 2003

The Northeast's first major storm of the season brought a blustery surge of sleet and snow yesterday, closing schools, making a mess on highways and triggering a rush on snowblowers and shovels.

Reversing the order of the ensuing events not only provides climactic and chronological order but also places the most important thing at the greatest position of emphasis—at the end of the sentence:

The Northeast's first major storm of the season brought a blustery surge of sleet and snow yesterday, triggering a rush on shovels and snowblowers, making a mess of highways and closing schools.

The revision also reverses the positions of "snowblowers" and "shovels," placing the most significant implement—"snowblowers"—last.

The following triads are excellent:

By Rebecca Santana
Cox News Service, March 28, 2004

GROZNY, Chechnya—They usually come at night, wearing masks, driving cars without license plates, always carrying weapons. They search houses without explaining what they're seeking. When they leave, they take people away who are sometimes never seen again.

Tennessean News Services, May 12, 2004

WASHINGTON—The way teachers see it, today's classroom environment often deserves a D—as in disrespectful, distracting and disheartening enough to drive many educators away.

The following example employs two triads in one paragraph.

By Susan Felt
Gannett News Service, July 7, 2005

The first wave of Gen-Xers is turning 40 this year.

The generation that grew up with "My Little Pony," Hot Wheels and Madonna will celebrate this birthday with bigger toys, fancier food and the cynicism that has come to characterize the 45 million people born between 1965 and 1979.

The principle of the triad thrives. Even the copy editor who wrote the headline for this feature couldn't resist a triadic flourish:

Exhibit Explains Why: Shoes Fit, Bras Shape and Lids Burp

By Elaina Sue Potrikus
Knight Ridder News Service, Dec. 13, 2003

WASHINGTON—Chances are you've never heard of culturally essential Americans such as Enid Bissett, Orla Watson and Earl C. Tupper. [note triad]

Their genius will be on display in a new Smithsonian Institution traveling exhibition of sketches, patent illustrations and factory drawings [another triad] for products that shaped the nation in profound but humble ways.

Two paragraphs, two triads. Nearly everybody employs the triadic principle:

One of the most dramatic uses of the triad (as well as the use of an excellent climactic paragraph) is illustrated in this eloquent address delivered by former President and General

Dwight D. Eisenhower before the American Society of Newspaper Editors, Washington, D.C., April 16, 1953—"The Chance for Peace":

> Every gun that's made, every warship launched, every rocket fired signifies in the final sense a theft from all those who hunger and are not fed, from those who are cold and are not clothed. This world in arms is not spending money alone; it is spending the sweat of its laborers, the genius of its scientists, the hopes of its children. This is not a way of life in any true sense. Under a cloud of threatening war, it is humanity hanging from a cross of iron.

Be conscious of the triadic pattern possibilities when writing. And arrange your examples or illustrations for maximum effect. Progress from the weakest argument to the strongest, from the least vivid image or language to the most vivid. Any other arrangement tends to be anticlimactic, stealing the wind from the sails of your reader.

SOME COMMON ERRORS OF COMMISSION: PART I

Having once captured your readers, you want to please and keep them with you.

Clichés: They Come a Dime a Dozen; Avoid Them Like the Plague

You would not want to bore those readers with clichés. At the end of this chapter you'll have the opportunity to read an article on this subject. Here is the beginning of it:

> LONDON—"At the end of the day" is the most irritating cliché in the English language.
>
> So says the Plain English Campaign . . .
>
> Second place went to "at this moment in time," and third to the constant use of "like," as if it were a form of punctuation.
>
> "With all due respect" came in fourth.
>
> "When readers or listeners come across these tired expressions, they start tuning out and completely miss the message—assuming there is one," said Plain English Campaign spokesman John Lister.
>
> Lister said people should follow the 1946 advice of writer George Orwell: "Never use a metaphor, simile, or other figure of speech which you are used to seeing in print."

Good advice from George Orwell.

Mixed Metaphors

Nor would you want to mix metaphors, as this congressman did, and have it recorded in the *Congressional Record:*

> With at least $263 billion already obligated to be spent by Congress over the next 40 years on public housing, we have dug a deep trench by obviously biting off more than we could chew.

Misplaced Modifiers

Nothing frustrates or irritates readers more than misplaced phrases and modifiers or misleading constructions, as illustrated by this example from the *Evansville (Ind.) Courier.*

> John Daley, out of golf since Aug. 28 after he scuffled with a spectator for 3½ months, will return to the PGA Tour in the 1995 season-opening Mercedes Championship.

Quite some prolonged scuffle, the reader says.

Yea! Boo!!

Avoid what may be called "yea-boo" constructions. In these sentences a reader or listener is led to believe one thing (yea!) only to have that belief negated later by a word or statement to the contrary (boo!). Ian Frazier, a *New Yorker* writer, was guilty of that: "I saw not many people I knew." That whipsawing around irritates the reader. Another example:

> Some students will celebrate Martin Luther King Jr.'s birthday tomorrow by learning about him in school; others will take the day off. But deep in their hearts many believe [yea!] little [boo!] in his dream of blacks and whites living in harmony.

This creation of momentary wavering in the audience's mind could have been eliminated by revising the sentence: "But deep in their hearts few believe in his dream of blacks and whites living in harmony."

Vocabulary Inflation

Among the many words being misused today (in what might be called vocabulary inflation or pollution) are "huge" and "issues." When sexual harassment surfaced in state government in Tennessee, the governor commented: "Anytime you mix men and women together in a work environment there's going to be issues."

Note "issues" instead of "problems." (Incidentally, anything wrong with using "there's"?)

And when the great woman's tennis champion, Steffi Graf, returned to the courts as a member of the Houston Wranglers, the chief executive officer of the World Team Tennis Pro League, remarked for the press: "It's huge that she is putting her toe in the water." (Ain't nothing "huge" about putting a "toe in the water.")

The Precise Word

Little things mean a lot. Without the precise word and vivid verbs and images, writing is not only uninteresting, it fails to communicate effectively. Mark Twain warned: The difference between the right word and almost the right word can be the difference between a lightning bug and lightning.

This quote from Jose Ortega y Gasset, the late Spanish philosopher and essayist, illustrates Twain's remark:

> We distinguish the excellent man from the common man by saying that the former is the one who makes great demands upon himself, and the latter who makes no demands on himself.

By "the excellent man" does Ortega y Gasset (or his translator) mean "exquisite," "fine," "sublime," "matchless" or "superb"—all synonyms for "excellent"? Or, given a moment to revise, would he change "excellent" to "outstanding," "exceptional," "superior" or "peerless"? For that matter, does he want "the common man" to be interpreted as the "simple man" or the "average man"?

We use words to communicate, not create questions of diction in a reader's mind.

In this fast-lane information era, try eliminating all momentary confusion in your communications. For example, forget about using "the latter" and "the former" in sentences. Just as readers did a double take on the use of them in the Ortega y Gasset quote, they would have a similar reaction to what Martin H. Fischer writes on the purpose of science: "Don't confuse hypothesis and theory. The former is a possible explanation; the latter the correct one. The establishment of theory is the very purpose of science."

Pretentious Writing

Think twice before using "the latter" and "the former." They not only provide momentary confusion, they verge on pretentious writing.

What is pretentious writing? Using those words or constructions that are too formal or stilted or archaic. You will want to erase from your writing vocabulary such words as "hence," "thus," "unbeknownst," "unbeknowing" and "betwixt." (Only slightly less stilted, and disruptive, is a word now gaining wide currency, "upcoming," instead of the plain "coming.")

Although you will read and hear mass communicators using those words, they create a momentary blockage of communication as the audience wonders at the quaintness of such usage.

> "I use 'thus,' all the time," a student in my classroom bridles at my advice against the use of the term.
>
> "Ever use it around the house talking with your Mother?"
>
> After a small pause, "Yes."
>
> That pause gave me the presence of mind to ask:
>
> "What did your Mother say when you used it?"
>
> "Laughed like crazy," he replied.
>
> An honest student.

If you have doubts about using those words, try them at home or on your friends.

Big Word, Small Word

We also do not intentionally use words to confuse. Ian Frazier, an excellent *New Yorker* writer who should know better, sent many readers to the dictionary when he recalled leaving home in "Out of Ohio:" "I hung around that summer until my presence became otiose." When a spokesperson from the University of Michigan Wolverines made the mistake of saying that the University of Southern California Trojans had "a finesse line," bad things happened. In the 2003 Rose Bowl, the Wolverines quarterback, sacked only 15 times in 12 games, was sacked nine times—three of them by end Kenechi Udezze. His postgame comment: "They said we had a finesse line. Half of us on the defense line can't even spell finesse. We were offended by it."

SOME COMMON ERRORS OF COMMISSION: PART II

Just as you guard jealously the beginnings and endings of sentences and paragraphs, so do you guard against the careless use of words and phrases.

No doubt Saddam Hussein was puzzled when former President George H. W. Bush said that he was "drawing a line in the sand" that Hussein had better not cross by invading Kuwait. Prior to this crisis, we had supported Hussein in his war with Iran. So what did "a line in the sand" mean to Hussein?

When I was a kid, we used the expression "I'm drawing a line in the dirt." If you crossed, you got your nose punched. That line could be seen for weeks after. How long does a "line in the sand" last in Iraq? Even without sandstorms that rise up to 5,000 feet, a "line in the sand" probably wouldn't be distinguishable the next day. Was this a subtle hint to Hussein that the U.S. would not look askance at his invasion of Kuwait?

Do speakers, specifically politicians, think carefully about the words they use? Not so far as "a line in the sand" is concerned. Ever since Bush said those words 15 years ago, they have been repeated ad nauseam by people in the news.

And, of course, Mark Twain would have chuckled at Defense Secretary Donald Rumsfeld's now-famous words when asked in December 2003 about reports that there were no known links between the terrorist organization al-Qaida and Iraq:

> "Reports that say that something hasn't happened are always interesting to me," he said, "because, as we know, there are known knowns; there are things we know we know. We also know there are known unknowns; that is to say, we know there are some things we do not know. But there are also unknown unknowns—the ones we don't know we don't know."

"In other words," columnist Trudy Rubin wrote in *The Tennessean*, "if I can be so bold as to translate Rumspeak—we had to act to avoid the risk of what we did not know."

A. A. Milne, the English humorist, wrote in *The House at the Pooh Corner*, "He respects Owl because you can't help respecting anybody who can spell TUESDAY, even if he doesn't spell it right." Unfortunately, the substance of what people say is invariably judged by how they say or write it. If you have any doubts about the importance of simply spelling words correctly, look at what an illiterate Abe Lincoln *might* have written on a brown paper bag when he penned the Gettysburg Address:

> For sore and seven years ago; our fathers brought fourth upon this contentment; a new nation conceived in liberty and educated to the preposition that all men are crated equal.

How would Lincoln's words have been received if the rest of the address contained similar errors and had been distributed to the news media instead of delivered orally? If somebody mentioned the Gettysburg Address today, we probably would expect a number and a street along with a zip code. That's one of the reasons spelling is stressed in journalism and mass communication classes. Misspellings erode the confidence of the reader in what you're writing.

ANALOGIES

What builds up the confidence in the reader is a comparison between dissimilar things that clarifies what you want to say or are in the midst of saying. Analogies tend to do that. Read this analogy about the Iraq war by Saritha Prabbu:

"Wake Up and Smell the Coffee"

The Tennessean, Nov. 7, 2005

Mention the Iraq war and I'm reminded of the perfume counter at the mall. After sniffing a half dozen perfumes, when you feel a little light-headed and are unable to distinguish the scents, the saleswoman sometimes hands you a jar of roasted coffee beans. "Smell this deeply," she explains, "it'll clear your head and you'll be able to smell the perfumes again."

So it is with this war—so many rationales, so many justifications that you find yourself from time to time looking for those coffee beans . . .

And, just so, Saritha Prabbu communicates with this excellent analogy.

LANGUAGE AND IMAGERY

Sensitive writers are always on guard against the use of colorless verbs and abstract detail. To replace them, however, takes effort. A freelance writer is eternally vigilant and disciplined. Anton Chekhov, the great Russian short story writer and playwright, underlines what that can mean in *The Sea Gull*. Trigorin, a character and writer in the play, describes his life, his passion:

> Day and night one thought obsesses me: I must be writing. . . . Why, now even, I'm here talking to you, I'm excited, but every minute I remember that the story I haven't finished is there waiting for me. I see that cloud up there, it's shaped like a grand piano . . . instantly a mental note. . . . I must remember to put that in my story. . . . A whiff of heliotrope. Quickly I make note of it: cloying smell, window's color . . . put that in next time I describe a summer evening. Every sentence, every word I say and you say, I lie in wait for it, snap it up for my literary storeroom . . . it might come in handy.

Vigilance will provide you with the concrete details that enable your readers to visualize what you saw and experienced.

"I got the mail" is dull compared to "I picked up a package from Heather Stitt at the University Center post office."

"I went to the hotel for refreshments" is boring compared to "I dropped in at the Brookshire Inn for a Heineken."

Perhaps nothing illustrates the importance of concrete detail so well as this brief poem by William Carlos Williams:

The Red Wheelbarrow
so much depends
upon
a red wheel
barrow
glazed with rain
water
beside the white
chickens.

When you read the phrase "a red wheelbarrow," an image of a red wheelbarrow forms in your mind. When you read "glazed with rainwater," you cast the red wheelbarrow image with a rainwater glaze, like icing on a cake. When "beside the white chickens" is read, you create the image of white chickens beside that glazed, red wheelbarrow. (William Carlos Williams uses a triad of concrete images in the poem. But, then, the whole of his poetry is based on the triadic principle.)

From this poem, you are able to see how little things—concrete details—mean a lot to your readers and, subsequently, to you, the writer.

You can enhance your writing by using a dominant theme of imagery or metaphor. However, if you start out using nature imagery in an article or story, you would not want to disrupt the unity of the work by switching, for no reason, to mechanical imagery. Having used such expressions as "gray mists" and "icy dew" and "cavelike opening," you would hesitate to shift abruptly to expressions such as "robotlike" or "metallic smell" unless the scene were invaded by some mechanical creatures from Star Wars.

WEAVING FIGURES IN THE CARPET

In freelance writing, terse, succinct phraseology is necessary. A novelist may devote half a page or more to describe a person or place in a book; you do not have that luxury. However, for your purposes, you needn't weigh a reader down with that much description. Let's look at how some characterization and settings are handled by other writers.

Character Description

> I stopped one of the students and asked why he was cursing the girls. He was red-faced and his black hair was covered with a blue knit skullcap.
> "What are you, a goy?" he asked.

Jeffrey Goldberg wrote this description for a May 2004 article in *The New Yorker* titled "Among the Settlers." The descriptions had to be brief. He interviewed many Jewish settlers in Israel, and used their actions, speech and physical description to create portraits of them. Here is what I mean:

Rabbi Levinger's "head is small, but his eyes are bulbous and his teeth outsized. His voice is deep, and his beard seems constructed of iron shavings. I said hello. He grunted a reply."

Anat Cohen is "one of the leaders of the Hebron Jews. A short woman in her early forties, she had a taut, windburned face and muscular arms and her fingernails were chewed and dirty."

Yehuda Liebman is "a thin and jumpy man, quick to show irritation."

Elizabeth Kolbert, writing for *The New Yorker* in a Nov. 2, 2006, article titled "The Darkening Sea," is equally succinct in her character descriptions:

"She is slight and soft-spoken, with wavy black hair and blue-green eyes."

And, "Caldeira is a trim man with wiry brown hair and a boyish sort of smile."

Vivid and succinct. But, of course, we don't have to go far afield to find such descriptions. Examples from this textbook follow:

"'He never knelt down to nobody,' his young, blonde wife of five years, Trina, reflected the other day. 'He didn't care who they were or how many there were. He didn't need nobody beside him.'"

The speaker, of course, is the wife of Ken McElroy.

Or, "Shreeves lost his first daughter, Debbie, 'the saint of the family,' in a fiery car wreck in 1972. She was 19." In "A Father's Tale," this description of Debbie is all that's needed.

Just a few descriptive words is all it takes. Of course, you have to be judicious in placing those proper words in proper places.

Setting Description

You describe a room or a place in the same succinct way as you characterize persons.

This description of landing zones in Afghanistan illustrates a superb grasp of setting description. The first paragraph sets the scene for that description:

By Jonathan S. Landay
Knight Ridder News Service, Aug. 21, 2005

> The landing zones were set high on the sides of the isolated Marah Valley, about 9,000 feet above sea level between massive peaks of the Deh Chopan district of southern Zabul province.
>
> Below, villagers tended fields and flocks and threshed wheat. Chimes of cowbells, brays of donkeys and cries of rollicking children drifted from hamlets of dried mud, carried on a languid wind tinged with the fragrance of mountain flowers.

By Amy Waldman
New York Times News Service, April 18, 2004

> MUDA, Nepal—With its simple mud homes, low roofs and string cots, this tiny settlement near the Indian border looks like any other in this part of western Nepal. Only the women suggest something different, garishly painted even in the morning's early hours.
>
> They loiter on a slope or around the tea stall, waiting for men, who banter, negotiate, then slyly walk one of the women to one of the village houses. The women's children play nearby and watch.

And, narrowing the setting down to a neighborhood, in a "Talk of the Town" brief a *New Yorker* writer described one this way:

> It was late afternoon, and a hot sun was burning through a thick haze. In the trafficless street, a tall, slender, graceful, barefoot girl of about thirteen was playing a lazy game of softball with three shaggy, fat, lumbering little boys, who were all wearing Yankee caps.

(Note how the last two lines describe those little boys.)

How would you describe your hometown in one paragraph? If you recall, here is how Jules Loh (see Chapter 3) described the town Ken McElroy intimidated:

> This is a small town: 440 people, filling station, bank, post office, tavern, blacktop street, grain elevator. Beyond are rolling meadows, ripening corn, redwing blackbirds, fat cattle, windmills and silos, a scene off a Sweet Lassy feed calendar.

Does the following Michael Satchell description resemble a gas station in your hometown? Here's Billy Carter's (see feature in Chapter 5) gas station in Plains, Georgia:

> The station is impossibly cluttered with tools, tires, cans of Campbell Soup and 10W40 oil all mixed up. On the wall is a saucy pinup calendar from the Kenna Auto Parts Co. Atop an 8-track tape deck, dusty and unused, are tapes by Lynn Anderson and Tammy Wynett.

How about a description of a room and a character in it? Perhaps that office in the "Lyle Starr Is Dead" essay might serve here:

You could run a lottery with the cigarette tray on Lyle's desk: "Guess the number of cigarette butts in the tray and win a trip to Las Vegas." I often wondered how the huge schefflera plant in the corner survived in all the smoke.

"Those cigarettes are going to do you in, Lyle," I once said.

"Naw," he replied. "They're the fuel that keeps me going."

I'm pleased that I was wrong about the cigarettes.

Among the other regular desk items was a top. When you spun it, and it stopped, it told you to buy stocks or not to buy stocks. Among other curios was a kaleidoscope. Though we never confirmed it, Lyle and I saw the world much same way: a configuration of bewildering shapes and colors that changed from moment to moment—a fascinating charade of characters and actions.

Of course there's more to characterization and setting description than these paragraphs, as you well know. Just try to put down those things that impressed you most in vivid and descriptive terms. That, along with your attentive reading of these examples, will give you a good start.

SHOW, DON'T TELL

Involve your readers in a conspiracy when you write. Don't "tell." "Show." Involving your readers in this conspiracy of discovery makes their reading experience more enjoyable. When readers work crossword puzzles, for example, do they have a solution before them, filling in the words from the solution? No. They'd rather work the puzzle out for themselves. The same holds true for an audience when they read or listen. When you're prone to write "Deby Rossie was in a happy frame of mind when she went to the candy store," write something like "Deby Rossie skipped all the way to the Russell Stover outlet."

Give them the joy of discovery. If you're describing a mother grief-stricken over the loss of her home to a tornado, don't write, "Margo Pantelone was grief-stricken over the loss of her home." That's "telling" the reader. Write: "Margo Pantelone, still dressed in the apron she wore when the tornado struck, picked up a towel from a twisted pile of clothing at her feet and dabbed at her eyes.

'It's gone,' she said, over and over, 'it's all gone.'"

Objective Correlatives

An even more sophisticated way of "showing" is to employ what poet T. S. Eliot called "objective correlatives." Describe an activity that correlates with the emotions, feelings or frame of mind of the person you're writing about. For example, if one kitchen wall stood with a window still intact after the tornado hit Margo Pantalone's house, and if it were raining and Margo Pantalone was looking at the raindrops coursing down the windowpane, you might write, "Margo Pantalone stood before the one kitchen wall still standing and looked at the raindrops coursing down the one windowpane in it." Those raindrops are objective correlatives for those emotions inside Margo Pantalone.

In the feature story titled "A Father's Tale" in Chapter 3, "Writing the Newspaper Feature," four daughters met violent deaths within a 10-year period. What activity might the mother of those daughters be engaged in that could serve as an objective correlative while you're interviewing her or her husband? If the mother is having a difficult time accepting the reality of the deaths, perhaps she's ironing one of the daughter's dresses even though the daughter won't return to wear it. Or perhaps she is polishing a brass kettle over and over—a kettle that obviously doesn't need any more polishing. The activity of ironing and polishing correlates with a frame of a mind so numbed by the tragedy that this mindless activity relieves the stress. The polishing, which eliminates the tarnishing, for example, can be the subconscious desire to restore those daughters to life and to a more innocent age.

One more example is useful. Robin Williams in the film *Awakenings* uses an experimental drug to awaken the catatonic victims of encephalitis. For 11 months the patients in the ward came back to life and then, despite increasing the dosage of the experimental drug, relapsed back into their catatonic state. During the "awakening" one of the patients sings this chorus to "Love's Old Sweet Song":

> Just a song at twilight, when the lights are low;
> And the flick'ring shadows softly come and go.
> Tho' the heart be weary, sad the day and long,
> Still to us at twilight comes love's old song,
> Comes love's old sweet song.

J. Clifton Bingham's chorus correlates perfectly with the twilight of the patient's awakening lives *"when the lights are low; And the flick'ring shadows"* of their past lives *"softly come and go"* and becomes a perfect objective correlative for what has happened and is happening to these patients. The doctor himself is awakened to life through this experience. (The film, incidentally, is based upon a true happening.)

All of this artistry takes vigilance, discipline and painstaking revision. But then, for good things, you usually pay a price.

WEDDING SENSE TO SOUND: THE ECHOES OF WORDS

Two of the most sophisticated things you can do to improve your writing are to consider the rhythm and flow of it and to wed the sense of what you are saying to the sound of how you are saying it. If you're just beginning your career, probably most of your writing should be cast in a conversational style. You're no doubt articulate. That being the case, if you write the way you speak, your writing will flow naturally. Although you may use words in writing that you do not use in speaking, writing still stems directly from speaking—we speak the words in our mind before we write them on paper. Writing the way you speak will endow your writing with a rhythm or flow. If you are exhausted or excited, you reflect that in your conversation. The words you choose determine how you will say them. Would you say "I'm tired" in an animated way? Of course not. You would say it wearily. You might even sigh.

The sense of what you are saying, then, should be echoed or reflected in the way you say it. If you're leaving a room hastily, you may say something like "I'm outta here!" If you're reluctant to leave, the reluctance might be reflected by saying "Well, so long. I guess I'll be going now." In these two examples, the flow of the sentence pattern reflects the sense of what's happening. The substance of what's being said is wedded to the form.

Michael Satchell employed sense/sound when he wrote about former President Jimmy Carter's brother, Billy Carter (see Chapter 6). Satchell describes what happens when work is over at 5 p.m.:

> At 5:02 p.m. precisely Billy bounces in, dives into a huge cooler, pulls out a handful of cans of beer, pops a couple, lights up a Pall Mall, sucks hard on it, gives a tubercular wheeze, and downs the can in a single guzzle.
> "Boy, I needed that," he said. "Here, have another."

By telescoping all the activity into one sentence, Satchell reflects the rapidity with which Billy Carter—a functional alcoholic at this time—gets a can of beer, pops it, lights up a cigarette and downs the can of beer. Satchell has wedded sense to sound.

The pauses, stresses, rhythm, sounds of words—all are considered in any serious writing. When you write, you should be able to call upon these stylistics. You've probably employed some of them already: You've no doubt talked of bees buzzing, dogs barking, cats purring. The words reflect the sound of the activity (the sense of what's happening) of the bees, the dogs and the cats. "Bark!" has a harsh sound. "Purring" has a soft, muted sound.

All writing can be enhanced by using sense/sound. When Steve Spurrier accepted the coaching position at the University of South Carolina, an Associated Press reporter wrote: "Spurrier seemingly could have stayed with the [Florida] Gators forever. But he resigned in 2001 and began a disastrous stint with the Redskins." The AP reporter could have combined both of these sentences into one, without even using a comma. But he didn't. Why not? By putting a period after "forever" the writer wanted to give the reader the impression of a football coaching eternity.

"When I Am Dead, My Dearest," Christina Rossetti

Want to validate the pronunciamento that ended the previous section? When Christina Rossetti wrote a poem for her husband titled "When I Am Dead," the first stanza begins: "When I am dead, my dearest, / Sing no sad songs for me; . . ." At the end of the stanza she wants her husband to have the freedom to do as he chooses after she is dead, so she writes:

> And if thou wilt, remember,
> And if thou wilt, forget.

She uses the word "remember" at the end of one line, because the sound of it reflects the sense of remembering, the lingering of something lost. The word lingers on, the way memories do. She uses "forget" at the end of the last line to tell her husband that she's giving him a choice other than remembering her after her death. "Forget," because of its abrupt ending, reflects the stopping of memories ("forget" cannot be drawn out in speech as "remember" can). Does this introduction of poetry to the discussion of prose writing sound reasonable to you?

In writing, as in speaking, the sense of what you are saying should be reflected in the way you say it.

"The Open Boat," Stephen Crane

Great writers observe the advice to reflect the sense in the sound. Listen to the sound of impending violence in these sentences from "The Open Boat" by Stephen Crane. A gull has landed on an open boat:

> The cook and the correspondent swore darkly at the creature. The captain naturally wished to knock it away with the end of the heavy painter, but he did not dare do it, because anything resembling an emphatic gesture would have capsized his freighted boat. . . .

The words selected to convey impending violence hit the ears hard: darkly, creature, knock, heavy, painter, did not dare, emphatic, gesture, capsized, freighted, boat.

The gull, however, must now be gently shooed away from the boat. Crane conveys the gentleness of this motion by slowing down the rhythm of the sentence with commas and by using soft-sounding words:

> . . . and so, with his open hand, the captain gently and carefully waved the gull away.

Crane interposed *gently and* between *captain* and *carefully* because placed together "captain" and "carefully" sound harsh and would not convey the gentle wave of the hand. Say "captain carefully" out loud. See how it is impossible to convey a sense of a gentle motion with those words together.

Treasure Island, Robert Louis Stevenson

Here are two more dramatic examples of words echoing the sense of what's being said.

Robert Louis Stevenson has his boy on the ocean in a boat. The first draft, if you fit the words to a wave image, read like this:

```
                              with me
                      up              gid
                  heaved                di
              now                         ly.
The          world
       whole
```

The final draft:

```
                        up,
                     ly     and
               di            now
             gid              rushed
           heaved              gid
             now                 di
The     world                     ly
    whole                           down
                                       ward.
```

"To Helen," Edgar Allan Poe

Edgar Allan Poe transports readers over waves and washes them safely onto the shore in his poem, "To Helen." He speaks of Helen's beauty and likens it to ships: "Helen, thy beauty is to me like / Those Nicean barks of yore / that gently o'er a perfumed sea,

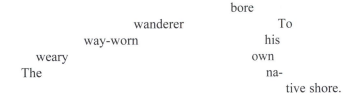

```
                        bore
            wanderer             To
        way-worn                his
    weary                       own
The                            na-
                                 tive shore.
```

Poe, of course, did not use this wave pattern when he wrote the poem. But the words, composed as they are, force the reader to read them as if they were a wave cresting, transporting the ship, with the wanderer on it, "to his own native shore." The sense of what is happening is echoed by the sound of what is happening. The substance is wedded to the form.

Can you see that in Poe's "To Helen"?

If you have some reservations about that passage, this wedding of sense to sound, or the sense being echoed in sound, how about this passage: "Over the river and through the woods to grandmothers house we go. . . ." The writer constructed the line so that there's a rollicking lilt to it that conveys the joy of sleigh riding on the way to a favorite place.

Stephen Crane, Robert Louis Stevenson and Edgar Allan Poe are more subtle, but they do the same thing—wed the sense of what they're saying to the sound. You can, too, when you use sound as a handmaiden to meaning. (You'll have a chance to do that in an exercise at the end of this chapter.)

To recapitulate a part of what has been discussed: To convey unrest or violence, use short, emphatic words and sentences, even sentence fragments. You may want to use words with hard-sounding consonants like *k, j, p* and *d*, and hard-sounding vowels like long *a, e* and *i*.

To convey the impression that all is at peace in the world, you may want to use longer words and flowing sentences, with soft-sounding consonants like *m, n, l, r* and *th* and soft-sounding vowels like *o* and *u*.

Any profound treatment of wedding sense to sound and the variety of ways it can be employed is impossible in these few pages, but a few more examples may be instructive.

"Cows," James Reeves

This poem, "Cows" by a seven-year-old English boy, James Reeves, captures the monotonous, boring life of the cows through repetition:

Cows
Half the time they munched the grass, and all the
     time they lay
Down in the water-meadows, the lazy month of May,
     A-chewing,
     A-mooing,
To pass the hours away.
     "Nice weather," said the brown cow.
     "Ah," said the white.
     "Grass is very tasty."
     "Grass is all right."

Half the time they munched the grass, and all the time
     they lay
Down in the water-meadows, the lazy month of May,
     A-chewing,
     A-mooing,
To pass the hours away.
     "Rain coming," said the brown cow.
     "Ah," said the white.
     "Flies is very tiresome."
     "Flies bite."

Half the time they munched the grass, and all the time
     they lay
Down in the water-meadows, the lazy month of May,
     A-chewing,
     A-mooing,
To pass the hours away.
     "Time to go," said the brown cow.
     "Ah," said the white.
     "Nice-chat." "Very pleasant."
     "Night." "Night."

Half the time they munched the grass, and all the time
    they lay
Down in the water-meadows, the lazy month of May,
    A-chewing,
    A-mooing,
To pass the hours away.

Death in the Afternoon, Ernest Hemingway

Finally, Ernest Hemingway, in *Death in the Afternoon*, wanted to produce the "sound" of a dead bull being pulled out of the arena through the sand. He selected and used words with a dominant consonant letter in them.

What is the letter? "*K*"? No. "*M*"? No. "*L*"? No. "*S*"? Yes. Why?

THE IMPORTANCE OF REVISION

An Arab Proverb

The errors noted in the "Common Errors of Commission" segments of this chapter remind us of an Arabic proverb: "Four things come not back: the spoken word; the sped arrow; time past; the neglected opportunity." As a motivation to revise, keep this proverb in mind.

> Easy reading is damned hard writing.

When the going gets tough, remind yourself of this (anonymous) "easy reading" comment, perhaps varying it to fit your situation: "Easy writing makes for hard reading."

As for how hard revision can be, read what one great English writer, Jonathan Swift, had to say about writing poetry:

On Poetry
Then, rising with Aurora's light,
The Muse invoked, sit down to write;
Blot out, correct, insert, refine,
Enlarge, diminish, interline

For Jonathan Swift, "putting proper words in proper places" took some doing. William L. Styron is a kindred spirit. He says, "I never write one word that I don't change seven."

PUTTING "PROPER WORDS IN PROPER PLACES"

How do you go about revising? When you have the luxury of time, these revision guidelines may engage your imaginative and creative talent as well as remind you of the craft of writing at your fingertips:

When you're through writing on a subject or return to it to revise, ask yourself what all that you've written means" Does it signify something more than what you initially had in mind? Does it signify less? What biases or prejudices have intruded? Do you want the intrusion? This self-examination will help you determine if you've taken the right point of view and the proper tone and rhythm. Then pick up your revision pen, knowing that you can improve what you've written.

First of all, *be aware of your mind.* It will tell you there's nothing wrong with what you've written, which is just what it tells you while you're writing. (Otherwise, if you see your actual words, you might not continue.)

Second, allow time to elapse between revisions. That enables you to view your writing more objectively.

Revise on the printed page of your draft, not on the computer. This will provide you with an esthetic "distance" from what you've written.

If you allow another time lapse before making revision changes on the computer, and then revise while making the revisions, you have the equivalent of still another revision.

Good writing does not come without struggle:

freelance writer who will be remembered is the one who writes as poetically as the subject matter and the audience can bear. Among the multitude of journalists who have left their signatures on history's register are William L. Shirer, Winston S. Churchill, William Manchester and David Halberstam. On the other hand, few current historians are registered in journalism annals. Why is that? One of the reasons may be that noted journalists have writing skills historians do not possess and their,

And although historians and journalists may cover much of the same territory, the journalists' impact upon our society is colossal. The media, sustained by journalism is a basic necessity in a democracy. Without the media and journalists, society could not function properly--people need current information to address major problems, to vote intelligently, buy intelligently, etc. As Paul Starr points out in *The Creation of the Media,*

"Newspapers made democracy possible; press freedom was the primary and central innovation of the new American nation; Zenger and Franklin and Jefferson and Paine, all journalists at heart, built this country. Crusading journalists ended slavery, urban graft, official indifference to [The Great] Depression poverty, McCarthyism, the Viet nam War, and the Nixon Administration." (Quoted by Nicholas Lemann in a book review for *The New Yorker,* April 12, 2004, p. 84. 82-84)

WHERE ARE YOU NOW?

Journalistic writing, and what we're advocating in this text, may differ from the many other forms of writing you've probably engaged in. And by this time many of you are developing a sense of news and social justice as well as a relentless curiosity trademarks of a professional writer. No doubt,

Poet Phillip Larken's eight-line poem, "Take One Home for the Kiddies," was begun in April 1954, and completed in August 1960. Editor Anthony Thwaite noted that Larkin, "after his graphomaniacal boyhood, became a scrupulously slow and patient reviser."*

Louis Menand, reviewing a book on punctuation, notes that

> . . . chattiness, slanginess, in-your-face-ness, and any other features of writing that are conventionally characterized as "like speech" are usually the results of laborious experimentation, revision, calibration, walks around the block, unnecessary phone calls, and recalibration. Writers, by nature, tend to be people in whom *l'esprit de l'escalier* is a recurrent experience: they are always thinking of the perfect riposte after the moment for saying it has passed. So they take a few years longer and put it in print. Writers are no mere copyists of language; they are polishers, embellishers, perfecters. They spend hours getting the timing right—so that what they write sounds completely unrehearsed.
>
> "Bad Comma—Lynne Truss's Strange Grammar" (*The New Yorker* 80 (June 28, 2004), 102, 104.

Harry Shaw, a noted teacher of freshman English and nationally known writer, always used to say, "There's no such thing as good writing—it's all good re-writing."

Follow the revision checklist provided in exercise 2 at the end of this chapter and your writing should improve dramatically. And when days grow cloudy and gray while revising, read again what Wallace Stegner, a poet and novelist, said about discipline ("To a Young Writer") at the beginning of this chapter.

What exactly do you cut out? What exactly do you improve upon? You can circle all the passive verbs you've used. Then circle all the "witches"—which is, which was, it was, they were, and so on. All the pronouns used in conjunction with verbs of being need to be circled and, probably, eliminated. When you do that, you'll find you've fashioned a more forceful sentence. But go to exercise 2 at the end of this chapter. It will go much more into detail on how to revise.

THE MENTAL BLOCK: PLUMBING THE DEEP WELL

How do you counteract a mental block? If you have an idea for the feature, article or commentary, the working title and the research you do should spur you to write. Once you've exhausted your research, outlining what you're going to write should propel you into writing. Recall the "Trouble in Suburbia" article in chapter 4? The accumulation of research previously unknown to you not only can get you started, but it can stir an excitement that motivates you still more. If you're writing about a personal experience and find yourself stymied, one way to overcome that frustration is to consider dipping into the Deep Well.

---

* John Updike, "The Well-Cared-for Poems of Philip Larkin," *The New Yorker* 80 (July 26, 2004), 84–88.

The Deep Well

John Livingston Lowes, when studying the creative process of the great English poet, Coleridge, who had photographic recall of what he read and experienced, described the poet's submersion in his mind into what he called the Deep Well.* The idea that nothing is lost in our life experiences is supported by psychologist Carl Jung's theory of racial memory, also stored in the Deep Well. It's all there in our minds. What we need is a mechanism to recall it.

Among those artists who enter that Deep Well are the author and poet John Hawkes; the poet Robert Graves, who once was told by his psychiatrist not to write any more poetry lest he lose himself in the writing; and the novelist Henry Miller, who describes his writing experience as hooking up with "the cosmic spirit."

How do you plumb that deep well of experiences?

Entering the Deep Well

The first step in entering the well is to find what Henry James might call "The Great Good Place"—in this instance, a quiet secluded nook where you will not be interrupted for at least

---

*This description of the Deep Well is drawn from Douglas Bement & Ross M. Taylor, *The Fabric of Fiction* (Harcourt, Brace @ World, Inc. New York, Burlingame: 1943), 5–16.

a couple of hours. Retire to it, and recline in a cushioned chair or on a soft sofa, with pen and pad by your side. Then close your eyes.

Recall the moment or incident, episode or event you want to write about. Let it crystalize in your mind, so that details materialize. You can actually see the tapestry, the figure in the carpet, the embers in the fireplace, the frown on your father's face, or hear your mother's sigh. Once that starts happening, you should be able to relive or reexperience the event.

When you are experiencing the event, not simply remembering it, pick up the pen and pad or use a laptop and write from that Deep Well. Dash it down on paper. Write without pause. Forget about the proper word (leave a space) or punctuation: You want to get the experience down while it is newly reclaimed in your mind. When you are through writing it, you may be exhausted and/or exhilarated.

When you revise it later, reexperience the event—reliving, not remembering. It may be a schizophrenic experience: reliving on the inside, revising on the outside. But then, revision, if done properly *is* a schizophrenic exercise: You read what you've written and revise as if you're another person, a reader going over it.

SUMMARY

Writing requires a profound knowledge of the craft and discipline. Editors are under tremendous pressure to select the most lively and significant fraction of available features, articles and commentary. As a consequence, freelance writers must develop ideas with succinct, varied and vivid phrasing.

What used to be cut-and-dried journalistic writing now verges on literature and poetry. Concrete details and imagery that show rather than tell are now matter-of-fact materials. The writer strives for writing with rhythm and flow enhanced by the wedding of the sense of what is being said with the sound or echo of the words. Writing should be as poetic as the subject matter and the audience will find agreeable. Although an initial writing can achieve some of the artistry described in this chapter, most distinguished writing stems from discipline and rewriting or, more precisely, revision.

Mental blocks can be avoided with exhaustive research and an outlining of that research into writing form. Personal experiences that provide writing material can be explored through plumbing the deep well.

ARTICLES FOR DISCUSSION

A. "Poll Identifies Most Irritating English 'Cliché'"

The Associated Press, March 25, 2004

LONDON—"At the end of the day" is the most irritating cliché in the English language.

So says the Plain English Campaign, which said the abused and overused phrase was first in a poll of most annoying clichés.

Second place went to "at this moment in time," and third to the constant use of "like," as if it were a form of punctuation.

"With all due respect" came in fourth.

When readers or listeners come across these tired expressions, they start turning out and completely miss the message—assuming there is one," said Plain English Campaign spokesman John Lister.

Lister said people should follow the 1946 advice of writer George Orwell: "Never use a metaphor, simile, or other figure of speech which you are used to seeing in print."

The Plain English Campaign, which offers annual awards for good use of the language surveyed its 5,000 supporters in more than 70 countries for the poll.

Other terms that received multiple nominations included: 24/7; absolutely; address the issue; around (in place of about); awesome; ballpark figure; basically; basis ("on a weekly basis" in place of "weekly" and so on); bear with me; between a rock and a hard place; bottom line; crack troops; glass half full (or half empty); I hear what you are saying; in terms of; it's not rocket science; literally; move the goal-posts; ongoing; prioritize; pushing the envelope; singing from the same hymn sheet; the fact of the matter is; thinking outside the box; to be honest/to be honest with you/to be perfectly honest; and touch base.

Formed in 1979, the Plain English Campaign is an independent group that campaigns against clichés, jargon and obfuscation, particularly in official and public documents.

Among my nonfavorite terms is "upcoming"—as in "the upcoming game"—instead of just "coming."

What's your cliché gripe?

B. "Martha Stewart Figures in Bad Writing Contest"

Tennessean News Services
July 20, 2004

SAN JOSE, Calif.—A Manhattan Beach, Calif., software developer won an annual bad writing contest with an entry that compared the end of a love affair to Martha Stewart ripping the vein out of a shrimp's tail.

Dave Zobel, 42, won first place in San Jose State University's 23rd Bulwer-Lytton Fiction Contest, an annual event that parodies the most atrocious beginning to an imaginary novel.

The contest is named after the British novelist Edward George Bulwer-Lytton, whose 1830 novel *Paul Clifford* begins with the now infamous phrase, "It was a dark and stormy night."

Zobel's winning entry came to him while he was in his kitchen cleaning fish.

"She resolved to end the love affair with Ramon tonight . . . summarily, like Martha Stewart ripping the sand vein out of a shrimp's tail . . . though the term 'love affair' now struck her as a ridiculous euphemism . . . not unlike 'sand vein,' which is after all an intestine, not a vein . . . and that tarry substance inside certainly isn't sand . . . and that brought her back to Ramon."

"I've entered the contest every year for the last six years," Zobel, a father of two, said yesterday. "This is the first time I've won anything. I never won and wasn't expecting to this year, but to be honest I'm a little jealous of people who won dishonorable mentions because that title would look better on my resume." He won $250.

Runner up was Pamela Patchet Hamilton, of Beaconsfield, Quebec, who described her style as "Dave Barry with a feminine twist." Patchet, who has written humor essays for *The (Montreal) Gazette* and other newspapers impressed judges with this putrid passage:

"The notion that they would no longer be a couple dashed Helen's hopes and scrambled her thoughts not unlike the time her sleeve caught the edge of the open egg carton and the contents hit the floor like fragile things hitting cold tiles, more pitiable because they were the expensive organic brown eggs from free-range chickens, and one of them clearly had double yolks entwined in one sac just the way Helen and Richard used to be," she wrote.

The contest is a labor of love for Scott Rice, an English professor at San Jose State. Rice reads thousands of entries, submitting what he thinks are the best to a panel of 15 people, many of them fellow professors or former contest winners. "The contest has been a much bigger success then we ever thought it would be, so we have no real plans to ever change it," Rice said.

The contest has many categories, from adventure to detective, romance and science fiction.

EXERCISES

1. A writer's self-analysis exercise. (See page 16. Note to instructor and student: If this exercise has not been assigned in Chapter 1, you may want to assign/write it now.)

2. A revision exercise. (Note to instructor and student: This exercise might be assigned last, after the various other exercises in this chapter that involve revision.)
   Select a feature story or a magazine article you've written—preferably a second or third draft. Follow the instructions below, marking, circling or underlining in red ink those words, phrases or sentences destined for revision. You may want to make several "runs" through your article, focusing on only one aspect of your writing during each "run." In any event, leave the actual revision until later.
   - Check to see if you have a hook, idea and transition in the lead.
   - Circle all "witches"—relative pronouns with verbs of being: which is, which was, which were, it was, they were, one is, there are, and so on.
   - Circle similar paragraph beginnings.
   - Circle trite phrases.
   - Underline with a wavy line each weak verb of being or overworked verbs—went, get, set, and so forth.
   - Note those sentences that feature your strong story points—could a periodic sentence add drama? Suspense? Emphasis? If so, place a "P" at the end of it.

- Note long sentences. For good readability, aim for a 14 to 17 word average.
- Forget about using semicolons except for using them to separate words in a series which include commas. Even Lynne Truss, who wrote the book about punctuation mentioned earlier, misused semicolons twice in the preface. Reviewer Menand (on page 217) also notes that "about half the semicolons in the rest of the book are either unnecessary or ungrammatical" (p. 102). (Remember, semicolons tend to confuse the reader, who is usually in trouble 50 percent of the time anyway.) Read more about this in Appendix A, "A Common Sense Approach to Punctuation."
- Do you "tell" rather than "show"?
- If there are quick or slow actions, or if there are pleasant or harsh scenes, have you employed the wedding of sense to sound (or substance to form)?
- When you give examples, have you used the triadic and climactic principles?
- Can you sharpen your character or setting descriptions?
- Do you need "Red Wheelbarrows" (specifics rather than generalizations), for example, "an English setter named Dora," rather than "a white-and-brown-spotted dog"?
- When you read your revised article aloud, does it flow naturally from sentence to sentence? Paragraph to paragraph? Are there awkward phrases or pauses? If so, mark them.
- Do you have a strong conclusion, or does it dwindle off?

3. Revise the following sentences into periodic sentences.
   a. Edgar Allan Poe was born in 1809 in Baltimore, Maryland.
   b. Andria Bowman became a painter the moment her mother put the first crayon in her hand.
   c. The drums beat lowly in the evening in darkest Africa.

4. Rewrite these sentences for the utmost emphasis:
   a. Stephanie Horne said, "I don't care how you do it, just get it done."
   b. "As a matter of fact, life ain't no crystal stair," Mark Holloway remarked.
   c. "The exam was easy," according to Sean Dietz.

5. Write three sentences from the following phrases (in capital letters) using the verb "stood" or some other verb. Emphasize a different phrase in each sentence. (Remember the positions of importance in a sentence? 2–3–1)
   BY THE SEA / WEATHER-BEATEN AND LONELY / THE HAUNTED OLD HOUSE

6. Rewrite the following paragraph so that it has a climactic sequence of the events that happened when the storm hit.
      We can't say it was a tornado, but it was definitely high winds that took the roof off the courthouse, tore up Mary Jean Delozier's barbecue and blew 10 trees down in the city park, said Matthias Gewelt, an Erie County sheriff's dispatcher.

7. In a column titled "Writing Tips" in The Associated Press Radio monthly newsletter, Barbara Worth posed a series of sentences that trail off at the end. Knowing what you do about periodic sentences and the importance of sentence endings (e.g., how less important phrases and attributions should be buried), revise the sentences for more forcefulness or impression. (Sometimes a periodic sentence can improve the sentence; sometimes a rearrangement of phrases will make a stronger statement.) As you finish revising each, compare your sentence with the one suggested by Worth at the end of this exercise. Are there any differences? Whose sentences are the best?
      Why?
   a. The total damage is expected to be in the millions from storms that swept the region.
   b. As many as 100 children may have died of starvation on the ship.
   c. A working dinner at the governor's mansion in Little Rock is under way.

d. The officer says the law must be respected by them.
e. The mayor worked all night, but a decision was not made.
f. The relief effort has problems that are not seen by officials.
g. They must meet so that a new treaty can be signed.

Worth's suggestions:
a. *Total damage from storms that swept the region is expected to be in the millions.*
b. *As many as 100 children on the ship may have died of starvation.*
c. *A working dinner is under way at the governor's mansion in Little Rock.*
d. *The officer says they must respect the law.*
e. *The mayor worked all night but did not make a decision.*
f. *Officials do not see the relief effort's problems.*
g. *They must meet to sign a new treaty.*

8. How can the following sentence be improved?
Ginger Stubblefield has collected more than 50 movies and I asked her if she had any favorites.

9. Rewrite the following trite phrases using fresh imagery:
a. Abby Gilbert's eyes were green with envy.
b. Brooke Wright's explanation was as clear as crystal.
c. Shannon Terry's hair was straight as a pin.

10. Ask a member of the class to sit on the desk at the front. Ask the student a series of questions. Then fill in the blanks below with 15 words or less:
a. When _____ smiled, her or his face _____ .
b. Talking to _____ was like _____ .
c. _____ sat on the desk like _____ .

11. Instead of "telling," "show." Rewrite the following sentences.
a. Laura Clemons took the turn into the driveway too fast.
b. Zachery S. Stewart looked tired.
c. Jane Day Jordan looked her age, 20.
d. Ronnie Dunn was preoccupied.
e. Lisa Eldridge was excited.

12. Write a brief description of your hometown similar to that written by Jules Loh in "The Saga of Ken McElroy" on page 150 paragraph 7. (This is a repetition of exercise 8 in Chapter 5.)

13. Describe a serene, peaceful scene in no more than a sentence or two that will tend to be long and flowing. Use letters like *l, o, m, n,* and combinations like "*ing*", "*oon*" (moons), and the like. Use pleasant-sounding consonants and vowels in phrases like "in the gloaming."

14. Describe in detail how you wedded sense to sound in the preceding exercise.

15. Describe a chaotic scene or episode or act filled with tension or conflict in three or four sentences that are short and staccato. Use *k, i, j,* long *e,* and/or combinations of sounds in words like "couth," "shriek," "strike," and other words with harsh-sounding consonants and vowels, like "wracking cough."

16. Describe in detail how you wedded sense to sound in the preceding exercise.

17. Show that James Hutcheson is sad by describing an action taking place in a setting. (See the objective correlative discussion on pages 210–211.)

18. Show that Monica Greppin is happy by describing an action taking place in that setting. (See, once again, the objective correlative discussion on pages 210–211.)

19. Plumbing the deep well: Write down three episodes in your life that had a major influence on you and might be re-created as a feature, article or commentary. Pair off with your neighbor and discuss your three biographical events for five minutes each. Decide which one seems the most promising to write about and examine the reasons for this. Then follow the instructions given for entering the deep well and experience again that event.

20. Describe the classroom in one paragraph.

21. Drawing upon the importance of wedding sense to sound presented to you in this chapter evaluate the following cases:

    a. Describe whether an audience is apt to receive enthusiastically the Bee Gees song "I Started a Joke." Base your conclusion not upon the incomprehensibility of its meaning, but upon the first two lines of song, the essence of which is the singer bewailing the fact that the joke he started ended up being on him. What indicates bad judgment in creating the lyrics of the song?

    b. General Motors decided to downsize its automobile lines, scrapping the Oldsmobile but keeping the Buick. An auto critic said that was like administering artificial respiration to a dead patient. Referring once again to the introduction to this question, what might we add to the list of reasons for the Buick automobile line to fail?

CHAPTER 8

THE ART OF INTERVIEWING

The Only Wheel in Town

First Gambler, arriving in town:	Any action around?
Second Gambler:	Roulette.
First Gambler:	You play?
Second Gambler:	Yes.
First Gambler:	Is the wheel straight?
Second Gambler:	No.
First Gambler:	Why do you play?
Second Gambler:	It's the only wheel in town.

—"The Only Wheel in Town"*

CENTRAL TO ALL MEDIA WRITING—INTERVIEWING

The interview is an age-old technique for eliciting information that will help fill the public's need to know what's behind newsworthy events or projects. The practice of journalism wouldn't exist without the interview. The goal of every interview is to elicit information and/or bring an interviewee or the topic closer to the public. Skill in interviewing is necessary to accomplish this.

---

*Eugene J. Webb and Jerry R. Salancik, *The Interview or The Only Wheel in Town.* JOURNALISM MONOGRAPHS No. 2, November 1966, p. 1.

But, as noted by Webb and Salancik, the authors of "The Interview or the Only Wheel in Town" (the source of the epigraph that opens this chapter), it's *A most perilous and unreliable method* . . .

> Reporters [writers] have four main techniques in gathering information: direct observation of an event, search of secondary and primary documents such as morgue clippings, police blotters and reference works, the receipt of unsolicited information via tips or from government or press agent handouts and direct interviewing of people who are involved in, concerned with or informed about a news event.
>
> Of these four, the most perilous and unreliable method is the interview. The observer's perception may be in error; documents may have been badly kept; and handouts may reflect the biases of vested interests. The interview, unluckily, has all these risks of error as the [writer and the] source join forces in distorting reality. . . . [Writers] should be less sanguine than they were about interviewing but more sensitive to devices that will reduce the risk of being deluded or deluding, misled or misleading. The interview, warped as it may be, is, after all, the only wheel in town. (p. 1)

Interviewing was introduced and incorporated in the media as a newsgathering innovation by the penny press revolution of the 1830s. The first printed interview was conducted by James Gordon Bennett in 1836 with a madam of a house of prostitution about a famous murder—the Ellen Jewett case. Techniques improving interviewing followed and were assimilated through the years. Those techniques are discussed in these pages.

Invariably, writing for the media requires employing this "most perilous and unreliable method." What are your career aspirations? Freelance writer? Newspaper feature writer? Magazine writer? Business publications writer? Public relations practitioner? Radio or television feature writer? If you want a career in any of these areas, if you want to crash glass ceilings, you must be able to write. And if you write, you must learn the art of interviewing because media writing involves gathering information. And that requires asking questions—interviewing. In the next few pages we will lead you through this information-gathering minefield so that you emerge on the media playing field intact and with a knight's proper coat of mail.

While gathering information involves interviewing, what's nice about asking questions is that the more you encourage people to talk about themselves, the more information you gather and the more they become impressed with you. Invariably people want to talk about themselves and their activities. Think about the last time you were at a social gathering. Did people ask you questions? Or did you do the questioning? In the last five years my wife and I have asked hundreds of questions and listened to the answers. Were we ever questioned? On only a couple of evenings. When you're interviewing try to remember the anecdote about a woman who had occasion to talk with two of England's great prime ministers:

After meeting with Prime Minister William Gladstone, the woman left his office exclaiming that Gladstone was the most brilliant man she had ever met. After a subsequent meeting with Prime Minister Benjamin Disraeli, however, she remarked, "He made me feel as if I were one of the most brilliant women he had ever met!" Disraeli did not dominate their conversation. Disraeli "conducted" an "interview."

REALITY AND HUMAN FRAILTY

What will also aid you in interviewing is to recall "The Only Wheel in Town," and the perils involved. Human frailty is ever present. An anonymous *New Yorker* writer noted this about "reality": "To avoid dissonance, we perpetually smooth and arrange reality to conform to our whims. We lie to ourselves and others, unthinkingly. When, occasionally—and only under external pressure—we see things as they are, we are unmasked."

Memories Are Made of This

The memory of the person being interviewed, then, is suspect. If the interviewee's memory of an event is triggered by a question from you, that memory is not lodged conveniently in one cell or even a multitude of cells in the same part of the brain. Recent studies have shown that the recall of an event takes place in the manner that a Broadway play has its run. In each performance the actors come together, the orchestra returns, the scenery is restored and the play is reenacted. However, an actress may have a cold, passages may be reconstrued, a refrain may be off-key or the set may be off the stage floor marks. The reenactment of the play is imprecise.

Recollections by the person being interviewed are complex: Different parts of the brain are called upon to present a performance that, at best, is slightly imperfect. Circumstances intervene. How long has it been between the event and the interview? Time changes things. The mind tends to reject the concept of chronology. Of course, attitudes also may change. Webb and Salancik note in their book the "half-life quality of memory and its rapid erosion" (p. 4). We are all familiar as well with "selective recall" (p. 4).

The following passage is written by a chronicler* of a novel who attempted to reconstruct what actually happened to a couple who were slain. He has an impossible mission:

> Though this record purports to be the truth, it is not the truth. No person can engage in exhaustive research of any happening and recreate the actuality of that event. Some persons refuse comment. Others fall prey to prejudices and biases, rumor and myth. From disparate backgrounds and experiences people form distortion screens through which they view life's moments and episodes.
>
> And memories keep badly. Just as molecules in glass shift with the passage of years, so, too, do experiences blend and muddle in the labyrinths of our minds. A little detail is added here, another forgotten there, until, like window panes in an old house, our memories gradually, imperceptibly, waver and distort and then reflect, not what actually happened, but what our mind wills to have happened. Such are the vagaries, the capriciousness, the human frailty of man and woman.

Or, as the philosopher Nietzsche would remark, we are condemned to view the world from a partial and distorted perspective, one defined by our interests and values.

". . . Pants on Fire"

If we grant the point that unintentional distortions of memory are part of everyone's experience, a particular individual may be suspect. Nowhere is this more true than in Washington, D.C. Our first president said, "I cannot tell a lie." Presidents following him had fewer

---

* Earl R. Hutchison, *The Echoes from Ole Forge Hill*, a novel under submission.

compunctions. Richard Nixon said, "I am not a crook," and then resigned to keep from being impeached. William Clinton, accused of having an affair with Monica Lewinsky, said: "I did not have sex with that woman." But, as later events proved, he lied. However, Charles Rangel, a Democratic Representative from New York, said that Clinton was morally obligated *to lie*—to protect his wife and child.

But, of course, other politicians lie. When Clinton was impeached for obstruction of justice in connection with the Monica Lewinsky episode, Republican politicians decried his immoral behavior. Then, in a stunning turn of events, the House majority leader, Newt Gingrich, stepped down from his leadership role when it was revealed he had a mistress and had asked his wife (in a hospital bed fighting cancer) for a divorce. Republican Bob Livingston, House Speaker-designate scheduled to replace Gingrich, had to acknowledge "I have, on occasion, strayed from my marriage" and gave up his role. However, Henry Hyde, a Republican from Illinois and chair of the impeachment committee, did not feel compelled to resign his position after what he described as "a youthful indiscretion" with a married woman. At the time of the "youthful indiscretion," Hyde was 48 years old.

As if this weren't enough to undermine a voter's confidence in the political arena, Jack Ryan, a Republican running for the Senate in Illinois, had to drop his campaign when his wife filed for divorce, charging him with forcing her to go to sex clubs with him. Ryan, as columnist Molly Ivins pointed out (in a June 2004 column), "was one of the 'family values' crowd who opposes gay marriage because it's such a threat to the institution."

All this tends to lend credence to what the character Gillian Loomis says about Washington, D.C., in Robert Rice's novel, *The Nature of Midnight*: ". . . it was a city of false smiles and barely sheathed claws, fingers crossed behind backs, of spins and bland lies and what's-in-it-for-me."

Of course, we know there are and were straight arrows in Washington—but still, all of this brings to mind Oscar Wilde's comment: "The Truth is rarely pure and never simple."

Fortunately, most of the persons you'll be interviewing will be like the mayor, Ada Haynes, or the working woman described by Niki Scott, later in this chapter.

A PRELIMINARY INTERVIEW

Before interviewing your subject, you'll want to investigate the background of the person and the topic you'll be discussing. How you conduct this research is covered in the next chapter, "The Search for Information." What is stressed here is the importance of it.

In a difficult interview, or any interview, good research is good armor. Being well versed in the subject matter gives you leverage when interviewing someone who is nervous, who is suspicious of the press or who gives vague answers to questions. A writer can keep the interview on track by supplying some facts the person can respond to directly and comfortably. (Marian Christy, *Invasions of Privacy*, cited in *Journalism Quarterly* Autumn (1985), 666–67, says if you want people to reveal something about themselves, you can encourage them by revealing something about yourself.) A command of the subject also suggests that the writer feels it is important. The result? Many people will respond to questions with enthusiasm and will refer you to other people who may be valuable information sources.

Let's preview some of the preliminary interviewing steps discussed in the chapter.

Assume you're a freelance environmentalist and you've become interested in a University City parks and recreation project that rests upon matching funds for a federal grant of $500,000. The Cane Creek Park project will also conserve some wetlands adjoining the city. You know your local newspaper and possibly the state wire service will be interested in the project and the possibility of the University City Council designating the matching funds. You phone the local editor, Gretchen Hollars, and ask her if she would be interested in a feature on speculation. With her own staff overextended on other stories, and no environmental reporter on the staff, Hollars is pleased you called. "Yes!" she says, "by all means." The Associated Press chief in the state capital, Whitney West, gives you another overwhelming "Yes!"

You call Mayor Ada Haynes of University City for an interview. The mayor, of course, is not hovering around a phone waiting to be interviewed by a member of the press. Will *any* person you call, for that matter, want to be interviewed by you? Perhaps. But on touchy issues or problems, you can't tell. Most politicians welcome the opportunity. Mayor Haynes, however, may be too involved in doing her job to spare the time. Other reporters may also have been trying to talk with her.

How do you approach the task of arranging that interview? With an air of assurance. After all, you are a representative of the public. You represent power. (You may even have voted Haynes into office.) All of this is important to any political figure you are going to interview. The mayor's political life may depend on the image the press projects, and you are now part of that projection apparatus. You dial Haynes' number. Her secretary forwards you to her:

"Mayor Haynes, I'm Sloan Trent, on assignment for *The University News*. I'd like to talk to you about your plans for the Cane Creek Park recreational project. Would it be possible to get together for about 15 minutes sometime today or tomorrow?"

"I'm sorry," Haynes replies, "much as I would love to talk with you about it, I have a very busy schedule through the rest of the week. Perhaps you can call me early next week."

Sympathize with her:

"I'm certain you do have a busy schedule, Mayor Haynes. I'd have trouble keeping up with it. That's why I'm only going to take up 15 minutes of your time. I'm thoroughly familiar with the proposed project and possible matching funds—I just need to clear up a few points on the planning of it and the Council's take on it. As a matter of fact, I only have six questions I want to ask you."

If the mayor still says, "No, I really can't spare the time," be persistent.

"Mayor Haynes, it's really important for the Cane Creek project that the public be more informed about it. That's exactly what I am prepared to do."

"I'm terribly sorry, and I know you're right," Mayor Haynes replies, "but I just can't see how I can spare the time right now."

What is your response to this? Do you capitulate? Of course not.

"Well, I'm sorry too, Mayor Haynes," you reply. "I've got to do this story, and I'd much rather get a balanced picture of the proposal. I've already arranged an interview with Councilman Bill Mackiney for his comments, but you are the central authority in this matter, and I'd like to have your thoughts on the questions I'm going to pose."

A moment of silence.

"Well, look," Haynes says, "if you really need to talk to me, I can arrange to see you just before lunch tomorrow in my office. Would that be convenient?"

"More than convenient," you reply. "Thank you."

What happened here? The major factors were: (1) you represent the public, (2) you were persistent (How can the Mayor *not* give 15 minutes for an interview?) and (3) you threw in the Open Sesame words, "Bill Mackiney"—the councilman from the opposition party. The mayor just couldn't stand the idea of Mackiney's comments standing alone in the press. It wouldn't be smart politics.

As a freelance writer, you want to be alert to what is news or what will be news, such as this Cane Creek project. This will lead you to feature stories, magazine articles or commentary that tie into news events, or ride on the coattails of them.

PREPARATION FOR THE INTERVIEW

Preparation for the interview will include not only the history and background of the interview topic, but research into the background and accomplishments of the person you will interview. Although the media library should be the first stop, if the project is a local one or the person is a hometown celebrity, the city's editor or reporters may also suggest background sources for you to check. If the person to be interviewed has written articles or books, the public library or a local bookstore may have copies of those books or the magazines the articles appeared in. Use a search engine to research the topic and/or the person. Read as much as you can prior to the interview so that you can ask fresh and intelligent questions. Record important details in a notebook or on 4 × 5½-inch slips of paper formed into a pad by folding 10 half-sheets together.

After gathering the background material, write your questions at the top of the 4 × 5½-inch slips and the answers received at the interview below the questions. Organize questions around subject-matter areas. To make certain you have complete coverage, enlist the services of the who, what, why, when, where and how questions, along with the what's-the-significance or consequence question. Writing the answers on the 4 × 5½ sheets during the interview does not take any more time than recording the answers in a notebook, and later you'll be able to shuffle the answers around like a deck of cards until they reflect the order they'll be appearing in the story. (When it comes time to write the feature or article, you'll compliment yourself upon ordering your materials in such an efficient fashion.)

Try to tape all interviews. Be overt about it, so that if a person does not want to be taped an objection can be made. No objection? You have tacit permission. Make certain your tape recorder has good batteries in it and that you have an extra tape in case the interview lasts more than an hour. It's added protection for you in libel cases or if a person denies making those comments.

CONDUCTING THE INTERVIEW

Before the actual interview begins, engage in some preliminary work.

Noticing Detail

Note the setting and the person being interviewed. Let your readers see—through characterization and setting description—what you see and hear. These details aid in your efforts at accuracy simply because we tend to eliminate details when reporting later.

If you are trying to determine how prosperous the business executive is, note what type clothing she or he is wearing. What aura does the person exude? Can you smell cologne? Is the person neat and well-groomed? Is the greeting genuine? Is the handshake firm or limp-fish fashion?

What is the dominant impression of the room or office? Cramped or spacious? How is the room/office furnished? What is on the desk? A thesaurus, a book of quotations, a letter opener with bright copper pennies embedded in the handle?

Although some details can mislead, more often than not their total impression will provide you with an accurate picture of the state of things.

In the Beginning, Put Them at Ease

The importance of starting off the interview correctly cannot be overemphasized. Put the person at ease. Perhaps you can remark about what happened to you on the way over to the interview. Or ask about the semiprecious rock collection on a shelf, a unique paperweight on the desk or an attractive travel print on the wall.

ROLE PLAYING IN THE INTERVIEW

As Webb and Salancik have noted, you have to assume some role in an interview. Just as you leave a role of son or daughter when you leave your parents and assume another as student or businesswoman or businessman, when you interview a person, you must assume another role.

Whose Side Are You On, Boy/Girl?

The role you elect to play when interviewing may be that of a representative of the all-powerful press, a protector, an absolver of guilt, a friendly companion or parent. The role no doubt will depend upon the topic of the interview. The role you assume may have an important effect upon the outcome. An example follows.

A Fatherly Role and the Compulsion to Confess

The most trying, frustrating and exhausting and then productive interview I ever conducted took place in a "third-degree" room in a Milwaukee police station. I was questioning two tough-looking vice squad detectives about how questionable materials were being censored in Milwaukee, for a research paper that later turned into a chapter for a book. I announced to the detectives at the onset that I was a doctoral student investigating the control of literature in Milwaukee. No matter what approach I took, no matter the questions I asked, I got non-committal or negative answers. However, I remained pleasant and courteous throughout. Finally, when I thought nothing and no one on this earth could soften up those two tough cops, I sighed, put away my pad and pen and picked up my briefcase. Then I happened to glance up at them. Their eyes had widened. I thought to myself, Okay, I'll try one more question:

"Before I leave, is there anything else I should ask you about?"

The question opened up a Pandora's box of admissions of illegal pressuring of book-store and drugstore owners to suppress magazines and books at the behest of the assistant district attorney in charge of prosecuting obscenity in Milwaukee.

What happened, I believe, involved two factors: First, there's a compulsion to confess in all of us. As children we readily confessed to our parents when questioned about something we did. This compulsion causes criminals to confess to cops. The Catholic Church embraces this compulsion. (And the Catholic Church is the dominant church in Milwaukee.) Second, although I announced my role as a doctoral student, I also presented another image. At age 35, with gray hair, dark-rimmed glasses and classic gray tweed jacket, I also represented a kindly father. That role, along with the compulsion-to-confess factor, I now believe, resulted in those confessions. At the time, I was unaware of the additional role I brought to the interview.

The moral? Remember the compulsion to confess. When you think the skies are so cloudy and gray that no ray can possibly break through, you may hear the persons you are questioning let loose a small sigh. You may see their eyes widen. They may start digging around in a desk drawer. When that, or something like it happens, be considerate. Ask them if perhaps it wouldn't be better to answer one or two more questions. Ask them if perhaps they haven't kept things to themselves too long. Chances are the little boy or girl in them will lead them into confession. When that happens, continue being considerate and pleasant and write everything down. Regardless of what they say, don't change your expression. Give them "tea and sympathy."

STILL MORE ROLE PLAYING

Interviewer Versus Interviewee

Both you and the person you're interviewing realize that you are in a confrontational situation. Whether it is an innocent or pleasurable situation or a semihostile or completely hostile confrontation, you are asking questions, and the person you're interviewing is being urged/forced to answer them. Some interviewer/interviewee roles:

"Do Gooders" and Those with the "Hunted Look"

"If I knew someone was coming to my door to do me good, I would run for my life."
—Anonymous

In this scenario you've been asked by the state Associated Press desk to check out what your district drug task force says is a meth problem in the little town of Monterey, Ohio, and write an article on it. (The Governor's Task Force on Methamphetamine Abuse had held a review of the state's anti-meth law yesterday. The review spurred the A.P. into action.) You get minutes of the Task Force meeting, a copy of the anti-meth law (supposed to be as stringent as Oklahoma's) and a record of meth arrests in the Monterey area. You arrange for a series of interviews with Monterey Chief of Police Roger Dale Phillips, Mayor Chuck Womack, and the high school principal, Dr. Xiao Mei Zhao.

Of course, you're upfront with them. You say you understand there's a meth problem in Monterey—the same as there is in surrounding communities—but that you've been asked to write an article about what's happening in Monterey in particular. Perhaps what's written will help parents and others realize the seriousness of the problem.

Will you be welcomed with open arms and answers? Not likely. Why not? You're just trying to do good. But it's still like the IRS greeting: "We're from the Internal Revenue Service, and we're here to help you."

Chief of Police Phillips will be reluctant to allow you to talk to cops on the beat because what they might say will reflect upon him. He will be reluctant to reveal the arrests made in the past year for the same reason, even though you have a copy of the Task Force's arrest record.

Mayor Womack will have an "Our Town" attitude. His administration may be discredited for not taking more measures to control the problem. Furthermore, he's trying to attract an auto parts plant to locate in Monterey, and the ensuing publicity from your story will cast a negative light upon the city.

Principal Zhao is in only her second year on the job and will be reluctant to arrange a meeting with student leaders for fear of what they will say. She's also reluctant to reveal violations of the school's drug policy because of the negative reflection upon her administration.

In situations such as this, you are the "do-gooder." You are looked upon sometimes with apprehension, at other times with ill-concealed horror.

"John, the Revelator" and Those to Be "Revelated"

The most hostile among the roles taken by the interviewer and the interviewee is that of the revelator (you) and those whose secrets are about to be revealed. The scene is usually hostile from the beginning. Those being interviewed are going to be forced to disgorge events that will place them in a bad light or cause them to lose their jobs. To expect a pleasant atmosphere is to be naive. Understanding this situation from the beginning provides you with armor to withstand hostile barbs.

THE RELUCTANT DRAGON: PART I

When stepping into the role of an interviewer (who can be viewed by interviewees in many roles other than those mentioned earlier), be prepared to assume the proper attitude for the role.

Who's in Charge?

Never forget that you are in charge of the interview.

Some people may try to dictate what will take place in the interview. See where this might take you. If you find the path not to your liking, insist upon a different path. If you do have to insist upon being in charge, be courteous and pleasant. Will the person you're interviewing be angry with your insistence? Not unless she or he is a control freak. If you allow politicians or other persons to dictate what will take place, you will not only "lose face" in their eyes, you will have lost a lever to pry from them answers to difficult questions. In *any* event, maintain a courteous and pleasant mien during your "insistence" and often enough you'll have gained respect from those being interviewed.

Ready, Set, Interview (Tape Recorders?)

Having arranged your questions in order from easy to complex, before asking the first question turn on your tape recorder.

However, tape recorders sometimes have strange effects on even sophisticated persons. If you find your tape recorder inhibits the interviewee, place it to one side. If it still bothers the person, put it away. If the sight of you taking notes on cards causes distress, write with the cards/pad on your knee below the desk top, out of sight. If the person is still disturbed, say that you want to be certain to get everything down the way it's said. If the person still is hesitant to answer your questions fully, put the pencil and cards away. After the interview, however, write down the answers immediately. Otherwise you may forget key words and phrases. Even if you use a tape recorder, you should take notes, writing answers down on your slips of paper. Tape recorders are used mostly for the record and to check some statements that warrant it once the interview is over. To do otherwise—listening to the tape after the interview and taking notes from it—is a needless waste of time.

About Those Persistent Questions

Questions that might be considered hostile, save until the very end. But no matter who is declining to talk   a celebrity, a scientist, a district attorney, the president of a large business or a labor leader—be tactful. Gentle persuasion works best with almost everyone.

The higher ranked the officials, the more celebrated the celebrity, the more they have been subjected to aggressive questioning, and the more likely they have been repulsed by it.

Still, knowing when to resort to more aggressive questioning may determine whether you get the information you need or whether you come away from a source with blank tapes and note cards. Sometimes aggressiveness earns you the respect of the person you're interviewing.

Reactions to the Questions

Once the answers start coming, listen not only to the words but how they are spoken. Myriad reactions may be noted: the inflection of a voice, an intonation, a hesitation, an evasive reply or a significant omission. Are the person's arms folded tightly in front? You'll have to open up that person by smiling and asking friendly questions. Is the person perspiring? Face pale? Does the person have trouble looking at you? Does she or he look at the floor when answering some questions? Blink a lot? Those things may mean a great deal. The Federal

Bureau of Investigation, for example, notes that when a person answers a question looking to one side and hands move sideways, the answer is suspect. If a person's hands move up and down to emphasize a point, that's an indication the answer is truthful. As an interviewer you have to determine what is happening and ask questions probing the subject matter that stirred those reactions and emotions. You will want to use some of those reactions when you write your interview story.

THE RELUCTANT DRAGON: PART II

As you know, some people are not willing fountains of information for a number of reasons. Perhaps their privacy is being invaded. Past unpleasant experiences with the press may make others wary, unwilling to talk or hostile. Loyalty to superiors or an organization may also create a reluctance to release revealing information. The degree to which your article will adversely affect a person's reputation or livelihood usually determines the degree of reluctance to divulge information. A stubborn streak of self-preservation is inherent in all but the most perverse human beings. To investigate thoroughly, you have to be ready to counter negative reactions and overcome them.

Once Again, Courtesy

A courteous and pleasant approach tends to disarm reluctant sources. When persons demur at answering questions, be pleasant. When they say they can't answer a specific question, be pleasant. If after 15 minutes, they still haven't answered one question, be pleasant. After all, you may be asking them to divulge information detrimental to themselves or others close to them. Why should they answer your questions? If you were in their place, would you answer them?

Always, and Again, Be Persistent

Once again (and persistently), a corollary to being pleasant and courteous is to be persistent. You will be rewarded by being persistent. At times you will need to extract facts that may jeopardize people's careers. But if you don't persist, you will not be fulfilling your responsibilities and you will have to face yourself in the mirror the next morning—not a pleasant experience. So be persistent.

You will talk to persons who will say they don't want to comment and who will then comment. If someone doesn't comment, if you find in your persistence that an edge is developing in your voice when you ask those questions, do not stop. If, toward the end of the interview, you find your questioning a little more aggressive than toward the beginning, that, too, is not a bad thing to let those interviewees experience. The combination of these things might move the person to answer.

If the person you are interviewing *still* does not want to answer your questions, assure her or him that answering the question is the best course of action:

"Senator Flagg, I can't imagine much being wrong with any answer that you may give to that question about the survey."

If Flagg still refuses:

"You know, Senator Flagg, that a balanced view of the situation is better than the one-sided view I'll have to write if you continue to refuse to comment. I'll be interviewing Senator Elizabeth Engle for answers to the same questions."

If Flagg still refuses:

"Senator Flagg, whatever you say about the survey will be better than my writing 'The senator refused to comment.' You know how active the voters' imaginations are."

Another refusal? Say, with a trace of weariness in your voice for the first time:

"Senator Flagg, you and I know it will all come out sooner or later. Won't it be better if your side is presented first, and by you?"

Flagg still refuses comment on that particular question? Don't give up. Continue with the interview and then at the end of the interview, say:

"Senator Flagg, all during this interview I've been thinking things over, and for the life of me I can't think of one reason why you shouldn't give your side about the survey. Now what is it that you really think is so bad about the survey?"

If, despite all these efforts, you still receive a refusal to comment, tell him that you feel certain that he's making a mistake. Leave your telephone number and ask him to call you if he changes his mind. Give him your deadline for the story. If you follow this line of questioning, you will have done all that is possible to get the answers to your questions.

Control Your Responses

Control your emotional responses to all answers. Nothing will conclude a line of questioning or an interview quicker than a look of surprise or a sharply drawn breath to a sensational answer. Try not to let the person being interviewed feel as though you are passing judgment on what is being said. Instead, nod encouragingly every once in a while. Encourage still more revelations by comments such as these:

- "I didn't know that" (stated in a matter-of-fact manner).
- "Tell me more about that, please." (Again, state this in such a matter-of-fact manner that it's impossible for the person not to continue elaborating.)
- "I'm not sure I understand what you meant when you said . . . ."
- "So what you're saying is . . ." (when you don't understand or, more importantly, when you want a reiteration or confirmation of a controversial statement).

OFF THE RECORD

What do you do if the person wants to preface comments with some "backgrounding" so that you will understand the full "implications" of the situation? The comments, of course, are "off the record." Your course of action depends on whether the background information will be forthcoming if you don't want to honor the off the record condition. Try to persuade the person to be "on the record." If you are not able to do so, say that although you would rather not, you will comply with the request. But also say that if you discover you can get the gist of the backgrounding comments in later investigative procedures, you may publish them.

After receiving the background material, try to convince the person that you should be free to publish it. Having revealed the background, the person may now have second thoughts about the restrictions.

In the middle of a line of questioning, an interviewee may say, "That's off the record." Reply that your understanding is that everything you are now talking about is on the record. And just what was so important about what was said, anyway? If the interviewee persists, say, "All right, but from this point on, *everything* will be on the record." If the person later says, "This is off the record," stop and say, "Just a minute. We had an understanding that everything being discussed is on the record. And it is." Be adamant. The person will probably see the comment, and the previous "off the record" comment in another light. If not, ask again later on. The interviewee may relent, and you'll be able to publish it with her or his blessing.

LISTEN TO THE ANSWERS

Listen to the answers to your questions carefully. In one televised presidential news conference, former President Reagan revealed that if the USSR attempted any move in the Persian Gulf, conflict would be imminent. More than 100 reporters asked eight more questions before one of them questioned the president about the foreign policy implications of his statement.

When Maria Sharapova defeated Serena Williams for the Wimbleton tennis championship on July 4, 2004, The Associated Press reported:

> Williams was gracious in defeat, embracing Sharapova.
> "It's great, she was so excited," Williams said. "I try not to be a bad loser."
> Williams said her own game "was way below par" and that she was only at 20 percent.

Try though she may, with that last comment Williams failed to make the grade of a "good loser."

When Pete Sampras, the great tennis player, retired, the interviewer noted this in his announcement in August 2004: "I'm 100 percent retired," Sampras said, his voice cracking. "I'm at peace with it. It's time to call it a career."

Sampras is not quite "at peace" with his retirement.

Other interviewers were not quite so perceptive:

Mark Fox, a first-string All American Rifle Team member eight times, was asked on television what went through his mind when he squeezed off those championship shots. "I hummed a little tune," he replied.

When John McEnroe devastated Ivan Lendl in a U.S. Open tennis championship match, the network interviewer asked him how he felt during the match. "I felt really good about my play. And I kept this tune going over and over in my mind, and things just fell into place," McEnroe said.

Neither of the interviewers listened to the answers carefully enough or had the imagination to ask what the name of the tune was that hummed through their minds at the moment of those great triumphs. (We *still* don't know.)

So when you write the answers down on a pad of paper during the interview, think about the significance and ramifications of what has been said. More than one skillful interviewer has been able to uncover a story (other than the assigned one) by following up on an answer that looked promising. For example, if Mayor Haynes is answering a question on urban renewal and mentions in passing a small snag or two that has to be eliminated, ask, "What are those snags?" "Who or what is behind the snags?" Then check on the facts and the persons mentioned. You may discover that a citizen's group has retained the best lawyer in town to file a suit to halt the renewal—a suit that might delay the construction for at least a year. Politicians like to slip in a hint of what may be big trouble so that later on they cannot be accused of hiding anything.

Straying Far Afield

Some persons may stray from the question you've asked. If they're evading the question, bring them back, courteously, at the first convenient pause: "Yes, that is interesting. But about the snag you mentioned just a minute ago—what exactly is that snag?" Some persons may stray from the questions simply because their speech patterns or thinking processes work that way. When that happens, listen for a minute or so to determine if anything newsworthy is being said. (Stray comments may lead to something important.) If there appears to be nothing newsworthy in the comments, once again, at a convenient pause, bring them back to the question: "Hmm, very interesting. However, I wonder if we might pursue the question about those snags you mentioned earlier."

THE LAST INTERVIEW QUESTION

Before concluding the interview, *always* ask this question: "What else should I ask you about?" More than one interview concluded in this fashion has been greeted with a laugh and then a retort like "Why don't you ask me about the incident that took place in the hallway right after the city council meeting about the Cane Creek project?"

Without smiling, ask immediately, "What happened in the hallway after the city council meeting about the Cane Creek project was adjourned?"

You've given the mayor an opportunity to talk about something she was reluctant to bring up herself in the interview. If someone now asks her why she mentioned that incident, she can reply, "I was asked about it by the reporter."

When you've explored all aspects of the interview and have it all down in your notes, conclude the interview in this way: "I think I have everything I need, but in case I've forgotten something, I'll call you. Will that be all right?" When the person agrees, it's your entry past the secretary or the agent.

This series of "tough" interview illustrations may be misleading. The vast majority of persons you will be interviewing as a freelance writer will be more than willing to talk about their project or hobbies or experiences.

TELEPHONE INTERVIEWS

If you feel you can accomplish the same goals in a telephone interview, it may not be necessary to push for a personal interview, but of the two, the face-to-face interview wins hands up.

Substitute a Telephone Interview?

In the case of Mayor Haynes, the parks and recreation story warrants a face-to-face interview. It's fairly complex and politically sensitive. A face-to-face interview will accomplish more and allow you to judge the response to your answers more perceptively. However, had Mayor Haynes said she was leaving that night for Japan to try to persuade a business concern to locate a plant in the city, you would have gone for a telephone interview. After all, the mayor had already been reached, and that in itself can be difficult enough.

The telephone is a valuable piece of equipment for a writer. The rush to wrap up features and articles is usually not quite so frenetic as hard news stories, but the telephone can still be the most convenient way to finish off your research.

Edna Buchanan Handles Rejections

The telephone interview has the advantage of saving time. However, it also is much easier for a person to sidestep a telephone call than a prearranged appointment for a personal interview. One can be "out" without really being "out" at all. If a person you want to question rejects you by hanging up the phone, do what former *Miami Herald* veteran reporter Edna Buchanan used to do. She covered *all* the major murders in Miami and had to interview those victims' families immediately after the deaths—not a pleasant prospect. Needless to say, she encountered many rejections when she phoned them. What did she do? She waited five minutes and then called again. In that time interval, other persons in the immediate family or friends may have intervened in her behalf, or the person may have changed her or his mind.

A Telephone Interview Checklist

Use this checklist when conducting a telephone interview:

Introduce yourself as a freelance writer. Briefly describe the story or project you're working on and the publication possibilities. Explain why it's important you have the interview.

Without face-to-face contact, rapport takes a little longer to establish. Having a list of prepared questions can keep the conversation moving. However, if the opportunity presents itself, depart from your prepared list and follow the train of thought your source introduces.

When you're finished, thank the person and say you might call back to double-check comments. Most people will be receptive to such callbacks, during which you can ask questions as well as clarify information given to you previously.

CELEBRITY INTERVIEWS

To ensure your celebrity interviews are distinctive, once you've completed your interview background research, think of the climb that person had to make to reach the celebrity pinnacle. Visualize that person at the foot of the mountain to be scaled. What preparations were necessary? Why were they necessary? How were they made? What obstacles had to be overcome? How were they overcome? How is it at the top? Anticlimactic? Disappointing? What now? How long does the celebrity anticipate being at the top? On the basis of what? Formulate your celebrity questions around these major points: preparations, obstacles, the top, and what now?

THE QUESTION-AND-ANSWER INTERVIEW

The material gathered by interviewing is usually written in the usual feature story format, such as "A Father's Tale" or "The Saga of Ken McElroy," both in Chapter 3. On occasion, however, the material may be presented in a question-and-answer format. The question-and-answer technique provides a deceptively simple approach to writing an interview story. Some question-and-answer interviews begin with a brief introductory paragraph to ensure a smooth transition into the body of the story. Some do not need one. However, a concluding paragraph may or may not be used to end the story. The structure generally follows that of the short or long feature.

Fortunately, Judy L. Thomas agreed to answer a multitude of questions about her investigation and writing of the feature on "hate groups" in Chapter 4.

"Judy Thomas on the Writing of 'Hate Groups'"

Q. Where did the idea for this specific article on hate groups come from? You? Your editor? What generated the idea?

Note that this question is actually two questions. They should have been asked sequentially.

A. The idea was mine. I covered the Oklahoma City bombing in 1995 for *The Wichita Eagle* before taking a job at *The Kansas City Star*. As a general assignment reporter on the metro desk of *The Star*, I continued to cover the bombing as well as the militia movement. As part of that coverage, in 1996, I visited Elohim City, the white separatist compound in northeast Oklahoma that received national attention when it was revealed that Oklahoma City bomber Timothy McVeigh called there just two weeks before the blast. Over the years, I continued to follow the bombing story and early this year told my editor that I would be interested in writing a story about what has happened to the militia and anti-government movement since the bombing.

Q. What were the points you made to the editor to persuade her or him?

A. The points I made to sell the story were that the 10-year anniversary of the bombing was approaching, and while numerous news organizations around the country would be writing pieces about the bombing itself and how it affected the city and the hundreds of victims, I wanted to look at the groups that were catapulted into the national spotlight after the disaster.

Other strong selling points were that the bombing had numerous Kansas connections—bombing accomplice Terry Nichols lived in the state, the Ryder truck used in the bombing was rented there, many of the materials used in the bombing were purchased there and the bomb was assembled there. And finally, recent incidents in Kansas City and across the country had brought the movement back onto the radar screen again. For example, the shooting of a federal judge's husband and mother in Illinois originally raised questions as to whether there was a neo-Nazi connection. And in Kansas City, we had just learned that the white supremacist Aryan Nations organization was planning to relocate its headquarters to the area. The editors all agreed that the story sounded like a good—and definitely timely—one.

Q. Did you outline the story before research or before writing?

A. I don't make any kind of formal outline, but I do sit down with my editor at the beginning and take detailed notes on what we think needs to be included in the story and who I want to interview. I'll add to that as I go, but it gives me a good start.

Then before I start writing the rough draft, I type up what you could call an informal outline—not like the kind we learned how to do in seventh grade English class, by any means—but one that helps me organize the story by sections. Under each section, I'll write short sentences or phrases about what issues and sources will be included in that section.

Q. Where'd you go for background material? *Star* library? Internet?

A. My research began by doing Google and Nexis searches to find out what had been written on the issue in the past few years. Although I had covered the bombing and the anti-government movement for years, I also worked on the projects desk of *The Star* and had been busy with other stories, so I felt a little "out of the loop" at first. I also checked out the Web sites of numerous militia, Patriot and hate groups to get caught up on what they had been doing. As I did that, I found that many of the militia groups that I had covered in the mid-to-late 1990s had dissolved. Only a handful appeared to still be active. (A great thing about Web sites is that many contain links to other sites that may also be useful. But don't get lazy and let this be your only method of research. The Internet should never replace good, old-fashioned networking with sources. Also be aware that some sites—particularly the racist ones—may be "toned down" so as to look more mainstream to the average reader.)

Q. Any problems doing research?

A. Another part of my research was to begin calling the leaders of the various groups I was writing about. I didn't encounter any problems and found that because I had covered them so extensively in the past, they remained willing to talk to me.

Q. When approaching sources, what preparation did you make?

A. When approaching sources, objectivity is crucial. If you lose your objectivity, you also lose your credibility. You need to put your feelings aside when covering controversial issues like this. That's not to say you can't have an opinion; just keep it to yourself. One thing I've found is that some people who are reluctant to talk to reporters are often caught off guard if I am courteous and professional and don't try to argue with their positions, no matter how distasteful. I don't have to approve of their beliefs, but I can listen to what they have to say. Once they see that I am genuinely interested in talking to them, they'll open up.

Q. When did you have a rough idea of where the feature would take you?

A. I had a pretty good idea of where the story would go after about a week of researching and interviewing sources. Going into it, and based on what I had been reading on a couple of list serves that I've been a member of for years, I had a feeling that the movement had dwindled since its heyday after the Oklahoma City bombing, and the research confirmed that. I was actually surprised at how candid some of the movement's leaders were in discussing their status. The one question I needed more confirmation about was whether authorities and others who monitor the movement were concerned despite the dwindling activity. And what I found became a major point of the story—that even though the movement was now rudderless and in disarray, there still was cause for concern. That's because, according to the experts, the lack of leadership had created a potentially explosive environment in which "lone wolves" were encouraged to carry out their agendas. I also learned that a new trend was developing in which some groups were starting to turn to the Internet to attract young recruits.

Q. How did you take notes? Note cards? Computer?

A. During an interview, I generally take notes on the computer. If I'm worried about the source becoming nervous when hearing the typing going on in the background, I'll take notes on a legal pad that I keep at my desk. If the subject is a controversial one, I'll tape the interview—with the source's approval—then transcribe it afterward.

Q. Did you write more than one draft?

A. I wrote several drafts beginning with a rough version, then keeping a copy before revising it on the computer. I usually make a printout of each version, marking the changes in red ink, then fixing them on the computer. I like to make hard copies so I can sit back and read them carefully—and sometimes out loud—instead of having my eyes glaze over while staring at a computer screen.

Q. What were the writing conditions? At home? At work?

A. I wrote this story at work, but took printouts home with me at night to go over. It always helps to go over a story again in a different and more relaxed environment.

Q. Any rituals involved prior to writing?

A. When I write, I often put headphones on—even though there's nothing playing—to help block out the background noise. It also helps keep others from interrupting as I write! I know some reporters can write a story without having the lead down first, but I'm not one of them. I always come up with some kind of lead, even if it's not that good, and go from there. Then, as I'm writing, a better, more polished lead will sometimes pop into my head.

Q. Any other preparations before writing? Coffee?

A. I'm not a coffee drinker, but I love Diet Mountain Dew, so there's almost always a can of it sitting next to me as I write.

Q. How long did it take to write the feature?

A. It took about three weeks to do this story, with the research taking more than two weeks. I wrote it over a two-day period, and it took about a day to go over it with my editor and answer any questions he had. We also had a meeting with the photo editor, a graphic artist and the front page editor the week before the story ran to determine what pictures and graphics would run with the piece and how it would be presented.

Q. Happy with the final draft?

A. I'm satisfied with the way the package turned out. I think it was timely and helped put into perspective what's happened to a subculture that surfaced after the bombing 10 years ago. My only disappointment—and this tends to be the case with many reporters' stories—is that a few cuts were made that I didn't necessarily like. For example, we ran a "Where are they now?"-type sidebar on what has happened to some of the leaders in the movement, and some bizarre and interesting details and quotes that I felt had enhanced the story were cut for space reasons. But that's just par for the course.

A greatly abbreviated feature on how married couples argue is presented below in question-and-answer form. The original article by Anthony Brandt appeared in *Psychology Today*.

"Avoiding 'Couple Karate'"

If you are happily married, chances are you possess good arguing skills. Anyway, that's what investigations of marital conflict by University of Illinois psychologist John M. Gottman indicate.

Q: How exhaustive was your investigation into marital conflict?

A: Throughout a nine-year period we studied some 487 couples, using aids such as videotapes and devices for measuring physiological reactions.

Q: What are some of your findings?

A: We discovered that skills in relating to one another were more important than wealth or education.

Q: What kind of marital discord were you studying?

A: Actually we found that most fights have three stages: agenda-building, then arguing and, finally, negotiating.

Q: You obviously have been able to help couples in conflict. What other relationship skills do you find important?

A: Helping couples to solve conflicts is obviously important. But no one yet has been able to instruct them in how to become friends. I intend to do that.

If you ask the right kind of questions in the right order and if you get the proper responses, you don't have to engage in much creativity in writing the interview. The creativity comes in shaping the answers so that they are succinct and still keep the spirit of the response. This creativity takes place in the background research that was necessary to formulate the questions.

Sometimes you may have just the right answer to end the story. Such was the case in "Avoiding 'Couple Karate.'" If not, you may have to use a concluding paragraph such as the following:

> Having helped couples resolve their conflicts, Gottman now intends to teach them how to become friends.
>
> "No one has done that yet," Gottman said. "That's my goal now."

THE "LET THEM DO THE TALKING" INTERVIEW

Even veteran feature writers often have difficulty letting the persons they're interviewing have free rein. Or the writers paraphrase when they should let the direct quotes stand. Niki Scott, in the following feature, "Working Woman," illustrates how vivid a feature can be when you keep yourself from obtruding:

"Working Woman"*

By Niki Scott

She spent one month crying, two months job hunting and three months cleaning her house.

It's been six months since she lost her job, and Laura is beginning to fear for her sanity.

She felt nothing when her boss called her in and smiled and chattered and asked how old her grandsons were. She felt nothing while he talked about cutbacks and profit margins and a temporary tightening of the belt. Then he informed her that she was out of a job.

"I thanked him for his time, walked out of his office, left the building and walked around the city for over five hours. I wanted to cry or scream, but all I could do was walk," she said softly.

"They transferred all the executives to Pennsylvania and laid off everyone else. I'm 54 years old. I worked for that company for 16 years. But I was as expendable as a box of pencils," she said bitterly.

"It wasn't just a job that I lost. It was where I went every day. In some ways, my identity was wrapped up in that job. I didn't just lose $312 a week, I lost a huge part of my life. And no one cares. No one," she said, swallowing hard.

"You'd think I'd be finished crying. I thought I was. I spent a whole month crying. I'm tired of crying. I'm afraid I may never stop. I'm afraid I'll never find another job. I'm afraid I'm going to lose my mind," she said, all in one breath.

She lit a cigarette with shaking hands. "After that first awful month, I stopped crying by getting up at 7 every morning, dressing up in my little suit and job-hunting. That was the most depressing experience of my entire life.

"I was either underqualified or overqualified. My experience was either not broad enough, or too broad and not specialized enough.

"What is true—and what no job interviewer dared say—is that I'm 54 years old and no company wants to hire someone who could retire in 10 years.

"After two months of interviewing, I stopped. I cleaned my house instead. And cleaned it. And cleaned it. When I wasn't cleaning, I cooked. And cooked. And ate and ate. I've gained 25 pounds from eating my own cooking, and my husband is begging me to stop because he's gained 10 pounds.

"Some days, I fear for my sanity. I have no support group—all my friends at work are scattered around town or have found new jobs, and I never did have friends who were at home because I've always worked.

"The worst part is the attitude other people have about this. If a man gets laid off, everyone sympathizes. They know how hard it is for him to be unemployed and they rally around, make allowances for him, encourage him.

"But if a woman loses her job, people assume she'll just stay home—and be happy about it—if she doesn't find another. If one more person says, 'But aren't you enjoying being home after all those years of working?' I'm going to scream."

---

* Reprinted with the permission of Universal Press Syndicate.

A NO-NO INTERVIEW

One type of interview currently making the rounds is, critized charitably, inane. Vince Young, University of Texas quarterback drafted by the Tennessee Titans, underwent this interview ordeal:

"Five Questions:
Vince Young, Quarterback"

Hidden talent: "Dressing."
Biggest pet peeve: "Losing."
One thing you can never
    forget on a road trip: "Clothes, drawers."
Most hated chore: "Washing dishes. I thought that was a woman's job."
First job: "'Just for Feet.' Selling shoes."

Here's what Tracey Lefevre, writer for the Public Affairs Office of Tennessee Technological University, has to say about the interview:

It's a good example of what not to do. The only thing it seems to do is satisfy the interviewer's personal curiosity. It reveals nothing about Young's early football influences, professional history, motivations, greatest personal achievement and challenge, or possible rituals he has before taking to the field.

Concise is good—irrelevant isn't!

THE MINI-PROFILE INTERVIEW

The following example of what I call a "mini-profile interview" further illustrates the gold you uncover when you let your source do the talking:

"Just an Old Basset Hound"*

By Jerry Hornsby

Ronald E. Cartwright, of Inglewood, a Metro Health Department rabies control officer, works at the Metro Dog Pound.

"We save as many dogs as we can, but, yeah, we have to put a lot of them to sleep.
We have 800 or 900 dogs a month, so we have to turn them over.

"Some go to Meharry and Vanderbilt for research purposes. Meharry usually
takes maybe 10 a month but Vandy will pick up 9, 10, 12 a day. Sometimes the
Humane Society will need some cats or dogs. But as I say, we have to put a lot of
them to sleep.

"Normally seven days is all we keep a dog, then we usually have to dispose of
it. Well, this old basset hound was brought in about three weeks ago. I sort of grew
fond of that old rascal, I started calling him Duke. After seven days, when he hadn't
been picked up, I said let's hold off on this one awhile, so we put him up front in
the adoption area. We kept hanging onto him for three weeks. He was just an old
basset hound.

"I couldn't have saved Duke but about one more week. Then this morning a lady
came and asked if we had picked up a basset hound, sort of old. I grinned and said
as a matter of fact we had. She walked back to look and she smiled and said, 'That's
him!' Then she hugged my neck."

———

*Reprinted with the permission of *The Tennessean.*

Another illustration is this mini-profile by a student:

"A Rose-strewn Path"

By Cathy Hill Postell

Cheri Seman is a graduate student in special education. Here is how she became
engaged.

"Over Christmas break, I went to visit my father who has just recently moved to
Kansas. I flew back on Christmas Eve, which is also my birthday. My boyfriend was
supposed to pick me up at the airport.

"When I got off the plane, the very first person I saw was his best friend, so I
thought to myself, 'Well, Chip couldn't make it, so he asked Mark to come instead.'
We were kind of saying hello, but then he handed me a rose. I was thinking, 'What
is going on here?'

"He directed me toward the rest of the people. I started walking, and the next
person handed me a rose. It turned out that everyone who was waiting for people to

come off the plane had a rose to hand me. I got to the end of the crowd, and Chip was at the end.

"He had a dozen roses, and an engagement ring. He got down on one knee and proposed to me in the airport in front of all those people, which was really embarrassing.

"Really, I was in shock because I really didn't think that Chip would do something like that. Even though I was getting the flowers and everything, I still thought that it was just because it was my birthday. I really didn't expect him to propose. I could barely speak. I kind of whispered, 'Yes,' and that's about as far as I got. Everyone applauded."

Good things happen when you let people talk.

SUMMARY

An interview will be successful if you conduct the background research necessary to ask the right questions and you are confident in your approach. Chances are a source has something to gain by granting an interview, but some people may fear they have something to lose. You may have to muster an arsenal of human relations experience to persuade a reluctant source to cooperate. In any event, the way a source responds may depend upon your preparation, persistence and professionalism.

The way you compose your feature or article may be suggested by something you notice while conducting the interview. Sometimes the personal traits and habits of interviewees or the way their offices or homes are furnished provide an angle around which many of the source's answers can be arranged. Use of detail may provide a story with a certain mood and give the audience the feeling of being an insider. These touches enhance a story. The goal of every interview is to elicit information and/or bring an interviewee or the topic closer to the public. Skill is necessary to accomplish this.

INTERVIEW FOR DISCUSSION

This interview for *Newsweek* by Brian Braiker of one of America's most well-known and prolific writers, Joyce Carol Oates, appeared, greatly abbreviated, under "This Week Online" on *Newsweek*'s Web site.

Braiker introduces the interview with an account of Oates' latest novel, *Rape: A Love Story.* "The book," Braiker says, "touches on themes Oates fans will find familiar: the construction of identity, fate, sex and the human body." Then he comments on her prolific writings and awards:

But this is just her latest offering. Since her debut in 1963, Oates has written more than 40 novels, 26 story collections, eight poetry compilations, five drama collections, nine books of essays, a children's book, and an opera libretto (which works out to an average of more than two works per year). The Princeton writing professor picked up along the way a Rosenthal Award from the

American Academy Institute of Arts and Letters, a Guggenheim Fellowship, the O. Henry Prize for Continued Achievement in the Short Story, the Elmer Holmes Bobst Lifetime Achievement Award in Fiction, the Rea Award for the Short Story, and in 1978, membership in the American Academy Institute.

Then Braiker enters a question-and-answer interview format:

"A Joyce Carol Oates Interview"*

Q: You must get tired of people asking you about how prolific you are.

A: It's not a question that means much right now because I am just sort of stumped with something I'm working on. I have all these notes in front of me—I often begin a novel or short story in so many different ways. I could have nine, 10 different openings, which is what I have in front of me right now. I'm not able to see what I'm doing yet. A lot of it's experimental and there's so much revising. So by the time an actual book comes out I have written and rewritten so many pages.

Q: Do you ever worry about running out of things to say?

A: I will never run out of things to say. I have pages and folders of notes. My problem is the structure, how to put it together. You meet someone on an airplane, he can tell you stories and stories. That's not the point: we're all brimming with stories. The difficulty is how to present the material. When you begin with one sentence, then you have another sentence and you have a first paragraph, then you're beginning that way and you're not beginning any other way. So you've excluded a lot of other things. I can write a whole chapter and I discover that wasn't the best choice and I go back and write another.

Q: You're so good at social commentary and observation. Are you paying attention to the election?

A: Well, yes. I'm not a fanatic. I'm obviously more of a liberal than the federal government is at the moment. But it's interesting to see the drama work itself out . . .

Q: You write a lot about boxing—which is a similar, if more violent, form of contest.

A: It's very much the same. There are strong athletes and personalities like Muhammad Ali and Joe Lewis and Mike Tyson. So if you're interested in American culture, they are iconic figures as well as human beings. I don't really pass judgment on these people; I'm fascinated by the unfolding of history and what is happening. If you read Henry Adams' "Democracy" which is set in the 1880s, it's the quintessential Washington novel. It's the first novel of its kind, a novel of manners. To read it now, so long after it was written, Henry Adams' view is so relevant, of democracy in America and the interplay of politics and the necessity of politicians to make compromises. Often they make deals—often they are very close to being corrupt—and yet without that, there isn't any democracy.

You can't have a pure politician. My point is that I'm like Henry Adams in the sense that I'm a novelist that's looking at the turmoil and the drama. You could say that it's an operatic drama; there's a lot of excitement there. But to say that I'm a fanatic for somebody or against somebody, I really don't see myself that way.

Q: What genre or style do you most enjoy writing in?

A: I find that the novel is most challenging. When I'm working on a novel, I'm always in a state of suspended anxiety, yet if I'm not working on a novel, I don't feel quite right. I know people do think of me as prolific, and I think statistically I am, but I don't experience writing that way. To me it's very heavily a matter of craft and I could throw out something I've been working on a couple of weeks and start over again in a halting way. But then when I get a draft, then I write the whole thing over and I feel very good, because the slack has been alleviated. For me, I love the novella form. I love to read novellas and I love to write them, but they are very difficult. If I could just write novellas like *Rape: A Love Story*, I would be very happy. But that form is difficult.

Q: In describing writing as a craft, you make it sound like something you can learn and get better at. What do you think your younger self would make of your current self rewriting *A Garden of Earthly Delights*?

A: Well, I'm not sure. The reason I rewrote so much of *A Garden of Earthly Delights* was that it was coming out in the Modern Library and being reprinted as an American classic. So I felt that this was an opportunity to go back and improve it. When I was a young writer—was 26 when I wrote it—I wasn't writing a classic then; I was an unknown writer. It was only my second novel; in a sense I was learning how to write by writing it. So when I went back to rewrite it, I excised a lot. I moved everything faster. I gave more space to voices in the characters' own language rather than my language. Young writers often tell stories, but older writers are more practiced; they allow the story to be told by the characters a little more. It just speeds it up a little; it's more dramatic.

Q: So it being designated a classic wasn't good enough for you?

A: Oh, we can always improve. It made me feel very humble and solemn in a sense that I should really make it the best I could do. I did that with "them" also. I mean, to see this book on the shelf, it's right next to William Faulkner *The Sound and the Fury*, his face and then my face. This is very daunting to a living writer. So I took the opportunity, in both cases, to revise. "them" I didn't revise too much. I made it better, definitely better.

Q: John Updike recently released a well-received collection of his early stories. Can we expect something similar from you?

A: No I don't think I would do that. John's a friend of mine. John collects everything that he has written and publishes everything. I don't have that philosophy. Even James Joyce could edit some of his work . . .

Q: Do you have stories, then, that you may never publish?

A: I do have some manuscripts in my archives that I'll never publish, novels that I just don't feel that I want to publish. My idea of a book is not like John's. I think he thinks of himself as a great writer—he is a great writer. He's a major American writer and he feels that anything that he writes and publishes would be of interest and should be in a book. I have a different position. I think of each book as a work of art in itself and the book in itself has to have an aesthetic shape to it. So just because I wrote something in 1969 and it won an award, I wouldn't necessarily put that in a book because now, shaping the book, I would have a different perspective. I would just flinch and cringe at the thought of a collected stories [anthology]. I would never allow that or want that.

Q: Do you ever worry about the sheer volume of your work diluting the impact of any individual book?

A: I think that's inevitable. If one publishes a couple books year, I don't think one can avoid that. But I'm not trying to create an image of myself or have a career that's necessarily sculpted or guided. I'm more interested in individual projects. So if I have an idea, I want to execute that idea the best I can. When it becomes published, like *Rape: A Love Story,* it passes over into what we call production. The editors find a cover for it and I work with them with the cover art and the design of the book, which to me is very exciting because it's an aesthetic production. To me it has a luminosity; there can be beauty in the physical look of the book.

Q: So you do judge a book by its cover?

A: I think everybody does perhaps subliminally.

Q: Was this book based on any real life events?

A: It's probably based on a composite of things. I have a strong feeling that something like this has happened or will happen—the mother, the daughter, just the mistake she makes to cut through the park. She would have known better, it's just that something whimsical—the moon was out and she and her daughter would walk through the park and save a 10-minute walk.

It's amazing how split-second decisions can change the course of a life. Well I've come so close to making these mistakes myself. But they're only mistakes in retro-spect. I've been in a car as a passenger and somebody cuts in front of us and just like that, in about half a second, we could all have been killed. This happened not too long ago on the [New Jersey] Turnpike. And it happened so fast. I think we think about these things all the time and for a writer it leads to all kind of dramatic possibilities.

Q: Paul Auster, who I'm a fan of, does that a lot.

A: Oh, yes. He's a friend of mine. He lives in my neighborhood, actually. I've seen him walking his dog.

He's a very nice man. He's shy. Listen, what you want to do is—you've read his work and you know how he likes these chance encounters—just go up to him very politely and quietly and say "Joyce sends her greetings." And he will look up with his big, brown eyes [and ask], "Joyce?" You say, "Not James Joyce. Joyce Carol Oates, your friend."

-----

*With some modifications the Oates interview was downloaded from Newsweekonline. MSNBC.com. Source: *Newsweek* Entertainment, January 24, 2004.

EXERCISES

1. Select one person from the class to engage in mutual interviewing. Interview each other for a feature or article in the University News.

2. Write a characterization of the person you interviewed in 25 words or less to introduce the inter-view. Concentrate on one central impression or characteristic (for example, she or he chewed on a pencil while answering the tough questions).

3. Write answers to these comments made to you by the person you are interviewing, or attempting to interview.
   a. "I really don't have time for you right now."
   b. "I don't want to talk about myself."
   c. "I don't want all this publicity."
   d. "Why should I talk to you about this?"
   e. "I really have to go now."
   f. "I'd rather not go into that aspect of the episode."
   g. "Why don't you ask me about my business partner's role in this whole thing?"

h. "I don't have to put up with this kind of questioning."
i. "That's an insulting question!"
j. "That's none of your damn business!"
k. "Your paper never reports anything accurately."

4. Clip a news-related feature interview from a local newspaper and paste it on the left-hand side of a page. To the right, critique it paragraph by paragraph.

5. Your U.S. senator is coming to campus to speak at an economic conference. Write a memo to the local newspaper editor about what you propose to cover in the interview and why (perhaps a-day-in-the-life piece).

6. The newspaper editor gives you the interview gig on the senator. Write 10 questions you will ask her.

7. Watch the following television news programs: CNBC'S Chris Mathews on *Hard Ball, Paula Zahn Now* on CNN, *The News Hour with Jim Lehrer, The O'Reilly Factor,* and *Lou Dobbs Tonight* on CNN. Compare the aggressiveness of the various reporters in questioning their sources. Do you approve of their questioning? What would you change if you were doing the questioning?

8. Create a "Let Them Do the Talking" brief from this newspaper story about a tornado survivor. You must use all direct quotes.

   Some paraphrasing is in the story, and attributions, but you're not allowed to engage in paraphrasing. However, note that the paraphrasing could easily have been eliminated because it stems from direct quote information derived from the person giving the account. Still, in real life, you'd replay the conversation over in your mind and use the exact words. Some news story sentences will have to be eliminated. Remember, don't close quotes until your person is through talking.

Tornado Survivor

By Brad Schrade and Leon Alligood
The Tennessean, April 4, 2006

All were accounted for at 1607 Biffle Road, home of Billy and Betty Sisk, and their two children, Erica, 13, and Brandon, 10. Betty Sisk said she didn't fully understand the expression "accounted for" until Sunday night's storm plucked her and her two children from the closet of their home, where they had prayed and linked arms as the tornado came closer.

"You could feel the walls start popping and hear the glass breaking and you could actually feel everything just falling apart," she said yesterday afternoon as family and friends sorted through the remains of their three-bedroom, two-bath home for mementoes and valuables.

Mother and children sailed through the air, landing about 50 feet from the front door, or what used to be the front door, she said.

"Everything just falls apart in front of you. You can feel stuff hitting you, flying by you, you just feel everything, the dirt slapping you in the face, you feel everything."

As the tornado moved the trio outside, the brute force wind wedged Erica from the mother's frantic armlock.

"I thought I had lost her. It pulled her away from me. She had to crawl back to us, and finally, I was able to grab her hand and pull her to me. I didn't let go," Betty Sisk said.

"The storm took 20 years of stuff, but my most precious possessions are still here—that's my kids."

After the tornado passed over them, she said she rose from the mud and called for the Sherrons, her next-door neighbors.

"Eddie," she shouted. "Eddie."

There was no reply.

9. Write a mini-profile (150 to 300 words) from an interview of a salesperson, perhaps similar to the following one that I did at Wal-Mart while being checked out. (Note: Seldom does a person talk about an experience in the way illustrated in previous profiles. Some quotes, of course, will have to be omitted. Your skill in composing a coherent, unified feature will be tested by how your quotes are linked together.)

"Brandie: What's in a Name?"

Brandie Hillman is a check-out clerk who has worked at Wal-Mart for five years.

"No, my mother was not a brandy connoisseur. And neither was my father.

"I was named after an old girlfriend of my father's.

"It all came about because I was the fourth child and both of my parents were looking for a name for me. It was my mother who suggested 'Brandie' because my father was always talking about her.

"My namesake lives in Kentucky, the same place my father grew up. When he came back from Korea, he met Brandie and they fell in love. The problem was, she was only 15 years old. Her parents told my father to come back in three years and they'd give their consent to a marriage. Brandie and my father swore to be true to each other.

"But when my father came back in three years, on the date they'd set, Brandie had married another man three weeks earlier.

"Like I said, my father always talked about Brandie. It didn't bother my mother. She told me once, 'She's in Kentucky, and I'm the one who's married to your Father.'

"I met Brandie once. She wasn't all that attractive. Rather common looking. It was just one of those things."

10. The Library of Congress is seeking volunteers to help record the memories of the 19 million living U.S. veterans. Go to www.loc.gov/folklife/vets to get a free Veterans History Project kit. It will have tips, resources and forms for recording and registering an oral history. Locate a vet and interview her or him. Your recording will be housed permanently in the nation's archives.

Before you receive the kit (it will take six to eight weeks to come) or download the forms for the interview, locate a veteran and write the questions you will be asking in the future interview. When the kit arrives compare what it contains with what you anticipated doing. Interview the vet. Complete the project.

CHAPTER 9

THE SEARCH FOR INFORMATION

A PRELIMINARY PRIMER ON RESEARCH

The message is clear: The way to construct your writing's house is to build a deep, sturdy foundation of solid research that prepares you to ask probing questions when interviewing and develop the freshest angle possible when writing. You accomplish this by taking as much care to refine your research skills as you do to improve your writing—being aware, always, of biases in your sources.

Once you are launched into freelance writing, nothing is lost on you. A government press release, a news story, a magazine article, a television documentary, a book, a conversation with a senator or a friend—all are noted and filed away, literally or mentally, in case they're needed for reference a month or a year later.

A change of rule in Yemen may spur a column on Yemen's changing relations with neighboring Arab countries. Protests in Bolivia might prompt a comment on that country's troubles. A source of pride to some Nigerians was a Nigerian satellite launch. About the same time as the launch, some Nigerian women stripped naked and picketed a U.S. oil company, demanding that water be supplied to their village and their men employed. In the photo accompanying the protest, shacks with tin roofs formed a background. That Nigerian story might be the spark for commentary on the misguided priorities of Nigeria and similar countries. It also could serve as a prompt to write about the desperate means women have used to bring about change in Africa or the Middle East, or lead to a historical account of women's protests.

When current events are the catalysts for writing about women's protests, writers open their files and their folders of clippings saved from previous assignments or past suspicions that just such a writing opportunity may await. The folders provide valuable background and leads. A review of the folder contents may call for updating the material. A trip to the library, a search of the Internet and a call to experts in the field will give you additional information.

A period of reflection on the information you have gathered usually follows this assembling of material. This reflection may suggest still other leads for more information. Usually outlining and writing will follow.

NEEDED: AN INQUIRING MIND

Any writing for the media involves research, which usually means proceeding from general information to specific information. Writers tend to develop a broad background in the area they're investigating or are interested in and then move on to specific target areas within it. In this way you frame a tentative outline about the subject matter and the questions you will ask primary sources when you interview them. Such a step-by-step approach to research, rather than a random gathering of facts and quotes from sources, saves time and assists you in being accurate, credible and objective. Working knowledge of a subject alerts you to newsworthy areas that call for additional scrutiny. Let's look at another example of this closer to home:

You're in Salem, Ore., where the city council is going to pass an ordinance banning nudity in public places—in reality, a law aimed at nude dancing. You call Ruth Vibelius, the state Associated Press editor, and ask her if she'd like a feature going into the background and complications of such an ordinance. Vibelius, beleaguered and understaffed, gives you a go ahead.

To write the feature, you need to know, at the outset, answers to these questions: What's meant by "nudity in public places"? Skinny dipping? By whom and where? Kids? Adults? How about nudes in art classes at the university? Nudity in theatrical productions? Who is behind the bill besides the council person sponsoring it? A county group called Citizens Against Sexual Exploitation drafted the ordinance. Who are they? They're affiliated with the National Coalition Against Pornography. What's its history? The ordinance infringes on freedom of expression, the First Amendment. What do the state and national chapters of the American Civil Liberties Union have to say about it? How does the ordinance compare with the state obscenity law? Does it go beyond it in banning nudity? For that matter, how does the state law compare with the Supreme Court definition of obscenity? If there is a difference, has the state law been tested in the courts?

Before you're through checking on the ordinance, you'll have received a current education on freedom of expression and the continual infringements on it attempted at the local, state and national levels. One of the nice things about being a freelance writer is that you find yourself enrolled in a continuing education program.

As noted earlier, features, articles and commentary can ride on the coattails of news events. Often news breaks so fast and the facts and figures change so rapidly that sheer lack of time prevents you from doing extensive research on a topic for a related article. So it's important to know where to go, quickly, to get information that will help interpret complex details for yourself and, ultimately, for your audiences. What sources can you call upon for the information you need to write? Some of the answers follow.

LIBRARIES

Your Personal Library

First of all, your personal library should have a good dictionary, a thesaurus, an almanac, an atlas and a couple of books of quotations. In addition, it's a good idea to have a CD-ROM of the *Encyclopedia Brittanica* and the *Oxford English Dictionary*. Of course, at www. m-w.com you have a free dictionary and thesaurus from Merriam-Webster. And although *The Columbia Encyclopedia* may not be the most comprehensive, it's free at www.bartleby. com/65. If you want world facts, then at www.cia.gov/cia/publications/factbook you have a guide to countries—their populations, governments, geography, agriculture, health systems, languages, and more—maintained by the CIA. Most of these sources are aids when writing. But when you find yourself stymied in your research, where is your port of call?

The Public Library

James Lee Burke in, *Last Car to Elysian Fields,* asks his reader:

> So where do you go to find a researcher who is intelligent, imaginative, skilled in the use of computers, devoted to discovering the truth, and knowledgeable about science, technology, history, and literature, and who usually works for dirt and gets credit for nothing?

His answer? A reference librarian.

Your local library is a good source for information about local affairs, politics and personalities. They usually carry back issues of community publications and employ a staff knowledgeable about community events. A municipal or county library usually has a close relationship with the local government. The staff can usually tell you where, in government or elsewhere, to search for the information you need.

Interlibrary loan and computer capabilities have brought greater sophistication to community libraries. And libraries at public colleges and universities are gold mines for freelance writers. In addition to large collections of books and back issues of popular periodicals, they also have special collections, sublibraries devoted to certain academic disciplines (such as medicine, engineering and architecture), interlibrary loan contracts with hundreds of other schools, special-interest magazines and journals, back issues of major newspapers and massive Internet reference resources. Writers can develop almost as many leads by browsing through libraries, *The Reader's Guide to Periodical Literature,* online computer systems and by talking to librarians as they can by developing contacts among subject matter experts. Here, too, librarians are likely to be able to identify additional sources for the writer in search of background information.

YOU CAN GET MOST ANYTHING YOU WANT...

When I wanted to use the most eloquent quote I had ever heard from former President Dwight D. Eisenhower in Chapter 7, I had only the quote itself to use as a source. When I asked the fellow who cited Eisenhower in a meeting of the Veterans for Peace where he got it, he didn't recall. So how did I find the time, place and occasion of the quote? I checked with a university librarian. Here is what the librarian emailed me: I chose Search "Quotations" from the pull-down menu and entered "every gun that is made" into the search field. Bartleby.com came up with this information:

> President DWIGHT D. EISENHOWER, "The Chance for Peace," an address delivered before the American Society of Newspaper Editors, Washington, D.C., April 16, 1953.—Public Papers of the Presidents of the United States: Dwight D. Eisenhower, 1953, p. 182.

The search machines in this information age are science fiction stuff. A universe of facts, figures, statistics and, most important, information are tingling on our finger tips on any subject we're interested in. Want to know sales ratings of various books or products? Call up Amazon.com. Got a baseball card or print you want to determine the market value of? Try eBay. Want to know which Web sites are most popular? Google will tell you. Whatever you want, it's probably out there in cyberspace.

When We Laugh: An Example

Let's say it's October and you're looking for an article idea for a magazine. You know you've got to get that article to a magazine three or four months in advance to meet their editorial schedule. Your friend, Hedy Russo calls up to tell you the latest joke she heard at the office party:

> A minister, a priest and a rabbi walk into a bar.
> The bartender looks at them and says, "What is this?
> A joke?"

You laugh to be polite. Then you say, "I'm having trouble with that."

"That's all right," Hedy says. "You're being English."

"Meaning what?" you ask.

"When the English hear a joke, they laugh the first time to be polite. They laugh the second time when others laugh. And they laugh the third time when they get it. You need to be in a crowd when you hear it." Hedy laughs. "Come with me to the ACLU bash on Saturday."

Maybe there's some synchronicity working here, you think, and enter "laughter" on Google. The results? You get 1,431,142 hits. You scan through a few of them and discover that April is "humor month." April is five months away. Synchronicity is alive and thriving, you think. You enter "laughter & health." You get 302,399 hits. In the first 15 entries you find, under "Laughter: Is It Healthy?" that Norman Cousins, former editor of the *Saturday Review of Literature,* started the laughter-health craze in 1979 when he developed heart problems. Under "Death: What's So Funny?" the reasons we laugh at death are explored. That topic doesn't appeal to you, but you think, perhaps, later, a mortician's magazine....)

Under www.howstuffworks.com/laughter.htm, one article explains what makes us laugh, what's going on in our brains when we laugh and how laughter can be good for our physical and emotional health. Another listing under laughter says "we laugh, as infants, reflexibly near the 10th week of life. When we're very old, we may...." You're intrigued by the ellipses and enter: Laugh when old. You get 5,900,000 hits. You've struck out. You try: Laughing when old. You get 3,810,000 hits. You're getting desperate. You try: Too old to laugh? All the entries indicate that it's never too old to laugh.

You decide to check this idea out further for the AARP magazine. But you're more intrigued with the idea of the laughter of a baby at the 10-week stage. You've seen babies at an earlier age than that laugh. A young-mother magazine would be an ideal market for it. Furthermore, *USA Weekend* just ran a cover story on the latest scientific findings about caring for an infant. Laughter wasn't included. You decide to let the three ideas idle in your mind for a couple of days before launching an article for the April humor month: Baby laughter, old age laughter or what causes us to laugh. You're leaning toward the baby laughter idea.

You're onto a good topic. *Reader's Digest*, you discover, is interviewing Robin Williams and titling it "The Power of Laughter."

Search Engines: Google, et al.

Millions of references are at your fingertips. Perhaps the most valuable general and specific research site of all is www.google.com. As Anick Jesdanun pointed out in a 2004 Associated Press story, *"an index of almost 4.3 billion Web pages and counting, makes Google the Internet's top search engine."* The following article tells us why:

By Robert S. Boyd
Knight Ridder News Service, Aug. 19, 2004

WASHINGTON—If you're considering investing in Google or you use this popular Internet searching system, you may wonder how the amazing thing works.

What computer magic makes it possible for Google to pick out in a fraction of a second the information you want from the incredible mass of material on the Web?

To answer users' queries, the system founded six years ago by two Stanford University graduate students has scanned and stored nearly 43 billion Web pages. If all those documents were printed, they'd make a stack of paper 300 miles high.

(Google's name, incidentally comes from the mathematical term "googol," an enormous sum written as a 1 followed by 100 zeroes.)

Some details of Google's methods are closely held trade secrets, but the broad outlines of how it and its competitors work are well known to computer scientists.

In computer jargon, Google's "search engines" use robotic "spiders," special software programs that "crawl" continuously along the myriad trails of the World Wide Web, "harvesting" documents as they go. A separate piece of software builds an index of every word that spiders find.

When a user submits a query, such as "Mount Everest" or "Bill Clinton," the search engine checks the index, fetches each document that contains those words, sorts them by relevance and returns the most pertinent ones first.

"For Google, the major operations are crawling, indexing and sorting," the system's founders, Sergey Brin and Lawrence Page, wrote in their original paper describing the system.

To improve the results, Google uses a patented method called "PageRank," a sort of popularity contest that tries to determine which documents are likely to be most valuable to the user.

For each page, the PageRank system counts the number of other pages that are linked, or connected to it. In essence, Google interprets a link from Page A to Page B as a "vote" by Page A for Page B.

In addition to the number of votes a page gets, the system analyzes the status of the pages that cast the votes. Popular pages weigh more heavily.

"Pages that are well cited from many places around the Web are worth looking at," Brin and Page wrote.

Google uses other tricks as well to determine a document's ranking. Words in a special typeface, bold, underlined or all capitals, get extra credit. Words occurring close together, such as "George" and "Bush," count for more than those that are far apart.

Finally, Google returns the documents that match a user's query, ranked in order of their relevance as determined by their page rank.

Here's how Google's stable of spiders known as GoogleBots go about their business.

A spider visits every Web page that isn't marked private, reads it and stores it in compressed form. The spider looks for any links that the page may contain to other pages. It follows those links to pages it hasn't seen before and continues the process until there are no more links to visit.

While the spider is chugging along, an "indexer" is creating a catalog or dictionary of every word it encounters, except for short grammatical terms such as "the," "in" or "where." For each word, the system keeps a list of all the pages that word appears in. It also records the exact position of the word in each document so it can be found quickly later on.

The lists can be extremely long, since some words appear in millions of documents. For example, a search for the word "carnival" returns about 5.6 million entries, far more than anyone could possibly use. The combination of "George" and "Bush" gets about 7.4 million hits.

In an interview published in the September issue of *Playboy* magazine, Google's founders explained why a page-ranking system is necessary to find the most important documents in the ever-expanding volume of material on the Web.

"Before Google, I don't think people put much effort into the ordering or results," Brin said. "We saw that a thousand results weren't necessarily as useful as 10 good ones."

Google Inc. provides Google Answers service where users can connect with researchers who will conduct online searches *for a fee.* But do you want to shell out money? Universities and government agencies offer most reliable help. What can you get on the Web that's free? You're sorting laundry and the washer has eaten your socks—again. Log onto this company site, www.10socks.com., for sock-buying solutions, laundry tips and Advice From Mom. Chain saw malfunctions? Sewing machine is skipping? Car windows won't roll down? Windshield wipers flipping out? Try www.howstuffworks.com.

If you want to write an article on drunk drivers and why they continue to be allowed to drive, first you'll need to find how many there are and the misery they cause. Click on The Transportation Department's Fatality Analysis Reporting. The system includes data on fatal vehicle accidents in the United States by state and county. Accident information is also broken down by age of drivers, alcohol and speeding: www.fars.nhtsa.dot.gov.

Looking for educational sites in the arts, sciences and other fields? Go to www.ipl. org—The Internet Public Library, sponsored by the University of Michigan. Links to psychology sites? Nearly 2,000 sites, including professional associations, may be found at www.psychology.org. If you're interested in archeology, archnet.asu.edu links you to museums and resources. An overview of major biological topics may be found at www.biology.arizona.edu. Life sciences reference tools are available through links at biotech.icmb.utexas.edu. Major universities generally house a research center or several small units: for example, the University of Maryland's Center on Aging, the Texas Real Estate Center at Texas A&M University and the Center for the Study of Women in Government at the State University of New York at Albany.

If you have a literary bent, you can hook up to more than 13,000 public domain books, including all of Shakespeare, *Moby-Dick, Aesop's Fables* and religious texts through www.gutenberg.net. You can download them and read the hard copy. Links to a range of literary sites, organized by era and genre, may be found at Andromeda.rutgers.edu/jlynch/Lit.

When you're researching a topic, the sources available appear limitless. Of course, you also can consult human sources to give your advice or comments more authenticity.

A Word of Caution

Not everything you see on the Internet is authentic or correct:

An item on singer R. Kelly circulating on the Internet was picked up by *The Miami Herald* and sent by Knight Ridder News Service to newspapers across the country in

November 2004. Kelly, facing trial on charges he videotaped sex sessions with an under-age girl, was falsely accused of making sexual advances to an underage sister of another singer.

According to *Herald* Executive Editor Tom Fiedler, the story was passed along to an editor of celebrity news by someone in the newsroom because it looked like an Associated Press story or appeared to be attributed to the A.P. The editor failed to verify that it had actually moved on the A.P. wire.

Moral? In the words of Walter Cronkite: "You say your mother loves you? Check it out."

GOVERNMENT OFFICES

If you establish yourself as a local and state Seymour Hersh—a writer who can investigate and write in-depth articles on the political scene for the local newspaper or press asso-ciation—you will want to develop political relationships with important individuals and not-so-important individuals such as aides, clerks and secretaries. You will also become familiar with the various jurisdictions of American government. Municipal, county, state and federal governments possess more data in files and on computer disks than anyone will probably ever read. Our system of government requires many points of contact with its citizens—through elections, tax filings, license applications, legal actions, jury duty, Social Security, Medicare and Medicaid, government financial assistance and other social services. Virtually every resident of the United States appears in one government database or another. An example is this story on government secrecy:

"Federal Agency Keeps Increase in Children Deaths Secret"

By Justin Blum
Gannet News Service (©1993 Gannet Co. Inc.)*

WASHINGTON — A federal agency kept secret a study showing a dramatic increase in deaths of children in car accidents so public outrage wouldn't force the agency to increase safety regulations, a consumer advocacy group charged yesterday.

The Institute for Injury Reduction released a federal study completed in 1990, but never revealed to the public, that shows the number of children under 5 killed in car accidents increased 30% between 1984 and 1989.

By contrast, the number of children in that age group increased only 4%.

"For nearly two years, [they have] known that alarming increases have occurred in cars and other private passenger vehicles, even while the use of seat belts and child restraints by those children was substantially growing," said Benjamin Kelley, presi-dent of the institute, an educational and research organization funded by a plaintiff's lawyers.

Ben Langer, a spokesman for the National Highway Traffic Safety Administration, the federal agency that compiled the study, claimed it made the statistics available to anyone who wanted them but did not publicize the information.

Langer said he "doubted sincerely" that pressure from the automobile industry had anything to do with not releasing the study. The industry has fought increased safety regulations.

The study showed deaths of children under 5 rose from 554 in 1984 to 721 in 1989. For children between 5 and 9, deaths rose from 365 to 513, a 40% increase.

The consumer institute blamed much of the increase on poor performance of rear-seat, lap-only seat belts found in many cars.

NHTSA has not recalled cars with lap belts but has ordered manufacturers to install shoulder belts in the back seats of new cars.

"The lap-only belts concentrate excessive force on the child's lower torso, exposing her or him to severe abdominal injuries and spinal column fractures," said Kelley.

---

*Published in Earl R. Hutchison's *Writing for Mass Communication,* 2d, Longman Publishers, 1996, p 228.

While writers need experts to interpret the findings of such studies, and those contacts may strongly disagree with the government's or official's point of view, the data the government uses in making law and writing regulations are extremely important. The different ways they are interpreted often make news, especially on the business pages.

Where to Go?

Learning which government office to go to for information is a challenge for beginning writers. Even local government can be quite complex. Most writers find government directories helpful, when they are available. Public affairs officers can point the way initially, but good reporters will do their own checking to make certain they have reached the most knowledgeable person as well as the appropriate office for the information they seek. This is how secondary sources become primary ones.

Among the valuable sources for information available to the freelance writer are the public records at the city, state and federal levels. Records of births and deaths, annual reports, committee hearings, commission hearings, court cases, property records—all these records and more are valuable sources of information. If you know what you want from the local, state or federal government, chances are records exist that will not only reveal part of what you want but also document it. If the bureaucrat, law enforcement officer or executive official does not allow you to see the records you want, you can file suit under the appropriate state or federal freedom of information act. The majority of states now have laws based on the 1974 federal Freedom of Information Act:

"Governor Accused of Sexual Harassment"

OLYMPIA, WASH. (AP) — A former press aide to Gov. Mike Lowry claims she resigned because he sexually harassed her—the second such complaint against the governor within a year.

Lowry, a first-term Democrat, denied harassing Susanne Albright.

"I left because of a very clear and very persistent pattern of unacceptable behavior by the governor toward me," Albright said Friday.

Albright, 37, who took the $48,000-a-year job in May 1993, has not filed a formal complaint and would not give details of the alleged harassment.

Her lawyer, Larry Finegold, said the accusation involved physical contact. He and the governor's office had been negotiating a settlement. The governor's office has hired an outside lawyer to investigate.

The allegations were made public Friday after reporters used the state's Public Records Act to get information on why Albright left her job.

POLITICAL AND CIVIC GROUPS

Political groups and civic associations may be counted on for a tremendous amount of information about legislation, zoning, development, schools, highways and traffic, community safety and security. These groups have a vested interest in who holds the reins of power and how it is exercised. Populating these groups are politicians, community activists, school board members, city and county council members, members of the state legislature, members of Congress, judges and the leaders of political parties. They range from the homemaker lobbying for expanded after-school programs at her daughter's junior high school, to the neighborhood association president, a lawyer who opposes a shopping center owner's plans to install a video arcade next door to a liquor store. They include the controversial circuit court judge stepping down after 25 years on the bench and the member of Congress who switches political parties to accommodate the swing in party loyalty in her or his district. All of these people and the organizations to which they belong can be excellent sources for the freelance writer working with a newspaper, or a public relations firm looking for ways to focus more attention on her or his company's activities in the community.

These individuals can be helpful because of the knowledge they have by virtue of their community involvement. They are excellent primary and secondary sources. They take opinion polls in their communities, gather information about government plans affecting their neighborhoods, go to public meetings where they demand disclosure of more information, examine and analyze budgets, and compare the performance of the Democrats and Republicans. The documents they produce as a result of their interests are superb sources for freelance writers because they reveal so much about the expectations and plans of those citizens.

PROFESSIONAL GROUPS

Trade unions, trade associations and membership groups are mainstays for writers doing research. Many of these groups are wealthy and powerful and able to finance studies and reports about their membership and relevant issues. Because press coverage is important to them, they are usually quite willing to share information with writers. Those with libraries will usually open them to freelancers who have a bona fide assignment for a newspaper, magazine, broadcast station or other medium.

PRIVATE SOURCES

Another type of organization, composed of persons with a strong personal (as opposed to employment-related) interest, is the special-interest group. These groups are formed by people who feel a formal organization is necessary to accomplish their goals. These groups know that organizing formally will improve their chances of having the press recognize them as authorities and use their comments and reports in the media.

Some of the best-known of these groups include the National Association for the Advancement of Colored People, the National Organization for Women, the 4-H Club, the Anti-Defamation League of B'nai B'rith, the American Civil Liberties Union and the Eagle Forum. They have local chapters eager to be tapped for information about their activities.

Not all special-interest groups are national in scope. Many have interests that are purely local. The Committee to Save Rhodes Tavern, for example, was a Washington, D.C., group that rallied to prevent the demolition of a historic building near the White House. Its members ultimately failed, and the decrepit little building fell to the wrecker's ball. But the group received much press coverage over several years that usually portrayed it as the little David fighting the huge Goliath of urban development.

Most special interests have a formal organization to promote them. The major organizations can usually be found by looking in the phone book; the smaller ones, by obtaining the name of the chief spokesperson or an officer.

RESEARCH ORGANIZATIONS

The evaluating and quantifying of our beliefs, feelings, attitudes and morals are taking place every minute of every business day, somewhere. Behavioral research is important to anyone concerned with future planning, whether she or he is in marketing, sales, communication, banking, national defense or other careers. These statistics can greatly help a writer interpret events because they can show what people have done in the past, what they seem to be doing now, and what can be expected of them in the future.

This research is done by opinion pollsters, such as Louis Harris and Associates and the GFK Roper and Gallup polls. Some pollsters are specialists, such as Cambridge Survey Research, which specializes in political polling. If you're working on a story on voting traditions in Vermont or a report on people's attitudes toward abortion, polls previously published by these groups on those subjects can give added depth to your story.

The federal government frequently releases reports about its survey research and will provide information about specific topics on request, although at times it may be reluctant to do so. When that happens you can use the Freedom of Information (FOI) Act to pry that information loose. (The FOI Act may also be called into service at the state and local levels.) The U.S. Census Bureau has divisions responsible for certain types of demographic information, such as the annual numbers of live births, marriages and divorces, and much more. The Justice Department's Bureau of Justice Statistics keeps records on crime, prisons, criminal behavior and sentencing. These are important sources for the writer because they are repositories of statistical information not readily available elsewhere, and because the information can be searched to cover exactly the geographic area or time frame under investigation. The following news story about increasing assaults against Peace Corps

Freedom of Information Act! What gives you the idea that you have any right to the Freedom of Information Act?!

volunteers illustrates the sources available and the dedicated research that may be necessary to present an accurate picture of a situation:

"Assaults Against Peace Corps Volunteers"

The Associated Press, Oct. 26, 2003

DAYTON, Ohio — Assaults against Peace Corps volunteers around the world more than doubled from 1991 to 2002, with almost 70% committed against women, the *Dayton Daily News* reports.

A Peace Corps database shows that assault cases jumped 125% during the 11-year period, while the number of volunteers increased only 29%, the newspaper said in a report for today's editions.

Peace Corps spokeswoman Barbara Daly disputed the newspaper's interpretation. She said that since 1997, the agency has had a 30% decrease in the rate of major sexual assault cases— excluding such things as touching and unwanted kissing—and a 35% decrease in the rate of rape cases.

The newspaper said that although the number of rape cases did decrease from 20 in 1997 to 13 in 2002, the number of all sexual assault cases increased from 73 to 94 during that period and the overall number of assault cases—including aggravated assault, simple assault, sexual assaults and death threats—rose from 251 to 283. A single rape or assault case could involve multiple workers, the newspaper reported.

The *Daily News* spent 20 months examining thousands of records and interviewed more than 500 people in 11 countries. It said that although many volunteers have little or no experience traveling outside the United States, some are sent to live alone in remote areas of some of the world's most dangerous countries and are left unsupervised for months at a time.

In 62% of the more than 2,900 assault cases since 1990, the victim was alone and in 59% the victim was a woman in her 20s, the *Daily News* said.

Peace Corps Director Gaddi Vasquez told the *Daily News* that his "No. 1 priority" is the safety of the 7,533 volunteers in 71 countries.

Two Peace Corps officials overseeing security in the past 12 years said they warned about increased dangers but the agency ignored many of their concerns.

Dan Gilmor, formerly with the *Detroit Free Press* and the San Jose *Mercury News*, is a firm believer in writers learning how to use many of the government databases. These include state driver records; criminal justice data, including felony disposition tapes; FAA Aircraft Service Difficulty reports and pilot disciplinary records; hazardous waste files; education records, including teacher lists; real estate and property tax records; campaign contributions and expenditures; and many others.

SUMMARY

A sturdy foundation of solid research prepares you to ask probing questions when interviewing and to develop the freshest angle possible when writing. As much care is needed to refine your research skills as to improve your writing. Because the amount of information available through private and public sources is increasing and is being made available in new formats, such as computer-accessed databases, today's freelance writer must develop greater research and reporting skills.

FEATURES FOR DISCUSSION

A. "Want My Love? Make Me Laugh"

By Kristi Gustafson
Gannett News Service, Aug. 11, 2004

Want to date Bill Stein? You'd better have a couple of good one-liners up your sleeve.

"You think all day at work," says Stein, 27 of Albany, N.Y. "You want to come home to someone who can make you laugh and who you can joke around with."

Stein is like most Americans, according to a survey done by the online dating website Match.com. Of 1,600 adults polled, 70% say they're more likely to fall in love with someone who makes them laugh than someone who makes them think.

Laughter is more emotionally intimate than intellectual discourse," says Trish McDermott, a vice president and dating service advice columnist with Match.com.

"When we laugh, we let down and open up in ways that create intimacy. There is a connection over laughter and a shared sense of humor that people find compelling."

And who can blame these fun-seekers, says Debbie Mandel, author of *Turn on Your Inner Light: Fitness for Body, Mind, and Soul.*

"Laughter is a natural de-stressor and raises serotonin levels," Mandel says. "People gravitate to positive people who make them feel good. Thinkers tend to brood, overanalyze, and often see flaws."

Thinkers can be bores, too, says Demetra Xythalis, an Albany 30-year-old.

"They say laughter is the best medicine," Xythalis says. "It makes you feel good."

And, in turn, it makes you feel good about the person you're with, says Steven M. Sultanoff, the creator of Humormatters.com and a psychologist and marriage counselor.

"Laughter is physiological. We feel good. Our muscles relax and it reduces tension so you're out on a date and you enjoy yourself more because it's a pleasurable physiological experience," he says.

"People will use humor to feel emotionally uplifted."

He points out that in personal ads people rarely, if ever, seek out someone who makes them think, but you frequently see requests for a mate with a good sense of humor" or "someone who can make me laugh."

But, of course, every relationship needs a combination of attributes to succeed.

"Thinking will have its day," says David Falcone, a professor of psychology at La Salle University in Philadelphia. "While we fall in love with those that make us laugh, we *stay* in love with those that make us think, as well."

Surf through the Internet for one or two quotations on love that might be suitable for this feature.

B. "A Slight Error in Goverment's Obesity Study"

By Daniel Yee
The Associated Press, Jan. 19, 2005

ATLANTA—Blaming a computer software error, the government says it overstated the nation's weight problem in a widely reported study last year that said obesity was about to overtake smoking as the No. 1 cause of death in the United States.

The study, conducted by the Centers for Disease Control and Prevention and published last March in the *Journal of the American Medical Association* said that obesity-related deaths climbed between 1990 and 2000 to 400,000 a year—an increase of 100,000.

In today's issue of the journal, the government ran a correction, saying the increase was a more modest 65,000 deaths or so.

CDC Director Dr. Julie Gerberding said yesterday that the agency regretted the computer error was not discovered earlier.

"Integrity is a core value of CDC, and the integrity of our science must be protected," she said. "We are improving our internal scientific review processes, including moving toward the adoption of electronic review processes."

The original study put the number of tobacco-related deaths per year at just under 435,000 and contended that more Americans soon could be dying of obesity instead of smoking if current trends persisted.

Despite the correction, the agency said the finding that obesity is a major cause of death still stands.

"The combination of diet, physical inactivity and tobacco are all leading causes of death, causing far more than a majority of total deaths in this country in the year 2000," said Donna Stroup, action director for the CDC's coordination center for health promotion. "Regardless of the controversy, it's clear to people these are the three underlying causes of death most important to the country."

The errors in the study were discovered soon after it was published, as scientists inside and outside the agency began to dispute its findings. That prompted the CDC to review the study using two independent statisticians.

What feelings are stirred in you by this revelation of an error in a government study?

EXERCISES

1. In one of the most widely reported celebrity crime cases in the history of this country, O. J. Simpson's lawyers attempted to limit the amount of domestic violence evidence put before jurors in his murder trial. (Simpson was accused of the June 12, 1994, slayings of Nicole Brown Simpson and her friend, Ronald Goldman.) Evidence of violence in the Simpson household was irrelevant, the lawyers argued. Allowing it would prejudice the jury.

   A Columbia University law professor, George P. Fletcher, sided with the defense lawyers. He was quoted in an Associated Press story: "Even if he engaged in spousal abuse, it's irrelevant. The premise that wife beaters tend to kill their wives is simply false."

   Your assignment:

   a. Are Simpson's lawyers and the Columbia University professor right? Call the local center for domestic violence in your hometown or university location. Ask for the number of cases reported last year and so far this year in the city and county. Get the number of cases reported 10 years ago for comparison. Ask if any of the victims were subsequently killed by their spouses in the last 10 years. Ask for the telephone number to call at the state level where they report those cases. Ask the state for information about those cases in which the husband killed the wife. How many were there last year? How many 10 years ago? Ask the state for the address and telephone number of the national center for domestic violence.

      Who does kill wives, if not wife beaters?

   b. Write a feature story based upon the statistics you've gathered.

2. An AIDS case is reported in your hometown—the second in a week. This case involves a prominent doctor—a surgeon.

Your assignment:

a. Check with the Centers for Disease Control in Atlanta, GA 30333 (phone: 404-639-3311). How many cases were reported in the last year and so far this year in your city and county? How many cases were reported 10 years ago in your city and county? How do your numbers compare to the average for your state? For the nation?

b. Write a feature story based on the statistics you've gathered.

3. What were your feelings when you read the news story in this chapter (pages 261–262) about the federal government keeping secret its study that revealed a 30 percent increase in the number of children under five killed in car accidents between 1984 and 1989?

Ben Langer, spokesman for the National Highway Traffic Safety Administration, claimed the statistics were available to anyone who wanted them. Does this failure by a federal agency to publicize the information amount to secrecy? Why?

4. Two teenagers are killed in two separate automobile accidents one night in your hometown or university location. Both were the drivers of the autos. The police investigating say there ought to be a curfew against teenagers driving at night. As a matter of fact, they continue, there ought to be a law against teenage drivers at any time. Are they right?

Your assignment:

a. Check with the police department and the nearest state highway patrol office for the number of fatal automobile accidents in your city and county during the past year and so far this year. Ask for the same statistics for 10 years ago. How many fatalities were teenage drivers? How many were women? How many were men? Check with your state department of safety.

How many fatalities were there in the state? How many were teenagers? Is the percentage of licenses issued to teenagers less than the percentage of accidents attributed to them? How many fatalities were women? How many were men? How many accidents were drug- or alcohol-related? In teenage accidents, what were the contributing factors: speeding? reckless driving? failure to yield? What is the percentage of those factors? Are more teenager drivers accident-prone during the night? Does the same hold true for men? Women?

Call the U.S. Transportation Department for a printout on similar statistics on a national level.

b. Write a feature story based on the statistics you've gathered.

5. Read again, "Women in Government" in Chapter 4. This feature illustrates how news events can be used as a springboard for a feature story. Although dated, it contains statistical data and is still lively. What does the writer do to make it so?

Here is an ambitious and sure-fire publishable feature idea: Using the "Women in Government" feature as a blueprint to follow, look up current data on women in government, insert the statistics at appropriate places, call upon the political figures and statisticians cited in this feature and elicit commentary from them reflecting on the current or impending political face of women in government.

In the lead use this Chinese proverb: "Women hold up half the sky."

After writing the article, query your local newspaper, the state Associated Press office and an appropriate magazine about publication possibilities.

6. Does your state have a public records law? Ask a city editor, news director or a member of the Society of Professional Journalism if your state law is effective in prying information loose from the government.

7. List 10 federal government local and regional offices located in your area. How did you get this information?

8. Select three of those federal agencies and describe their functions and services.

9. List three local special-interest groups in your area. How did you get this information?

10. What major lobbyists have offices in your city? How did you get this information?

11. What are the tax rates for your city? How did you find this information?

CHAPTER 10

FOCUSING, OUTLINING

Pulling It All Together

AN INTRODUCTION TO OUTLINING

The outline undergirds your confidence in your writing and allows your mind to be more creative. Not having to think about what will be taken up next (it's in the outline) or where you've been, you are free to develop new and related ideas, incidents or illustrations to amplify the writing or thoughts at hand.

Although this chapter may be a ho-hum recapitulation for you, it's probably necessary, not only to recall your memories, but to illustrate the importance of outlining and how it is used in writing and in research.

Most of the previous chapters have each featured basic outlines to follow. It seems logical and natural, before discussing the importance of outlining in general, to briefly recall each of these organizational patterns—to pull them together and use them as a launching pad. The first pattern presented was that of a short feature.

THE SHORT FEATURE STRUCTURE

The feature story is something other than a straight news story both in structure and, most times, in subject matter. Some of the differences:

A straight news story may or may not have a featurized lead and begins by answering seven questions (five Ws and H and what is the significance) in a straightforward manner, usually beginning with "What happened?" See the figure on page 24. A featurized lead would have another rectangle on top.

The rectangle the inverted pyramid rests upon, incidentally, represents the last paragraph of the news story.

A short feature stems from events that have human interest and/or emotional appeal or comic relief. The lead piques the interest of the reader with a narrative hook, presents the idea of the feature and serves as a transition into the body of the story. It saves, for the very end, a punch line that releases the tension created by the suspension of knowing how the event is going to end.

The graphic representation of the short feature is diametrically opposite from that of the straight news story, as the illustration on page 25 shows.

THE LONG FEATURE STRUCTURE

What are the differences between the long feature and the long news story? The basic subject matter of long news stories and long features usually differ. The organization of both is more complicated than mere graphic representations of pyramids.

A long news story, such as a story about a city council or school board meeting, will have three or more major news elements involved. The lead and the body of the story will have to reflect that complexity. Those major story elements will have to be mentioned within the first two or three paragraphs so the reader will know what's coming in the following 10 or 15 paragraphs.

A long feature, meanwhile, lures the reader in with a lead similar to that of the short feature. The writer is then relatively free to roam a literary field, building on that reader interest to climactic paragraphs and an ending. The graphic representation for a long feature may look something like the drawing on the left, and the complex news stories usually look like the representation on the right:

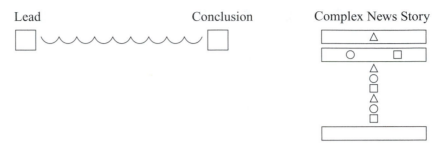

The left rectangle in the left-hand drawing represents the lead for the long feature. The up and down wavelike line represents valleys of exposition and peaks of reader interest—connected nuggets of information that will inspire readers to read on to the ending represented by the concluding rectangle. All of this should parallel a constantly mounting plane of reader interest. The drawing on the right represents the various elements of a news story and where they appear in the story.

THE MAGAZINE ARTICLE OUTLINE

To represent the depth and length of the magazine article, a ramp is called into play: "the reader interest plane."

The Reader Interest Plane

While the lead of the newspaper feature and of the magazine article is basically the same (narrative hook, idea and transition), the article writer organizes her or his notes along designated areas of the reader interest plane (developing, generating and climactic paragraphs), keying them to a mounting article interest ending with a lingering impression. While both features and articles strive to attain a unity of impression, the schematic diagram of the reader interest plane offers a more rigorous plan to achieve it.

"Once More to the Lake," keyed to the reader interest plane, looks like this:

"Once More to the Lake" (Reader Interest Plane)

    I. Narrative Hook
       Reminiscence about childhood and lake in Maine
   II. Developing Paragraphs
       A. More reminiscence about lake
       B. Setting description of lake
       C. Illusion of dual existence—he being his son
          1. Same illusion—no passage of time motif
          2. Enchanted sea—no passage of time motif
       D. Dinner at the farmhouse
  III. Generating Paragraphs
       A. Summertime! Life indelible!
       B. More remembrances
       C. Motorboat noise

        1. Sets years moving
        2. Dying flywheel revolution—eversing years
  IV. Climactic Paragraphs
     A. Description of week at camp—illusion persists
     B. Thunderstorm on lake presages father's fate?
   V. Lingering impression and Concluding Paragraph:
     As son pulls wet swimsuit on, the father feels in his groin the chill of death.

OUTLINES FOR COMMENTARY

While commentary outlines delineated here may in some instances be distinctive, for example, the persuasive and review formats, most other commentary can be written using the reader interest plane as a guide. However, it's important that commentary, like all writing, embrace the general principle of unity of impression.

Writing to Persuade

The reader interest plane provides valuable guidance without dictating specific structure. Writing persuasively, however, has this more instructive matrix:

1. An introduction to the issue and your stance
2. Arguments in support of your position
3. Arguments in opposition to your position and a refutation
4. A reaffirmation of the stance taken in the opening paragraphs, but phrased differently

The Review Format

Until you feel more comfortable without it, keep this review format in mind:

    An overall appraisal or assessment of the work being reviewed is presented in the lead. The aim or purpose of the artist is also stated early in the review. The initial appraisal of the work is substantiated by comments, illustrations and examples, along with a synopsis or description of the scope of the work and a suggestion for the audience as to whether the event or publication is worth reading or attending.

    You may want to approach other categories of commentary with the reader interest plane in mind.

THE VALUE OF OUTLINING

Why all this fuss about outlining? It's important. All the other instruction for outlining that has preceded this chapter does not suggest the magnitude of the value it has for a writer.

You Say You Don't Outline?

Every newspaper, feature and article lead instruction and graphic representation you incorporated in your writing to date is a form of outlining.

We're all outline freaks. When we get up in the morning, we think about what we're going to be doing the rest of the day and outline in our mind how we're going to go about doing it. If you're going out on a date, you plan what to wear, where to go, what to order if you're dining, what to say. If you're going to do some serious grocery shopping, you're no doubt going to make a list. There's a whole lot of outlining in most persons' lives. If you *really* don't outline, you'll find yourself wandering around haphazardly from the university to the grocery store back to the university and then to the drug store and then back to the university and then ... who knows where? The same thing can happen when you set out to write something without a plan of action in mind.

Writing practically *anything* begins with the formulation of a rough outline in your mind of what you're going to say before putting it down on paper. If you don't believe in the detailed outlining we advocate, you nevertheless begin *all* writing with an outline in mind. It may be a vague, shadowy thing, but it's an outline.

How an Outline Figures in Research

If you're investigating how love begins as a romance and eventually dies in marriage and is supplanted by a love that lasts or doesn't last, depending upon the marriage relationships, you're going to have to decide what to look for in the library and on the Internet. You'll begin with a vague outline in your mind. Perhaps you may or may not write the outline down. Once you start collecting information, if you've written the outline on paper you'll be able to put that information in the various sections of that outline—either mentally or physically. A quarter of the way into your investigation, you'll discover some information that you've collected doesn't fit into the rough outline you started with, so you create another section in the outline for it.

Halfway through your investigation you'll realize that the makeshift, data-collecting outline is so out of shape that you have to refine it to accommodate the information you now have. *If you're into halfway outlining,* this is what you'll be doing. If not, you'll have accumulated a pile of notes (some 50 of them) on your desk or in your computer. That is exactly what they are: "a pile of notes." What are you going to do with those notes when you start to write?

If you spread them out so you can read them without shuffling through them, you'll spot a couple that you might use in the beginning—so you start with them. Once you've incorporated them into the beginning of your article, you look through the other notes to see what can next be included. What you're doing, of course, is what all of us have at one time or another done before we took the outline path: You're wallowing in a graveyard of notes. If you aren't careful, a feeling of hopelessness will overwhelm you and kill the article you were so intent upon writing.

The "Rejected Poet" Interview Notes

Let's look at one "graveyard" of notes (notes collected haphazardly) and how that maze of information can be converted into a coherent pattern for writing.

You obtained the following series of items by interviewing an unpublished poet for a newspaper feature. Judging by the order presented by the notes, the poet had poetic license to ramble freely during the interview. The items need to be arranged in the order you'll be writing about them.

"An Unsuccessful Poet Continues Composing"

>	rejections of poems (first rejection, etc.)
>	present-day efforts
#	nursery rhymes
#	miner's strike
=	serious efforts & poem examples
&	Prufrock motif
~	wife's view of his poetry
^	poet's muse
*	triumphs
+	army troop train efforts
#	"Village Blacksmith"
*	poem to wife
=	humorous poems & examples
^	writing rituals—place, pen, time, etc.
&	Hymen Ensor Xmas letter
~	last rejection
+	high school explications
*	writing workshops
~	friends' views of his poetry writing

If you're not an outline believer, you'd simply look through them pick one to use as a lead, another to follow, and another and another until you're wallowing in the middle of the note graveyard.

How do you go about arranging the notes in a coherent fashion? As you read through this list, you notice I've placed a symbol before each item—the preliminary stage of rendering the notes coherent. The symbols indicate the different blocks of subject matter that the notes fall into. If there are enough notes in a particular block, that block may form a major section of an outline. An outline may have three to five major sections, in addition to the introduction and the conclusion. (While it is difficult to develop a subject thoroughly with fewer than three major sections, more than five or six run the risk of overstating the case.)

After sorting the free-form data into blocks by symbols (all * in one place, all + in another, and so on), arrange the notes in the order you'll be expecting to write from them. Create an outline for the feature. While constructing the outline, better titles may come to mind, as it did in this case. The rejected poet outline might look like this:

"The Life and Times of a Rejected Poet"

I. Introduction
   Lead reflecting the fact that no matter how he tries, no matter how trivial the market or poetry contest, the poet is rejected—and at times totally dejected. How did he get started in this life of rejection?

II. The Early Years
   A. Nursery rhymes
   B. Coal miners' strike—was taught haunting poetic lines

    C. Elementary school—recitation of "The Village Blacksmith"
III. Later Years
    A. High school poetry explications
    B. WWII troop train efforts
    C. Present day efforts
        1. Muse
        2. Rituals
IV. Triumphs
    A. Friends' views of efforts—"that's what friends are for"
    B. Writing workshops—needed the money
    C. Prufrock motif in prose sermon—a semi-poetic effort
    D. Poem to wife—a poetic proposal she accepted
V. Rejections
    A. First rejection & others
    B. Last rejection
    C. What got rejected
        1. Humorous poem:
          "On the highway of our love she littered."
        2. Serious poem:
          "Umbrellas of love furl and unfurl in life's wintry storms."
VI. Conclusion
    Feelings on getting rejections. How he bears up. Statement to the effect that he will keep on writing poetry, knowing he will never achieve fame.

This outline is acceptable. The chronology of the events determines much of the outline. Only one item has been omitted ("Hymen Ensor Xmas letter")—an extraordinary occurrence. You will discover when you outline that some items just do not fit comfortably into the feature. When that happens, omit them. Better to find that out here rather than in your feature revision. Most of the time you should gather so much information that one-third to one-half of it has to be discarded.

One way to organize these blocks of topics is according to similar subject matter and on a rising climactic plane. Your outline may be entirely different, however, and still be a good outline. What we want to stress now is how to go about organizing your materials and what an asset an outline is. Without an outline, when you are writing you can be cast adrift, floating on the currents of your impulses.

In the Beginning: The Outline

Once you've finished investigating and jotting down those notes, facts and ideas that have occurred to you in the investigation, you'll need a detailed outline to organize still further those items for a more formal written (or oral) presentation, as noted earlier.

In the beginning, the detailed outline aids you in these ways:

1. The outline forces you to think about your subject matter: to know it more thoroughly and to organize it for presentation.
2. The outline forces you to survey your materials more exhaustively. If the material and facts are lacking, the outline exposes the thin spots and saves you from being

stranded in the middle of a presentation, an article, column, editorial or essay for lack of research.

3. The outline brings a sense of proportion to your undertaking. Is one idea more important than another? Do more facts support this concept than other concepts? If so, that should be reflected by the idea's position in the article and the amount of space and notes devoted to it.

4. The outline clarifies the relationship of one idea to another. Coherence and good transitions will follow.

While You Are Writing: The Outline:

While you are writing, outlining has these beneficial effects:

1. The outline is the foundation of your confidence. You know what you're going to say and usually how you are going to say it.

2. The outline forces you to focus on the task at hand while providing a boulevard for your mind to follow.

3. The outline frees you to think. A good deal of creativity takes place as you write. Not having to think about what will be taken up next (it's in the outline) or where you've been, you are free to develop new and related ideas, incidents or illustrations to amplify the writing or thoughts at hand.

4. The outline frees you to write. You can ponder the best word, the best phrase, the best figure of speech, the best image. "Putting proper words in proper places" is made easier.

THE MASTER OF THE OUTLINE

However, once you've composed your detailed outline and are writing, remember that you, and not your outline, are the master. You need not follow it slavishly. If a deviation from the outline appears to be the best path, consider it fully. If it is the best path, take it.

SUMMARY

In essence, outlines are procedures to follow to organize the information you've gathered to make it easier to write. The writer of a short news feature and news story may utilize a schematic pyramid as an outline guide. However, the news story will utilize an inverted pyramid with answers to important questions in the lead. The short news feature, meanwhile, will have a lead composed of a narrative hook, an idea and a transition into the main body of the feature. Unlike the news story, rather than revealing all the facts at the beginning the feature builds to a climax at the end.

The structures of the long news story and long feature story are different. A graphic representation of the long feature may be a wavelike line representing valleys of exposition and peaks of reader interest generated by examples and illustrations of what was noted in the preceding valley of exposition. The peaks inspire readers to continue on to the ending represented by a rectangle. All of this should parallel a constantly mounting plane of interest.

The magazine article format is represented by a ramp designated "the reader interest plane." The article writer organizes the article along designated areas of the reader interest plane (developing, generating and climactic paragraphs), keying them to an article interest ending with a lingering impression.

While commentary outlines may in some instances be distinctive, depending on their purpose, most writers may employ the reader interest plane to accomplish their tasks. Commentary, like all writing, should embrace the general principle of unity of impression.

If you remain master of the outline, you will discover it is a valuable aid in all phases of writing: Not having to think about what will be taken up next (it's in the outline) or where you've been, you are free to develop new and related ideas, incidents or illustrations to amplify the writing or thoughts at hand. You can ponder the best word, the best phrase, the best figure of speech, the best image.

"Putting proper words in proper places" is made much easier.

FEATURES FOR DISCUSSION

A. "Music Doth Not the Beast Soothe? (or, 'There Goes That Song Again')"

By Eric R. Danton
The Hartford Courant, May 8, 2003

Remember when folks like the Moral Majority said that exposure to music with violent lyrics can prompt aggressive behavior? Seems they're right, according to a study published in the May issue of the *Journal of Personality and Social Psychology*.

The study, conducted by researchers in Iowa and Texas, found a link between listening to violent song lyrics and feelings of aggression and hostility, bolstering arguments that such content can lead to violent behavior. It is a finding that belies the notion that violent music provides a cathartic release for anger and negative feelings.

That may not come as a shock given that studies examining violence on TV, in movies, and in video games have reached similar conclusions. This study, "Exposure to Violent Media: The Effects of Songs With Violent Lyrics on Aggressive Thoughts and Feelings," extends the same hypothesis to another pop-culture medium, lead researcher Craig A. Anderson says.

"There really hasn't been much research on music lyrics, certainly no conclusive research had been done prior to this, so this research, in a sense, fills a gap," said Anderson, chairman of the psychology department at Iowa State University. We've known for years from TV research and movie research and, more recently, video game research that content matters."

The study consisted of five experiments designed to measure participants' reactions to violent songs. The first two assessed the effects of violent lyrics on hostile feelings and aggressive thoughts that college student volunteers demonstrated after listening to a pair of songs by the band Tool, one with lyrics deemed violent and one considered nonviolent. The third experiment expanded on the first two by adding a larger selection of songs, including pairs of tunes by Suicidal Tendencies, the

Beastie Boys and Run D.M.C. The last two experiments studied the combined effect of violent, but humorous, song lyrics on aggressive thought. They included tunes by Johnny Cash—"A Boy Named Sue"—and "Weird Al" Yankovic.

"Each study has its own particular strength and weakness, and by doing multiple studies on the same hypothesis, but with slightly different design—in some cases different measures, in other cases different songs—if in doing that you get similar results, then you should be more confident that you're actually converging on a correct answer," Anderson says.

Results from all five experiments strongly suggest that listening to songs with violent lyrics increases feelings of aggression, at least in the short term. Such feelings can influence the way people view social interactions, leading them to interpret ambiguous actions as hostile and react more aggressively in turn, writes Anderson and his colleagues, Nicholas L. Carnagey from Iowa State and Janie Eubanks from the Texas Department of Human Services.

The findings support what moral watchdogs have argued for years and one of them, Sen. Joseph Lieberman, D-Conn., says the paper is an important tool in understanding the effects of violent music.

Lieberman says he will soon propose a federal program to fund more research into the positive and negative consequences of electronic media use.

That's fine, says a record-industry lobbying group, but the ultimate responsibility still rests with parents.

"We agree that parents should be educated so they can make their own determinations about what media content is appropriate for their children," says Amy Weiss, a spokeswoman for the Recording Industry Association of America.

The group made no comment concerning the study's findings.

B. "More Ugly Americans: A Slippage in Manners"

By Donna Cassata
The Associated Press, Oct. 15, 2005

WASHINGTON—Americans' fast-paced, high-tech existence has taken a toll on civility.

From road rage in the morning commute to high-decibel cell phone conversations that ruin dinner out, men and women behaving badly have become the hallmark of a hurry-up world. An increasing informality—flip-flops at the White House even—combined with self-absorbed communication gadgets and a demand for instant gratification have strained common courtesies to the breaking point.

"All of these things lead to a world with more stress, more chances for people to be rude to each other," said Peter Post, a descendant of etiquette expert Emily Post and an instructor on business manners through the Emily Post Institute in Burlington, VT.

In some cases, the harried single parent has replaced the traditional nuclear family, and there's little time to teach the basics of polite living, let alone how to hold a knife and fork, according to Post.

A slippage in manners is obvious to many Americans. Nearly 70% questioned in an Associated Press-Ipsos poll said people are ruder than they were 20 or 30 years ago. The trend is noticed in large and small places alike, although more urban people report bad manners, 74%, than people in rural areas, 67%.

Peggy Newfield, founder and president of Personal Best, said the generation that came of age in the times-a-changin' 1960s and 1970s are now parents who don't stress the importance of manners, such as opening a door for a woman or girl. So it was no surprise to Newfield that those children wouldn't understand how impolite it was to wear flip-flops to a White House meeting with the president—as some members of the Northwestern women's lacrosse team did in the summer.

A whopping 93% in AP-Ipsos poll faulted parents for failing to teach their children well.

"Parents are very much to blame," said Newfield, whose Atlanta-based company started teaching etiquette to young people and now focuses on corporate employees. "And the media."

Sulking athletes and boorish celebrities grab the headlines, while television and Hollywood often glorify crude behavior.

"It's not like the old show *Father Knows Best,*" said Norm Demers, 47, of Sutton, Mass. "People just copy it. How do you change it?" Demers would like to see more family-friendly television but isn't holding his breath.

Nearly everyone has a story of the rude or the crude, but fewer are willing to fess up to the boorish behavior themselves.

Only 13% in the poll would admit to making an obscene gesture while driving; only 8% said they had used their cell phones in a loud or annoying manner around others. But 37% in the survey of 1,001 adults questioned Aug. 22–23 said they had cursed in public.

Yvette Sienkiewicz, 41, a claims adjustor from Wilmington, Del., recalled in frustration how a bigger boy cut in front of her 8-year-old son as he waited in line to play a game at the local Chuck E. Cheese.

"It wasn't my thing to say something to the little boy," said Sienkiewcz, who remembered that the adult accompanying the child never acknowledged what he had done. In the AP-Ipsos poll, 38% said they have asked someone to stop behaving rudely.

Bernard F. Scanlon, 79, of Sayville, N.Y., would like to see one railroad car set aside for cell phone users to ensure peace and quiet for the rest. Amtrak has taken a stab at that by banning cell phones and other loud devices in one car of some trains.

But if those trains are sold out, the Quiet Car service is suspended and anything goes.

How rude.

EXERCISES

1. Outline the article on hate groups in Chapter 4. (Perhaps in class compare your outline with a classmate's. If they differ, why?)

2. Outline the first article in the Features for Discussion in this chapter: "Music Doth Not Soothe the Beast." (Perhaps in class compare your outline with a classmate's. If they differ, why?)

3. Outline the second article in the Features for Discussion in this chapter: "More Ugly Americans: A Slippage in Manners" (Perhaps in class compare your outline with a classmate's. If they differ, why?)

4. Take the outline completed in Exercise 3 and place it on the reader interest plane—that is, denote where each section of the outline will fall on the reader interest plane. (Once again, in class compare your outline with a classmate's. If they differ, why?)

CHAPTER 11

TO MARKET, TO MARKET

The Business Side of Freelancing—Part I

To write what you are interested in writing and to succeed in getting editors to pay for it, is a feat that may require pretty close calculation and a good deal of ingenuity. You have to learn to load solid matter into notices of ephemeral happenings; you have to develop a resourcefulness at pursuing a line of thought through pieces on miscellaneous and more or less fortuitous subjects; and you have to acquire a technique of slipping over on the routine of editors the deeper independent work which their over-anxious intentness on the fashions of the month or the week have conditioned them automatically to reject.
—Edmund Wilson, Journalist/Critic

The literary landscape is littered with noted authors who have been rejected: James Lee Burke's *Lost Get-Back Boogie* was rejected 52 (fifty-two!) times by New York publishers before being published by the Lousiana State University Press. The novel was nominated for a Pulitzer Prize, and landed Burke a movie contract. His *Neon Rain* was rejected 97 times! Other authors: John Grisham's *A Time to Kill* was rejected by 28 publishers. William Golding's *Lord of the Flies* was rejected 21 times. Pearl Buck's *The Good Earth* was rejected 14 times. Mary Higgins Clark's first short story was rejected 40 times.

Are you getting the idea that rejections are a major part of a freelancer's life?

Nevertheless, once you've written an article, whether it's a feature, magazine article or commentary, you'll want to send it to a market. Unlike Emily Dickinson, who kept her poetry to the very end, you'll want immediate gratification. And you're entitled to some reward for all your efforts. The gratification, strange as it may seem, comes with sending your manuscript to a market, always believing that, this time, the editor will smile upon it. As Edmund Wilson indicates in the quote that opens this chapter, the road may be long and hard. But let's hit the road.

SELECTING MARKETS

Newspaper or Magazine?

If you have an article that can be sent to either a newspaper or a magazine, chances are you'll opt for a magazine first. And for the reasons freelancer Vince Passaro notes:

THE MAGAZINE

Magazines pay more—often, quite substantially more. To paint the picture most dramatically, you can model it on the *New York Times*, which has a magazine as well as many "newspaper" sections that use freelance writers. If you propose a piece to the *Sunday Magazine*, and they take it, you might make anywhere from $5000 to even $10,000, depending on a number of factors. If you fail to interest the magazine in the piece, however, and turn around and sell the idea to the City Section, or the Styles section, which are in newspaper format, you make $400 or $500. This has to do with many things, including culture and habit, but most of all advertising: ads in the magazine bring in a lot more money than newspaper ads, and the editorial copy that are their excuse for existence is treated like that much more valuable a commodity. And the magazine is more selective: It's harder to sell them an idea, and they put you through many more edits and revisions and guidance sessions. They fact check vigorously; they worry over every word.

The second advantage of magazine writing is length. You can do more substantial pieces for magazines.

The third advantage is that book and movie deals are made from magazine pieces but rarely from newspaper pieces.

The Newspaper

Newspapers have an advantage though in several ways: there is much more need for copy, and a much broader range of things you can sell them. What you write generally gets published quickly and with minimal fuss. People read it. You can write and be edited and published and cover greater territory with much greater frequency writing for newspapers.

Newspaper and Magazine Markets

In both magazines and newspapers, with very few exceptions—perhaps *Harper's* and *The Nation*—you'll be prevented from saying anything dramatic or radical. The editors wouldn't have attained their desks and their titles if they were not inherently and permanently allergic to those kinds of ideas. Cf. Noam Chomsky. So if you want to say anything really challenging, plan on writing a book.

Where to Look

Just as there exist numerous ideas for the freelance writer to explore, numerous markets in both newspapers and magazines exist for those ideas which have come to fruition. You look under allied subject matter headings on the internet and in such books as *Writer's Market,* which lists more than 4,000 markets. Other market listings are included in *The Directory of Little Magazines & Small Presses,* 700 pages of listings, and Bacon's *Magazine Directory,* with more than 14,000 listings of business, trade, professional and consumer publications in the United States, Canada, Mexico and the Caribbean. Bacon's *Newspaper Directory* includes listings of daily and community newspapers as well as news services and syndicates. They include 1,565 daily and 10,298 community newspapers in the United States and 117 daily and 1,517 community newspapers in Canada. (Although Bacon's directories primarily provide media and editorial contacts for news releases, they may also serve as a source for freelance writer markets.) Finally, the AA Independent Press Guide, a free online resource for writers at http://www.thunderburst.co.uk, has detailed listings on over 2,000 literary and genre magazines and publishers from around the world, plus links to over 750 Internet magazines.

Market Categories

The categories of markets for article ideas range all the way from that of consumer, professional and company trade journals, to narrower categories such as women, men, children, farm, sports and health. Magazines and newspapers specify what articles they publish and the kinds of material they want freelancers to produce. Generally, freelancers contribute familiar material, while editors look to their staff to research and write about innovative topics.

The Writer's Market

If there's one book freelance writers opt to keep on their bookshelves, it's *Writer's Market*—"the writer's bible." (It lists a broad category of markets for articles—nonfiction, fiction and poetry.) Once an idea for an article occurs to you, the *Market* can be used to select the most prestigious and best-paying markets for it.

Two typical examples from *Writer's Market*:

American Profile

American Profile, Publishing Group of America, 341 Cool Springs Blvd., Suite 400, Franklin TN 37067. (615)468-6000. Fax: (615)468-6100. E-mail: editorial@americanprofile.com. Website: www.americanprofile.com. Editor: Peter V. Fossel. Contact: Joyce Caruthers, associate editor. 95% freelance written. Weekly magazine with national and regional editorial celebrating the people, places and experiences of hometowns across America. The four-color magazine is distributed through small to medium-size community newspapers. Estab. 2000. Circ. 3,000,000.

Pays on acceptance. Byline given. Buys first, electronic, 6-month exclusive rights. Editorial lead time 3 months. Submit seasonal material 6 months in advance. Accepts queries by mail, e-mail, fax. Responds in 1 month. Writer's guidelines online.

Nonfiction: General interest, how-to, interview/profile, travel. No fiction, nostalgia, poetry, essays. Buys 250 mss/year. Query with published clips. Length: 450–1,200 words. Pays expenses of writers on assignment.

Photos: State availability with submission. Reviews transparencies. Buys one-time rights, non-exclusive after 6 months. Negotiates payment individually. Captions, identification of subjects, model releases required.

Columns/Departments: Health, Family, Finances, Home, Gardening.

Tips: "We appreciate hard-copy submissions and one-paragraph queries for short manuscripts (less than 500 words) on food, gardening, nature, profiles, health and home projects for small-town audiences. Must be out of the ordinary. Please visit the website to see our writing style."

Campus Activities

Campus Activities, Cameo Publishing Group, P.O. Box 509, Prosperity SC 29127. (800)728-2950. Fax: (803)321-2049. E-mail: cameopub@aol.com or campusactivities.org. Website: www.cameopub.com. Editor: Laura Moore, Managing Editor: Robin Hellman. Contact: WC Kirby, Publisher. 75% freelance written. Magazine published 8 times/year covering entertainment on college campuses. Campus Activities goes to entertainment buyers on every campus in the US. Features stories on artists (national and regional), speakers and the programs at individual schools. Estab. 1991. Circ. 5,200. Pays on publication. Publishes ms an average of 2 months after acceptance. Byline given. Offers 15% kill fee if accepted and not run. Buys first, second serial (reprint), electronic rights. Editorial lead time 2 months. Submit seasonal material 2 months in advance. Accepts queries by mail, e-mail, fax. Accepts simultaneous submissions. Responds in 1 month to queries; 2 months to mss. Sample copy for $3.50. Writer's guidelines free. Nonfiction: Interview/profile, photo feature. Accepts no unsolicited articles. Buys 40 mss/year. Query. Length: 1,400–3,000 words. Pays $250. Sometimes pays expenses of writers on assignment.

Photos: State availability with submission. Reviews contact sheets, negatives, 3×5 transparencies. Buys one-time rights. Negotiates payment individually. Identification of subjects required.

Tips: "Writers who have ideas, proposals and special projects requests should contact the publisher prior to any commitment to work on such a story. The publisher welcomes innovative and creative ideas for stories and works with writers on such proposals which have significant impact on our readers."

After reading through hundreds of market listings such as these, you'll be aware of a whole wide world of publications out there, waiting for your manuscripts. Those descriptions of the kind of articles wanted by the various magazine editors tend to generate article ideas for you.

TAKE FIVE (MARKETS)

When you have an idea that you're going to turn into an article, or if you've taken an idea and completed an article without consulting markets, go first to *Writer's Market* and select the five most prestigious and/or best-paying markets for that idea or article. Write the names of the editors and the magazine addresses on 3×5-inch cards or in a markets file in your computer under the title of the article. While you are doing this market search, write down a title or two from some of the articles you read so that they can be mentioned in your query letters to the editors or letters accompanying articles submitted. That suggests you are familiar with the magazine and will be observing its editorial style.

Writing with a Market in Mind

You'll be writing your article with markets in mind (a good approach), so study the editorial styles of the magazines. Note the kind of article leads used—dramatic, question, and so forth. What kind of style is preferred—breezy, formal, first-person point of view? Are authorities cited in the articles?

When you're doing this preliminary selection of those markets, you'll also be aware of other editorial policies. Do the markets welcome young writer submissions? Or is there a requirement that an agent submit manuscripts? What subject matter is encouraged? What's banned? What lengths are tolerated?

Before writing or sending an article to a magazine, a query letter may be sent to the editor. No matter whether you write an article before you query or not, if an editor wants a query it may (or may not) pay to accommodate her or him. But what exactly is a query letter?

WHAT IS A QUERY LETTER?

What makes an acceptable query?

A query is a compact letter that sells your article idea to the editor. Address your query to the appropriate editor, feature editor, article editor, commentary, and so on. Sometimes two or three editors are listed for the same area. Should you select the first of these editors? She or he is probably inundated with manuscripts. If your topic is about women and you have a choice between a man or woman editor, select the woman. Perhaps the name of an editor appeals to you. Select that editor. When I queried Soft Skull Press of New York City, I had a choice of four editors: Sander Hicks, David Janik, Tennessee Jones and Chris Teret. The novel I was intending to submit to them had a setting on a cattle farm 35 miles from Nashville, Tennessee. Want to guess which editor I elected to send the query (with three sample chapters) to? Within three weeks Tennessee Jones emailed me to send him the rest of the novel. (Five weeks later he emailed me a rejection.)

Your query should comment on the significance and timeliness of the article and its particular suitability for the magazine. The letter will include the proposed length of the article, the title and opening paragraphs, and a rough outline or summary. It should also list the sources you will use in writing the article, and your qualifications. A self-addressed, stamped envelope (SASE) should be included along with your email address.

An Acceptable Sample Query Letter

Note this sample query letter:

> Route 10 Woodview
> Salem, Oregon 97301
> August 15, 2007

> Sarah Grace Johnson, Articles Editor
> *Campus Voice*
> Whittle Communications L.P.
> 505 Market Street
> Miami, Florida 37902

Dear Ms. Johnson:

Would you be interested in a 1500-word article about student graduation fears? People tend to believe that day is a time of elation and joy, but more often than not, graduation day stirs in the seniors not only feelings of elation but also fears of the freedom and unknown out there in the world after graduation day.

Entitled "Graduation Daze—Butterflies and Dragons," the 1500-word article focuses on graduating students' fears and how to cope with them. At this time of year, I believe the article will be ideal for *Campus Voice* readers.

In addition to using my personal experience in writing this article (I'm a graduating senior), I will be interviewing other seniors as well as conducting a mini-random survey of graduating students at the University of Oregon. In addition, I will be gathering information from three psychologists in the counseling center and at least one professor from the psychology department.

If this is of any significance to you, I have had more than thirty news stories and articles published in the university newspaper. I have also served as managing editor.

But let me know how you feel about "Graduation Daze."

Sincerely,
Dorris J. Anthony

P.S. I particularly enjoyed the "The Art of Unblocking" by Noah Stefanick in the last issue of *Campus Voice.* As a matter of fact, it unblocked me so that I could write this query to you.

Should the student list or not list publications? In this query I list them because the number of them indicate a budding writer. And serving as a managing editor or sports editor of a university newspaper is quite an achievement. If articles have been published in a regular commercial newspaper, mention them. If you have no publications or they are minor, don't mention them.

An Unacceptable Sample Query Letter

The query letter below is guaranteed to find its way to a wastebasket:

Route 10 Woodview
Salem, Oregon 97301
February 15, 2007

Sarah Grace Johnson
Campus Voice
Whittle Communications L.P.
505 Market Street
Miami, Florida 33132

A first-name familiarity is not welcome.

Dear Sarah—

Would you be interested in an article about students graduating and the fears that event engenders?

People tend to believe that graduation day is all peaches and cream but more often than not, that is not the case as I can truly vouch for this scenario.

The tone of these paragraphs will not appeal to an articles editor or "engender" confidence in this writer's ability.

There's great fear of the unknown out there, unknown to those who have not tread that path.

I haven't worked up a good title for it yet, but I will, you can bank on it.

If you haven't published, don't tell.

And although I haven't published any articles yet, you can bank on my doing a bang-up job for you on this subject, using myself as a prime example.

But, hey! I'm wasting valuable time. I'm going to start that article for you as soon as I sign this letter and put it in the mail, 'cause I know you can tell an up-and-coming writer when you see one. And the same goes for article ideas.

As if the present *Campus Voice* needs improvement.

Yours for a better *Campus Voice,*
Dorris J. Anthony

Busy editors are not prone to correcting articles. This request automatically casts the writer into the amateur category.

P.S. When you get my article, if, somehow, it doesn't come up to what you want it to be, I can change it. Just let me know.—DJA

TO QUERY OR NOT TO QUERY, THAT IS THE QUERY

Among the things *Writer's Market* will tell you is whether you should query the magazine before sending an article to it. The arguments pro and con follow:

You Should Query

If the editor says "query," I suppose you should query. Most writers usually determine the market for an idea and then query. Freelancer Vince Passaro comments:

> Well, I wouldn't write something without knowing someone wanted it unless it was something that I really really wanted to write anyway (like an essay I recently wrote, failed to sell to a major publication, and eventually published in a quarterly). The only scenario in which I can picture this being a good idea is if you know (1) that you can't get through to a particular editor because she or he doesn't know you and isn't taking unsolicited calls or something, and (2) that if she or he saw the final copy it would definitely be wanted or close to enough to establish your credibility. To do commercial, journalistic pieces without a place waiting for them is a bit of a time waster I think.

If given a go-ahead by an editor, freelancers can write the article with that market in mind. Their reasoning for querying first? They know that wherever the article is eventually published, it will have to observe the particular magazine's editorial guidelines. Why go through an unnecessary editorial revision? Revisions take time, and time means lost money.

The editor of that market may not want to take an unqueried article based upon what a future revision by the author might look like.

However, if the article to be written involves expensive outlays of money and time, as a matter of course you will query before investing in such an article. An example would be writing about a canoe and fishing trip through international waters from Ely, Minnesota.

Reasons for Not Querying

On the other hand, just about anything you write, if it's written well, can be marketed in one or more newspapers or magazines. Passaro notes this:

> Anyone with a modicum of talent can find some publication out there, online or in print, that needs copy. From there, one can have clips. And having clips, one can solicit more work. It's a long process but the main trick is finally finding someone who likes your work and remains supportive of it. From there it gets easier.

And Susan Freinkel remarks:

> I can see writing a personal essay—something that I just want to get out because I need/want to write it for myself. But financially it's pretty risky to invest time in something without knowing that someone will buy it. I certainly wouldn't do that with a reporter piece since most editors have an idea of what they want. But I am thinking about bigger magazines—maybe that's fine for someone starting out or writing for local publications that are really eager to fill their pages.

Because of the multitude of markets, many writers may write an article first and then select the market. Sometimes I take this writing/marketing approach because it guarantees an enthusiastic first draft with my mind unencumbered with a market's do's and dont's. And, of course, once you've got the article written, you can still query the editor before sending the article.

And despite warnings against sending unqueried articles, most editors will look at an article sent without a query.

A COVER LETTER IS NEEDED

Whether or not you choose to query, a cover letter accompanies the article. It should be short and to the point as exemplified by the following letter. Send it to the appropriate editor by name:

1544 Landscape View
Potsdam, New York 53410
June 12, 2007

Frank Zachary, Article Editor
Town & Country
1700 Broadway
New York, New York 10019

Dear Mr. Zachary:

The enclosed true, humorous article, "If You Think You're Having Problems with Your Lawn...," seems particularly suited for *Town & Country*. In 1,500 words it chronicles the efforts of my wife in creating the "woodsy look." Before the "woodsy look" was completed, we had created, under eight layers of newspaper pages and a foot of leaves, a haven for black snakes.

In case you're wondering, I've published 10 articles in commercial newspapers in the surrounding communities.

Let me know how you feel about "If You Think . . ."

Sincerely,
Damon Thomas
Email: ddthomas@hotmail.com

P.S. I particularly enjoyed the barn-building article by Laurie Robertson in the last issue of *The Country Gentleman*.

If you do not hear from the editor within the period of time the *Writer's Market* notes the magazine usually responds wait another week or two, as your article may still be going through the editorial process, (You're no doubt working on another article during this time.) Then write a brief note to the editor:

1544 Landscape View
Potsdam, New York 53410
August 2, 2007

Frank Zachary, Articles Editor
Town & Country
1700 Broadway
New York, New York 10019

Dear Mr. Zachary:

About six weeks ago (June 12) I sent you a true, humorous article, "If You Think You're Having Problems with Your Lawn...," that I believe is particularly suited for *Town & Country*. I have yet to hear from you. (The *Writer's Yearbook* indicates you respond within four weeks.)

If you're still considering the article, please forgive this inquiry. My fond hope, of course, is that you've made an editorial decision and are in the process of mailing me a check. Is that the case?

I'll be awaiting your reply. Thank you.

Sincerely,
Damon Thomas
E-mail: ddthomas@hotmail.com

If you queried the editor earlier and received a positive reply, remind the editor of his or her positive response to your query, but point out again how well suited the article is for the magazine, and comment about still another article you've read in the magazine.

WHY MENTION ARTICLES IN THE EDITOR'S MAGAZINE?

Why comment about articles read in query and cover letters? As mentioned earlier, your comment assures the editor that you are familiar with the magazine and the editorial content of it. It tells the editor that you are a reader of the magazine. ("At least someone out there is reading my magazine!") It can get lonely for that editor in an editorial office. Your little postscript at the end of your letter touches the editor and puts her or him in the proper frame of mind to read your query or article in a positive light, and so gives you a little advantage over other manuscripts being submitted for publication.

PACKAGING YOUR ARTICLE: MANUSCRIPT FORMAT

You received a positive answer to your query letter to the editor. After you have completed the research for your article, outlined it along one of the suggested paradigms or the reader interest plane, written the first draft and revised it numerous times, you are ready to type it in final manuscript form. You'll want to package it attractively because it can bring about an acceptance or a rejection depending on how it's handled.

On the first page, in the upper left-hand corner, single-spaced, type the title of your article, enclosed in quotes. Underneath it, type: A 1500-word article/feature/commentary (whichever is the case). Round the count out to the nearest 50 words—nothing less, nothing more. If you should type 1,579 words, for example, the editor may visualize you painfully counting each word and peg you for a beginner. On the third line type your full name.

Some writers recommend typing name, address, email address and telephone number in the upper right-hand corner, also single-spaced. I believe this simply clutters the page. That information is included in the cover letter.

Start the text of your article one-third down the page. Set it in 14-point New Times Roman font, line spacing 1.5, with these margins: left margin 1.5 inches, right 1.5 inches and 1 inch at the top and bottom of the page. Page numbers should come at the bottom of each page, centered. At the end of the article, in the middle of the page, two spaces after the last line, write "The End." Needless to say, your article should be free from errors.

Manuscripts under eight pages may be folded once and mailed in a 6-by-9-inch envelope. Longer manuscripts should be mailed in 9-by-12-inch envelopes, with a cardboard insert to keep the pages wrinkle-free. Use a paper clip for the pages. Stapling them leads to frustrating editing, if the editor elects to run your article. Use the correct postage for the envelope addressed to the editor. Include a self-addressed, stamped envelope to return the manuscript to you if the article is rejected. Editors are not likely to return manuscripts unless you provide an envelope and pay the postage.

THE EDITOR ACCEPTS

After many weeks, perhaps months, of waiting, you've got an email from the magazine editor. The editor likes your article and wants to publish it. You shout! Run about! Time for celebration, perhaps with other freelance writers who are friends over a bottle of champagne or Perriers. However, the next few lines give you pause: The editor likes the article, all right, but with a few editorial changes. Could you change the lead so that it does not proclaim the article to be "the definitive article" on the primary sources of *The Scarlet Letter?* The editor also found a citation discrepancy in a comment you made in the fourth paragraph of the article compared to one in the next-to-last paragraph. Could you rectify this discrepancy? And would you accept a payment of $200? (It's $100 less than noted in *Writer's Market* for the magazine.) The editor wants first North American publishing rights and will schedule your article for publication within the next six months. What do you do?

First of all, you continue in a jubilant mood and set the stage for a celebration. After all, the article had been turned down by seven other magazines and you were about to retire it for a couple of years. You look at the editor's suggestions for change. Although you like the lead—it *is* the definitive article—you can tone the braggadocio down without downgrading the importance of the article too much. You check the other discrepancy noted and find the editor is right. You can, and want, to correct it.

Should You Accept the Offer?

You're going to acquiesce to the editor's requests. They're minimal. And the *Arizona Quarterly* is a prestigious magazine. You write in a letter:

> I'm pleased you want to publish "Mythology and Antiquity in *The Scarlet Letter*: The Primary Sources" in the *Arizona Quarterly* as the lead article in the January issue. And thanks for noting the discrepancy in the citation—I'll take care of that immediately. Although I believe strongly in the article's definitiveness, I'll also tone the lead down a little.
>
> You've offered payment of $200 rather than the $300 pay scale noted in *Writer's Market.* Any particular reason for that? Can we settle for, let's say, at least $250?

With this reply to the editor you've portrayed yourself as a writer who is not obdurate and one who can take instruction. Most important, you've thanked the editor for noting a minor discrepancy in the article. Unless that magazine is under great financial stress, the editor will be inclined to pay you $250 or give you a good explanation for not coming up to the *Writer's Market* quote.

WHAT HAVE YOU SOLD? COPYRIGHTS

So you made the sale. But what did you sell? The first North American publishing rights of your article? Probably. That means you can't do any more marketing of it until the *Arizona Quarterly* publishes it in January. The important thing is, in most instances: You keep the copyright. You can sell it again if you find a market. If you're putting together a book of articles and want to include it, you don't have to go to the *Arizona Quarterly* to get the editors to relinquish their hold on it.

Whenever possible, you'll want to keep the copyright of what you've written. You've earned the right to profit as much as possible from your efforts. If the publication has a policy of keeping forever the copyright to your article, try bargaining with the editor. This brief overview of copyright law explains the situation in more detail:

In general, copyright law rewards the production of creative works by providing the owner with the exclusive right to reproduce those creative works in any tangible medium of expression. Works of authorship may include almost any imaginable artistic or creative endeavor, from literary and dramatic works to sound recordings and architectural and choreographic works. If the work was created on or after January 1, 1978, it is under copyright from the date of its creation for the life of the author plus 70 years after death.

However, if an employer hires an employee to create a work, the employer is considered to be the author and owns the copyright.

(A more detailed explanation of copyright is provided in Appendixes C and D.)

REJECTIONS: SURVIVING THE AFTERMATH

But what if some indiscriminate, inept, incompetent editor rejects your article? And other editors follow her or his lead? Doom and gloom? Do not despair. Any freelance writer will tell you rejections play a major role in your writing career, especially in the beginning, when rejections are least welcome and most devastating. What do you do? Take action!

Don't let the shock of being rejected keep you from pursuing your goals as a writer. Rejections are a large part of a writer's life.

Seek Comfort in the Log

Go to the manila folder where a hard copy of your article is stored (or to the computer file). On the inside of the folder you've created a log for your article, where you've listed other markets to send the article to if the first market rejects it:

Article		Market	Date sent	Returned	Comments
1.	*"They Drew a Circle"*	*Elle*	12/8/05	3/30/06	form reject
2.	" "	*Women's World*	4/2/06		
3.	" "	*Women Alive*			
4.	" "	*Woman's Life*			
5.	" "	*Woman's Day*			

Fill in the columns for the rejected manuscript. Below this rejection market you've noted four markets which might also be interested in this particular article, along with their pertinent address information (editor's name, etc.). If the pages of your article have been damaged or wrinkled in some way, print the article again. (No editor likes to receive obvious rejects from another magazine.) Then mail the article, with a cover letter, to your next market. Queries, incidentally, may be handled in logs the same way you track articles.

After the article has been rejected three times, it might be worth reading it over in light of comments made by the editors to see if a revision would improve it. Form rejects, obviously, won't help here, except to tell you these markets aren't buying. However, what has taken place, even with form rejections, is a passage of time. As noted in Chapter 7, "The Art of Writing," with this time lapse you will have established an aesthetic distance from your article. This allows you to see more easily the words and phrases and organization needing to be revised. Rejoice! There's life in rejections after all!

The log is valuable to you for a number of reasons:

1. As a freelancer, you'll have a number of articles in the mail at any one time—I've had as many as six. You'll be able to keep track of them and avoid sending two at the same time to the same market.

2. Another reason for keeping a log is that newspaper, magazine and book publishing editors play musical chairs all the time. If you know you have a good article and you've exhausted the markets for it, wait three years and check the editors of those markets. Chances are they now have different editors and perhaps different tastes that correspond even more to your article. After taking a hard look at what you've written, and if you're assured it's worthy of publication, start the article on the market rounds again.

3. You'll want logs available for income tax purposes, as evidence that you're actually a small business. (More about this in the next chapter, "Home Again, Home Again.")

A WASTELAND OF LITERARY REJECTIONS

Among my rejection stories: I sent the humorous article "The Woodsy Look," mentioned in a cover letter earlier, to 32 different markets before *Inland Steel* paid me $300 for it. Then, while the article was in galley proofs, the magazine folded during a recession. After 10 other rejections, *Word Play* magazine published it.

But, as noted earlier, rejections play a major role in a freelancer's life.

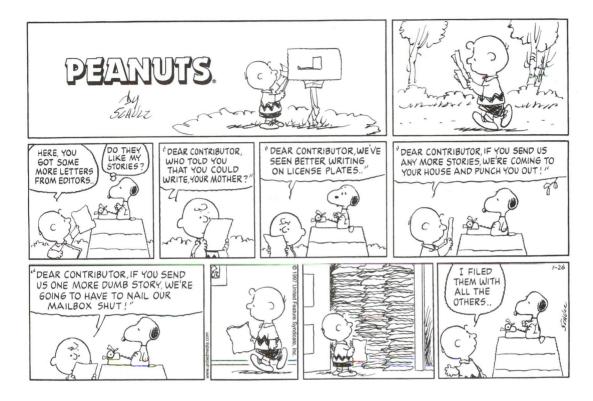

Hibiscus magazine editors wrote this about rejections:

> Rejection slips are part of writing. Each one hurts. Writers and poets, being sensitive, may feel this is a rejection of them personally. It is not. . . .
>
> There is no way the writer or poet can know the biases of all the magazine editors publishing in the English language. Writers and poets must write as well as they can and submit their work to editors. If it is rejected, they must send it out again and again and again. At least ten times. After the tenth rejection they may say, "The world is not ready for my work," and file the piece.
>
> Allowing a lapse of some time, the story or poem should be retrieved and re-read with critical eyes. If its creator believes it to be a sound work, the submission cycle should begin anew.

MULTIPLE SUBMISSIONS: TO DO? OR NOT TO DO?

Knowing what you now know about the rejection tide that will carry you in and out, month in and month out, you might begin wondering about multiple submissions of an article. Should you do it, or not? My advice? Do it. For a number of reasons:

1. Some editors keep your submissions overly long, so if your article is on a current topic and you receive a rejection, the article has lost its timeliness.
2. An editor may hold on to a timely article to keep the competition from running it.

3. If an article is kept two to three months before a rejection, and you have 10 rejections before it is published, you've waited a couple of years for that acceptance.
4. While most editors don't particularly favor multiple submissions, they understand and tolerate them.
5. There's nothing unethical about multiple submissions. Book publishers, for example, understand the time constraints operating on the author.

If an editor notes in *Writer's Market* that multiple submissions are not acceptable, you can observe her or his cautionary guidelines.

WHILE YOU ARE WAITING: THE EDITOR AT WORK

While you're going through all these marketing throes, you might want to consider what that editor is doing. An editor's role is to play the skeptic, to fine-tune already good work for clarity of thought and correctness of syntax. Sometimes that means cutting an article and rephrasing thoughts. Is she or he poised, with blue pencil, over your manuscript? The editor would rather not have to blue pencil any article. Pride of authorship bolsters the foundation of the writer, and most editors try not undermine it. If you view an editor as a collaborator you can be flexible in your thinking and writing and accept suggestions for changes gracefully.

Most writers benefit from an editor's objective scrutiny. Few writers are so polished that their work can go from a computer directly into print. However, freelance writers cannot depend on others to correct spelling, punctuation and organization errors.

Little can compare to the excitement of receiving an acceptance from an editor about an article you've just written. But before that acceptance, chances are the article came under the scrutiny of one or more of the unsung heroes and heroines of the writing world—the copy editors who point their pencils at or set their cursors on words and phrases and eliminate an offending construction and errors that can result in a rejected manuscript.

BEWARE OF EDITORS BEARING ILL TIDINGS

When you've decided, after three rejections, to take another look at what you've written, be wary of some of the editor's comments. Some criticism may be constructive, and if so, take it. Other objections may not be valid, and, indeed, counterproductive.

One editor wrote the following criticism about a short story I sent her, titled "Saturday Morning with the Burnside Circle: Jake Madigan and the Black Irish":

> This story lacks focus, mostly because the narrator is largely uninvolved. I think you should dump the first person narrator & tell it in 3rd, or narrate it in 1st person from the point of view of one of the most involved characters—either Madigan or Seivers. The first two pages lend absolutely nothing to the story. . . . If you want to try these ideas, I'd like to see it again. If not, I'll look at something else, if you like.

Of course, when she said, "I'll look at something else, if you like." I thanked her for her comments (they totaled a full page) and sent her another story. This is what you should do when you get such an invitation—and do it immediately. As a matter of fact, I sent her two more stories. She was not impressed with those stories either. She had still more problems with "point of view."

In contrast, a couple months later, *The Sun*'s editor, at the bottom of a form letter, wrote in ink,

> Earl,
> "[indecipherable word—maybe "thanks"] for an engaging, well-written story.
> —Sy

One year later, *The Roanoke Review,* a more impressive periodical than the initial market, printed "Saturday Morning with the Burnside Circle…" exactly as I had written it. The editor even complimented me on my writing.

University and Commercial Publishers Rejects

Five university presses and a state historical society rejected a book of narrative essays I was marketing, titled *Growing Up on the Illinois Prairie During the Great Depression and the Coal Mine Wars* (a Portayal of Life the Way It Was). One university press kept it for a year, while the historical society kept it for two years! It was published in 2006 by The Edwin Mellen Press. Ten commercial presses rejected another book I coedited with Dr. David G. Clark titled *Mass Media and the Law.* John Wiley and Sons eventually published it.

So be judicious in taking editors' advice and comments. Some may be on target, others may be kicking up clods of dirt on it.

Keep Your Sense of Humor

Whatever is the case, it eases things when you can view their comments with some humor. For your edification, here are three satirical rejections:

"Sorry, But—"

Dear Mr. Burroughs:

Your story is certainly unusual, but we feel the idea of a man living with apes in the jungle is a little too much to ask our readers to swallow. Also, the name

"Tarzan" seems a bit forced. Something like Oscar, which is a name everyone knows, might go over a little better.

Is the remote African locale really necessary to the story? Give us some area we can visualize. If you could change this piece from "Tarzan and the Apes" to, say, "Oscar and his Dogs," and put the locale in one of our Midwestern states, we would be very interested in considering your work.

Sincerely,
Oscar C. Hitch, Editor

Sorry, But—

Dear Mr. Tolstoy:

We like your story *War and Peace* very much. However, we think it needs more character development, and the length is a little too long for our magazine.

If you could polish this up and cut to about 5,000 words we would be very interested in looking at your work again.

Sincerely,
Ivan Krincheviszyenov
Editor

Sorry, But—

Dear Mr. Twain:

You write very well, but we feel that a story about young boys on a raft does not have the appeal readers look for in our magazine.

Ours is essentially a family magazine, and thus subject to certain taboos. It is not our policy to encourage children to leave home and endanger themselves on our rivers and lakes.

If you have any more work dealing with less touchy subjects we would be glad to look at it.

Sincerely,
Bascomb L. Bascomb
Editor

EXPANDING YOUR PUBLISHING HORIZON

If you have a knack for writing commentary and columns, especially humorous columns, and a local newspaper is printing them regularly, try expanding your market. Take three of your published columns (or features or articles) and query the other newspapers in the state to determine whether they'd like to carry a weekly column of yours starting at $50 a column. (See Editor Sweitek's invitation in Chapter 1.) You might find yourself opening a column service.

Or you might query feature syndicates with three or four columns to determine if those editors are interested.

A FINAL WORD TO KEEP YOU WRITING

Whatever you do, don't let the shock of being rejected keep you from pursuing your goals as a writer. No matter how many rejections you receive, though there may be enough to set you up in the wallpapering business, do whatever is necessary to keep writing. When you get a rejection, sing "Yes, Jesus loves me." Or sing the "Sam Hall" song the way I do sometimes. How does "Sam Hall" go? I first heard this old English ballad sung by Carl Sandberg at the University of Illinois. The first verse follows:

O, my name it is Sam Hall, it is Sam Hall.
O, my name it is Sam Hall, it is Sam Hall.
O, my name it is Sam Hall,
And I hate you one and all,
Yes, I hate you one and all,
God damn your eyes!

I'm not so certain what singing the "Sam Hall" will do for you as far as your character is concerned, but my main point is to *do whatever it takes to keep writing.*

If you get rejections from national magazines, lower your sights a bit and try local and regional publications and magazines with smaller circulations. Remember James Lee Burke's 52 rejections. Remember what William Faulkner did. He kept a log of his rejected short stories, and when he finally wrote his first novel best-seller, editors and publishers called his agent begging for something to publish. He sent them the identical stories they had rejected, with inflated price tags on them. They paid the price. Gladly.

SUMMARY

Once you've written a feature, article or commentary, it's only natural to want to send it to the best market possible for publication. With so many market possibilities you will want to investigate up to five and note the editorial requirements in the *Writer's Market* along with the appropriate editor and address.

A query letter comments on the significance and timeliness of your article and its particular suitability for the magazine. Your letter will usually include a rough outline or summary of the article as well as your qualifications and the sources you will consult.

Strict manuscript preparation is necessary. First impressions are important, so note the instructions for manuscript preparation given in the market listing and in this chapter.

If your article is accepted, celebrate with fellow writers. If rejected, seek solace in the article log. Register the rejection data and send the article to the next market of the five you entered in the log. The time lapse between rejections can bring about an aesthetic distance that will enable you to enter into a profitable revision of the article.

If you view the editor as a collaborator, you will be able to accept more gracefully comments critical of the article. However, beware of unwarranted criticism. The literary landscape is littered with noted authors who have been rejected.

Rejections can be devastating but they are a major part of freelancing. Unfortunately, most rejections come at the start of a freelance career. But they continue coming in the mail throughout the years, whether successful or not. Make a major determination, perhaps through creating a rejection ritual, to persevere and continue writing.

EXERCISES

1. Select one article idea that you want to develop. Choose and analyze the market for that article from *Writer's Market*. Examine issues of that magazine published in the last two years.
   a. Record brief comments about what you have discovered. Is the *Writer's Market* description accurate? On what does it agree? Where does it apparently differ?
   b. What kind of leads are favored in the magazine? What point of view is used? What is the tone of the articles?

2. In the magazine you chose in exercise 1 for your market, find an article similar to your article idea.
   a. Analyze it according to the reader interest plane, paragraph by paragraph. Comment on the article's title, purpose, sources, tone, flow and descriptions.
   b. Note what you will have to do in writing your article so that it will have the best chance of being accepted by the magazine editor.

3. Using the *Writer's Market*, select three magazines for each of three article ideas you listed in exercise 1. Repeat the article ideas here, listing three prime markets for each. Note the pay you'd expect to receive from each.
   a.
   b.
   c.

4. Select one article idea that you want to develop. Choose and analyze the market for that article. Examine issues of that magazine published in the last year or so. Record brief comments about what you have discovered.
   a. Is the *Writer's Market* description accurate? Where does it apparently differ? (When Tennessee Jones rejected my manuscript, his reasons were directly contradictory to the *WM* description.)
   b. What kind of leads are favored in the magazine? What point of view is used? What is the tone of the articles?

5. In the magazine you chose in exercise 4, find an article similar to your article idea. Analyze it according to the reader interest plane. Comment on the article's title, purpose, sources, tone, flow and descriptions. Analyze it paragraph by paragraph. Note what you will have to do in writing your article so that it will have the best chance of being accepted by the magazine editor.

6. Write a letter to the editor of a magazine you'd like to work for. Tell the editor that you're a journalism major and would like to be a contributing freelance writer to her or his magazine. Ask the editor for advice on the best way to achieve that goal. Be sure to cite one or two articles that you read in the magazine. Include a SASE. (You'll be surprised by the positive response.)

7. Write a query letter to the editor of the magazine you analyzed in exercise 5. Follow the guidelines and format provided in this chapter.

CHAPTER 12

HOME AGAIN, HOME AGAIN

The Business Side of Freelancing—Part II

Income is not required to claim deductions. But obviously, the more income produced, the better the argument that writing is a trade or business. The burden of proof is on the writer to show a profit motive in the writing activity.

—Lyle Starr

FAILING TO ITEMIZE COSTS TAXPAYERS MONEY

Billions of dollars are lost by taxpayers each year because they fail to file for deductible expenses. Many freelance writers who have yet to complete a sale may have some reservations about filing for expenses incurred in their writings, especially when the Internal Revenue Service preys upon the audit fears of citizens.

However, a freelance writer is, in effect, a small business owner, and entitled to the government subsidies awarded to small businesses. Although no sales have been registered, the freelance writer is serving an apprenticeship. A log of articles sent out to markets and rejections received serve as evidence of a freelance writing business. Too few freelance writers acknowledge this apprenticeship.

Noting that many deductions go unclaimed, Curt Anderson, an Associated Press tax writer, wrote this article in 2002:

> WASHINGTON (AP)—Tax payers are cheating themselves out of nearly $1 billion in overpaid income taxes simply because they fail to claim itemized deductions.
>
> "One of the big mistakes that people make is that all of a sudden they rush to get their tax returns finished and they aren't careful in organizing their records so they overlook things," said Toni Bardi, a tax professional licensed by the Treasury to represent taxpayers before the IRS.

A Closer Look at Losing Taxpayers

After reading those paragraphs, I said, "I know one person I'd lay money on who isn't cheating himself—Harry."

I became friends with Harry at the State University College in Potsdam, New York. (Harry later took the chair of the Bridgeport [Conn.] University physical education department.) He and I formed a poker club with five other members of the faculty. (We called it a seminar in statistics.) One night in late March the seminar convened at the home of Don, a sociology professor. The other seminar participants were Walter (history), Harry (psychology), David (history) and Joe (sociology). The professors were all bemoaning the impending IRS onslaught in a couple of weeks—except for Harry. Harry was rubbing his hands in anticipation.

"How come you're so gleeful, Harry?" I asked.

"Well, the IRS has been taking money from me all year long," he replied. "Now it's my turn to take the money back."

"How you going to do that?"

Harry listed the many legitimate deductible expense avenues of a professor who wrote articles for newspapers and magazines, refereed football and basketball games and designated a room in his house as a business office. I took notes from Harry that night, and, later, from George Oberst, a Clarkson College business professor and also a certified public accountant in Potsdam. Still later I learned from Lyle Starr, a former IRS employee, in Nashville, Tenn.

All the while, I gathered more information and articles from writers magazines, on tax consultants' suggested deductions. I passed all on to friends and my freelance writing classes.

UnAmerican Not to Deduct Legitimate Expenses?

The funny thing about listening to Harry that night was that none of the other professors in the seminar were buying.

Years later, I walked into the faculty lounge at George Peabody College, Nashville, for lunch, and Jack Miller, an education psychology professor, got up from an easy chair and greeted me with a handshake.

"Hello, fellow American!" he said.

"What's this all about?" I asked.

"I've just been telling these professors," Miller said, waving to the room, "what they can deduct as business expenses. I find out that you're the only other professor they know who does what every American should do—deduct business expenses when filing their income tax returns. And they're too scared to file."

"I can't believe it," I replied. "It's unAmerican not to deduct expenses—to let the government intimidate you."

"Just what I've been telling them," Miller said, clearly exasperated.

DOES THE IRS PLAY THE FEAR FACTOR?

I've experienced Miller's exasperation when I've attempted to convince other professors and friends of missed dollars because of failing to deduct legitimate expenses. What's working on almost all of them is the fear factor: fear of being audited. Does the IRS prey on this fear? Well, after reading the next few paragraphs, what do you think?

One year the IRS actually created public service announcements stating that it's all right to file for refunds, but if the refund topped $700 you were more likely to be audited. (So watch those deductions, the IRS was warning.) The announcements were broadcast widely.

Columnist Ellen Goodman is aware of IRS tactics. When Leona Helmsley, of the Helmsley Hotels, was sentenced for income tax evasion, she went to prison. On what date? Read what Goodman writes:

> In the wee hours of April 15, when the average mathphobic American taxpayer was still desperately rummaging among little piles of receipts for some last-minute deduction, a car pulled up to a prison gate in Lexington, Ky.
>
> Out of it emerged Leona Helmsley, the most famous and scorned tax-evader since Al Capone.
>
> If you think the timing of Mrs. Helmsley's incarceration was an accident—a mere astrological coincidence—take a rebate for credulity. What the hell, take two, they're small.
>
> The April 15 date for Leona's appointment in Lexington was designed to send a chill up the pen of any taxpayer who has ever thought about charging lunch with mom as a business expense. It was a pre-emptive strike against any

deep, dank, dark suspicion that the very rich do not pay taxes like thee, me and a White House canine author named Millie.

—*The Tennessean,* April 21, 1992

If You're Eligible, File for Deductions

Under these pressures, should you file for income tax refunds? Is it unAmerican not to do so? Certainly it's unAmerican not to stand up to government when it engages in despicable scare tactics and when you, personally, are involved, especially when you are justified in doing so. Why would I make that remark, aside from the fact that Henry David Thoreau is a sometime hero of mine? Let's look at the justification for filing an income tax return as a freelance writer and listing deductible expenses.

Tax Deductions Are a Part of Freelancing

You are a small businesswoman or -man, and if you do not take those deductions that's tantamount to tearing up a check you've received for a story or article that you've toiled over for months and finally sold to a magazine. Income tax deductions are as much a part of freelance writing as rejection slips. These deductions apply salve to the wounds inflicted by those rejection slips. In the first few years you'll find deductions more of a balm than acceptance checks because of the absence in the early years of those checks.

Small Businesses Are Entitled to Subsidies

Because you are operating a small business, you are entitled to some government subsidies. A major government subsidy is income tax deductions. As a matter of fact, if you contact the nearest IRS office you can get a free Business Tax Kit, which will give you basic tax forms and information pertinent to most businesses.

Throughout the years, filing for income tax deductions has become more and more complicated and overwhelming. Subsequently, the best course to follow in filing for those legitimate expenses is to locate a good certified public accountant and take all your receipts and expense estimations to her or him. The accountant's expertise should save you money. Although the IRS offers free service in filing a tax return, year after year news stories indicate that the IRS's own surveys post a 20 percent to 50 percent error rate in performing those services. (Perhaps that's why the IRS warns citizens that government help in preparing a return is not legally binding.)

DO YOU HAVE TO PUBLISH TO DEDUCT EXPENSES?

If you've established yourself as a freelance writer who writes weekly columns for newspapers across the state (let's say, perhaps, six newspapers) for $50 a column and you work out of your home, you'll have little commerce with the IRS. But what if you have not sold anything yet? No income whatsoever. Do you have legitimate tax deductions coming to you? Yes.

Making Money Without Sales

In the first four or five years you do not have to have published *anything* to declare expenses as a freelance writer. Why? Just as small businesses, like a dry-cleaning business, just starting out do not have to show a profit while operating to declare expenses, you, a small business operator, are serving, in effect, an apprenticeship. In a few years when your business is thriving, and you're selling articles to national magazines, the IRS will reap its benefit.

After four or five years, without any income resulting from your labor, you may have to reconsider filing. But leave that decision up to your accountant—if he's a Lyle Starr kind of accountant.

Some Tax-deductible Items

Let's note some of those tax deductible items:

If you declare a home office—a room in which the preponderance of freelance activities takes place, or a part of a room, whichever is the case—one way of determining a deduction is to list a fair rental value on that furnished room or portion of that room (for example, $500 per month). Another way is to determine what portion of the house the room comprises. If you have a seven-room house and one room is devoted to freelance activities, one-seventh of the household expenses (heat, electricity, water, phone, etc.) is deductible.

If you take this last route, list the furnishings of the room, placing a fair market value on each of them. Let's say you have an overstuffed chair, sofa and computer desk in the room. You also have a rug, two lamps, two end tables, a television set, radio, computer, printer, monitor, camera and so on. Your library consists of some 50 books you refer to on occasion, including encyclopedias, atlases, *Writer's Market*, thesaurus, dictionaries. (Perhaps worth a total of $1,000?) Once you've listed these furnishings with their estimated value, add them up and place them on a five-year depreciation scale. If, for example, they total $5,000, you have a $1,000 deduction you can take for five years. If you buy any of these items during the year— let's say a computer set-up for $3,000—under the tax rules at this writing, you can write off the entire $3,000 as a deduction rather than placing it on a depreciation scale. This is a prime example of a government subsidy to encourage business enterprises, large and small.

Other Legal Deductions

As a freelance writer you must be an informed citizen of the world. All newspaper subscriptions, magazine subscriptions, Internet and television cable expenses, as well as the books you buy and the movies, concerts and plays you see to stay abreast with what's going on in the world are income tax deductible. Make a list of those expenses as they occur, with dates, and keep receipts.

All expenses incurred in your writing, phone calls, lunches attended, trips taken (mileage is computed at around 46 cents per mile and room and board at around $204 per day as of this writing) are income tax deductible. Also included are purchases of paper and ink cartridges, camera expenses, repairs to computer or television, and the like.

As you can see, these expenses mount up, especially if you arrange an article on speculation about spelunking along the Mississippi River, writing about a unique Mardi Gras celebration or embarking on an international waters canoe experience between Minnesota and Canada.

If the expenses you've listed total from $6,000 to $9,000, you'll get approximately one-third of those dollars back. The flat deduction allowance the IRS lists at the time of this writing is $5,350 if you are single, or married and filing separately. (For heads of households, it is $7,850.) If you are married and filing jointly, you are allowed $10,700. If your spouse did not have any additional expense deductions and you filed jointly, you'd lose money because at the outside your deductible expenses total only $9,000. Your best bet in this instance would be to file separately.

Most of the time, you should be able to benefit from itemizing your expenses.

ESTABLISHING FREELANCE WRITER STATUS

To establish proof of claim to freelance writer status, keep logs of various writings sent to markets (features, articles, columns, stories, poems, plays, etc.) and rejection slips. Write brief narratives of trips taken in pursuit of subject matter for articles and the mileage, if you drive. Keep receipts of hotel bills paid, meals eaten, etc.

WHAT ABOUT AN AUDITED RETURN?

Perhaps with all that has been presented, you're having second thoughts about declaring tax deductions—especially with the thought of the IRS auditing your return. My advice? Scrap those second thoughts. Odds are long that you won't be audited. Furthermore, you're entitled to declare all that you've listed or will be listing.

You may be thinking, "Why me? Especially when there must be 50 corporations worth billions that are not paying any taxes at all because they've hired 50 lawyers each to seek out those tax loopholes created for them by legislation?" But read what the AP tax writer John Luther has to say about the audited return:

"We're from the IRS and We're Here to Help You"

By John Luther
AP Tax Writer, March 2, 1994

WASHINGTON (AP)—There are more dreaded phrases than "IRS audit," but not a lot.

Perhaps it is fear of the unknown. After all, chances a given tax return will undergo an Internal Revenue Service audit—or examination, as the IRS calls it—are about one in 100.

There was a time when the IRS was accused of using fear of an audit as a weapon to ensure compliance with the tax laws. Now the agency cultivates a "customer-friendly" image, telling taxpayers they have a right to be treated with consideration and to pay the least amount of tax that is possible within the law.

Nevertheless, an audit is not something to be coveted. It can be time-consuming, disruptive—and expensive, if you lose.

Most individual tax returns routinely face a type of audit every year. If your only sources of income are wages, interest and dividends, your return is checked automatically by computer. It makes sure that every dollar of income you earned shows up on your return.

If the computer finds the reports filed by employers, banks and brokers don't match your return, it quickly kicks out a form letter asking you to pay up or explain.

You don't have to assume the letter is correct. If you challenge it, send documentation for your case along with a check for what you think is right. The IRS will let you know whether it agrees.

Unlike the fast computer-generated letters, it can take the IRS 12 to 24 months to inform you that your return was selected for a formal audit.

Most audits are initiated because the IRS suspects deductions were overstated or some cash payments were not reported. In those cases, the audit generally is restricted to the items questioned by IRS.

On the other hand, if your return is picked at random for the Taxpayer Compliance Measurement Program, the IRS can require you to prove every item on the return. These audits are conducted to get a benchmark for gauging the income, deductions and tax liability of people at various economic levels.

In many cases, audits are conducted by mail. If the IRS demands a meeting, the 1988 Taxpayer Bill of Rights makes two guarantees:

A lawyer or accountant may represent you at the audit and you won't have to attend unless the IRS has issued an administrative summons for you personally. If you are there alone and not the subject of such a summons, you may demand at any time the audit be interrupted until you confer with your representative.

Notify the IRS 10 days in advance and you will be allowed to make an audio recording of your audit session. Or, if the IRS tapes the meeting, you may buy a transcript.

If you don't agree with the auditor's finding, you may ask for an on-the-spot review by a supervisor. If you accept the verdict, you sign Form 870, which authorizes an immediate assessment and limits the interest you will be charged, and pay up. You thus give up any right to fight the IRS in Tax Court, but you may file suit in U.S. District Court of the Court of Claims seeking a refund.

Assuming you and the IRS still can't agree—or if the audit was conducted in your home or office—you will be mailed a "30-day letter" that offers you a chance to accept or to ask for an appeals conference inside the IRS.

A Negative Audit Experience

Let's say you've filed expenses for a trip the IRS does not think is allowable. You combined a trip to Savannah, Ga., to describe the many beautiful mini-parks in that city, with a visit to George and Barbara Hofer who are old college friends of yours, and you stayed at their home for three days. The local newspaper or state magazine turned down your article. You're listing perhaps $300 as expenses, and the IRS has presented a strong case for not allowing the expenses. (It was a pleasure trip to visit your friends.) What are the penalties you face? You will have to repay $100 plus something like 6 percent interest for six months—at the outside, something like a total of $103. You've still represented yourself well and legitimately.

A Positive Audit Experience

You've been called in to explain why expenses of a canoe trip with your friend or spouse to international waters should be deductible when you have no published article to show for your trip.

With your shoe box of receipts in tow and your tax consultant, you represent the trip as one on a speculative article for the *Chicago Tribune.* You point out that you have motel receipts, canoe rental receipts, outfitting receipts from Bob Carey's Outfitters and the letter from the *Tribune* stating their acceptance of the article idea on speculation, along with another letter expressing their regret that they couldn't use the article.

To top it off, you bring with you to the meeting a receipt for the purchase of a $300 Canon camera that you'd neglected to declare.

You not only justified your tax declarations, you registered a $300 additional deduction and get a check back for $100 more.

Not only that, the IRS will note that you may be the kind of tax payer who neglects to declare an expense so that you can spring it if you're audited. Lyle Starr indicated that procedure can get you a yellow tab on your folder, meaning "Let this person be."

SHOULD YOU EMPLOY AN INCOME TAX CONSULTANT?

I recommend employing an income tax consultant, but make certain she or he is the right consultant for you. When I described to a contractor friend of mine how my consultant (Lyle Starr) assisted me at income tax time, he complained that his consultant was unassertive about deductions and challenging the IRS. How do you choose that "right" consultant? If other writers have consultants, ask them about their experiences. At an initial meeting with a consultant, ask her or him if a freelance writer can be considered a small business-woman or -man. Ask if expenses can be deducted without publishing in the first three or four years of the business. If the consultant does not agree to the legitimacy of freelance expenses, pass on her or him and go to another consultant, and another, until you find one you can bond with. If consultants are unaware of artist-deductible expenses, they are not well versed in their field.

Use a consultant for a number of reasons:

1. The IRS constantly changes its guidelines. Even income tax consultants use income tax interpretations by specialized publishing companies like Kleinrock Publishing because of the complexity of the guidelines.
2. You'll feel more secure and comfortable with an ally—a good tax consultant.
3. The consultant should increase your refund check by suggesting still other avenues of tax-deductible expenses that may not have occurred to you, such as mortgage expenses if you're declaring a fair rental value on a room.

A TASTE OF IRS GUIDELINES

As an example of IRS guidelines, look at section 25.1 of the IRS tax code, which states that all ordinary and necessary expenses incurred during the year in carrying on a trade or business are allowable deductions. After pointing out that duplicate expenditures are not allowable, the IRS states that expenditures must be "ordinary" and "necessary." A discussion of what is ordinary and what is necessary follows. Here are Kleinrock's interpretations (Kleinrock is a tax service provided to consultants, for a fee.):

> a. Ordinary
>
> Ordinary in this context means normal, usual or customary. It does not imply that the expense must be habitual or normal in the sense that the taxpayer must incur it frequently. <18>. Rather, it refers to expenses that are normally or customarily incurred in response to a particular circumstance. <19> Thus, an expense may be ordinary although it happens only once in a taxpayer's lifetime. *Welch v. Heivering,* 290 U.S. 111 (1933). The determination depends on whether the expense is one that has occurred or could occur in connection with businesses similar to the business claiming the expense deduction....
>
> ....
>
> b. Necessary
>
> Necessary generally means appropriate and helpful as opposed to required or obligatory. *Welch v. Heivering,* 290 U.S. 111 (1933). An expenditure is necessary if it is appropriate and helps develop and maintain the taxpayer's business. <24>

Kleinrock then provides examples and court cases to further clarify the discussions. While the interpretations are understandable, to the layman the tax code itself may not be.

SUMMARY

A freelance writer is a small business owner, and therefore entitled to the government subsidies. Although no sales may have been registered in the first few years of one's career the freelance writer is serving an apprenticeship. A log of articles sent out to markets and rejections received serve as evidence of a freelance writing business.

While the chances of being audited are remote, unless outlandish expenses are claimed, the audit can be a profitable event if you've forgotten to file for something like a camera. Even if an error in filing is made, the penalty is mild—a disallowance of the deduction and roughly 6% interest on the monies owed the government.

An income tax consultant service eases your chores in filling out your tax. The IRS code is difficult to interpret (even tax consultants subscribe to an interpretive service). Chances are the consultant will suggest more avenues for deductions that you haven't thought of.

EXERCISES

1. Query a freelance writer in your community on these points:
   a. Does she or he file for freelance writing expenses?
   b. If not, why not?

    c. If so, does she or he employ an income tax consultant?

    d. If so, why? What are the deductions taken?

    e. Has she or he been audited?

    f. If so, ask the person to describe the experience.

    g. Does she or he fear being audited?

    h. If so, does the freelancer see the IRS as preying on that fear?

2. Go to the local IRS office and ask for an income tax kit for a small business.

3. Query the chief IRS officer as to the legitimacy of a freelance writer filing for expenses incurred in writing without having sold any articles.

4. If the IRS is amenable to deductible expenses such as those in exercise 3, ask the officer how many years a freelance writer is entitled to this "apprenticeship" status without any sales.

5. Ask an educator:

    a. If she or he does a portion of preparation for teaching or research in the home.

    b. If the educator does not, ask if she or he has ever considered filing for expenses incurred in this preparation. If not, ask why not.

    c. Ask the educator what the deductions might be if she or he chooses to file.

    d. Ask if she or he would consider newspapers, magazines and television expenses as such deductions?

    e. If a negative answer comes in exercise 5d, ask the educator if she or he is required to be an informed citizen in performing educational duties, and note that these media keep her or him informed.

A COMMON SENSE APPROACH TO PUNCTUATION

No punctuation system is utterly foolproof. But this common-sense approach takes care of two arch villains—the comma and the semicolon—quite adequately. It also gives you something other than a bewildering array of punctuation rules to memorize. (And this simple learning device may prove so interesting that you'll be moved to go to the freshman English handbook and study punctuation, by the rules.)

This system is based on punctuation according to the way you read. After writing a sentence—simple, complex or compound—read it aloud. Wherever there is a natural pause, a punctuation mark is needed. All that remains for you to do, is to determine which mark to use.

Since you know what a question is, you need not concern yourselves with that mark. The same is true of a declarative sentence. So the period need not be considered. Exclamation marks usually fall into the same category as question marks. If a person yells "Fire!" or shouts, use an exclamation mark; otherwise, forget about it. Within a sentence, the vast majority of pauses in reading must be punctuated with either a comma or a semicolon. Sound simple? Not so simple: Ninety-nine percent of all punctuation errors are either comma or semicolon errors.

How can you be sure of using commas and semicolons properly to eliminate those punctuation errors? The answer is simple: Memorize the three instances in which the semicolon is used:

1. Use semicolons when independent clauses are not joined by conjunctions: Robert Goodson learned to box; Heather Burgess learned karate.
2. Use semicolons with independent clauses that have commas in the clauses and are joined by conjunctions: Goodson learned to box as a lark, not caring whether he would use this skill later in life or even at all; however, Burgess learned karate in preparation for life in the big city.
3. Use semicolons in series that already contain commas: Helen Haggard and Candee Gentry walked to the store and bought apples, oranges and carrots; milk, yogurt and cheese; and pork chops, a roast, and a leg of mutton.

Determine if any of these instances apply to the natural pauses when you read sentences aloud. If they do, use a semicolon. If they don't, use a comma.

The best way to avoid making errors with semicolons is to avoid them, except in words in a series. Since readers are generally in trouble 50 percent of the time, use a period instead of a semicolon. Your sentences will also be more emphatic as a result.

Other pauses may occur in sentences that may not be resolved by the comma or semi-colon. These may require a colon or a dash.

A colon points to what follows. In media writing it is usually used to introduce a series too long to be prefaced by a comma, such as: Elected at the meeting were: Lorie D. Mathis, president; John Glenn Lively, vice president; Krista B. Paschal, secretary-treasurer.

A dash marks a separation more intense than a comma—the sentence dashes off in another direction: Amanda Miller sat serenely behind her desk—scurrying around the makeup tables was April Idalyn Wiencek. The dash can also be used to set off a parenthetical expression: The time for the meeting—2 o'clock to be exact—was set by Susan Lynne Stapleton.

Follow these rules, and the majority of your punctuation problems are solved.

WORDS COMMONLY USED AND ABUSED: A LIST TO AID SPELLING AND USAGE

absence
absent
absolutely
accept (receive)
access (entry)
accidentally
accommodate
accompanied
achieve
acknowledgement
acquaint
acquire
across
adapt (modify)
adequate
adherence
admirable
adolescent
adopt (take up)
advantageous
advice (n.)
advise (v.)
affect (v. usually)
aggravate
aggressive
agreeable
aisle
alien
allegedly
allies
allot (assign)
all right
already

altar (podium)
alter (change)
amateur
ambiguous
ambulance
analysis
analyze
angle
anxious
apologize
apparent
appreciate
appropriately
arduous
arguing
argument
arousing
arrangement
arriving
ascent (rise)
assent (agree)
assessment
athlete
attach
attendance
attitude
audience
authority
available
balance
bargain
basically
believable

benefited
bipartisan
boisterous
brilliant
burglar
business
campaign
canceled
cancellation
capital (city)
capitol (building)
career
careless
casualty
category
caucus
cautious
ceiling
cemetery
ceremony
certainly
character
chief
choose (select)
chose (selected)
circuit
cite (name)
clothes
coarse (rough)
coincidence
column
combated
commitment

committee
compel
competent
complement
   (adjunct)
compliment
   (remark)
concede
conceivable
condemn
conference
conferred
confident
conscience (n.)
conscious (adj.)
consequently
considerable
consistent
continuous
controlled
controversial
convenient
corporation
correspondence
council (group)
counsel (advice)
courageous
course (path)
courteous
criticism
criticize
curiosity
debt

decent (proper)
decision
defendant
definite
definition
delinquent
delivery
dependable
dependent
deplorable
descent (fall)
describe
description
despair
desperate
despise
destroy
deterred
develop
different
disagree
disappear
disapprove
discipline
discussed (talked
    about)
disgust (abhorrence)
dismissal
dissatisfied
dissent (objection)
distant
disturb
doubt
drowned
drunkenness
dyeing (coloring)
dying (expiring)
effect (n. usually)
elegant
eliminate
eloquent
embarrass
eminent
    (prominent)
emphasis
emphasize

encore
encouraging
enormity (horror)
enormousness (size)
ensure (guarantee)
equivalent
especially
evidence
exaggerate
except (exclude)
excess (surplus)
excitement
executive
exhilarate
existence
expel
experience
explanation
extraordinary
extremely
familiar
fantasies (n. pl.)
fantasize (v.)
farther (literal
    distance)
fascinating
favorite
feasible
field
finally
flexible
friend
friendliness
fundamentally
further (figurative
    distance)
gambling
generally
government
gracious
grief (n.)
grieve (v.)
guarantee
guard
guidance
handicapped

harass
hysterical
identical
ignorance
illegible
illiterate
illusion
immediate
imminent
    (impending)
imperative
implied (hinted)
inaugurate
incident
incongruous
incredible
independent
inevitable
inference
    (deduction)
influence
inherent
innocence
innocent
innocuous
inoculate
inseparable
insistent
insure (cover
    with insurance)
intelligent
intercede
interrupt
involvement
irrelevant
irresistible
irritable
its (of it)
it's (it is)
judgment
kidnapped
knowledge
knowledgeable
labor
laundry
lay (set)

laziness
legislative
legitimately
leisure
lie (recline)
liveliest
loneliness
loose (unattached)
lose (mislay)
losing
luxuries
lying
magnificent
maintenance
marriage
mechanic
medicine
merchandise
miner (worker)
minor
minuscule
miscellaneous
mischievous
misconduct
mission
misspell
monopolize
moral (proper;
    lesson)
morale (spirit)
mortgage
muscle
muscular
mysterious
naturally
necessary
negotiate
neighbor
noticeable
nuisance
obedience
observant
obstacle
occasion
occurred
occurrence

omission
opportunity
organize
origin
outrageous
pamphlet
paragraph
parallel
paralysis
paralyze
patience
peaceful
peculiar
penetrate
perceive
perform
permanent
permit
persistent
personal
(of a person)
personnel
(employees)
perspiration
persuade
pertain
pervade
photograph
phrase
piece
political
portray
possess
possible
practically

precede
prefer
prejudice
presence
present
principal (chief)
principle (basis)
privilege
probable
proceed
prominent
prospective
protester
pursue
quality
quantity
quiet (silent)
quite (very)
radioactive
readily
recede
receipt
receive
recognize
recommend
reference
referred
regardless
relevant
reliable
relieve
reminisce
repentant
repetition
represent

resistance
responsible
revise
rhythm
ridicule
righteous
safety
scarcely
schedule
scholar
secretary
seize
sensitive
separate
several
severely
shield
significance
similar
simultaneous
sincerely
site (location)
solemn
sophomore
source
specifically
stationary (fixed)
stationery (paper)
stature
straight
subsequent
subtle
summary
supervise
supplement

suppose
suppress
susceptible
suspense
symbolize
systematically
tangible
tentative
their (of them)
there (at that place)
they're (they are)
thief
tolerance
tranquil
tranquillity
transferred
tremendous
variable
various
vengeance
vigorous
violence
violent
weather (atmospherics)
weight
weird
whether (if)
who's (who is)
whose (of whom)
wield
worrisome
worshiper
wrist
yacht
yield

THE ASSOCIATED PRESS TOP TEN MYTHS ABOUT REWRITING SOMEONE ELSE'S NEWS REPORTING*

1. All News on the Internet is in the Public Domain.
   News on the Internet—or on the radio, television, or in newspapers—is not automatically in the public domain. In fact, copyright law and state misappropriation law protect news, including text, photographs, videos, graphic images, and audio found on the Internet, in a newspaper, on television or radio, or anywhere else.

2. It's OK to Rewrite Someone Else's Story for My News.
   Courts protect the investment of news organizations in gathering facts through the law of "hot news" misappropriation. While the news is "hot," you can't take it from someone else. Copyright law protects the story and the aggregation of facts in the total story. Don't cheat. Only use news you are licensed to use or gather yourself.

3. Copyright Protects Only "Artistic" Works.
   Copyright does not protect just "artistic" works like movies, novels, and songs, but news as well. This includes news stories, photos, videos, graphic images, and audio found on the Internet, in a newspaper on the television or radio, or anywhere else.

4. Because I'm Using Material for "News Purposes," It's Automatically OK.
   There is no general "news purpose" exception to copyright infringement—especially if you use the copyrighted works of another news organization in creating your news. Taking news from a competitor or another news organization is almost never going to be considered a "fair use."

5. Copying Seven Seconds of Audio Is a "Fair Use."
   Copying any portion of audio, text, video graphics, photographs, etc., can violate the copyright law. There is no minimum amount for copyright infringement—copying two notes of music has been alleged to be a copyright infringement.

6. As Long as I Give Credit to My Source, I'm OK.
   Some people believe that they can take news from someone else as long as they give the source credit (e.g. "According to The Associated Press..."). However, attribution is no defense to copyright infringement or to misappropriation. Only use news you are licensed to use.

---

*Reprinted by permission of The Associated Press.

7. Unless There Is a © or Other Copyright Notice on Material, I Can Use It.
   Long ago this was true—but not any more. Even if there is no copyright notice on a work, it is protected by copyright law. And because copyright law is a "strict liability" law (like speeding), you can be found guilty even if you didn't know you were taking someone else's material.

8. I Got My News From a News Service, So I Have No Worries.
   Just like speeding tickets, copyright liability is a "strict" liability. In other words, if the source you used for news took it without permission, your use of that news on your station makes YOU guilty of copyright infringement as well—even if you didn't know. Make sure you know your news service's source for its news. With thousands of staff and over 240 bureaus worldwide, you can always count on AP.

9. Copyright Penalties Are Small and Meaningless.
   Copyright violations are subject to several penalties—including criminal penalties with jail time. Courts can award up to $150,000 per story copied—even without any showing of actual loss by the copyright owner. Furthermore, courts can make you pay the attorneys' fees for the copyright owner, which can be even higher than the penalties!

10. There Is Nothing I Can Do About People Stealing My News.
    Protect your investment in your own news—AP does. Federal and state laws prohibit people from using your news without your permission. If you see someone doing it, ask him or her to stop. If you see someone stealing AP news, contact us at iprights@ap.org and we will take action.

THE ASSOCIATED PRESS COPYRIGHT GUIDELINES*

Copyright is the right of authors to control the reproduction and use of their creative expressions that have been fixed in tangible form. The types of creative expression eligible for copyright protection include literary, graphic, photographic, audiovisual, electronic and musical works. In this context, "tangible forms" range from film to computer disks to material posted on the Internet. Personal letters or diaries may be protected by copyright even though they may not have been published and may not contain a copyright notice.

Not all uses of copyright material constitute infringement. The broadest limitation on the reach of copyright law is the ideas and facts are never protected by a copyright. Rather, the copyright pertains only to the literary, musical, graphic, or artistic form in which an author expresses intellectual concepts.

This page can show the distinction between protected expression and non-protected ideas and facts. Despite the copyright protecting this page, a subsequent author is free to report the facts it contains. The subsequent author may not, however, employ the same or essentially the same combination of words, structure, and tone, which comprises the expression of those facts.

While copyright generally prohibits the use of another's protected expression, the doctrine of "fair use" permits, in certain circumstances, the use of copyright material without its author's permission.

To determine whether a particular use is fair, courts are required to evaluate and balance such factors as: (1) the purpose of the use; (2) the nature of the copyright work that is used; (3) the amount and substantiality of the portion used in relation to the copyright work as a whole; and (4) the effect of the use upon the potential value of the copyright work.

News reporting, criticism, and comment are favored purposes under the fair-use doctrine, but "scooping" a copyright holder's first use of previously unpublished material is not. Note, though, that "purpose" is only one of the fair-use factors. Thus, a use for a proper purpose may nevertheless constitute an infringement if other factors weigh against that use's being fair.

Some general guidelines:

Fair use is more likely to be found if the copyrighted work is informational rather than fictional.

---

*Reprinted by permission of The Associated Press.

Fair use is more likely to be found if the copyrighted work is published as opposed to unpublished.

The greater the amount of the copyrighted work used, the less likely a court will characterize the use as fair. The use of an entire copyrighted work is almost never fair. Size alone, however, is not decisive. Courts have found uses not to be fair when the portion used was small but so important that it went to the heart of the copyrighted work.

Uses that decrease any potential market for the copyrighted work tend not to be fair. For instance, if a literary critic reproduces all five lines of a five-line poem, the potential market for the poem will be diminished because any reader of the critic's piece can also obtain a copy of the poem for free.

The First Amendment provides no greater right to use copyrighted materials than those provided by the copyright law. Moreover, proper attribution cannot transform an infringing use into a fair one.

In using copyright material in a news story or column, writers should make sure that no more of a copyrighted work than is necessary for a proper purpose is used, and that the work is not used in a way that impairs its value.

It is always possible to obtain permission from the copyright holder. Reporters and editors having questions about whether their use in a news story or column of copyright material is a fair use should review these factors. No mathematical formula can yield the answer.

SOCIETY OF PROFESSIONAL JOURNALISTS: CODE OF ETHICS*

PREAMBLE

Members of the Society of Professional Journalists believe that public enlightenment is the forerunner of justice and the foundation of democracy. The duty of the journalist is to further those ends by seeking truth and providing a fair and comprehensive account of events and issues. Conscientious journalists from all media and specialties strive to serve the public with thoroughness and honesty. Professional integrity is the cornerstone of a journalist's credibility. Members of the society share a dedication to ethical behavior and adopt this code to declare the society's principles and standards of practice.

SEEK TRUTH AND REPORT IT

Journalists should be honest, fair, and courageous in gathering, reporting, and interpreting information.

Journalists should:

- Test the accuracy of information from all sources and exercise care to avoid inadvertent error. Deliberate distortion is never permissible.
- Diligently seek out subjects of news stories to give them the opportunity to respond to allegations of wrongdoing.
- Identify sources whenever possible. The public is entitled to as much information as possible on sources' reliability.
- Always question sources' motives before promising anonymity. Clarify conditions attached to any promise made in exchange for information. Keep promises.
- Make certain that headlines, news teases and promotional material, photos, videos, audio, graphics, sound bites, and quotations do not misrepresent. They should not oversimplify or highlight incidents out of context.
- Never distort the content of news photos or videos. Image enhancement for technical clarity is always permissible. Label montages and photo illustrations.
- Avoid misleading re-enactments or staged news events. If re-enactment is necessary to tell a story, label it.

---

*Reprinted by permission of the Society of Professional Journalists.

- Avoid undercover or other surreptitious methods of gathering information vital to the public. Use of such methods should be explained as part of the story.
- Never plagiarize.
- Tell the story of the diversity and magnitude of the human experience boldly, even when it is unpopular to do so.
- Examine their own cultural values and avoid imposing those values on others.
- Avoid stereotyping by race, gender, age, religion, ethnicity, geography, sexual orientation, disability, physical appearance, or social status.
- Support the open exchange of views, even views they find repugnant.
- Give voice to the voiceless; official and unofficial sources of information can be equally valid.
- Distinguish between advocacy and news reporting. Analysis and commentary should be labeled and not misrepresent fact or context.
- Distinguish news from advertising and shun hybrids that blur the lines between the two.
- Recognize a special obligation to ensure that the public's business is conducted in the open and that government records are open to inspection.

MINIMIZE HARM

Ethical journalists treat sources, subjects, and colleagues as human beings deserving of respect.
  Journalists should:

- Show compassion for those who may be affected adversely by news coverage. Use special sensitivity when dealing with children and inexperienced sources or subjects.
- Be sensitive when seeking or using interviews or photographs of those affected by tragedy or grief.
- Recognize that gathering and reporting information may cause harm or discomfort. Pursuit of the news is not a license for arrogance.
- Recognize that private people have a greater right to control information about themselves than do public officials and others who seek power, influence, or attention. Only an overriding public need can justify intrusion into anyone's privacy.
- Show good taste. Avoid pandering to lurid curiosity.
- Be cautious about identifying juvenile suspects or victims of sex crimes.
- Be judicious about naming criminal suspects before the formal filing of charges.
- Balance a criminal suspect's fair trial rights with the public's right to be informed.

ACT INDEPENDENTLY

Journalists should be free of obligation to any interest other than the public's right to know.
  Journalists should:

- Avoid conflicts of interest, real or imagined.
- Remain free of associations and activities that may compromise the integrity or damage credibility.

- Refuse gifts, favors, fees, free travel, and special treatment, and shun secondary employment, political involvement, public office, and service in community organizations if they compromise journalistic integrity.
- Disclose unavoidable conflicts.
- Be vigilant and courageous about holding those with power accountable.
- Deny favored treatment to advertisers and special interests and resist their pressure to influence news coverage.
- Be wary of sources offering information for favors or money; avoid bidding for news.

BE ACCOUNTABLE

Journalists are accountable to their readers, listeners, viewers, and each other.
  Journalists should:

- Clarify and explain news coverage and invited dialogue with the public over journalistic conduct.
- Encourage the public to voice grievances against the news media.
- Admit mistakes and correct them promptly.
- Expose unethical practices of journalists and the news media.
- Abide by the same high standards to which they hold others.

THE ASSOCIATED PRESS ON LIBEL*

WHAT IS LIBEL?

"Libel is injury to reputation.

"Words, pictures or cartoons that expose a person to public hatred, shame, disgrace or ridicule, or induce an ill opinion of a person are libelous."

Civil libel suits are filed mainly as a result of news stories that "allege crime, fraud, dishonesty, immoral or dishonorable conduct, or stories that defame the subject professionally, causing financial loss either personally or to a business."

THE DEFENSES AGAINST A CIVIL LIBEL ACTION

[1] The facts stated are provably true.

[2] The statement is absolute or qualified privilege.

"Absolute privilege means that certain people in some circumstances can state, without being sued for libel, material which may be false, malicious and damaging. These circumstances include judicial, legislative, public and official proceedings and the contents of most public records. . . .

"The interests of society require that judicial, legislative and similar official proceedings be subject to public discussion. To that extent, the rights of the individual about whom damaging statements may be made are subordinated to what are deemed to be the interests of the community" (269).

Qualified privilege means that the private defense "can be lost or diluted by how the journalist handles the material" (269). If "there are errors in the report of the hearing, or if the plaintiff can show malice on the part of the publication or broadcast outlet," (269) the privilege defense is lost or diluted.

There are two key points: a. "Does the material come from a privileged circumstance or proceeding?" b. "Is the report a fair and accurate summation?" (269)

[3] The "press enjoys a great protection when it covers the affairs of public officials. To successfully sue for libel, a public official must prove actual malice...that the editor or reporter had knowledge that the facts were false or acted with reckless disregard of the truth" (277).

[4] Fair comment and criticism is a defense where defamatory matter consists of comment and opinion. [Whatever facts are stated must be true.] The right of fair comment is summarized in Hoeppner vs. Dunkirk Pr. Co., 254 N.Y. 95:

---

*Reprinted by permission of The Associated Press.

Everyone has a right to comment on matters of public interest and concern, provided they do so fairly and with an honest purpose. Such comments or criticism are not libelous, however severe in their terms, unless they are written maliciously. Thus it has been held that books, prints, pictures and statuary publicly exhibited, and the architecture of public buildings, and actors and exhibitors are all legitimate subjects of newspapers' criticism, and such criticism fairly and honestly made is not libelous, however strong the terms of censure may be. (271)

PUBLIC RELATIONS SOCIETY OF AMERICA MEMBER CODE OF ETHICS 2000*

PREAMBLE

>   Professional Values
>   Principles of Conduct
>   Commitment and Compliance

This Code applies to PRSA members. The Code is designed to be a useful guide for PRSA members as thety carry out their ethical responsibilities. This document is designed to anticipate and accommodate, by precedent, ethical challenges that may arise. The scenarios outlined in the Code provision are actual examples of misconduct. More will be added as experience with the Code occurs.

The Public Relations Society of America (PRSA) is committed to ethical practices. The level of public trust PRSA members seek, as we serve the public good, means we have taken on a special obligation to operate ethically.

The value of member reputation depends upon the ethical conduct of everyone affiliated with the Public Relations Society of America. Each of us sets an example for each other—as well as other professionals—by our pursuit of excellence with powerful standards of performance, professionalism, and ethical conduct.

Emphasis on enforcement of the Code has been eliminated. But the PRSA Board of Directors retains the right to bar from membership or expel from the Society any individual who has been or is sanctioned by a government agency or convicted in a court of law of an action that is in violation of this Code.

Ethical practice is the most important obligation of a PRSA member. We view the Member Code of Ethics as a model for other professions, organizations, and professionals.

PRSA MEMBER STATEMENT OF PROFESSIONAL VALUES

This statement presents the core values of PRSA members and, more broadly, of the public relations profession. These values provide the foundation for the Member Code of Ethics

---

*The PRSA Assembly adopted the Code of Ethics in 2000. Replaces the Code of Professional Standards (previously referred to as the Code of Ethics) last revised in 1988. Reprinted by permission of the Public Relations Society of America.

and set the industry standard for the professional practice of public relations. These values are the fundamental beliefs that guide our behaviors and decision-making process. We believe our professional values are vital to the integrity of the profession as a whole.

Advocacy

We serve the public interest by acting as responsible advocates for those we represent.

We provide a voice in the marketplace of ideas, facts, and viewpoints to aid informed public debate.

Honesty

We adhere to the highest standards of accuracy and truth in advancing the interests of those we represent and in communicating with the public.

Expertise

We acquire and responsibly use specialized knowledge and experience.

We advance the profession through continued professional development, research, and education.

We build mutual understanding, credibility, and relationships among a wide array of institutions and audiences.

Independence

We provide objective counsel to those we represent.

We are accountable for our actions.

Loyalty

We are faithful to those we represent, while honoring our obligation to serve the public interest.

Fairness

We deal fairly with clients, employers, competitors, peers, vendors, the media, and the general public.

We respect all opinions and support the right of free expression.

PRSA CODE PROVISIONS

Free Flow of Information

Core Principle

Protecting and advancing the free flow of accurate and truthful information is essential to serving the public interest and contributing to informed decision making in a democratic society.

Intent

To maintain the integrity of relationships with the media, government officials, and the public.

To aid informed decision-making.

Guidelines

A member shall:

Preserve the integrity of the process of communication.

Be honest and accurate in all communications.

Act promptly to correct erroneous communications for which the practitioner is responsible.

Preserve the free flow of unprejudiced information when giving or receiving gifts by ensuring that gifts are nominal, legal, and infrequent.

Examples of improper conduct under this provision:

A member representing a ski manufacturer gives a pair of expensive racing skis to a sports magazine columnist to influence the columnist to write favorable articles about the product.

A member entertains a government official beyond legal limits and/or in violation of government reporting requirements.

Competition

Core Principle

Promoting healthy and fair competition among professionals preserves an ethical climate while fostering a robust business environment.

Intent

To promote respect and fair competition among public relations professionals. To serve the public interest by providing the widest choice of practitioner options.

Guidelines

A member shall:

Follow ethical hiring practices designed to respect free and open competition without deliberately undermining a competitor.

Preserve intellectual property rights in the marketplace.

Examples of improper conduct under this provision:

A member employed by a "client organization" shares helpful information with a counseling firm that is competing with others for the organization's business.

A member spreads malicious and unfounded rumors about a competitor in order to alienate the competitor's clients and employees in a ploy to recruit people and business.

Disclosure of Information

Core Principle

Open communication fosters informed decision making in a democratic society.

Intent

To build trust with the public by revealing all information needed for responsible decision making.

Guidelines

A member shall:

Be honest and accurate in all communications.

Act promptly to correct erroneous communications for which the member is responsible.

Investigate the truthfulness and accuracy of information released on behalf of those represented.

Reveal the sponsors for causes and interests represented.

Disclose financial interest (such as stock ownership) in a client's organizations.

Avoid deceptive practices.

Examples of improper conduct under this provision:

Front groups: A member implements "grass roots" campaigns or letter-writing campaigns to legislators on behalf of undisclosed interest groups.

Lying by omission: A practitioner for a corporation knowingly fails to release financial information, giving a misleading impression of the corporation's performance.

A member discovers inaccurate information disseminated via a Web site or media kit and does not correct the information.

A member deceives the public by employing people to pose as volunteers to speak at public hearings and participate in "grass roots" campaigns.

Safeguarding Confidences

Core Principle

Client trust requires appropriate protection of confidential and private information.

Intent

To protect the privacy rights of clients, organizations, and individuals by safeguarding confidential information.

Guidelines

A member shall:

Safeguard the confidences and privacy rights of present, former, and prospective clients and employees.

Protect privileged, confidential, or insider information gained from a client or organization.

Immediately advise an appropriate authority if a member discovers that confidential information is being divulged by an employee of a client company or organization.

Examples of improper conduct under this provision:

A member changes jobs, takes confidential information, and uses that information in the new position to the detriment of the former employer.

A member intentionally leaks proprietary information to the detriment of some other party.

Conflicts of Interest

Core Principle

> Avoiding real, potential, or perceived conflicts of interest builds the trust of clients, employers, and the public.

Intent

> To earn trust and mutual respect with clients or employers.
> To build trust with the public by avoiding or ending situations that put one's personal or professional interests in conflict with society's interests.

Guidelines

A member shall:

> Act in the best interests of the client or employer, even subordinating the member's personal interests.
> Avoid actions and circumstances that may appear to compromise good business judgment or create a conflict between personal and professional interests.
> Disclose promptly any existing or potential conflict of interest to affected clients or organizations.
> Encourage clients and customers to determine if a conflict exists after notifying all affected parties.

Examples of improper conduct under this provision:

> The member fails to disclose that he or she has a strong financial interest in a client's chief competitor.
> The member represents a "competitor company" or a "conflicting interest" without informing a prospective client.

Enhancing the Profession

Core Principle

> Public relations professionals work constantly to strengthen the public's trust in the profession.

Intent

> To build respect and credibility with the public for the profession of public relations.
> To improve, adapt, and expand professional practices.

Guidelines

A member shall:

> Acknowledge that there is an obligation to protect and enhance the profession.
> Keep informed and educated about practices in the profession to ensure ethical conduct.

Actively pursue personal professional development.

Decline representation of clients or organizations that urge or require actions contrary to this Code.

Accurately define what public relations activities can accomplish.

Counsel subordinates in proper ethical decision making.

Require that subordinates adhere to the ethical requirements of the Code.

Report ethical violations, whether committed by PRSA members or not, to the appropriate authority.

Examples of improper conduct under this provision:

A PRSA member declares publicly that a product the client sells is safe, without disclosing evidence to the contrary.

A member initially assigns some questionable client work to a non-member practitioner to avoid the ethical obligation of PRSA membership.

RESOURCES

Rules and Guidelines

The following PRSA documents, available online at www.prsa.org provide detailed rules and guidelines to help guide your professional behavior.

PRSA Bylaws
PRSA Administrative Rules
Member Code of Ethics

CHECKLIST FOR REVISION/GRADING

NEWSPAPER FEATURE (MAGAZINE ARTICLE) GRADING FORM

Heading at top of page single spaced as per following example :
"Featuring the Greatest of Grading"
A 500-word feature
D.J. Anon   yes ____   no____

Hook, Idea and Transition clear to you?   yes ____   no____
Comments?
An improved feature lead might be:

Is the feature coherent? (Logical sequence?)   yes ____   no ____
Comments?
A more logical progression of paragraphs, sentences:

The conclusion wraps up the feature in a neat bow?   yes ____   no ____
An improved conclusion might be:

Does the feature "flow" from sentence to sentence and
    paragraph to paragraph?   yes ____   no ____
Are there similar paragraph beginnings?   yes ____   no ____
Overly short paragraphs?   yes ____   no ____
Is there a change in points of view?   pv   yes ____   no ____
Is there a change in the "tone" of the feature?   to   yes ____   no ____
Are attributions buried?   yes ____   no ____
Are "witches" negligible?   yes ____   no ____
(It is, was, we were, there are, they were, which
    was, were, he was, one is, etc., e.g., pronouns+verbs
    of being   yes ____   no ____
Passive verbs used instead of action verbs?   yes ____   no ____
Overused verbs like "get" or "set"?   yes ____   no ____
Are there trite phrases?   yes ____   no ____
Are there "be specific" possibilities?   bs   yes ____   no ____
Is there "telling" instead of "showing"   tell   yes ____   no ____
Possibility for better characterization   cd
    or setting description?   sd   yes ____   no ____
Diction problems?   yes ____   no ____
Illogical statements?   ill   yes ____   no ____
Concluding comments:

SYMBOL SHEET FOR REVISION/GRADING

A	Action verb needed
Agr	Agreement (subj.-verb)
Am	Ambiguous
Arr	Improper arrangement
AU	Article unity violated
Ask	Ask about this in class
BS	Be specific, (not dog, "beagle")
≡	Capital letter(s) needed: Paris
C	Clichéd, trite
CD	Character description
✓✓✓	Choppy sentences, subordinate
Coh	Clearer order needed
Con	Poor conclusion
There is amount	Delete
ᴧᴧ	Diction, word choice
DT	Show, don't tell
E	Emphasis rules violated
Eif	Error in fact!
Exp	Expression, Explain
Fig	Inappropriate figure
Fog	Foggy, Vague
Frag	Sentence fragment
G	Good!

H	Improper hyphen use or lack thereof
Id!	Error in identification!
Ill	Illogical
Im	Improper, or lack of Imagery
Ital	Italics needed
K	Awkward (phrase, sentence)
Lead	Poor lead
Lib	Libelous statement
LI	Lingering impression needed
/	Lower case needed: Let my people
MM	Misplaced, dangling modifier
NSFI	Note suggestions for improvement
MS	Format incorrect
NY	Funny. Potential New Yorker filler material-not good.
Org	Organization
P	Punctuation

PR	Pronoun reference	Su	Sentence unity
¶	Paragraph or none needed	#	Space needed between lines, etc.
¶Tr	Paragraph transition		
¶U	Paragraph unity	T	Tense shift
		To	Tone change
PV	Point of view change		
		⌣	Transpose: Would you
Q	Questionable statement		
Quo	Use quotes, misused quotes	Tsk!	For shame! (That you err so.)
		22	(something's wrong: instructor's catch-22.)
R	Rhythm or flow		
Ref	Faulty reference, vague		
Rep	Repetitious	U	Unity violated
Run	Run-on sentence,	UD	Underdeveloped
◯	Misspelled word: thier or spell out:	V	Variety needed in sentences, paragraphs
SD	Setting description	W	Wordy, verbose, prolix, nimiety
SS	Sense-sound needed	Wow!	Misspelled name
Sty	Style error		
S tr	Sentence transition needed	X	Carelessness

CREDITS

INDEX